T0167955

复旦—胡佛近代中国人物与档案文献研究系列

Hoover Institution and Fudan University Modern China Research Series:
Leadership and Archival Documents

宋子文驻美时期电报选

Select Telegrams between Chiang Kai-shek and T. V. Soong

(1940—1943)

吴景平　　郭岱君　编

Edited by Wu Jingping & Tai-chun Kuo

復旦大學 出版社

Fudan University Press

吴景平，1990年于中国人民大学获法学博士，现为复旦大学历史系教授、亚洲研究中心主任、中国金融史研究中心主任，兼任复旦大学校务委员、国务院学位委员会学科评议组成员、国家社会科学基金评审专家、上海市人大代表。主要著作、编著有《宋子文评传》、《中德关系（1861—1992）》、《上海金融业与国民政府关系研究》、《近代中国的经济与社会》、《上海金融的现代化与国际化》等。

Wu Jingping is Professor in the Department of History, Fudan University. He received a Ph.D. in Law from Renmin University of China in 1990. At Fudan, Dr. Wu is the current Director of the Asia Research Center, the Director of China Financial History Center, and the university committee member. He is also appointed as member of the Commission of Academic Degree Appraisal of the State Council, the National Social Science Foundation Appraisal Expert, and the Representative of Shanghai City Congress.

Dr. Wu's major publications include *Biography of T. V. Soong; Sino-German Relations during 1861-1992; On the Relation between Shanghai Financial Industry and the Nationalist Government; The Economy and the Society in Modern China; The Modernization and Globalization of Shanghai Financial Industry.*

郭岱君，史坦福大学胡佛研究院研究员，专研经济发展、中国政经现势、社会科学研究方法、近代中国历史档案等。曾任史坦福大学东亚研究所客座讲座、台湾淡江大学美国研究所副教授。主要论著有《宋子文与战时中美外交》、《领导、改革及制度变迁：中国第一个市场经济》、《中共研究方法论的探讨》、《毛泽东的权力与人格》等。

Tai-chun Kuo is research fellow at Hoover Institution, Stanford University. Prior to this position, she was a visiting lecturer at Center for East Asian Studies, Stanford University and associate professor at the Graduate Institute of American Studies, Tamkang University (Taiwan).

Her major publications include *T. V. Soong in Modern Chinese History; China's Quest for Unification, National Security, and Modernization; Watching Communist China, 1949—79: A Methodological Review of China Studies in the United States of America and Taiwan; The Power and Personality of Mao Tse-tung, etc.*

RESORT HOTEL IN THE NATION'S CAPITAL

The SHOREHAM
Connecticut Avenue at Calvert Street
Washington, D.C.

耀煌兄来电 借胡使相商 请兄速回进行 令使此
时拟各期使四国赤知有否不便之虑如遇
罗总统请以中言转达此不妨美德以助
法之私机及其他物资之投只要十分之一助
华则华不难了浮胜利且了固美助华而
浮後兴兵中国应史上最不能忘美国之
国情高昂矣此除罗总统以外洪祁可望
扵其他另二人所能行也希以此意相机
进言如可又闻美雅清大使之浦主脱回美
中势膊其事华使高等致向赤知可尽
请致之 中正叩卅二 (书)

1940年7月12日蒋介石致宋子文电

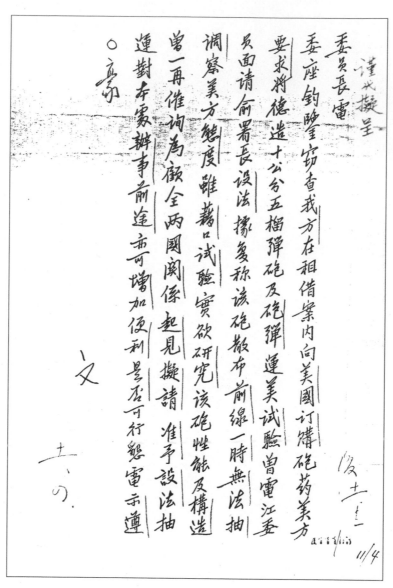

委員長電

委座鈞鑒竊查我方在租借案內向美國訂購砲藥美方

要求將德造十公分五榴彈砲及砲彈運美試驗曾電江委

員面請俞署長設法撥复称該砲散布前線一時無法抽

調察美方態度雖藉口試驗實欲研究該砲性能及構造

曾一再催詢為顧全兩國關係起見擬請准予設法抽

運對本案辦事前途亦有增加便利是否可行懇電示遵

○文

文

十一〇

謹擬呈

俊堂三

11/4

1941年11月4日宋子文致蔣介石電

总　目

"复旦—胡佛近代中国人物与档案文献研究系列"总序

　　复旦大学历史悠久,在自然科学、医学、经济金融、政治外交、思想文化等领域的研究与教学,享誉中外。百年来,对中国现代化的进展,贡献卓著。复旦大学在近代中国人物和档案文献研究方面,也有相当的积累和成果,并积极与海内外学术机构交流合作。

　　史坦福大学胡佛研究院是世界著名的智库,除了杰出的学者之外,还有享誉全球的图书及档案蒐藏。自 1919 年创办以来,胡佛研究院档案馆一直注重近代人物档案文献的征集、整理和开放,最近更扩大近代中国档案的蒐藏及研究。新公开的档案包括蒋介石日记、蒋经国日记、国民党党史资料、宋子文文件等,对于近代中国政治、经济、外交诸领域的研究,极具价值。

　　保存历史、还原历史,是我们的初衷;进一步阐明历史、从历史中学习,是我们的心愿。自 2004 年起,复旦与胡佛的学者开始合作整理与研究胡佛典藏的近代中国人物档案。2005 年,双方合作举办了"近代中国档案文献研究"学术研讨会;2006 年共同举办"宋子文与战时中国(1937—1945)"学术研讨会。为了更进一步推动中国近代史研究的合作交流,并促进有关机构及时开放历史档案文献,双方决定共同编辑和不定期出版"复旦—胡佛近代中国人物与档案文献研究系列"。

本研究系列包括档案史料汇编、研究著作、专题论集、口述历史稿、照片图册等。入编档案史料以胡佛研究院典藏中外文档案为主,也欢迎其他来源的珍档。档案文献的选编校注均从尊重历史、体现原始文本样态的准则,著作、专题论集则代表各相关作者的观点。

此项研究系列的出版得以实现,首先要感谢复旦大学和胡佛研究院的大力支持,还有许多参与写作、整理、编辑、出版、校对等工作的同仁,以及对本研究系列热忱协助的朋友及档案所有人家属,在此表示诚挚的敬意和感谢。

吴景平(复旦大学)

郭岱君(胡佛研究院)

2008 年 3 月 8 日

Preface: Hoover Institution and Fudan University Modern China Research Series: Leadership and Archival Documents

The Hoover Institution is a public policy research center located at Stanford University. It is world-renowned for its scholarship and research on domestic and foreign affairs, and the repository of valuable archival and documentary material from Europe and Asia. Many documents date from before World War I. The Hoover Institution Archives is now a repository of the diaries of Chiang Kai-shek and his son, Chiang Ching-kuo, as well as copies of the vast historical records from the Kuomintang, the dominant political party in China before 1949 when it moved to Taiwan (The Kuomintang remained as the ruling party in Taiwan until 2000).

Fudan University is the leading university in Shanghai, China, known world-wide for its research facilities in the natural and social sciences. Its Department of History has been researching the work of modern Chinese leaders and their influence on the modernization of China.

In 2005, Hoover Institution and Fudan University collaborated on the first seminar on the management, collection, and preservation of Chinese materials from the Nationalist period. A second seminar in 2006, "T. V. Soong and Wartime Nationalist China, 1937 - 1945" was held in Shanghai, and scholars from the United States, Japan, Korea, Taiwan, Hong Kong, and Mainland China could now examine the role of T. V. Soong during World War II.

It is from this second seminar that the Hoover Institution and Fudan University are pleased to publish some of these historical documents in a new series, *Hoover Institution and Fudan University Modern China Research Series: Leadership and Archival Documents*. The first volume presents the telegrams exchanged between T. V. Soong and Chiang Kai-shek from 1940 - 1943. The second consists of photographs of T. V. Soong, many taken from his personal family album. The third volume is the proceedings of this 2006 seminar.

Future publications will continue to collect the writings, oral histories, private correspondence, and personal photographs of many major and important figures in modern Chinese history. This series is now promoting an exciting and new understanding of modern China.

We want to express our deepest gratitude to the Hoover Institution, Stanford University, and Fudan University. Their support has made this series possible. We also want to thank the many colleagues, friends, and donors for their participation in this project. We appreciate their hard work, devotion, and generosity to make this series successful.

Tai-chun Kuo, Hoover Institution, Stanford University
Wu Jingping, Department of History, Fudan University
March 8, 2008

编者说明

一、本辑资料均选自美国史坦福大学胡佛研究院典藏之宋子文档案第59盒至61盒，并经得胡佛研究院及冯宋琼颐女士同意列入"复旦—胡佛近代中国人物与档案文献研究系列"，予以正式出版。

二、本辑资料所收绝大部分为宋子文蒋介石往来电报稿，个别为宋子文托他人带给蒋介石的函稿；大部分为已发电文稿，个别是否发出不详。所有原稿均为手写。

三、各电函稿的标题，包括发件人、收件人及第三人的姓名均为编者所加。电函稿中的称谓、署名及第三人称中外人士，有用字、号、职衔的，或外人不同之译名，均照原件未加更改，并酌加注释说明。标题的日期，首先依据原稿末之韵目；若无韵目或韵目不清，则按照原稿首末标出之日期；原稿无韵目、无日期的，则据内容推断。原稿中之标题（如"委员长来电"、"重庆来电"、"致委员长电"）后之汉字数字系原文所有，表示实际收到或发出之日期。部分来往电稿在原标题和日期之后,还注有"复"、"已复"加月日数字,均照辑录。

　　四、各电函稿文字内容全文照录,标点为编者所加。原稿中不通顺的文句,为存真起见,均照原件辑录。大部分原稿有修改情况,仅辑录改定后的文字,删改情况不一一注明。

　　五、部分往来电稿原件起首处有英文字母和数字组成之编号,照录。部分电稿末有宋子文拟复电稿,或宋子文及他人所加注,均予以辑录,内容置于"[ ]"内,附于该电稿后。

　　六、原稿格式,大部分首行首字与次行首字持齐,少部分首行首字缩字位;原稿有全文不分段的,也有分段另起行的;序数词有加圆括号"( )"的,也有未加的。以上均照原文,未予更改。

　　七、宋子文所发电稿多为文秘人员代拟稿,宋子文签发。因避讳原拟稿署名处为○（或○○）加韵目代日(或再加支时);也有宋子文亲签"文"字于韵目之前的情况,均照原稿辑录。宋子文在原稿纸左下方签发"文"字,以及下有之月日数(或无),现统辑录于署名处之后。凡署名处之"文"字非宋子文亲签者,均加以注明。少数电稿正文中也有以○代"文"的情况,均辑录"文"字,并加以注明。

　　八、少数电稿有拟稿人姓名,照录或予以注明。

　　九、原稿中误字、别字予以保留,更正字置于【 】内,缺字、不可辨认字以□□表示,能断定者添补脱字于〈 〉内,讹误但难以确定以【?】标示。现文稿内的圆括号及括号内之数字、文字,均原稿所有。

　　十、人名、地名、国名、机构、重要职衔、重大事件,通常在首次出现时加注释。另在书末附索引。

　　十一、本辑资料原稿为中文,现翻译为英文。全书编排顺序如下:中文编者说明、中文目录、中文导论、中文电函稿、英文编者说明、英文目录、英文导论、英文电函稿、中文索引、英文索引。

　　十二、本辑资料由吴景平、郭岱君主编。注释由吴景平、曹嘉涵完成。英文翻译为林孝庭、蒋劭清。中英文导论分别由吴景平、马若孟(Ramon H. Myers)撰写。索引由曹嘉涵、王丽、石涛、李辉完成。全书校对为吴景平、曹嘉涵、王丽、石涛、万立明、田兴荣,英文校对为郭岱君、林孝庭、蒋劭清。

目　录

胡佛研究院藏宋子文驻美时期
电报函稿的研究价值

吴景平

《宋子文驻美时期电报选（1940—1943）》（以下简称为《电报选》）收入的是1940—1943年宋子文驻美期间与蒋介石往来电报函稿。在其编竣付梓之际，我想谈谈这本资料书的研究价值。

宋子文1933年辞去行政院副院长、财政部长和中央银行总裁之后的相当长的时间里，被排除在中央决策层之外。虽然宋子文辞职后即被委任为国务委员，且在抗战初期仍有此"宋委员"身份，他的一些故旧甚至在职的高官一直在当面和函稿中仍称宋为"宋部长"，但"宋委员"只是一个虚衔，"宋部长"也要过了整整八年之后才名副其实。1935年4月初，宋子文出任改组后的中国银行董事长。此后一直到太平洋战争爆发前，中国银行在开展国际汇兑业务和维持法币汇率方面起了十分重要的作用，这方面的作用一定意义上甚至连中央银行也不可替代。可是，与中央银行总裁不同，中国银行董事长只是财政部在该行确定的常务董事中所指定的，并非特任、简任的官员。也就是说，出任中国银行董事长并不意味着宋子文重新回到国民党中央政府任职。

随着抗日战争的爆发，国民党政权的政治体制开始转入高度集权，战时外交的决策中枢，从国防最高会议过渡到国防最高委员会，但作为战时大本营的军事委员会却是真正的外交决策机构。作为外交行政机构的外交部以及驻外使馆，虽然在体制文本中直属于行政院，实际运作中往往向军事委员会负责。另外，蒋介石本人在抗战爆发之初因其军事委员会委员长的身份，已经被授予最高统帅权和"对于党政统一指挥"之权；1938年成为国民党总裁；1939年成为国防最高委员会委员长。蒋介石本人成为执掌最高、最后决定权的领袖，统驭重大内政外交方针政策和人事进退的决定权。

抗日战争初期，宋子文在仕途上并没有什么大的进展，仍然只是国民政府委员和中国银行董事长。虽然蒋介石和一度出任行政院长的孔祥熙①曾委托宋子文同英方接洽借款,但当时宋并没有重新进入国民政府高层决策圈。从1938年初起,宋子文同英国驻华大使克拉克·卡尔(Sir Archibald Clark Keer)在香港多次商谈对华借款事宜。卡尔大使对宋子文的才干十分欣赏,认为中国要在战时维持其财政金融局面,非宋子文莫属,因而向蒋介石提出过这一建议。1938年4月,卡尔在武汉同蒋介石谈起英国对华贷款问题,他明确向蒋表示,英国希望宋子文取代孔祥熙出任财政部长。但蒋介石答称无法同宋子文合作,拒绝了英方的要求。同年7月,卡尔大使再次就英国对华贷款问题,向蒋介石提出启用宋子文管理财政的建议②,但依然没有下文。

蒋介石要利用宋子文在财政金融领域的才干和对外交往中的影响,较典型的是1938—1939年期间宋子文受命与汇丰银行、麦加利银行的代表商谈共同设立平准基金,其间宋子文与英方代表,尤其是与后来担任中英平准基金会主任的罗杰斯③,建立起良好的关系。但蒋介石此时并不愿意让宋子文重新回到权力核心,这依然限制着宋子文在内政外交方面的作为和阐发自己的主张。

1940年6月,宋子文以蒋介石代表的身份赴美;1941年12月太平洋战争爆发后,被委任为外交部长,继续在美从事外交活动。对于宋子文驻美代表的身份,蒋介石自重庆致函美国总统罗斯福,作如下说明:"因世界局势之剧变,余觉有与阁下交换意见并请畀予援助之迫切需要。因余不能亲来承教,特派宋子文先生为代表,前来华府晋谒,彼固为阁下素所熟悉者。余已授予宋先生代表中国政府在美商洽一切之全权,彼受余完全之信任,且其对国内之情形与对外之关系完全明了。敬请阁下惠予亲切之洽谈,一如与余私人接触者然,不胜企盼。"④在这里,宋子文的身份非常明确:在对美交涉时,宋子文是蒋介石的私人代表,也是国民政府的全权代表;交涉的内容,一是交换意见,二是获得美国的援助。

从1940年6月下旬起,宋子文便长驻美国;1942年10月中旬离开美国经印度回国,至1943年2月下旬返抵美国;然后于1943年10月回国。换言之,战时宋子文驻美的实际时间有整整三年。

驻美期间,宋子文主持和亲自进行了许多重大问题的谈判交涉,取得不少成果,其中主要方面有:

---

　　①　孔祥熙同时担任财政部长、中央银行总裁。1939年12月孔辞去行政院长(由蒋介石兼任),担任行政院副院长。

　　②　A. N. Young, *China and the Helping Hand 1937 - 1945*, Harvard University Press, 1963, pp. 73、75.

　　③　罗杰斯(Cyril Rogers),英国英格兰银行专家,1935年随李滋罗斯来华,后被中央银行聘为顾问。

　　④　《中华民国重要史料初编》第三编战时外交(一),第274页。

　　一、达成多项财经援助。主要有中美之间的钨砂借款协定、金属借款协定、平准基金协定、5 亿美元财政援助借款协定、中英第二次平准基金协定。

　　二、争取军事援助。除了在钨砂、金属借款额度内采办可用于军事用途的货品也可视为争取军事援助外,更主要的和更直接的是获得租借法案援助,包括争取对华租借额度、提出军品货单、落实货品、组织运输抵达中国内地,相应的交涉对象包括白宫、政府各部门、军方以及制造、供销、运输、保险、银行等方面,为此宋子文专门设立了中国国防供应公司(China Defense Supplies, Inc.),负责具体落实。而 1942 年宋子文签署的《中美抵抗侵略互助协定》,也含有军事上互相支持的内容。

　　三、重大战略协商,最重要的当数 1942 年宋子文参加签署的《联合国家共同宣言》,以及参加盟国领导人和高级幕僚之间的重要会议,如在华盛顿举行的太平洋军事会议、加拿大魁北克会议等。

　　这一期间中美之间达成的重要文件之中,唯一不是由宋子文签署的,便是 1943 年 1 月 11 日的《中美平等新约》(由中国驻美大使魏道明与美国国务卿在华盛顿签署),那时宋子义在重庆签署《中英平等新约》。

　　以往业已出版的史料中,有不少涉及宋子文在美期间的史事[1]。但是,更值得指出的是,1981 年中国国民党中央委员会党史委员会出版的由秦孝仪主编的三卷本《中华民国重要史料初编》第三编战时外交(以下简为《战时外交》)。这是迄今为止研究国民政府战时外交最重要的中文档案文献集。《战时外交》收入了宋子文驻美时期与蒋介石之间往来电报共 282 封,其中蒋介石致宋子文电文 94 封,宋子文致蒋介石电文 188 封。根据《战时外交》分类,这 282 封电报主要包括"一般交涉"、"财经援助"、"军事合作"三个方面的内容(共 207 封),另外还涉及"居里来华"、"拉铁摩尔来华"、"蒋介石访印"、"开罗会议"、"史迪威事件"、"中美中英平等新约"、"联合国组织经过"等重要问题[2]。

　　在宋子文驻美期间,虽然先后有胡适、魏道明两任驻美大使,但无疑在美从事外交最重要的角色是宋子文。另一方面,战时中国外交、军事、政治诸领

　　① 如上海市档案馆编:《颜惠庆日记》(上海市档案馆译,中国档案出版社,1996 年);《胡适任驻美大使期间往来电稿》,中国社会科学院近代史研究所中华民国史组编,中华书局,1978 年;《胡适的日记》(手稿本),台北远流出版事业公司,1989—1990 年;《顾维钧回忆录》第 2 至 5 分册,中国社会科学院近代史研究所译,中华书局,1983—1988 年;《摩根索日记(中国)》(*Morgenthau Diary, China*),Dacapo 出版公司,纽约 1974 年。

　　② 由中国第二历史档案馆编、江苏古籍出版社 1997 年出版的《中华民国史档案资料汇编》第 5 辑第 2 编(外交)之中,关于宋子文驻美期间与蒋介石电文,仅见一封,即 1940 年 12 月 4 日宋子文与胡适一起致蒋介石电,报告美国援华政策情况。见该书第 317 页。

域的最高领导人是蒋介石。所以,宋子文驻美时期与蒋介石之间的往来电报,对于研究这一时期的国民政府对美外交,甚至对英、苏等国外交,具有不可或缺的意义。

《战时外交》是以蒋介石档案为来源,当然是非常权威的。而《电报选》出自史坦福大学胡佛研究院藏宋子文个人档案,而且选自 2004 年才解密的第 59 盒。整个第 59 盒为宋子文与蒋介石 1936—1947 年间往来电报。胡佛藏宋子文档案从第 59 盒起的分类均根据捐赠提供时的状态。换言之,把宋子文与蒋介石往来电报稿与其他文件分开保管,正是宋子文自己生前的安排,可见其重要性。

《电报选》所依据的宋子文驻美期间与蒋介石往来中文电报函稿,均为手稿,其中致蒋介石电报函稿均经过宋子文亲笔修改定稿,署名"文"同意发出,部分则是宋亲拟稿。蒋介石来电稿通常注明收电、复电时间,蒋介石署名"中正"之后通常有韵目及以括号标示的代日;以及宋子文阅读后的署名"文",或"阅"字,或打钩。部分来电稿、发电稿有流水编号。有少量呈蒋介石稿是拟电稿和函稿。

这部分电报函稿总数有 500 余封,目前《电报选》收入电报函稿的总数达 418 封。其中,蒋介石致宋子文电报共 123 封,宋子文致蒋介石电报函稿则多达 295 份。如果把若干份蒋介石来电稿后宋子文的拟复电稿计算在内,宋子文致蒋介石稿的数量超过 300 封,《电报选》收入文稿的总数要比《战时外交》中的宋子文驻美期间与蒋介石往来电报多 136 封。从内容上来看,《电报选》收入的电报稿中有 63 封业已收入《战时外交》,其余的 355 封则是新刊布的。由此可见《电报选》为相关时段研究者们提供了较多的新刊档案史料。

《电报选》收入的那 63 封电报稿,与《战时外交》相应电报稿相比,两者之间内容基本一致,但都有个别字词上的不同。试看几份电文内容之比较结果,正文括号内除序数词外,为《战时外交》不同于《电报选》之处。

《电报选》载有 1940 年 7 月 7 日"蒋介石致宋子文指示军械飞机定购数量及借款数目请兄相机决定电":

A102　委员长来电　七.八
(宋子文先生:)耀密。各电均悉。甚慰。(一)军械数目(量)请照俞大维交兄物单中之最大数量,即三千万元美金之数相商。(二)驱逐机如能定(订)购,以百五十架为准,其式样请令现驻美国之王承黻决定,已令其来谒兄。(三)借款数目请兄相机决定,务望在美要务办妥后,再赴欧可也。诸事勿念。小(舍)儿纬国来见时,请代教诲为盼。中正。阳(七日)。

按《战时外交》该电文的日期作"1940 年 7 月 6 日",电文结束署名之后没有韵母及所代之日;《电报选》则根据档案原件末的"阳(七日)",把蒋介石发电日期写作"1940 年 7 月 7 日"。《电报选》有收电登记号"A102"、来电方和收电日期"委员长来电 七.八",《战时外交》则无。《战时外交》有称谓"宋子文先生",《电报选》则无。《电报选》中的"数目"、"定购"、"小儿",在《战时外交》中则为"数量"、"订购"、"舍儿"①。

这份电文两个版本的几处差别,并不影响主要内容的一致性。但是,以下两例中的一字之差,表示的含义有很大不同。

电报选载有"宋子文致蒋介石建议直接电请居里向军部催提高射机枪电(1941 年 9 月 26 日)",其电文为:

> S426　呈委员长电　九.廿六日
> 委座钧鉴:本月内美方应给我之半寸径高射机关枪,闻因苏俄战况紧急,有转给苏俄之说。请钧座作为不知此事,直接电致居里,告以华中战事激烈,军队急需防空器,请其向军部催请提议速拨一千枝,电交麦寇由转拍。当否仍候钧裁。○宥。文。九.廿六

而在《战时外交》中,"速拨一千枝"为"速拨二千挺"②。这种差别形成的原因,只有在查核蒋介石档案中相应的原件之后,才有可能搞清楚。

《战时外交》收入宋子文 1941 年 7 月 12 日致蒋介石电,其中第三部分文句如下:

> 丙、真电体谅周至,益增钦感,适之使美,仰蒙俯允,尤佩荩筹。国际风云日亟,更非有外交方面之协助,不能相与有成。此次向总统商陈各要务,经过几回周折,始得其切实答复,处境困难,可想而知。长此以往,不但文不能尽责,有负委任,适之亦属难堪。惟有恳请毅然处置,迅予发表。钧座如一时以为未便,文在此期间,谨当循分株守贷借案之职责。钧座必能鉴谅苦衷,曲予宽容③。

作者多年前读到这段时,便对其中的"适之使美,仰蒙俯允"句有疑惑:胡适

---

① 《中华民国重要史料初编》第三编战时外交(一),第 409～410 页。
② 同上书,第 466 页。
③ 同上书,第 144 页。

1938 年便被发表为驻美大使且赴任了,为何到了 1941 年 7 月,却还要由蒋介石再来"俯允"呢?而且前半部分与后半部分明显体现了不同的取向。这次看到了宋子文该电文的发电稿(发电登记号 S378),发现同一段中第一个"适之"处,为"植之",即"植之使美,仰蒙俯允"。

植之,即施肇基(1877—1958),浙江杭县人,早年就读于圣约翰大学,后留学美国康乃尔大学,获博士学位。施肇基外交生涯的起点比顾维钧更早,他 1905年便随端方等五大臣出洋考察时任一等参赞,民元后曾任唐绍仪内阁交通总长,先后出任过驻英、驻美公使,是出席巴黎和会和华盛顿会议的中国代表之一。1931 年前后,施肇基为中国驻国际联盟理事会全权代表。1935 年施在驻美公使任上时,两国外交关系升格,施便成为中国首位驻美大使。

回到上述《战时外交》和《电报选》关于"适之使美"与"植之使美",究竟宋子文发出的电文稿是何者呢?是否可能胡佛档的稿本"植之"是错的,实际发的就是"适之使美"呢?

《电报选》另收入了提到施肇基的两份电报,其一为 1941 年 3 月 3 日蒋介石致宋子文电:

A195　委员长来电　三.五
径(廿五)电悉。施植之到美协助,弟当赞成。请兄以中之意代邀可也。中正。江(三日)。

这份电报表明:宋子文于 1941 年 2 月 25 日曾致电蒋介石,推荐施肇基协助宋子文开展对美外交。

其二则是 1941 年 7 月 6 日宋子文致蒋介石电:

S375　呈委员长电　卅.七.六日　复　七.十一
密急译呈委座钧鉴:前托石曾先生带呈一札,计邀钧察。窃文到美年余,一切秉承钧命,黾勉从公,幸免颠蹶。惟各事进行之中,尤以特别之对外工作,非无困难波折,有时不得不避免手续问题,向美方军政最高当局直接商洽,以致引起各方对文越轨之责难,而使事务进行阻滞。高斯前有以后凡与其政府有关各电,皆请用正式手续之表示,即其明证。是以反复思维。四月艳电有副院长名义之渎请,当时为公心切,冒昧陈词,未能顾及立法手续问题,致烦廑虑,委曲成全,尤深感激。副院长名义提出困难,惟冀有精明干练之驻美使节,彻底合作,以便各事之顺利进行。目今施植之在美,人地最为相宜。当此国际风云,瞬息万变,中美外交所关益巨。如文仅负责办理借贷事宜,外交上之关系尚浅,如兼顾国际特别工作,则非有外交使节同心协力,不足以求事功。文久历艰懔,深荷知遇,钧座必不以文为个人利禄之谋,私人恩怨之故,有此于渎。是否可行,伏乞裁夺,无任急切待命之至。○鱼亥。文。七.六

如果说,蒋介石3月3日的来电,没有点明宋子文推荐施肇基赴美具体担任什么职务的话,那么宋子文7月6日致蒋的电报,就非常明确地表示了对胡适作为驻美大使的不满,也非常明确地提出,施肇基是继任驻美大使的合适人选。与此相应的,宋子文7月12日向蒋介石表示"仰蒙俯允"的,只能是"植之使美"而不可能是"适之使美"。当然,当时蒋介石没有马上召回胡适,后来也是发表了魏道明而不是施肇基作为召回胡适后的下一任驻美大使。然而,作为宋子文圣约翰大学的学长、资深外交家,施肇基深受宋的尊敬和钦佩,施除了继续在中国国防供应公司帮助日常事务外,宋子文有不少需与美方上层官员联系的事项,是让施代表他去做的。在胡佛藏宋子文档案中,有不少关于施肇基以及宋施关系的中英文资料,可以提供更多的史实。

从以上几份电报内容的比较分析中,我们可以看到,《电报选》中即便与战时外交内容相同的电报稿,也存在着诸多不同点。导致两种版本之间种种差异的原因很多,比如宋子文方面致蒋介石的正式发电稿,就是从拟电稿修改而成的,《电报选》收入的是拟稿而非正式的发电稿。然而,与正式发电稿不同的拟电稿,也是有其研究价值的。

明确了这一点,那么《电报选》中与《战时外交》内容不重复的350多封电报的价值,则可以提供更多的史料,其中不乏十分重要的史实。另外,《电报选》附有约360个中文索引,包括中外人名、机构、地点等,从中可见《电报选》新选入电报包含内容之丰富。

比如,史迪威事件是战时中美关系一大公案,甚至蒋介石与宋子文的关系也一度因之陷于危机。《战时外交》第三卷在"史迪威事件"专题下,总共收入了90份文件,时间从1942年3月到1944年10月,是迄今为止刊行的研究史迪威问题最重要的中文文献。其中到1943年9月宋子文离美之前的文件共44份,包括宋子文与蒋介石往来电报23封。《电报选》收入1943年之前的与史迪威直接相关的电报(包括译名作史梯威的),共有50份,其中15份与《战时外交》内容相同,另有35份内容不同。也就是说,对于至1943年10月宋子文回到重庆之前属于第一阶段的史迪威事件,《电报选》提供了相当数量的新史料。试举例说明。

《战时外交》收有 1942 年 5 月 20 日宋子文致蒋介石电,其中第一句便是"十九日皓申电计达钧览"。《战时外交》并未收入该皓电,而《电报选》收入了:

> 加码　呈委员长电　卅一.五.十九
> 委座钧鉴:本日午后见空军参长亚诺,告以既谓双马达运输机足可应用,今以两星期为试办,期间如成绩不佳,仍须照拨四马达飞机,等语。
> 史梯威不久抵印,务请命其来渝详商:
> (一)中印空运每月最少吨位及运输机种类;
> (二)我需要之驱逐机及轰炸机;
> (三)中国派军入印训练及军械配备详细计划等等。
> 盖美军部以史梯威有全权,每有所商请,辄以史梯威并未要求,为不负责任推诿之词,谈及空运亦然。是以此后史梯威应令常依左右,遇事随时饬办,勿使远驻印度,否则种种计划进行愈感延滞。伏乞钧裁。○皓申。卅一.五.十九

　　看了皓申电最后一部分宋子文对美国军部与史迪威之间关系的分析,就较容易理解宋子文在次日的电报中建议蒋介石命令史迪威"设法策动军部,尽力增派"中国所需飞机[1],的确是点到了中国争取美援飞机难以奏效的症结所在。

　　又如,1943 年中英之间关于西藏问题的交涉,《战时外交》收入了 1943 年 5 月 31 日宋子文致蒋介石长电,有关于宋子文与丘吉尔激烈争辩的内容[2]。《电报选》不仅收入上述电报,还收入了多封后续交涉以及反映蒋宋关于西藏问题应持立场的往来电,如 5 月 22 日蒋介石电示宋子文:"西藏为中国领土,藏事为中国内政,今邱相如此出言,无异干涉中国内政,是即首先破坏大西洋宪章。中国对此不能视为普通常事,必坚决反对,并难忽视。"5 月 23 日宋子文致蒋介石电提醒"关于西藏事,在此危急之时,务恳避免冲突"。当日蒋介石致宋子文指示应向罗斯福严重表示;5 月 25 日蒋介石致电宋子文告以关于西藏问题"如罗总统有勿因此发生意外之语,则我更应申明立场主权为要,否则其他军事要求与我之主张,更被轻视,以后一切交涉,皆必从此失败矣"。5 月 25 日宋子文复电蒋介石报告当重复声明我国立场与主权。此外,当月宋子文还相继去电向蒋介石报告分别与罗斯福和英国外相艾登谈西藏问题的内容。

---

① 《中华民国重要史料初编》第三编战时外交(三),第 594 页。
② 同上书,第 233～235 页。

《电报选》还有不少重要内容,如:

1940 年 7 月即宋子文抵达美国不久,蒋介石便密示宋子文,在美交涉借款事,不必与胡适商量,以及在较长一段时间里蒋宋之间为替代胡适出任驻美大使的人选、召回胡适的时间等问题交换意见。

宋子文希望以行政院副院长的身份从事在美外交,蒋介石虽然原则上同意,但对于能否通过有顾虑。

蒋介石指示宋子文,在美购机事不可委托世界公司,该公司为陈光甫在美设立,实际上受孔祥熙影响。

1941 年春蒋介石为皖南事变多次向宋子文保证,这一事件绝不会影响中国的政治与外交,绝无分裂与内战之可能。

1941 年 5 月宋子文为宋庆龄主持的保卫中国同盟辩护,但最终在蒋介石的压力之下不得不退出。

《电报选》在编辑方面的一些安排,如:尽可能保存电报函稿的原始样态,视原稿情况尽可能注明收电、发电的登记号,注全发电、收电、复电的日期,不遗漏韵目及其代日;保存宋子文本人所有签署的"文";为每份电报确定了体现主要内容关键词的标题,在目录和正文部分同时出现;附中外人名、地名、机构索引等。上述安排在体现尊重历史的前提下,也提升了整个《电报选》的学术价值。

最后,还要强调的是:胡佛研究院藏宋子文驻美期间与蒋介石往来的中文电报稿,并不限于第 59 盒。这一时期宋子文与蒋介石之间还有英文函电稿;宋子文赴美前、自美回国后,与蒋介石之间有大量的函电往来;宋子文与亲友、部属、诸多中外人士之间,有着大量函电稿;宋子文与国外政要之间的许多会谈有纪要、记录、备忘录。而宋子文档案资料的使用,还要结合相关的其他文献。所以,《电报选》的学术价值是相对的,只是对宋子文档案整理出版的第一步,更是整个"复旦—胡佛近代中国人物与档案文献研究系列"的起点。

宋子文驻美时期电报选
（1940—1943）

1. 蒋介石致宋子文嘱见罗斯福时须说明各点电（1940 年 6 月 26 日）

A101　委员长来电

本日计已安抵美国为祝①。自法降德后，国际形势剧变，然亦无足为奇。英法既海军仍能联合作战，欧局不至速了。惟在此时期内，日本在远东必肆无忌惮，偏所欲为，变本加厉，尤其对于安南停运②，实于我军心民心大受影响。美国若傍【旁】观到底，不速干涉，则我抗战不利，甚想美政府必能为我国设法援助也。见罗总统③时，请先注重第一点，即欧战现阶段，中国因法降德对于远东影响太大，尤其安南交通断绝，中国抗战形势甚为不利。其对于中日问题解决之法与和战之道，请其详示。其他以下各点，请相机进言：（甲）美舰现在太平洋者是否可久驻，不调往大西洋。（乙）日本如果侵略安南，则其第二步必侵占和属印度④无疑。故对安南及运输问题，只望其以美国之权益与立场，及时出面维持正义。此实无形中遏制日本之南进政策，惟□时机也。（丙）美对俄最近之关系有否进步，美俄对日本之方针究有合作一致之可能否。（丁）日机每日狂炸重庆，美国如能警告其停止滥炸，否则即实行禁运汽油，必能生效也。中正。宥（廿六日）。

---

① 宋子文作为蒋介石的私人代表，于 1940 年 6 月 26 日抵达美国纽约。
② 指法属越南当局屈服于日本方面的压力，宣布自 1940 年 6 月 20 日起禁止中国假道越南运输货物，使得中国的国际运输遇到极大的困难。
③ 即时任美国总统的罗斯福（Franklin D. Roosevelt）。
④ 和属印度，即荷属东印度，今印度尼西亚。

2. 蒋介石致宋子文指示军械飞机定购数量及借款数目请兄相机决定电（1940 年 7 月 7 日）①

A102　委员长来电　七·八

耀密。

各电均悉。甚慰。（一）军械数目请照俞大维②交兄物单中之最大数量,即三千万元美金之数相商。（二）驱逐机如能定购,以百五十架为准,其式样请令现驻美国之王承黻③决定,已令其来谒兄。（三）借款数目,请兄相机决定,务望在美要务办妥后,再赴欧可也。诸事勿念。小儿纬国④来见时,请代教诲为盼。中正。阳(七日)。

3. 蒋介石致宋子文关于俞大维购械料之呈文电（1940 年 7 月 10 日）

A103　委员长来电　七·十二

耀密。

据俞大维呈称:前奉子文先生面嘱开二千万美金订货单,以备向美洽购,并云购械无把握,以购材料接洽较便,当开购械、购料各一千万美金单交之。械单内所开为轻机关枪一万挺,子弹三万万发。如能将购械范围增至二千万美金,则盼增购步枪、战车、防御炮、山炮,数量须得美价格后方能规定,已面告宋。等语。祈台洽。中正。蒸(十日)。

4. 蒋介石致宋子文指示向美方接洽驱逐机轰炸机电（1940 年 7 月 10 日）⑤

A104　委员长来电　七·十二

耀密。

请照鱼(六日)电各项进行。美国往日售法之各种飞机,如能转让于中国,现在美国若有最新式驱逐机三百架、远距离轰炸机五十至一百架助我,则抗战必能加速

---

① 该电文已收入《中华民国重要史料初编》第三编战时外交(一),台北:国民党中央委员会党史委员会,1981 年,第 409～410 页。

② 俞大维,浙江绍兴人,时任国民政府军政部兵工署署长、军事委员会作战部副部长。

③ 王承黻,时任国民政府航空委员会参事。

④ 即蒋纬国,浙江奉化人,时在美国麦斯威尔基地航空兵战术学校、装甲兵学校实习。

⑤ 该电文已收入《中华民国重要史料初编》第三编战时外交(一),第 410 页。

胜利。如遇罗总统时,请以余言告之。并告其每次我军之所以不能得到最后胜利,完全在我空军数量对日不及百一之故也。务望其于飞机能特别助我也。中正。灰(十日)。

5. 蒋介石致宋子文密示借款事不必与胡适相商请兄径自进行电(1940 年 7 月 12 日)

A105　委员长来电　已复　七.十二

耀密。借款事不必与胡使①相商,请兄径自进行为便。此时拟召胡使回国,未知有否不便之处。如遇罗总统,请以中②言转达如下:如美能以助法之飞机及其他物资之数,只要十分之一助华,则华不惟可得胜利,且可因美助华而得复兴,是中国历史上永不能遗忘美国之盛情高义也。此除罗总统以外,决非可望于其他第二人所能行也。希以此意相机进言何如。又闻美驻法大使蒲立脱③回美,中想聘其来华任高等顾问,未知可否,请酌之。中正。震(十二日)。

6. 蒋介石致宋子文告以英停止缅甸运输之后果电(1940 年 7 月 16 日)

A109　委员长来电　耀密　已复　廿九年七.十七

震(十二日)电已收悉。(一)缅甸运输如果停止,则对美借款除金融借款外,其他皆不能见效。(二)俄尚有半数之价款未并,以陆运甚难,自为原因之一。(三)美货经俄来华恐难有望。(四)英停止缅甸运输,使我国人对英美一切援助皆成泡影。(五)如美有决心,能与俄切实协商,对远东共同负责,则其事或有转机。(六)行政院新设经济作战部,暂任兄为部长,由中兼代,待兄回时或临时再易他部亦可。以该部关系重要,不能不从速成立,次长人选先以顾翊群④及曾养甫⑤二人,待兄回国可再另商也。中正。铣(十六日)。

---

① 即胡适,字适之,安徽绩溪人,时任中国驻美国大使。
② 蒋介石名中正,电文稿中常自简称"中"。
③ 蒲立脱(William C. Bullitt),即蒲立德,时任美国驻法国大使。
④ 顾翊群,字季高,江苏淮安人,时任广东省政府委员、财政厅厅长。
⑤ 曾养甫,广东平远人,时任管理中英庚款董事会董事、滇缅公路督办。

7. 蒋介石致宋子文嘱请美国阻止英国对日关于滇缅路妥协电(1940 年 7 月 17 日)

A110　委员长来电　耀密　七·十八

元(十三)寒(十四)电均悉。(一)苏联自上月与日订诺门坎协定①后,对我应交之货,口头尽管说可以就来,但迄无一物运到,想因近东问题未决,而欲与日妥洽一时。故此时欲以美借款购苏械及军械,希望甚少。已订者尚且不来,新订购者更难免借词延宕。观彼不欲得罪日本,纵与之商量,恐亦无确实答复也。目前若真欲加强我抗战力量,断难靠远水以救近火。除非美国直接帮忙,并由美切实运用苏俄,美俄间对远东问题有一确切办法。来电所称美货经海参威运华一节,自当向苏方交涉,但亦必须美国从中促成之,否则恐亦无□。(二)目前西北交通线虽未被日封锁,然事实上已等于封锁。今可靠者只滇缅路一条。此点关系重要,必使美国明了,并盼其速用一切方法,阻止英国对日本关于滇缅路之妥洽。(三)中国于英国态度之谈话,昨晚发表,想已见及。中正。篠(十七日)。

8. 蒋介石致宋子文嘱请美当局阻止倭寇侵略安南并从速金融救济电(1940 年 8 月 11 日)②

A113　委员长来电　耀密

各电均悉。此时我国抗战最大难关是经济,而武器尚在其次。此时米价比去年已贵至八倍以上,通货澎涨【膨胀】,不能再发。若不能在金融上设法处济,则民生饿冻,加之共党必从此捣乱,则抗战必难久持。如美能真正援华,请直告其当局:(一)此时必须以行动上阻止倭寇侵略安南,或当有效。否则不久倭必假道安南占领云南。如云南果为倭占领,则英美虽固守新加坡亦不能援华矣。(二)美国若不在金融上从速救济,则中国内外情势实难久持。务望美当局能于最近期内能将以上二事见之于行动,以助我一臂之力也。中正。真(十一日)。

---

① 指苏联和日本之间为解决两国军队在中国边境诺门坎地区武装冲突而达成的协定。
② 该电文已收入《中华民国重要史料初编》第三编战时外交(一),第 277 页。

9. 蒋介石致宋子文嘱向美当局疏通照准西南运输处设马尼拉分处电(1940 年 8 月 14 日)

A114　重庆来电　廿九年八月十四日

译转宋委员子文兄：西南运输处拟在马尼拉①设立分处，经菲方电美请示，赫尔②国务卿尚未作肯定答复。除令外交部正式交涉外，请兄就近向当局疏通照准。中正。寒申。

10. 蒋介石致宋子文告以行政拟改组整顿早日回国为盼电(1940 年 8 月 15 日)

A115　委员长来电　八.十五

瑞典政府购美飞机，如美政府能转售我国，彼不反对。如此只要美能转售于我，宜无问题。以后入口道路，如在缅甸不能入口，则在新加坡与印度装配后亦可直飞中国，只要英美果能有诚意助我耳。前电请恳惠美借款，兄可斟酌当地情势处理，词句亦不必照原电直□也。行政拟改组整顿，兄能早日回国为盼。中正。删(十五日)。

11. 蒋介石致宋子文告以加强行政机构事待兄来方得决定电(1940 年 8 月 23 日)

A116　委员长来电　耀密　八.廿四

删(十五)等电悉。加强行政机构事大要如兄所言者相同，待兄来方得决定。回国时能便道经俄亦好，尽其在我而已。中正。漾(廿三日)。

12. 蒋介石致宋子文指示药材运华安排电(1940 年 9 月 2 日)

A117　重庆来电　廿九年九月三日到

译转宋委员子文兄：俭电悉。该项药材为便利起见，由仰③运昆④，拟请红十字会负责，自昆至渝⑤则由西南运输处拨车，仍请红十字会供给汽油。惟在美起运

---

① 即菲律宾首府马尼拉(Manila)。
② 赫尔(Cordell Hull)，时任美国国务卿。
③ 即英属缅甸首府仰光。
④ 即中国云南昆明。
⑤ 即中国重庆，时为国民政府的战时首都。

时,请先电知香港柯士甸道一一一号中国红十字会王儒堂①先生。希察洽。中正。冬侍总渝。

13. 蒋介石致宋子文告以钨砂事已嘱经济部照办电(1940年9月11日)

A118 委员长来电　耀密　九.十九

钨砂事已嘱经济部照办。中正。真(十一日)。

14. 蒋介石致宋子文指示借款请全权办理电(1940年9月26日)②

A119 委员长来电　已复　九.廿六

漾(廿三)电悉。五千万美金③实不能济急,然却之不恭,且不无补益,自当承受。惟此五千万元全数希望其能一次付足,否则对外发表时,书面上亦应称总数五千万元。至于其中半数须过相当时期再商一句,不提更好,如此于对外声势与对内心理上,或更多补益也。据庸兄④之意,只要钨砂抵品能按期付足,保持信用,即可承借。请兄全权办理可也。中正。宥(廿六日)。

15. 蒋介石致宋子文告以三国同盟已证实美对我必有更进一步协助电(1940年9月28日)

A120 委员长来电　九.廿八　已复　九.廿九　十.二

德意倭三国同盟⑤消息刻已证实,则美国对我必有更进一步之协助。请兄特别注意此事,并望美能于最近期内再有一批金融借款贷我也。如美国果有意与我合作,则我所望其接济之武器惟飞机而已,而主要之接济乃在经济与金融,以安我抗战之民心与军心,使能持久抗战为惟一要求。此外无何要求也。又,俄国态度亦请在美特别注意。以现在三国同盟之精神,实由于防共协定⑥之脱胎而来,

---

① 即王正廷,字儒堂,时已卸任中国驻美大使,正兼任中国红十字总会会长,驻香港负责接收侨胞及国际援助。

② 该电文已收入《中华民国重要史料初编》第三编战时外交(一),第280页。

③ 即中美钨砂借款,当时宋子文向国内报告的该项借款数是5 000万美元,但后来正式达成时只有2 500万美元。

④ 即孔祥熙,字庸之,山西太谷人,时任国民政府行政院副院长、财政部部长、中央银行总裁。

⑤ 德国、日本、意大利于1940年9月27日签订《三国同盟条约》,正式组成法西斯轴心国集团。

⑥ 即德、日、意三国于1937年11月6日订立的《反共产国际协定》。

无论其同盟条件不关涉俄国,或俄最近态度如何,其最后必为此同盟之制命耳。甚望英美俄能与我联成阵线,共同制裁侵略,则幸矣。然此关键在美国,故我只可相机运用,而非我所能强求。如操之过急,或反被其怀疑。请兄从中运用,使不失时机为要。中正手启。俭(廿八日)。

16. 蒋介石致宋子文告以美新借款所需偿还钨砂产量和运输电(1940 年 10 月 1 日)

A121　重庆来电　廿九年十月二日到

译转宋子文先生:据翁部长①报告,美新借款所需偿还钨砂,每年约七千吨之数,就目前产量论,可无问题,所可虑者实为运输,现正商洽赶运,等语。特电知照。中正。东。

17. 蒋介石致宋子文告以借款签字事请相机处理及购办飞机计划电(1940 年 10 月 1 日)

A122　委员长来电　十月一日

宥(廿六)、感(廿七)、沁(廿七)一二各电均悉。借款签字事②,已照兄意电胡大使③照办,余可请兄相机处理。关于购办飞机计划,日内当可奉告。以后如新嘉坡为敌占领,则飞机用汽油亦甚为难。最好能预备大型运输机,由菲列滨④运汽油到重庆或桂林等地接济。如我方至明年二月秒再无新型驱逐机五百架、重轰炸机一百五十架到华接济,则抗日实无法维持。此意不□先示意美国也。中正。东(一日)。

18. 蒋介石致宋子文告以倭年内或大选以前必向英美先取攻势电(1940 年 10 月 2 日)

A123　委员长来电　十.三　已复　十.五

据密确消息,此次倭寇侵越南,其目的在由越境联系泰国军队图攻新嘉坡。此系

---

①　即翁文灏,字咏霓、咏年,浙江鄞县人,时任经济部部长兼资源委员会主任委员、工矿调整处处长。
②　中美 2 500 万美元钨砂金属借款协定,于 1940 年 10 月 22 日在华盛顿签署,中方由宋子文代表国民政府、李干代表中央银行、吴志翔代表资源委员会签字。
③　即时任中国驻美国大使的胡适。
④　菲列滨,即菲律宾。

德方授计,且德确定美国大选以前对英美开始总攻。届时西方助西班牙攻直布罗①,远□中由意大利攻苏彝士②纳【?】,东方则由倭泰协攻新嘉坡、香港,使英处处受敌,逼令屈服。此计中以为其必如期实行,且倭如对英美此时若不下手,一过明年以后则其力量更不及英美,只有让英美宰割。故中料其年内或大选以前必向英美先取攻势。惜英美行动迟疑不决,坐失时机,处处为轴心国吹制机先。若英美此时对新嘉坡复不迅即联防,积极进行,则新嘉坡危而太平洋大势去矣。望明告英美当局为盼。中正手启。冬(二日)。

19. 蒋介石致宋子文指示应购飞机及油料弹械电(1940 年 10 月 4 日)③

A124　委员长来电　十月六日　已复　十.八

应添之飞机及油料、弹药、器材如下:(一)飞机数量:(甲)驱逐机三百,其中一百五十架对轰炸机战斗者,一百五十架对驱逐机战斗者。(乙)轰炸机二百架,一百架单发动机有俯冲性能者,并由其中抽一部充实侦察中队,一百架双发动机。备份飞机每月以百分之卅计,每月须补充:(甲)驱逐机九十,依前项两种性能各购半数;(乙)轰炸机六十架,依前项单双发动机各购卅架。(二)飞机式样:以现在美国军部使用当为主。因制造需时过久,故拟尽量就美国军部现用妥善飞机适合我国使用者,并更换新发动机后,期能迅速运华。(三)飞机之发动机:以装气凉式发动机为主。因我国空军机械经验对气凉式佳,如 WRIGHT 公司之 CYCLOE F G 各式之发动机,及 PRATHWHITUCY 公司之 WASP 及 TWIRWOSP 发动机均有经验。至液凉式发动机,如 ALYSON,因经验较少,且液凉需凉剂如 GLYCOL 之供给及配合较为困难。希望目前略予供给装用液体凉式发动机之飞机,以资练习。(四)飞机零件:飞机装备武器之口径一二点七及七点六二与六三点均可适用。照相机、描【瞄】准具等须最现代化者。其备份零件部分,轰炸机之前舱,即机身首部,与轰炸机及驱逐机之起落架尾轮、翼尖、螺旋浆【桨】等,其数目希望至少在百分之一百。(五)照上项之飞机数目及训练用,年需汽油二千五百万至三千万加仑,及配合适当之滑油。(六)照上数之飞机数目,年需炸弹三万吨、枪弹七点六卡【?】一万万发、一二点七一千万发、炮弹二三 MM 二百万发。(七)飞机交货:上

---

① 直布罗,即直布罗陀,是连接地中海和大西洋的重要门户。
② 苏彝士,即苏伊士运河,位于埃及境内,是连接欧、亚、非三大洲的重要航道。
③ 该电文已收入《中华民国重要史料初编》第三编战时外交(一),第411~412 页。

项飞机及油料弹药器材等最好尽量立刻运华,以免以后运输断绝。至于人员之训练,(一) 地点为补给不感困难并美政府许可时,任在美国或菲列滨均可。但菲岛距我较近,费用亦省,尤为有利。如分地训练为有利时,美籍华侨请其尽量代为训练,并另以官校之高级班学生,或器材困难时,即自中级起调往受训。此项计划如能实施,则官校高级班之教育器材可移交士校使用。(二) 人数暂定为一千名。除训练飞行华人外,并以同时训练一西轰炸员,请少数机械人员为宜。至其兵科人数之百分比,俟订购飞机机种机数确定后再行分配。(三) 期间暂定为三年。(四) 计划拟交裘伟德上校专〈一〉认真办理。此项补充之飞机为求迅速获得,不受美参战后所生之影响,及得外交之声援起见,以能立即于美国所现用之飞机先行商让为盼。希与前途切实洽商,早日决定为要。中正手启。支(四日)。

20. 蒋介石致宋子文告以俄机终未来急需美国新式飞机接济电(1940 年 10 月 7 日)

A125　委员长来电　十月七日　已复　十·八

支(四日)、支二电悉。(一) 俄机已允而终未交来,但其飞机即使交来,其性能亦不能与敌现用之飞机作战,徒使我空军死伤而已。以其速度与各种性能相差太远。最近敌空军在成都猖獗无阻,军民抗战心理渐起动摇,非由美国更新式飞机接济殊难持久。(二) 我在浙江尚有空军根据地大机场,衢州、丽水、玉山等三① 个对日本国内各军港根据地距离最近,如美能助我新式重轰炸机维持每月二百架,及驱逐机前电之数,则日本主力舰队不难在数月内扫荡尽净。此非夸语,请美注意。(三) 美在陆军与空军上如有与我合作诚意,我即可派员来美洽商。(四) 合【俄】对华症结是在要我脱离英美,独与俄合作,否则无论如何彼不愿助华。至于对中俄合作办法,自当在时时设法也。中正手启。阳(七日)。

21. 蒋介石致宋子文指示获得美国新式飞机为唯一急务电(1940 年 10 月 7 日)②

A126　委员长来电　十月七日　已复　十·八

两电谅达。敌驱逐机近日由宜昌可直飞蓉渝两地,掩护其轰炸机随意所至,肆无

---

① 原稿为"(三)",但根据上下文,此处应为基数词。下文之"(三)"、"(四)",原稿为"(四)""(五)"。
② 该电文已收入《中华民国重要史料初编》第三编战时外交(一),第 413 页。

忌惮。以俄式驱逐机升高速度至六千公尺须十五分钟以上,而敌机只要六分钟就可升至六千米以上,故对之望尘莫及,只有让其猖獗。此与兄在渝时空战情形完全不同。以后俄国即使供给我飞机,亦为不能望其以新式飞机交我也。以后我若无新式美驱逐机与敌机一打击,则军心民心实难持久。故此时以获得美国新式飞机为唯一急务,特再为兄陈之。中正手启。虞(七日)。

22. 蒋介石致宋子文告以美联社电文查询结果电(1940 年 10 月 9 日)

委员长来电   十月十日

前据感(廿七)电,经转庸之①兄查询。据复:美联社宥(廿六)日渝电系合众社所发,但原电并无官方发言人字样。原电谓滇缅路苟仍封锁,则钨砂无出口途径,是故为中国与各和平国家之贸易计,滇缅路实有开放必要云。检查人员以其意在促成缅路开放,故予放行。细译原文确无恶意等语。特达。中正。佳(九日)。

23. 蒋介石致宋子文告以美空军义勇队来华甚为欢迎电(1940 年 10 月 12 日)

A129   委员长来电   十.十二   已复   十.十四

美空军义勇队来华助战,甚为欢迎。如果美愿与我合作,则将派陈纳德②与我国要员飞美接洽。如其有决心,则进行应快,否则恐交通运输皆发生障碍也。上海陆战队届时与我合作当不成问题。惟平时须先介绍其驻沪陆战队与我方认识,而可不说明其认识之目的也。中正手启。文(十二日)。

24. 蒋介石致宋子文告以拟派毛邦初来美电(1940 年 10 月 15 日)

委员长来电   十.十六   已复   十.十七

美政府召陈纳德顾问回美陆军航空部服务,中拟派邦初③同其来美,以备兄咨询空军合作计划。未知美政府之决心如何,请探明,以便邦初决定行止。中正手启。删(十五)。

---

① 即孔祥熙。
② 陈纳德(Claire L. Chennault),美国退役空军飞行员,抗战爆发后任国民政府航空委员会顾问,曾帮助中国训练飞行员,当时在美游说争取援助,后成为中国空军美国志愿大队指挥官。
③ 即毛邦初,字信诚,浙江奉化人,时任国民政府军事委员会航空委员会委员。

25. 蒋介石致宋子文并转胡适告以十八日与美大使会谈内容电（1940 年 10 月 20 日）

A132　委员长来电　十·廿一

并转胡大使：中十八日接见美大使①，略谓：自滇缅路禁运后，不独美国货品无从运入，即苏联之来源亦已停止。尤以近二月来中国共党日见猖獗，于前途不无顾虑。此乃中国危机之一。滇缅路禁运后中共在文字上虽无反对中央显著之动作，但在其宣传上已有反对之言论。此种实□只愿美政府知之。倘此次滇缅路不能重开，而美国此次如不贷款于中国，则我国□□与经济皆将发生严重之影响。此乃中国危机之二。余深信我国现在陆军实力绝不能受日军摧残，所虑者惟中共猖獗与民众抗战意志之减低耳。最近一星期局势已有好转，此固由于滇缅路之重开，而苏俄对我态度之改良亦不无关系。如欲维持苏俄此种改善态度，与安定我国之人心使能继续抗战，非有美国在事实上之积极援助不可。我国所期望于美国者为飞机与经济援助。此次英国重开滇缅路，得罗斯福总统之鼓励实多，此为中国抗战历史上转败为胜、转危为安之最大关键。中国政府与人民对罗斯福总统之厚意不胜感谢。宋子文先生现正与美政府商讨援助我国之具体方案。总之，国际形势不论如何发展，中国必与美英□□到底。惟今后美国之援助其最要者为日【时】间问题，盖援助须在滇缅路受敌机狂炸交通中断之前始克有济。进而言之，敌人如进攻新加坡，则海运必断，此时美国虽欲助我亦不可能，故时间急迫实为最要问题。余切盼二三月内能得美国大量装制齐备之飞机，庶可鼓励我国军民继续抗战。我国每年需机数只五百至一千架，但须于交通未断二三个月内能先运到五百架以济眉急。浙江省现有完备空军根据地多处，即可由此轰炸台湾与日本各大军港。我国如有此数量飞机即可□□日本海军之实力。此实美国惟一替待【代】对日作战之良策也。即使美日发生战事，只要中国有新式空军以助我陆军之作战，则美国海军虽不驶来远东亦无妨碍，盖中国陆军与美国空军之一部分已足以消灭日本海军，而永奠远东安定之基础矣。除供给上述飞机外，美国空军志愿飞航人员能来华助战则更佳，否则中国空军人员稍加适当训练亦可驾驶新式飞机。美大使答称，倘能实现此项计划，余完全赞成，深盼有以报命，当将谈话要点电告华盛顿。中谓：在中美英合作中我国当随美国之领导自无待言，□此美国三次借款共七千五百万美金业已发生良好之影响，深盼今后对我贷款能化零为整，一次贷我以巨款，必可激励我人民抗战之情绪。总之，

---

① 即时任美国驻华大使的詹森（Nelson T. Johnson）。

我人至今已不患日寇敌军之侵略,而患国内经济与社会现状之崩溃。惟美之空军与经济之援助乃足以固我摇动之经济与民心。如能得此中【美】国援助,则中共自无所施其技矣。因之须知中国抗战如果失败,不惟日本独霸东亚为□虑,而共党起而为患,则于远东将来之影响亦甚足忧也。美大使允将此节一并报告政府。云云。中正。号(廿日)。

26. 蒋介石致宋子文补述与美大使谈话要点电(1940年10月20日)①

A133　委员长来电

前电谅达。兹又补充与美使②谈话要点如下:(一)余愿于交通线未断以前能得大量飞机运入中国,已拟有具体计划,由宋先生洽请贵国政府之协助。此项飞机期于三个月内可以应用,故向厂家订购时间已不许可,必须于美国已经制成或美国军部现有之飞机分拨来华,方可鼓励军民继续抗战。(二)中国抗战之始,即公告国民以三年为期,今抗战已逾三年,尚未能败敌获胜。当七、八月间敌机来袭,我尚有少数飞机应战,故民心未若今日之动摇。惟至今我空军消耗已尽,再无法起飞应敌,所以敌机敢在全国各地狂施轰炸,横行无忌,此实使最近民众转侧不安,尤以商民为甚,常转相问曰如美国再〈不〉筹拨援助我国,则我继续牺牲果有何益乎? 倘美机答〈达〉以前国际交通再断,则人民□战局势更为动摇矣。等语。以上二意最为重要,恐美大使对其政府报告遗漏未能详尽,请兄再对美当局申述此意为盼。中正。号二。

27. 蒋介石致宋子文告以斯大林对三国同盟立场电(1940年10月23日)

A135　委员长来电　十.廿三

昨接史太林③篠(十七)日直接复我之电,其意甚含蓄,但其关于三国同盟事,明言我中苏两国之利害相同,最后并含有中苏两国皆无对日妥协余地之意。而其最注重之点,则谓相信中国有精强之陆军在握,必可求得国家之独立自由,摧破一切困难云,请兄注意。但须守密,非有重要□故,不对任何人说明也。邦初等约廿六日由港飞美,特闻。中正。梗(廿三日)。

---

①　该电文已收入《中华民国重要史料初编》第三编战时外交(一),第103页。
②　即美国驻华大使詹森(Nelson T. Johnson)。
③　即斯大林(Joseph V. Stalin),时任联共(布)中央委员会总书记,为苏联最高领导人。

28. 蒋介石致宋子文转告俞大维关于襄助购械报告电(1940 年 10 月 26 日)

A129　委员长来电　二十七日

据俞大维告：拟派江灼①率技术人员往美襄助购械,在该员等未抵美前,由本署现驻美协助陈光甫②先生购兵工材料工程师韩朝宗③、王乃宽□□,宋先生随时指导。等语。除复照准外,希知照。中正。寝川侍参。

29. 蒋介石致宋子文嘱转告美当局总期年内有三百架美机到华电(1940 年 10 月 27 日)④

A136　委员长来电　十.廿九

美国飞机务期其售给瑞典飞机全数让我之外,并望其在售给法国或安南之飞机中拨购二百架,尤以新式驱逐机为最急。请将此意转告美当局,总期今年之内能有三百架美机到华,以坚军民抗战心理也。中正。感(廿七)。

30. 蒋介石致宋子文告以滞越美货情况嘱请美方积极交涉电(1940 年 10 月 29 日)

A138　委员长来电　十.卅一　已复　十一.十

据子良⑤寝(廿六)港电称：据报,海防信臣洋行⑥所租之法船西江号,装货满八千五百吨,敬(廿四)日敌陆海军官员登船查验,搜得防毒面具,指为军用品,要求全船卸载。越态度软弱,税务司现作最后努力,希望甚微。等语。查该轮所载物资,系各机关于六月间售与美商信臣洋行。该行在美国德拉维亚州注册,实系美商卖买,及付款手续均已合法办妥,故该项物资实为美国资□,与我国无关。至面具为防毒卫生用品,与普通商品相同,不应视作战斗品。似应由我方告知美大使,俾明真相,设法交涉放行。至胡大使方面应否告知并乞核示。等语。请转请美方积极交涉,使法船美货能如期运出为盼。中正。艳

---

① 即江杓,上海人,时任国民政府军政部兵工署驻美国代表。
② 即陈辉德,字光甫,江苏镇江人,时任国民政府财政部贸易委员会主任委员。
③ 韩朝宗,字海波,河南孟津人,时任军政部兵工署兵工研究委员。
④ 该电文已收入《中华民国重要史料初编》第三编战时外交(一),第 413～414 页。
⑤ 即宋子良,宋子文二弟,时任军事委员会西南运输处主任。
⑥ 信臣洋行,即美国远东贸易公司(United States Far Eastern Trading Corporation)。

（廿九日）。

31. 蒋介石致宋子文指示高射枪炮与飞机同时订购起运电（1940 年 11 月 14 日，附宋子文拟复电稿）

A139　委员长来电　十一.十四　已复　十一.十五

各种高射枪炮，务请照前寄之单，与飞机同时订购起运，以应急需。如何，盼复。中正。寒（十四）。

［宋子文手拟复电稿如下：当遵嘱同时进行，邦初今可抵此。文。］

32. 蒋介石致宋子文告以中国银行代央行领收美新借款请直接电达孔祥熙电（1940 年 11 月 22 日）

A141　委员长来电　十一.廿二

皓（十九）电关于二千五百万美元借款由中国银行代中央银行领收事，请直接电达庸兄，想已用正式手续办理矣。又，孟余①事只要孟余承允，当照办。中正。养。

33. 蒋介石致宋子文告以俄大使面告武器预备完妥即可开始运输电（1940 年 11 月 25 日，附宋子文拟复电稿）

A142　委员长来电　十一.廿六　已复　十一.廿七

昨俄大使②面告，其政府已将前约武器预备完妥，即可开始运输云。此可知俄德与俄日之关系，并未以莫洛托夫③访德而有所增进，或至比前恶化亦未可知。请以此意酌告英美当局，作一参考材料。但俄货必须待其到华后方能作数耳。中正。有（廿五）。

［宋子文手拟复电稿如下：一、承示俄大使告武器开始输运，甚感。起运日期亦请届时告。惟此项消息尚未成事实，请暂勿告任何人，恐英美以为既有后援，不必太出力援我。二、政府（以下稿断）］

---

①　即顾孟余，字梦渔，浙江上虞人，时任国民党中央宣传部部长。
②　即时任苏联驻华大使的潘友新（Alexander Semenovich Paniushkin）。
③　莫洛托夫，时任苏联外交人民委员。

34. 蒋介石致宋子文密示美金两千万借款签字后暂不发表电(1940 年 11 月 29 日)

A143 委员长来电 十一.卅

沁(廿七)二电悉。现允借美金二千五百万元,务望签字后暂不发表,必须待中所提方案成立后同时发表,否则于我国民心影响甚为不利。而且日本承认伪组织时,如美在经济方面对我不有大借款发表,则于我政府地位与社会心理,必发生动摇,抗战局面万难久持。美既不愿在形式上有任何合作行动,则对中所提丙项具体办法是否可以允许,务希详询。又,对于华西各种经济建设,拟速定一个整个计划,如美愿协助,亦可在此时讨论进行,以免将来恢复和平时日方有所要求。亦请兄研究探询,最好能促其派经济团来华进行也。中正。艳(廿九日)。

35. 蒋介石致宋子文嘱告美当局推动合作开发华西电(1940 年 11 月 30 日)

A144 委员长来电 十一.卅 已复 十一.卅

昨电谅达。华西物资与宝藏,日人常称为以后三百年虽用东亚全力开发此富源,亦不能完尽,可知其垂涎之切。我国以后经济建设之基础,与国防工业之建立,亦全在华西,川、康、滇、桂、黔、粤、湘、赣诸省皆在内。万一中日恢复和平,其对我华西物资之开发,必争先着,有所要求,故此时不得不先为之。所以我国战后之经济建设全赖美国,否则日本必先争取,如此时中美对华西有一合作基础,订立条约,或即以我所提三万万美金为美国预付之资金亦可。如此则敌对华西之经济不敢再有所觊觎。但此时要有整个计划与设计,故须先催其派经济、交通、军事顾问来华切实进行也。希以此意转告美当局从速推动为要。中正。卅。

36. 蒋介石致宋子文告以日已与汪伪组织签约嘱把中国之意转达罗斯福电(1940 年 11 月 30 日)

蒋总裁①来电 廿九.十一.卅

日本与汪伪组织已正式签字,条约②事实上已经承认。此时英美如无严重表示

---

① 即蒋介石,在 1938 年 3 月召开的中国国民党临时全国代表大会上被推举为中国国民党总裁。
② 指 1940 年 11 月 30 日汪伪政权在南京与日本当局签订的《中日调整国交条约》,亦称《中日基本条约》。

及大量助华之事实发表,对我国民心理与经济状态必发生不测变化。如美国不愿与英共同宣言,可否两国先商定共同之原则,而作平行各自之宣言。如能以大量借款同时发表,则助我之效更大也。务请以此意转达罗总统为盼。中正手启。

37. 蒋介石致宋子文告以张心一调甘请另物色替人电(1940年11月30日)

蒋委员长来电　十二月一日

沁(廿七)电悉。张心一①君调甘,业经明令发表,请另物色替人,并催张君早日赴任,以重边政。中正。卅亥。

38. 蒋介石致宋子文指示请先赴英办理借款再速回美电(1940年12月3日)

A146　*委员长来电　十二.四　已复　十二.四*

美借款既发表,所拟补助飞机说帖已交美英,可一面催其早决,务望其于兄由英回美时,飞机交涉能完全解决相约也;一面请兄先赴英办理借款完成,再速回美为盼。中正。江(三日)。

39. 蒋介石致宋子文并转胡适借款完成乃二兄努力之功效无任感谢电(1940年12月3日)

A147　*委员长来电　十二.四　已复　十二.四*

并转胡大使:此次借款完成,乃二兄努力之功效,无任感谢,并祝康健。中正手启。江(三日)二。

40. 蒋介石致胡适并转宋子文告以法越当局损害外国物资并侵犯美国权益电(1940年12月4日)

A145　*重庆来电　廿九年十二月四日*

胡大使适之并转达宋子文兄:据西南运输处转海防报告:(一)敌军以卡车运输美商信臣洋行前装西江轮之货,并闻另行装船外运,应请转美政府向法抗议,或扣押法在美资产。(二)西贡方面奉越督命,将我方官商过境货物解倭馆。我方

---

① 张心一,又名继忠,甘肃河州人,1940年11月起任甘肃省政府委员兼建设厅厅长。

在越资产权利,系托美领代管。现美领李德密嘱请胡大使商华盛顿起诉,扣押东方汇□□千万金。等语。此事法越当局不但损害我国物资,且并侵犯美国权益,自应迅采对抗处置办法,即希斟酌所陈意见,就近洽办。中正。支机印。

41. 蒋介石致宋子文嘱对英借款至少凑足一万万之数电(1940 年 12 月 6 日)①

A148　委员长来电　十二.七

豪(四日)、歌(五日)各电悉。闻裴律普②到美,中亦以为兄不必赴英。适接歌(五日)电,正合鄙意也。对英借款至少要其凑足美金一万万元之数,请以此意告之。美国借我总数已一万万五千万美金,而英国如承〈借〉我,数量上至少亦要有一万万美金也。但其方式与交款办法,则可设法使英国战局不受影响也。中正手启。鱼。

42. 蒋介石致宋子文密告日方与美油商商定由美运沪转日电(1940 年 12 月 9 日)

重庆来电　廿九年十二月九日

探报,敌为挽救石油恐慌,曾派斋藤某赴美,与美油商商定以上海为转运站,秘密由美运沪转日。等情。即希知照。中正。庚川佳六。

43. 蒋介石致宋子文准购买大号汽车电(1940 年 12 月 9 日)

A149　委员长来电　十二.十

宥(三日)电悉。所拟自办矿产运输,由借款内拨给美金购买大号汽车一节,可予照准。并已知照孔副院长③及翁部长矣。中正。佳(九日)。

44. 蒋介石致宋子文告以英已内定贷华总数一千万镑电(1940 年 12 月 9 日)④

A150　委员长来电　十二.十

确知英政府已内定贷华总数为一千万镑,其中以信用与币制借款各五百万镑。

---

① 该电文已收入《中华民国重要史料初编》第三编战时外交(二),第 222 页。
② 裴律普,即菲利普(Sir Frederick Phillips),时任英国财政部次长、中英平准基金英方谈判代表。
③ 即孔祥熙,时任国民政府行政院副院长。
④ 该电文已收入《中华民国重要史料初编》第三编战时外交(二),第 230～231 页。

中刻召英大使①来见,说明如只有总数一千万镑,则切勿正式发表,必须足有二千万镑之数同时发表,方足有助于我抗战,及我人民对英国方不失望。与之讨论二小时之久,彼必以为甚难。最后中嘱其以中意见直告其政府。如果为难,则发表时总数仍须定为二千万镑。除一千万镑为币制借款外,其余一千万镑之信用借款现在不须急用,姑待以后另议办法。万一英国真困难,不能全数支付,则中国亦决不强求,但发表总数必须为二千万镑也。彼勉允电达其政府,并约星期四日可得复电,则可知此借款将于本星期三、四发表。请兄速与在美之英友切实声明,如果仅止一千万镑总数,则暂勿发表为要。惟其内定之总数,并非英大使之言,亦不必与美友肯定其事,只说见之于报上消息可也。中正手启。佳(九日)。

45. 蒋介石致宋子文嘱与英方切商贷我二千万镑电(1940 年 12 月 10 日)②

A151　重庆来电　廿九年十二月十一日

即转宋子文兄:顷据路透息,英政府已正式宣布,将贷我以一千万镑。务请仍照中前电,向英方力争,必须贷我二千万镑。如彼以此数已经确定,亦切商此一千万镑专作为币制借款,对于信用贷款,必须另行续商订借。除电复初③兄外,务希照此速与英方切商,并复。中正。灰亥侍秘印。

46. 蒋介石致宋子文告以自由英镑办法已转英方电(1940 年 12 月 11 日)

A152　委员长来电　十二.十二

阳(七日)电悉。关于自由英镑办法,已嘱卡尔大使转达英方矣。中正。真(十一日)。

47. 蒋介石致胡适并转宋子文嘱密告美方苏联援华已转趋积极电(1940 年 12 月 11 日)

A153　重庆蒋总裁来电　廿九年十二日十二日

胡大使并转子文兄同鉴:外交部转来胡大使微(五日)电悉。可以下列之意密访美外部,口头答复之:苏联对我物质援助系根据签定之信用贷约,用以货易货之

---

① 即时任英国驻华大使的卡尔(Sir Archibald Clark-Kerr)。
② 该电文已收入《中华民国重要史料初编》第三编战时外交(二),第 235 页。
③ 即郭泰祺,字保元,号复初,时任中国驻英国大使。

方式。最近鉴于日本求和失败,我国抗战坚决,对于履行契约应交我方之物资,特数次派员向中表示,愿积极运交。其种类包括野炮及机枪等,惟飞机数量不多,亦未预告确数与运交确期。再苏方人员并向中探询,美国委我军需有无成议,且表示希望美国充分援华之意。故苏联援华之前途实已转趋积极,且与美国态度有密切之关系也。上述各语,并希互约守密为要。中正。真(十一日)。

48. 蒋介石致宋子文嘱分别译致罗斯福等四人电稿并分转电(1940 年 12 月 12 日)

A154　委员长来电　十二.十三

下列四电请分别译成英文由兄分转为要。

(一) 致罗斯福大总统电如下:

当此日本承认伪组织与日伪签订条约,正在敝国危急之秋,贵大总统适于此时宣布贷与我国以币制与信用巨款①,所以增强敝国对侵略者抗战力量,提高我军民自信心与安定社会经济之基础者,裨益实无限量。阁下此种扶弱抑强维持正义之精神,实予侵略者以最大之打击,已辟太平洋上和平光明之大道。望风遐想,敬佩何如。深信远东局势之澄清与永久和平之确立,必由阁下贤明之政策与伟大之精神而完成,此为余五年以来一贯不变之认识,即敝国全体军民所一致信赖而至今更日益坚强者也。此后关于远东和平与建设问题,更待吾人共同努力,当盼阁下随时赐示,俾作南针。兹因另有密件托宋子文先生面陈,如有公暇,务盼早日召见,是为至幸。特电敬谢,并祝康健。

(二) 致赫尔电如下:

余对于总统及阁下所采取之实际办法,一面援助中国,一面抑制侵略者,至为感荷。此次在华盛顿所议订之贷款,又足证明美国愿于中国需助最切之时予以援助,更使余深信总统及阁下对于中国所必需之考虑,与主持美国对远东局势每采一种重要步骤,吾人对美国之感荷则更深一层,而抗战至最后胜利之意志益为坚决。特电伸谢。

(三) 致摩根索②电如下:

中国为自由独立而抗战,阁下屡示同情,余实欣感。美国迭次对华予以财政上之援助,均赖阁下周旋之力。此次贷款又足证明美国对于正以全力在太平洋抵抗侵略之国家愿予充分之援助。特电致谢。

---

① 币制与信用巨款,指次年签署的中美平准基金借款 5 000 万美元和金属借款 5 000 万美元。
② 摩根索(Henry Morgenthau Jr.),时任美国财政部部长。

(四) 致琼斯①电如下:

美国迭次对华贷款,裨益我抗战非浅。此次贷款之效用必将更大。贵国政府所定援助被侵略者之政策,由阁下负责实行。余对阁下为此事之努力无任欣感,特电驰谢。中正。震。

49. 蒋介石致宋子文嘱译转致罗斯福函稿电(1940 年 12 月 13 日)②

A155　委员长来电　十二．十四

译转罗斯福大总统阁下:十二月十二日谢电谅已达览。敝国目前在抗日侵略战争上之需要,在经济方面既承贵国贷与巨款,复因此获得英国之响应,一时已不致有何困难。惟在空军与武器补给方面,仍不得不切望大力主持。兹将余之计划及请求要点,为阁下详述之。余以为西欧战争与中国抗战已不可分,且在解决之程序上,对于遏制日本侵略之范围较易,而且可使中日之战事先行结束,远东形势获得早日安定,而后西欧之战事亦易着手解决,世界和平乃能实现。此为世界大局之枢机,想已早为阁下所察及。然为达此目的,必须在日本尚未发动及扩大其南进战事以前,对其空军与【予】以甚大之打击,或使之不断消耗而与【予】以有力之牵制。据余所得情报,日本在明年四月以前,不致发动南进攻势,亦不致大量撤退其在华之陆军,而转用于南洋之攻击。因之在目前与日本空军以攻击与牵制,阻止其南进军事之扩大,甚至根本打消其南进之企图,在远东与世界大局上实为必要而不可或缓之发动,而此种计划决非不可能之事。余且深信其必可以少数之力量而收获重大之效果,其关键要在短急时期内能予敌军以出其不备之打击耳③。盖现在日本空军实力,其有作战能力之飞机约在二千五百至三千架之数,且其装炸弹与飞行速率不及于美国最新式之飞机。依敝国过去作战之经验,此时敝国若有美国新式飞机五百架,即足以牵制一千五百架日机之战斗。换言之,即日机有半数以上不能作南进之用。若中国空军有此数额之优良武器,能继续补充与之持久空战,更可进一步与【予】日本空军以不断之消耗。如此日本之陆海军无充分空军之掩护,必无发动南进扩大侵略之可能。即令其有上述南进之准备与计划,亦不能不被迫中止。故目前消除日本在太平洋上侵略之祸患,根本之计无逾于此。余所以迫切要求阁下对于敝国空军之接济与充实,决不

---

① 琼斯(Jesse Jones),时任美国联邦债务署主任。
② 该电文已收入《中华民国重要史料初编》第三编战时外交(一),第 427~429 页。
③ 原稿中,"其关键要在短急时期内能予敌军以出其不备之打击耳"为后加。

在获得少数或一二百架飞机,仅以保护运输路线与重要都市。余确信打击日本军事之计划,必须采取攻势,不能仅取消极的守势,且必有充分空军力量作积极整个之反攻,方为有效。如每次只能得到数十架至一二百架之飞机,不独绝无整个反攻之力量,且陆续接济,则彼对我新到飞机反可陆续轰炸,不断与我以消耗。如此我在发动反攻以前,即有受其分次击破之可能,而外来之接济与援助反成为虚耗,而辜负阁下之嘉惠。余在发动下期反攻之目的,不仅使我空军可掩护陆军以反攻日本之陆军与打击日本在华之空军,而且必须我空军能派遣至日本国内轰炸其空军根据地与制造厂,及其重要之军事设备与工业中心。如此方能发生决定胜败之效用,而根本结束中日战事。为达到此目的,必须在一定期间以前,获得贵国最新式飞机至少五百架整批之供给,而且必须有最精良而为日本所无之远程空战工具。综括上述理由,余在明知美国□□及供给之状况下,特提出二点最低限度之请要:(一)由贵国所造英美两国需用之飞机总数量中至少抽拨百分之五至十以助我,且提先运交,务使在三四个月内能得到五百架以上之飞机。然此事非经阁下特别设法批准,恐不能实现余之计划。务盼迅赐特准,饬令实施,俾我国最低限度之充实空军计划得以完成,而能实施有效之反攻。(二)请助我以贵国所制之空中保【堡】垒若干架,俾我能发挥远程战斗之力量,予日本国内以更重大更有效之打击,暴露其军阀之弱点,促起侵略者根本之觉悟。去年日本与俄国在诺门勘作战,俄国实只以不足五百架新机在半月之间即击毁日机足在六百架以上。从此日本即对俄屈服,不敢再向俄尝试挑战。此为日本对空战失败之实例,亦为其现实教训之先例也。余抱此计划实已蕴蓄已久,不愿托之空谈。今日亦且为贡献于远东大局着想,故不惮向阁下坦白直陈。至于详细技术上贵部人员及配备、补充等问题,以及运交之日期与方法,特托宋子文先生面洽,请嘱主管机关与之切商。总期贵国一向援华之好意能不失时机而收最大有利之效果,亦使中国能彻底打击日本,消灭远东祸患,而有俾于世界和平。务盼大力主持,早日批准,不胜厚幸。蒋中正。元(十三日)。

50. 蒋介石致宋子文指示前拟中英美空军合作提议不宜再提并召胡适回国事当须研究电(1940 年 12 月 13 日)

A157　委员长来电　十二.十四

军事方面此时美仍忌与英国有合作之形式,故前拟中英美三国空军合作提议不宜再提。现只要求美国照中致罗总统电意设法进行,或较方便也。胡大使在美不得力,故中在正式提出方案以前召其回国。然现在电召或调换,据中所得消息,彼或仍留美,不愿奉召,故对此事处理当须研究至当方能决定也。中正手启。覃(十三日)。

51. 蒋介石致宋子文嘱请译转诺克斯函稿电(1940年12月13日)①

A158　委员长来电　十二.十五

译转诺克斯②海军部长阁下:麦寇③少校携示十一月十五日大函,诵悉感佩。余已与麦少校接谈,告以中国抗战之实况与军事上之需要,以便向阁下报告。中国在抵抗侵略者作战以后,屡得贵国之同情与财政上及其他之援助,足使吾人能为正义必获胜之自信。而此种种援助之日见增强,固出于贵国大总统之英断,更多由执事之远见与热诚促成。此尤为余及全国军民所共感,自当益加奋发,继续努力,与扰乱远东安宁之野心国家以极大之打击,而根本遏止太平洋上之祸患。为达此目的,在军事器材补给尤其空军需用之飞机等,实盼望贵国能与【予】以及时之接济,俾中国在野心国家断然发动南洋侵略以前,能施行有效之反攻。余已将余之意见托宋子文先生提陈贵国大总统,深信阁下本于军略上之见地,必予以深切之赞助。务请多方促成,俾得迅速实现,不胜盼幸。蒋中正。问(十三日)。

52. 蒋介石致宋子文指示英借款既正式公布我方不必再争电(1940年12月14日)④

A156　委员长来电　十二.十四

尤(十一日)电悉。英借款⑤既在其议会正式公布,则我方不必再争,免伤感情,并表代谢之意。兄应即允其待美完全商洽后访英。惟未赴英以前,可托复初与秉文⑥先行开始协商。如美事能早日就绪,则请速前往以报其厚意也。中正。盐(十四日)。

---

① 该电文已收入《中华民国重要史料初编》第三编战时外交(一),第430页。
② 诺克斯(Frank Knox),时任美国海军部部长。
③ 麦寇,即麦克猷(James M. McHugh),美国海军陆战队军官,时任美国驻华大使馆参赞、海军武官。
④ 该电文已收入《中华民国重要史料初编》第三编战时外交(二),第238页。
⑤ 1940年12月,英国同意向中国提供总额为1 000万英镑的平准基金借款及信用贷款。
⑥ 即郭秉文,字鸿声,江苏江浦人,时任中国驻伦敦贸易委员会委员兼驻英大使馆财务参赞。

53. 蒋介石致宋子文嘱在致罗斯福元电内增补一语电(1940年12月15日)①

A155　委员长来电　十二.十五　已复　十二.十六

致罗总统元电内"以少数之力量而收获重大之效果"一节以下请增补一语曰:"其关键要在短急时期内能【予】敌军以出其不备之打击耳。"如前电尚未转交,请照加入为盼。子良、子安弟②有否到美,甚念。纬国已安抵重庆矣。中正。删(十五)。

54. 蒋介石致宋子文告以关于上海对付伪银行办法电(1940年12月17日)

A160　委员长来电　十二.十七

关于上海对付伪银行办法,此间处理方针与兄相同,勿念。至于借款为公债方面之议,此间并无所闻。中致罗总统电中所谓与【予】敌方以出其不意之打击一语,乃有闪电攻击之意。如相见时,请口〈头〉加以补正。中正手启。篠(十七日)。

55. 蒋介石致宋子文告以此时惟有调顾维钧使美较宜电(1940年12月18日)

A161　委员长来电　十二.十九　已复　十二.十九

铣(十六)、谏(十六)二电均悉。史致中电此间除二三人外并无人闻知,大约由莫斯科使馆方面泄漏,故至今英法亦皆有此传闻。至于美使人选经过,外人已多猜测,自不能免。中意此时惟有调顾少川③使美较宜。但时间如何,请兄酌复。中正。巧(十八日)。

56. 蒋介石致宋子文指示须先有驱逐机相当数量电(1940年12月23日)④

A162　委员长来电　十二.廿三　已复　十二.廿三

飞垒⑤非先有驱逐机充分掩护准备不可,否则未用飞垒以前被敌机毁灭,故必先有驱逐机相当数量方能从事。而且飞垒跑道至早须至三月底方能使用,一个月

---

① 该电文已收入《中华民国重要史料初编》第三编战时外交(一),第430~431页。
② 即宋子文的幼弟宋子安。
③ 即顾维钧,字少川,江苏嘉定(今属上海市)人,时任中国驻法国大使。
④ 该电文已收入《中华民国重要史料初编》第三编战时外交(一),第432页。
⑤ 即美制 B-17 重型远程轰炸机,亦称"空中堡垒"(Flying Fortress)。

内无论如何准备不及也。中正手启。漾(廿三)。

57. 蒋介石致宋子文圣诞贺电(1940 年 12 月 24 日)

委员长来电

敬祝圣诞并颂康健。中正。敬(廿四)。

58. 蒋介石致宋子文称宋子良病一时不能回任不如辞去西南运输处职务电 (1940 年 12 月 24 日)

A163　委员长来电　十二.廿六　已复　十二.廿八

子良弟病状如何,约需几时可痊,甚念。现在西南运输处自良弟①去后,业务日坠,内容复杂,头绪纷烦,负责无人,最近运输力照预定者不及三分之一。此种情形,对于军事与运输前途危险殊多。现在名义与责任仍皆由良弟负担,将来更多牵累。中意如良弟病一时不能回任,则不如辞去此职,而令各部分负责人员仍照旧安心服务。中另派亲信有能力之人负责代理或继任,则负责有人,则良弟可安心治病,不致心挂两地。但必须严令现有处员一律均属继任之人,不准其辞职,以免公务停顿。如此公私两全,□□责亦可减免矣。未知良弟之意如何,盼复。中正手启。敬。

59. 蒋介石致宋子文告以关于核准借款条件大纲及指派签字代表电(1940 年 12 月 25 日)

委员长来电　十二.廿六

戌(十一日)、号(廿日)函件均悉。合约②已分转庸兄及资委会存查。关于核准借款条件大纲及指派签字代表之记录,已嘱庸兄查明检寄矣。中正。有(廿五)。

60. 蒋介石致宋子文嘱迅向美洽订机枪山炮及弹药电(1940 年 12 月 26 日)

A164　委员长来电　十二.廿七　已复　十二.卅一

请迅向美洽订:(甲)七九轻机枪一万挺;(乙)七九步机弹三万万发;(丙)七

---

①　即宋子文二弟宋子良,军事委员会西南运输处主任,当时正在美国就医。
②　即中美金属借款合同,该协定于 1941 年 2 月正式签署。

五山炮一百廿门,每门配弹三千发;(丁)半英寸高射机枪一百廿挺,每挺配弹五千发。轻机枪与步机枪为储备械弹中之决不可少者,尤盼迅洽电复。中正。宥(廿六)。

61. 蒋介石致宋子文告以罗杰士来渝相商后将赴美电(1940年12月29日)

A165　委员长来电　十二.卅　已复　十二.卅

罗杰士①来美庸兄并未不准,惟请其面谈来渝相商后,将此间意见托其赴美与兄研究也。中正手启。艳(廿九日)。

62. 蒋介石致宋子文告已转达美政府派兄等签字电(1941年1月5日)

成都来电　卅年一月五日

译转宋委员子文先生:先电悉。已电胡大使转达美政府,照派兄等三人分别代为签字矣②。中正。歌侍秘印。

63. 蒋介石致宋子文告以赞成参加平准基金会电(1941年1月5日)

A166　委员长来电　一.五

世(卅一日)、冬(二日)、江(三日)各电均悉。庸兄复电谅达,请兄察照核办。至于兄参加平衡基金会事,中与庸兄皆赞成,请照办可也。中正手启。歌(五日)。

64. 蒋介石致宋子文询问毛邦初有否接见记者电(1941年1月5日,附宋子文注)

A167　委员长来电　一.五　已复一.六

上月底纽约论坛报载有毛邦初谈话,未知果有其事否,并问其为何要接见新闻记者,以后应绝对禁止为要。中正。微(五日)。

---

① 罗杰士(Cyril Rogers),英国政府派驻中英平准基金会的英方代表。
② 1941年2月4日,宋子文(代表国民政府)、李干(代表中央银行)、吴志翔(代表资源委员会)三人与美国进出口银行总经理皮尔逊签署了5 000万美元金属借款合同。

[宋子文注:交邦初洽。文。]

65. 蒋介石致宋子文指示西南运输公司不变更组织电(1941年1月5日)

A168　委员长来电　一月六日　已转

世酉电悉。良弟开刀后病状如何,甚念。关于西南运输公司,现决定照旧不变更组织,派陈副主任体诚①正式代理主任,负责主持。并由俞樵峰②以运输统制局参谋长名义前往滇缅路指挥监督,期增进效能。只要由良弟切嘱各部人员绝对服从樵峰命令可也。中正手启。歌。

66. 蒋介石致宋子文嘱购机事不可委托世界公司电(1941年1月7日)

A169　委员长来电　一·八　已复　一·八

微(五日)电悉。购机事不可委托世界公司③。请兄要以此为重要任务,全力以赴之。中正手启。虞(七日)。

67. 蒋介石致宋子文嘱在借款内拨购卡车电(1941年1月8日)

A170　委员长来电　一·九　已复　一·十

请在美借款④内拨购三吨载卡车一千辆,以便航空委员会运输之用。中正。齐。

68. 蒋介石致宋子文询是否再须令派空军人员电(1941年1月9日,附宋子文1月13日拟复电稿)

A172　委员长来电　一·十

麻(六日)电悉。沈德燮⑤之外,是否再须另派空军人员,抑仅派兵工技术人员即可,请详复。中正。佳(九日)。

---

① 陈体诚,字子博,福建闽侯人,原为福建省建设厅厅长,时任西南运输处副主任兼代理主任。

② 即俞飞鹏,字樵峰,浙江奉化人,时任军事委员会后方勤务部部长,兼任运输统制局副主任、参谋长。

③ 即世界贸易公司,1939年由陈光甫在美国注册设立,以商业公司的名义为国民政府在美从事贸易活动。

④ 即美国向中方提供的5 000万美元金属借款。

⑤ 沈德燮,福建福州人,时任国民政府航空委员会训练总监。

[宋子文手拟复电稿如下：佳电奉悉。沈德燮足以应付。此外并请派兵工技术人员,其人须知美国或欧洲兵工情形者。〇元。文。]

69. 蒋介石致宋子文转知孔祥熙要求平准基金全数一次交足电(1941年1月10日)

A171　委员长来电　一.十

前接漾(廿三)日两电。经转据庸之兄复称：(一) 关于财政部表示不放弃沪法币一节,数年来财政部并无放弃某地法币之说。月前以有人造谣,经即以英文谈话方式声明政府对法币政策并无变更,自借款①成立,准备益加雄厚,劝令人民勿信谣言,堕其术中。(二) 外汇政策目前并无变更。□为免生枝节起见,该项借款自以全数一次交足为是。等语。特达。中正。蒸(十日)。

70. 蒋介石致宋子文答复托世界公司办理手续可照办电(1941年1月10日)

A173　委员长来电　一.十三

齐(八日)电悉。托世界公司出面办理,手续自可照办。中正。灰(十日)。

71. 蒋介石致宋子文关于西南运输处事项电(1941年1月15日)

委员长来电　一.十六　已转　一.十六

宋子文先生电悉。转子良弟静养,并代留。只要令西南运输处人员绝对照中意改良与服从俞部长②指挥可也。中正手启。删(十五)。

72. 蒋介石致宋子文赞同对英说帖复文电(1941年1月18日)

委员长来电　一.十八

青(九日)电悉。照片十张已付邮飞寄。对英说帖之复文,中亦与兄同一感想也。中正。巧(十八日)。

---

① 指1941年4月达成的5 000万美元中美平准基金借款。
② 即俞飞鹏,时任军事委员会后方勤务部部长。

73. 蒋介石致宋子文告以已将新四军全部解决电(1941 年 1 月 18 日)

A174 委员长来电 一.十八 已复一.十八

删(十五)电悉。新四军抗命谋叛,兹已将其全部解决①,明令撤消其名义番号,故江南共军已经肃清,以后可无后顾之忧。共党因无实力,故只有扩大宣传,摇撼国际视听,一面以内战不利于中央名义,使中央对其不敢制裁。其实中央抗日之外,确能控制国内一切,决无他虑也。□外人不明底细,易为共党谣惑,请详告各友放心为盼。中正。啸(十八日)。

74. 蒋介石致宋子文询带美专本收到否电(1941 年 1 月 21 日,附回电稿)

重庆来电 三十年一月二十一日 已复 一.廿一

胡大使译转宋委员子文:宋主任子良带美专(本)收到否? 乞查示。机要室。
[原文回电稿:重庆军事委员会机要室鉴:电悉。密本已由宋主任带到。特复。宋○○②。马。]

75. 蒋介石致宋子文指示办理交通素有经验美籍雇员先聘来华电(1941 年 1 月 23 日)

A175 委员长来电 一.廿四 已复 一.廿七

对于办理交通运输素有经验之美籍雇员,可否设法先聘,并嘱其早日来华何如。中正。梗(廿三)二。

76. 蒋介石致宋子文告以罗杰士言行不正希加注意电(1941 年 1 月 23 日)

A176 委员长来电 复 一.廿四

罗杰士言行不正③,希加注意。金融及外汇权必须操之在我,不可信赖外人也。中正。梗(廿三)。

---

① 指皖南事变,1941 年 1 月,新四军军部及直属部队在皖南地区遭国民党第三战区部队围攻,新四军军长叶挺被俘,副军长项英牺牲。
② 宋○○,即宋子文,电文起草者避免直接使用宋子文姓名。
③ 原来电誊稿为"言? 不正",宋子文另加"论行"二字,现取"行"字。

77. 蒋介石致宋子文关于罗斯福任命居里赴华考察电(1941年1月25日)①

A178 委员长来电 一.廿五 复 一.廿五

华盛顿廿四日国际电称:罗斯福总统宣布,任命秘书居里②赴华实地考察中国经济情形,国务院同时宣布美国对于中国国共之内争曾表示关怀之意。居里为经济学专家,渠即将携罗总统致蒋委员长之问候函,赴重庆一行。据讯美政府曾训令居里调查国民党指摘共产党抗命叛变及其他阴谋之情事,与共党反责国民党剥削农民之情事。美政府关怀中国内部摩擦之结果,已使拟议通过中之五千万美金贷款③缓期实现云。此息如何,最好请美政府声明否认,并将交款手续从速完成。中正手启。有(廿五)。

78. 蒋介石致宋子文关于美国志愿军条件原则可照办电(1941年1月27日)

A180 委员长来电 一.廿七

关于美国志愿军事,其条件与原则皆可照来电办理,但须注意其权利与义务之详细规定,并须绝对服从统帅之命令为要。中正手启。感(廿七日)。

79. 蒋介石致宋子文告以新四军案实情已于本日发表电(1941年1月29日)

A181 委员长来电 一.卅

沁(廿七)电悉。新四军案实情已于本日中正讲演发表。其实国内对此皆知共党兵力极弱,不及全国军队总数百分之二。以中国最近有百十九军之多,而新四军与第八路军不过共数两军耳。请兄以实状告之。中正。艳(廿九)二。

80. 蒋介石致宋子文告以敌平汉南段攻势不久可击退电(1941年1月29日)

A182 委员长来电 一.卅

沁(廿七)申电悉。敌在平汉④南段发动攻势,仍如过去一样,不久就可击退。请勿念。中正。艳(廿九)。

---

① 该电文已收入《中华民国重要史料初编》第三编战时外交(一),第535页。
② 居里(Lauchlin B. Currie),时任美国总统罗斯福的行政助理。
③ 是时美国已宣布向中国国民政府提供5 000万美元平准基金借款。
④ 即从北平至汉口的平汉铁路线。

81. 蒋介石致宋子文告以英美同盟计划我国如能正式加入更好电(1941 年 1 月 30 日)

A183　委员长来电　一.卅一

艳(廿九)电悉。英美同盟计划我国如能正式加入更好,否则间接使之发生关系,以其同盟关系中对中国经济全力支持亦可。俄国态度无论军事政治皆一如往常,并无变更征象,武器亦如常运来。中共今已正式表示服从命令,不再冲突矣。美报有否载中对合众社记者谈话?影响如何?中正手启。卅。

82. 蒋介石致宋子文告以新四军问题绝不影响政治与外交电(1941 年 2 月 3 日)

委员长来电　二.三　复　二.□

世、世亥各电悉。此时对美宣传不必过重辩白,不久事实必能大白也。自新四军事发表后,俄械于上星期内已到甘肃者,有新式飞机一百五十架、野炮一百门等武器,当可证明新四军问题决不影响政治与外交也。但此点对美要人非万不得已不必明告也。至于受德国恶意挑拨,更为反宣传无稽之谈,反则俄国何能对我再加援助乎?惟望美国当局注意第三国际此种宣传,其作用在破坏中美之感情,更使中国人民心理惟其自赖而已。中正手启。江(三日)。

83. 蒋介石致宋子文告以居里约明日到渝电(1941 年 2 月 6 日)

A185　委员长来电　二.七

邦初已回来。居里昨到港,约明日到渝,与其接洽人员以庸兄与孟余为正副主任。兄能于三月杪回最好。如届时交涉未完则缓行亦可。空中炮垒事究能如原约飞来否?此间机场约三月杪可完成一切准备也。中正手启。鱼(六日)。

84. 蒋介石致宋子文告以处理新四军事件绝不牵及政治或党派问题电(1941 年 2 月 8 日)

A186　委员长来电

此次中央处理新四军事件纯为严明军纪问题,绝不牵及政治或党派问题。故中央虽明知新四军与中共有关,但对中共仍抱定宽容态度,绝无压迫中共党人,或停止其刊物之举。现我国抗战部队共二百廿余军,都四百余万人,而受共产主义影响之正规军队实际不过数万人,仅占总数百分之一二。即使中共始终执迷不悟,亦决不能造成大规模内战,以妨碍我抗战军事之进行。中央始终认定全世界反侵略势力应联合一致,□与英美苏三国尤应密切合作,共同行动。若中共则倡此反帝口号,反对中国与英美接近合作,以妨碍本党对外政策与抗战国策之实行。中共此点阴谋务使英美政府特别了解,并详悉共党用意所在。希妥为转达,并详细说明为盼。中正。庚。

85. 蒋介石致宋子文告以决无分裂与内战之可能电(1941 年 2 月 13 日)

A187　委员长来电　二.十三　复二.十三

旧俄总顾问①回俄,与新总顾问②已来华继任,是去年十二月决定之事,乃在新四军未出事之前也。中共除宣传以摇撼中外观听外,决无分裂与内战之可能。中央决更不愿有内战之事。可勿虑。中正手启。元(十三日)。

86. 蒋介石致宋子文指示向美接洽核办新借款电(1941 年 2 月 21 日)

A190　委员长来电　二.廿五　复　二.廿五

国际宣传处派驻纽约李复③报称:美众议员 Rep. Andrew L. Somers 及 Mr. Thomas K F Moloney 与总领事于焌吉④曾作面告,正式会谈磋商向美交涉新借款一亿五千万元,利用美国闲废工厂专为中国生产军火。□提议此项借款将来当中国便利之时或以美金或以货物□□,其办法与目下国会辩论之军火租借法案大致相同,不加利息,偿还日期亦□限定。是项工厂则由中美合资办理,管理权则□之中国。该议员颇同情中国,自称有提出国会促其□之把握。等语。请兄接洽核办。中正。马。

87. 蒋介石致宋子文告以居里约廿八日由渝起程电(1941 年 2 月 25 日)

A191　委员长来电　二.廿五

卡雷⑤约廿八日由渝起程,所有材料托其带来,勿念。共党设立军事委员会确有

---

① 即 1939 年 11 月至 1940 年 12 月担任国民政府军事总顾问的 К·М·卡恰诺夫。
② 即 1940 年 12 月起任国民政府军事总顾问的 В·И·崔可夫。
③ 李复(Earl H. Leaf),英国人,时为国民党中央宣传部国际宣传处驻美办事处负责人。
④ 于焌吉,字谦六,河北文安人,时任中国驻美国纽约总领事。
⑤ 即居里(Lauchlin B. Currie)。

此事,但其作用在恐吓敲诈。总之共党行为是在使国内外空气紧张,并非有任何实力行动可畏也。其他共党提条件及扣留周恩来等,绝无其事。共党在外宣传,对政府提出条件,且在各处□无名条件,而其对政府并不敢有一条正式提交,可知其完全为宣传作用而已。中正手启。有(廿五)。

88. 蒋介石致宋子文告以滇缅铁路由兄负责主持交涉电(1941年2月27日)

A192　委员长来电　二.廿八

寝(廿六)电悉。滇缅铁路准即由兄负责主持与英美交涉。已嘱孔副院长与张部长①照办,速派杜君②飞美矣。中正。感(廿七)。

89. 蒋介石致宋子文告以滇缅路问题行政院已通过电(1941年3月2日)

A194　委员长来电　三.二

感巳电悉。关于滇缅路问题,行政院已据英大使所提同样意见由院议通过接受,并对英方滇缅界务意见亦予采纳矣。中正。冬。

90. 蒋介石致宋子文告以施植之到美协助当赞成电(1941年3月3日)

A195　委员长来电　三.五

径(廿五)电悉。施植之③到美协助,弟当赞成。请兄以中之意代邀可也。中正。江(三日)。

91. 蒋介石致宋子文指示待居里到美时速接洽高级空军军官来华电(1941年3月5日)

A194　委员长来电　三.五

(一)居里行前建议美国派遣高级空军军官来华考察,待居里到时速接洽。(二)美国空军志愿队何日能来华工作,请复。并请在美定购中自用大号坐机及运输机各

---

① 即张嘉璈,字公权,时任国民政府交通部部长。
② 即杜镇远,湖北秭归人,时任滇缅铁路工程局局长。
③ 即施肇基,字植之,浙江余杭人,时任外交部顾问,旋即应宋子文邀请赴美国,在中国国防物资供应公司负责日常事务。

一架。坐机约可容二十人为度,该机希能由美直接飞渝为盼。中正。微(五日)。

92. 蒋介石致宋子文指示平准基金迅速签字更为重要电(1941年3月13日)

A196　委员长来电　三.十三　复　三.十三

居里谅已回美京。军货贷借案通过以后,各种援华案能早日办妥,尤其对于平衡基金迅速签字更为重要,勿使共党反宣传摇撼人心。其次空军志愿队与空中堡垒,及前定空军整个计划之数量与运输办法,皆望能早日决定具体方案。此次军政部俞大维所开之武器单,以及如何分期接济,亦望有一确定也。中正手启。覃(十三日)。

93. 蒋介石致宋子文嘱请促成美志愿军来华电(1941年3月13日)

委员长来电　三.十三　复　三.十五

据航委会转沈德燮江电称:陈纳德组〈志愿军〉事暂停顿。职意新机接收,本会应先促成人员为妥。等情。查苏机正在接收,航委会驱逐人员不敷美机支配。仍请促成美志愿军来华为盼。中正。元(十三日)。

94. 蒋介石致宋子文关于中国银行官股董监电(1941年3月21日,附宋子文注)

A198　委员长来电　三.廿二

删(十五)电悉。所请派吴、王两君①为中国银行官股董监一节,已交孔部长②核办矣。中正。马(廿一日)。
[宋子文注:电告宋汉章③、贝淞荪④。]

95. 蒋介石致宋子文告以改良制造植物油车已请孔院长转饬就近派员参加电(1941年3月22日,附原加注)

A199　委员长来电　三.廿三

上月元(十三)电请派专家办理改良制造植物油车一节,经查国内现无适当人才,

---

① 即吴鼎昌、王延松,时分别被派任中国银行官股董事和官股监察人。
② 即孔祥熙,时任国民政府财政部部长。
③ 宋汉章,名鲁,字汉章,时为中国银行常务董事兼总经理。
④ 贝淞荪,即贝祖诒,字淞荪,江苏吴县人,时为中国银行副总经理。

惟贸委会①在纽约第五大道六百卅号所设之环球公司②经办美贷款采购事宜，并有主持机械工程人员。已请孔副院长转饬就近派员参加矣。中正。祃（廿二）。
[原加注：已告宋子良先生。三.廿四　C S. Lui③]

96．蒋介石致宋子文告以交居里带去关于冻结存款函大要电（1941年3月24日）

A200　委员长来电

马（廿一）电悉。二月廿七日交居里带去关于冻结存款函大要如下：（一）贵国对于欧洲若干被侵略国人民在美之存款及所持证券，已实行某种步骤。若此项步骤能施于远东，则于中国大有裨益。请阁下予以考虑。（二）远东局势变动，以及种种谣传，均足造成人心惶惑，促起投机，以形成通货再度外溢之现象，使中国维持法币面值益增困难。（三）通货之性不坚定，遂多以贵国为□〈通〉逃薮。倘贵政府能实行冻结中国私人存款，使受中国政府之管理与支配，或即用以作借款抵押品，进一步加强中国实力财政，则不特裨益我战时经济，且有益中国一般财政情况。（四）更有进者，历来中国由输出贸易所得及华侨汇归款项之美金外汇，向为上海外汇投机家所吸取者，皆将因此转入中国政府之手，用以购买急需之美国货品。（五）上项步骤之实行，英国政府之平行行动自有其功用。余亦拟妥筹以敦促。英国现在正加紧于外汇之限制，故敢预断英国亦愿杜塞其在上海最后之隙漏。（六）余深知在贵国政策下之签证出口制，对侵略国与被侵略国一视同仁，则欲封闭日本在贵国之存款，自有待此项政策之更新。但日本侵略者以掠得中国之财富售与美国，易其迫切需要之美元。倘贵国能将此签证制推及于日本之存款，则日本欲得美元，必将确属日本生产之货物输出以易之，此可闭塞日本掠夺中国财富之途径。（七）如蒙采纳，则实行时务望勿露声色，以免在美国有存款者过入美人之户。诸祈请阁下特加注意，鼎力玉成。等语。特达。中正。敬（廿四）。

97．蒋介石致宋子文告以江杓等可于四月内赴美电（1941年3月27日）

A201　委员长来电　三.廿七

号（廿日）电悉。据俞大维称，江灼【杓】等可于四月内启程赴美。特复。中正。

---

① 即国民政府财政部贸易委员会。
② 即世界贸易公司。
③ 即刘景山，为宋子文秘书。

感(廿七)。

98. 蒋介石致宋子文指示兵工交通器材请照原表接洽电(1941 年 3 月 30 日)①

A202　委员长来电　三.卅　复　卅

感(廿七)电悉。(一)兵工交通器材种类繁多,详单函寄。请先照原表分类大纲总数接洽,此项应用最急。(二)关于军械部分,似无须分急需与可缓交二类,可将原单甲、乙两项归并,加成总数交美方。惟须注明最急需者为轻机枪一万五千挺,子弹五万万发;山炮四百八十门,每门附弹两千发;高射机枪一千挺,每挺附弹五千发,三七战车防御炮三百六十门,每门配弹一千五百发。其他各项亦盼美方尽先由库存供给我用。(三)中型与轻型二种战车,照美国现有装甲师之编制,足敷两个至三个师之战车数量与多种配属武器,但可延至本年十月以后应用。(四)关于载重汽车,请照交居里单洽购。中正。卅。

99. 蒋介石致宋子文告以康印公路计划请予以推动电(1941 年 4 月 9 日)

A203　委员长来电　四.十

三月宥(廿六)电悉。查康印公路计划②原系由杜局长③拟呈,经饬交部尽先勘察与准备,限期于一年半内完成。并指派杜负责筹办,并请庸之兄速筹的款,如期完成。电询各节,除由交部航寄外,查该路虽经过山地,工程并非特别艰难。以英保守党过去认为,欲保印度必保印度东北高原与山地之中立区,不愿打通西藏,使我势力及于哈啸【?】。即在近今,对于接近西藏国际道路线犹现踌躇之色。该路关系边区西南国际交通甚巨,且趁此开扩西边政治经济亦属良图。为促英国之决心,亦惟有利用此时机,并借美国经济之力量,予以推动,方可冀其有成。特请默识此点而应用之。至技术问题请就询杜镇远可也。中正。佳(九日)。

---

① 该电文已收入《中华民国重要史料初编》第三编战时外交(一),第 441~445 页。
② 即 1940 年国民政府与英国达成的修筑中印公路的计划,该公路自西昌经盐源、永宁、中甸、德钦、盐井等地进入印度,与印度阿萨密省塞地亚铁路车站相接。
③ 即时任滇缅铁路工程局局长的杜镇远。

100. 蒋介石致宋子文转知军政部说明筹购物资清单电(1941 年 4 月 10 日)

A204　委员长来电　四.十

冬(二日)电悉。询据军政部称,前开卅年拟向国外筹购物资清单内 THIONOL 颜料四种,系染草黄色及灰色之用,并非布匹。又,医药设备器材等已饬林可胜①开具清单寄美矣。中正。蒸(十日)。

101. 蒋介石致宋子文询问代聘教官与招集空军志愿兵事宜电(1941 年 4 月 12 日,附宋子文注)

A207　委员长来电　四.十五　复四.十五

灰(十日)申电悉。此代聘昆校教官与招集空军志愿兵事是否两事? 志愿兵有否招募? 盼复。中正手启。文。

[宋子文注: 交沈副主任②。文。]

102. 蒋介石致宋子文请急问美当局对华方针电(1941 年 4 月 14 日)③

A205　委员长来电　四.十四

俄日中立友好条约④,据日讯其中有互认外蒙与满州二地领土完整之条,此必属实无疑。以后俄对华外交方针自当更□□也。请急问美当局对华方针,如其果真援华,则望速提具体有效之整个计划与保证,以慰我人民怀疑之心理。又此次菲律滨美、英、荷会议究为何事? 不使我国预闻,殊令人失望也。请以此意转达为盼。中正手启。寒(十四)。

---

① 林可胜,福建海澄(今龙海)人,时任国民政府军政部卫生行政人员训练所主任。
② 即沈德燮,1941 年 4 月起任国民政府航空委员会副主任。
③ 该电文已收入《中华民国重要史料初编》第三编战时外交(一),第 129 页。
④ 1941 年 4 月 13 日,苏联与日本签订中立条约,同时发表宣言,称苏联誓当尊重"满洲国"之领土完整与神圣不可侵犯性,日本誓当尊重"蒙古人民共和国"之领土完整与神圣不可侵犯性。

103. 蒋介石致宋子文告以中英平衡借款已派兄及李干代表签字电(1941 年 4 月 14 日)

A206 委员长来电 四.十四

真(十一)电悉。中英平衡借款已交由孔副院长派兄及李干①代表签字矣。中正。盐(十四)。

104. 蒋介石致宋子文告以邵力子与莫洛托夫晤谈苏日订约电(1941 年 4 月 17 日)

A208 委员长来电 四.十七

刻接邵力子②兄电称:本日下午五时半晤莫洛托夫,遵询第二条是否包括中日战局。莫答此次苏日订约基于保持苏联和平,并不涉及中国问题,双方谈判时亦并未提及中国关系;又称苏联对中国继续□□,毫无变更。关于继续援华一点,遵示未提询,但因其态度良好,对于援助表示谢意,并告以现时与对外贸易部商谈运输物品,时感困难,可否转告该部长特别多方协助。莫初称此为运输问题,且其原因在中国方面,继称对于满足贵大使之希望未见有何困难,据此对继续援助应无问题。等语。特闻。中正。洽(十七)。

105. 蒋介石致宋子文指示平衡基金如不一次交付不得签字电(1941 年 4 月 17 日)③

A209 委员长来电 四.十七

咸(十五)、删(十五)电悉。俄接济武器至此刻正仍照常运华,并无变更。俄大使④接其政府今日来电,并未有对华变更政策之表示云。刻面嘱美大使⑤托其转告政府,对于平衡基金如不一次交付,则我人民对于美国好意将发生误解。而美财部对我政府似太不相信,若分期交款,反失我政府内外威信,故嘱兄不得签字,务望其政府谅察我政府之苦衷。至于军火贷借办法,则与兄对美总统所说者相

---

① 李干,字芑均,江苏无锡人,时任中国驻美国大使馆商务参赞、经济部驻美国商务办事处参事。
② 邵力子,字仲辉,浙江绍兴人,时任中国驻苏联大使。
③ 该电文已收入《中华民国重要史料初编》第三编战时外交(一),第 135 页。
④ 即时任苏联驻华大使潘友新(Alexander Semenovich Paniushkin)。
⑤ 即美国驻华大使詹森(Nelson T. Johnson)。

同,总望其先签借贷整个物品总数之约,至于交货日期之迟早,则可另商。此乃慰我国民对美援华急切之心理,以增强我抗战之心理也。至中共惟第三国际之命是从,而其所谓信仰三民主义者,完全为烟幕欺人之谈。此次俄日协定发表后,全国青年与智识阶级对苏联与中共发生重大刺激,中共过去之宣传皆归失败,此后中共内部亦必分裂,殆无疑义。至于中共在抗战兵力方面,可谓毫无实力,更不能阻碍我抗战耳。中正手启。篠(十七)。

106. 蒋介石致宋子文嘱基金委员应屈就电(1941年4月22日)

A212　委员长来电　四.廿二

皓(十九)申电悉。基金委员兄不可辞①,应屈就,勿使误会。中正手启。养(廿二)。

107. 蒋介石致宋子文告以致居里转罗斯福电大意电(1941年4月24日)

A213　委员长来电　四.廿五

顷致居里转罗总统一电,特电达大意如下:苏日协定发表后,我军民悲愤激昂,咸认远东局势即有严重发展。愚意希、南战事②之失利,不无影响我中国之士气,以致我闽、浙沿海之战事不甚顺利。日本此次侵扰闽、浙,已使用其向所不肯轻用最精锐之部队。我中国政府临此重要局势,切盼美国之援华行动速有积极而决定之表现。贵国军火租借法案包括援华部份,业蒙一再□□,对于中国所请求贷借军器之数目详单,极盼贵国总统速将□□实行之整个总数正式发表。此项表示盼能愈速愈佳。云云。蒋中正。敬(廿四)。

108. 蒋介石致宋子文嘱平准委员仍应勿辞为要电(1941年4月25日,附宋子文4月25日拟复电稿)

A214　委员长来电　四.廿五

养(廿二)未电悉。仍应勿辞为要。中正手启。有(廿五)。

[宋子文手拟复电稿如下:有电敬悉。万恳勿发表文名为祷。子〇。径。文。四.廿五]

---

① 当时宋子文力辞出任中英美联合平准基金委员会的中方委员。
② 即1941年4月,德军分别攻占希腊和南斯拉夫。

109. 蒋介石致宋子文告以对沪金融人员绝不妨碍电(1941 年 4 月 25 日)

A215　委员长来电　四.廿五

祃(廿二)申电悉。我方特务人员对沪任何金融人员决不妨碍也。中正。径(廿五)。

110. 蒋介石致宋子文告以平准委员已改派贝淞荪接充电(1941 年 4 月 27 日)

A216　委员长来电　四.廿八

径(廿五)电悉。兄既不能兼顾,已由孔副院长改派贝淞荪接充矣。中正。感(廿七)。

111. 蒋介石致宋子文指示飞机种类与数量从速商订电(1941 年 4 月 27 日)

A217　委员长来电　四.廿八　复　四.廿九

兄电中所谓曲射炮,是否为山炮? 又飞机种类与数量亦请从速商订。盼复。中正手启。沁(廿七)。

112. 蒋介石致宋子文询问机枪火炮坦克车等订货情况电(1941 年 4 月 27 日)①

A218　委员长来电　四.廿八　复　四.廿九

敬(廿四)电悉。(一) 七九机枪及弹为目前最急需者。美方现虽不能交货,仍盼迅筹制造交货。制造七九枪弹所需一切图样已由俞署长②寄美。(二) 美方允交之点三机枪一万五千挺,盼迅交运,每挺须配弹二万发。(三) 各项火炮中以山炮需用最急,来电称,须明年六月底方可交清,期限太长。请与美方商洽拨让库存提前交清。(四) 其他各类火炮及坦克车请催美方迅速交货,并电告交货详数及交货日期。(五) 来电所称曲射炮八百四十门,想系七五山炮四百八十门之误。又,所称机械化七五野战炮一百四十门,查原购械单内并无此项,是否由美方自动提出,抑系电文有误? 盼电复。中正。沁(廿七)酉。

---

① 该电文已收入《中华民国重要史料初编》第三编战时外交(一),第450页。
② 即时任国民政府军政部兵工署署长俞大维。

113. 蒋介石致胡适并转宋子文平衡基金合同签字感念劳苦电(1941 年 4 月 28 日)

重庆来电　卅年四月二十八日

胡大使:有电悉。并转子文兄:平衡基金合同签字,感念劳苦,欣祝成功。对摩财长①并请代为表示感忱。中正。俭。

114. 宋子文致蒋介石称参加保卫中国同盟系孙夫人邀文列名电(1941 年 5 月 6 日)

S328　委座

支电奉悉。文参加反战大同盟②,系当时孙夫人③募集捐款,邀文④列名。现既有不稳报告,已电港查明内容,以便遵嘱应付。文。鱼西。五.六

115. 宋子文致蒋介石孔祥熙询军械贷借事是否与胡适共同负责办理电(1941 年 5 月 6 日)

委员长　孔部长　复　五.十

关于进行军械贷借事,孔部长冬电所称诸盼共同努力一语,是否嘱文与胡大使共同负责办理,敬乞示复,俾明责任也。○鱼。文。五.六

116. 蒋介石致宋子文告以副院长事尚不敢断行电(1941 年 5 月 6 日)

A219　委员长来电　卅.五.七　复　□□

副院长事⑤屡想提出而未果者,总以官制不能常变,犹恐为他人所讥评。且此案必须经过立法手续,决非如普通提议或一纸手令所能发表也。故中于此尚不敢断行,必须待其他官制亦有改革时提出,乃不着痕迹,其事较易。此时惟

---

①　即美国财政部部长摩根索(Henry Morgenthau Jr.)。
②　指由宋庆龄于 1938 年 4 月在香港发起成立的保卫中国同盟,旨在广泛争取国际援助,支持中国抗战。
③　即孙中山夫人宋庆龄。
④　此处原稿为○。
⑤　蒋介石曾考虑任命宋子文为行政院副院长,并以此身份在美寻求援华。

有经济会议主席,为中自兼,拟推兄屈就,或恢复经济委员会①,推兄为委员长。此皆不必经立法程序,故其事较顺耳。未知兄意如何? 盼复。中正手启。歌(六日)。

117. 宋子文致蒋介石孔祥熙报告福克司为平衡基金美方委员电(1941年5月7日)

S329　委座　孔部长

美国务部称财长毛根韬②推荐现任关税委员会委员福克司③君 A. Manuel Fox 为平衡基金委员会美方委员,现任财部货币司职员台洛君 William H. Taylor 为副委员。福克司要求年薪美金二万五千元加津贴每日十元,台洛要求年薪一万元加津贴每日八元,另支来往飞机票。如荷同意,请即电示以便转复,并由政府正式任命福克司为基金会委员,副委员毋须发表。文。虞。五.七

118. 宋子文致蒋介石询棉布军装数字电(1941年5月7日)

委座

前居里单棉布一项,列二百万匹,约合八千万码。此项数字,系按士兵若干人计算,每人可合军装几套。请饬□查示,以备美方提询。文。阳申。五.七

119. 宋子文致蒋介石报告太平洋大西洋美军调动情况电(1941年5月8日)

S330

委座钧鉴:友人密告美政府已令调太平洋大部海军至大西洋。据一般内部推测,数星期内美德将武装冲突。至太平洋方面,美已集中大批陆、空军及海军一部于孟尼拉,预备应付倭寇南犯。敬密闻。〇齐。文。五.八

---

① 即 1931 年成立的全国经济委员会,1938 年并入新成立的经济部。
② 即美国财政部长摩根索。
③ 福克司(A. Manuel Fox),时被推荐出任中英美平准基金委员会美籍委员。

120. 宋子文致蒋介石报告孙夫人主持之机关从未反对政府之宣传电(1941年5月9日)

S331

委座钧鉴：据港电，孙夫人主持之机关系 China Defense League，译称保卫中国大同盟。该机关专为难民筹款，从未有反对政府之宣传。至钧座支电所谓反战大同盟，文未曾参入此项组织。是否即系郑彦棻①任秘书长之国际反侵略会？抗战以始，各种救国机关，五花八门，分别不清也。○佳。文。五·九

121. 宋子文致蒋介石请令饬运输机关红会物品优先运输电(1941年5月14日)

S338　委座

美红会②救济物品，存仰极多，无法内运，颇有烦言。文③函红会会长台维斯，声明滇缅路运输，已在改进中，以后运输力量，可增二三倍。顷得台复函，内称根据文④所述运输进步之可能性，美红会已核准于原送救济物品外，增加其他医药品等值九十万元，购后即运。文已代钧座致谢。务乞钧座令饬运输机关特加注意红会物品优先运输为祷。文。盐。五·十四

122. 宋子文致蒋介石报告福克斯等将首途来华电(1941年5月15日)

委座　孔　复　五·十七

虞电计达，至盼复示。因福克斯⑤等即将首途来华也。○咸。五·十五

123. 宋子文致蒋介石报告贷借首批物品预期七月六日可抵仰光函稿(1941年5月15日)

函稿

委座钧鉴：美军货贷借首批货品，已经装船，预期七月六日可抵仰光，兹谨开具

---

① 郑彦棻，广东顺德人，时任广东省政府委员兼秘书长，国际反侵略大会中国分会执行部主任。
② 即美国红十字会。
③④ 此处原稿为○。
⑤ 即前注之福克司。

货品清单,奉尘【呈】钧察。本批货品中,两吨半军用汽车二百四十辆,建□极为坚固,任何崎岖之路均可通行。再最初数批货品到仰光后之卸货费用,美方已允担任,嗣后仍待续商。专布。敬请钧安。五月十五日

124. 宋子文致蒋介石询汤姆生机枪是否需要电(1941 年 5 月 15 日)

S339

委座钧鉴:轻机枪交涉颇不易。惟现有现货汤姆生零点四五手提机枪一万支,附子弹每支二千发,是否需要,乞核示。○删。五.十五

125. 宋子文致蒋介石报告财部顾问杨格现将回渝电(1941 年 5 月 16 日)

委座钧鉴:财部顾问杨格①去年随文来美,现将回渝。可否告孔部长,如关于滇缅路飞机运输等事,文须其在渝或仰光等处转达意见时,财部可准其奔走。○谏申。文。五.十六

126. 宋子文致蒋介石报告与哈利法克斯会谈情形电(1941 年 5 月 17 日)②

S332

委座钧鉴:(一)顷哈利法克使③面告,英政府决不致再封锁滇缅公路,且以彼判断,日政府明了英国立场,亦不至有此项请求,如松冈④或重光⑤有此类要求,英外部必电知其本人。(二)文略告哈,美在军械贷借法案下,除接济我军火外,并供给卡车、汽油、滇缅公路所需技术人员,及滇缅铁路材料一千五百万元,英能助我由缅境至内地之运输,实予我抗战莫大助力。文建议英政府应指派驻缅大员,协助我方专责办理下列事宜:(甲)迅速完成腊戍⑥至滇边铁路;(乙)康印公路之测量及建筑;(丙)加强滇缅公路运输力量。哈允将以上建议电达英政府,同时请钧座直接向卡尔作同样之建议。(三)庚电关于空军志愿队⑦事,居

---

① 杨格(Arthur N. Young),美国人,时任国民政府财政部顾问。
② 该电文已收入《中华民国重要史料初编》第三编战时外交(二),第 78 页。
③ 哈利法克使(Lord Halifax),时任英国驻美大使。
④ 即松冈洋右,时任日本外相。
⑤ 即重光葵,时任日本驻英国大使。
⑥ 腊戍,缅甸北部城市,滇缅公路的缅方起点。
⑦ 即由陈纳德负责指挥的中国空军美国志愿大队。

里主张日内先与总统商定办法,再向英方接洽,故文见哈时,尚未提及此事。至国务部方面,在未得总统准许前,当然不愿向英方实告也。〇篠。文。五.十七

127. 宋子文致蒋介石报告嘱核购汽车配件已并入贷借案办理电(1941年5月19日)

致委员长电

真电嘱核购万国牌汽车配件,已并入贷借案办理矣。〇皓。文。五.十九①

128. 宋子文致蒋介石报告第一批贷借物资内容电(1941年5月20日)

S333

委座钧鉴:第一批运出贷借物资七月六日可到,载重七千吨,包括野战运输卡车二百五十辆,兵工厂用铝二千吨、铜一千余吨,及飞机用汽油、机器油等。详单另寄。〇哿。文。五.廿

129. 宋子文致蒋介石建议郭泰祺回国请其取道仰光电(1941年5月21日)

S334　呈委员长电　五.廿一日　复　五.廿四

委座钧鉴:复初回国,鄙见请其取道仰光,缅督与其素有交谊,就便可以商讨滇缅铁路、康印公路等问题。若回国之后专程前往,不免引起注目,恐非英方所愿。如何之处,敬候饬遵。〇马。文。五.廿一

130. 宋子文致蒋介石报告第二批部分军械飞机日内可望批准电(1941年5月22日)

S335　呈委员长电　五.廿二日　复　五.廿七

委座钧鉴:军货贷借法案,我方所需物品,经与美方交涉,迅速陆续起运。第二批一部份军械及飞机,总统日内可望批准。嗣后在渝、仰与国内各机关接洽之事必多,运输交接事宜,必更繁琐,须有专人代表子文在渝、仰接洽办理,始能迅捷

---

① 原稿末写有"C S Liu 5/19"。

便利。兹拟请钱昌照①兄在渝兼办及前中国银行仰光经理陈长桐②驻仰光主持其事,重要事项仍当由文径呈钧座。可否之处,敬乞示遵。○养。文。五. 廿二

131. 宋子文致蒋介石报告军械贷借第二次批准货品电(1941 年 5 月 24 日)

S336

委座钧鉴:军械贷借于今晨第二次批准,计开:(一)山炮六百门,配备齐全,附弹一百廿万发;(二)七五机械化野炮一百四十四门,附弹十四万四千发;(三)坦克车三百六十辆,附武器及配备;(四)野战轻便小汽车一千辆。以上四项总值美金四千九百万元。交货期洽定后再电陈。○敬。文。五. 廿四

132. 宋子文致蒋介石乞准予宋子良辞去西南运输公司职位电(1941 年 5 月 27 日)

S340 呈委员长电 五.廿七日 复 五.卅

委座钧鉴:子良弟病,三次手术,迄未大痊。顷据面陈,西南运输公司事繁任重,身负其名,不克到职,深为不安,一再恳辞,所称当属实情。伏乞准予所请,一俟病体全愈,再图报效。仍候示遵。○沁酉。文。五. 廿七

133. 宋子文致蒋介石报告拟由霍亚民代表驻渝接洽电(1941 年 5 月 27 日)

S341 呈委员长电 五.廿七日 复 五.廿九

委座钧鉴:感(廿七)电敬悉。钱昌照不宜兼办,谨当遵命。兹拟由中国银行副总稽核霍亚民③代表子文驻渝,遇事与各机关接洽,以资便利。可否之处,仍候示遵。○沁。文。五. 廿七

---

① 钱昌照,字乙藜,江苏常熟人,时任国民政府经济部资源委员会副主任委员。
② 陈长桐,名传桐,字长桐,福建福州人,1896 年生,美国科罗拉多大学商业及银行专业毕业,时任缅甸、印度等地中国银行经理。
③ 即霍宝树,字亚民,时任中国银行副总稽核。

134. 宋子文致蒋介石提议滇缅铁路公债可否撤销电(1941年5月27日)

S342   呈委员长电   五·廿七日   复六·四

委座钧鉴：据此间新闻社重庆消息,我政府发行滇缅铁路公债美金一千万元,又闻派有华侨邝炳舜来美推销。等情。国务部私人表示,事前未接我方通知,颇以为异,且示不满。就华侨方面观察,亦未必能募集此数。事果属实,可否撤消,或另筹办法之处,出自钧裁。再,郭大使①颇知此事经过,伏乞垂询,上贡【供】参考。○感申。文。五·廿七

135. 宋子文致蒋介石报告已遵谕声明退出保卫中国同盟电(1941年5月28日)

S343   呈委员长电   五·廿八日

委座钧鉴：前奉支电。顷接董显光②寄来反战大同盟共党宣传品,借文③名义,在外招摇。已遵谕发电公开声明退出。谨闻。○俭申。文   五·廿八

136. 宋子文致蒋介石报告钨砂在美作价情形电(1941年5月28日)

S344   呈委员长电   五·廿八日

委座钧鉴：钨砂、金属两借款,钨砂作价,原系根据美矿业杂志所载市价,现约每单位十六七元,即每吨一千零五十元左右。顷美以日本在波利维亚高价收购钨砂,美金属准备公司亦向波以高价定购三年全部钨产,作价每单位约廿一元,合每吨一千三百六十余元。公司因此所受损失由国库贴补。上届欧战,钨砂价格虽曾飞涨,但现时美国主要物品均受统制,不准涨价。每单位钨砂作价廿一元,高于现价甚多,即为将来着想,似亦不致吃亏。经文饬属与金属准备公司接洽,要求我钨砂作价三年内与波砂同等待遇。美方对此原则已可接受。事关借款担保,特电呈核,并乞转饬资委会复示意见为叩。○勘。文。五·廿八

---

① 即郭泰祺,时任国民政府外交部部长,此前任国民政府驻英国大使。
② 董显光,浙江鄞县人,时任中国国民党中央宣传部副部长。
③ 此处原稿为○。

137. 宋子文致蒋介石报告各种军械表及技术文件早经函请颁发电(1941 年 6 月 2 日)

S346　复委座世电

委座钧鉴：世电奉悉。各种军械之操典、教范、编制、配角等表，以及有关技术文件，早经函请美军部颁发。惟事关机密，手续繁重，迄今仅得一部份，已于本日饬兵工组①随收随寄。谨复。○冬申。文。六·二

138. 宋子文致蒋介石报告卡车工程修理车装运订购情形电(1941 年 6 月 2 日)

S347　呈委员长电　六·二日

委座钧鉴：勘电敬悉。黄总监镇球②未呈请以前，业已装运 GMC 野战用四吨卡车二百五十辆，运输武器，颇为适用，约两月后可到仰光。又空军用游动工程修理车，亦已向美方要求订购三十五辆。谨复，并乞转饬知照。○冬。文。六·二

139. 宋子文致蒋介石报告居里来言催请批准飞机电(1941 年 6 月 3 日)

S348　呈复委员长东电

委座钧鉴：东电敬悉。居里来，言钧座此电仍以由其本人呈递为是，藉此可以催请批准飞机，以应急需，以后再用正当手续。高斯③所言如彼。足见彼方人员之内幕及我方在华府人事之布置，不得不深切考虑。石曾④先生知之甚详，伏乞垂询为叩。○江申。文。六·三

140. 宋子文致蒋介石报告与居里同见拉铁摩尔情形电(1941 年 6 月 3 日)⑤

S348　呈复委员长电　六·三日　复六·六

委座钧鉴：顷与居里同见宁【?】拉铁马尔⑥。此君通华语，对我北方情形及远东

---

①　即中国国防供应公司(China Defense Supplies, Inc.)下属的兵工组。
②　即黄镇球,字剑霆,广东梅县人,时任国民政府航空委员会防空总监。
③　高斯(Clarence E. Gauss),1941 年 5 月接替詹森任美国驻华大使。
④　即李煜瀛,号石曾,时正往返于欧美、香港和重庆之间从事外交活动。
⑤　该电文已收入《中华民国重要史料初编》第三编战时外交(一),第 725~726 页。
⑥　即拉铁摩尔(Owen Lattimore),美国著名汉学家、蒙古学家,时任约翰·霍普金斯大学教授,当时被美方推荐出任蒋介石的政治顾问。

问题甚为熟悉,与总统并不相识,惟精神学识均佳,愿为钧座个人顾问。文与其商定条件如下:一、先试用六个月,如届期解聘,除旅费外,给予美金一万元。二、如一年以上,除旅费外,每年给予一万五千元。居里主张,如蒙俯准,即由文通知。因系个人顾问,毋须经过大使馆。如何之处,伏乞钧裁。○江西。文。六.三

141. 宋子文致蒋介石报告昨晤前任缅督情形电(1941年6月3日)

S349　呈委员长电　六.三日　六月十日由张公权①复

委座钧鉴:昨晤前任缅督,据称缅方极欢迎滇缅空运早日成功,并愿在米芝那②地方建筑机场,等语。我方云南驿机场完成后,即可得一稳捷航线,直接通航。美方对中航公司③颇有信用,愚见滇缅空运,莫若并归该公司办理,关于让机等事,较为便利,且中航公司四年约满,即可收回自办。如蒙采纳,乞饬交通部与该公司商洽进行为叩。文。江。六.三

142. 宋子文致蒋介石报告安司丹于廿四日飞渝电(1941年6月3日)

S350　呈复委员长先、冬两电　六.三日

委座钧鉴:先冬两电敬悉。已嘱安司丹④率所带技术人员,于(廿四)日飞渝,到时请赐接见。贝克为铁路会计专家,无公路运输经验,久居我国,深谙世故人情,但为居里所荐,如屈居安下,居里不无悒悒。不若以贝克为督察长,安司丹为副督察长。安为公路运输专家,如钧座嘱贝克多假以事权,必能尽其所长,两人当可融洽合作。仍候钧裁。再,居里所称恩斯坦,即安司丹,原为霍金⑤介绍于文及居里,经历函呈。合并陈明。○肴。文。六.三

---

① 即国民政府交通部长张嘉璈。
② 米芝那(Myitkyina),即密支那,缅甸北部交通重镇。
③ 即中美双方合资组建的中国航空公司(China National Aviation Corporation, CNAC)。
④ 安司丹(Daniel G. Arnstein),1941年夏访华的美国交通专家代表团团长。
⑤ 即霍普金斯(Harry L. Hopkins),时任美国总统罗斯福的政治顾问。

143. 宋子文致蒋介石密告美对日关系有不愿尖锐化之势电(1941 年 6 月 4 日)

S351 呈委员长电 六.四日

委座钧鉴：日本驻美大使野村①，曾向美国务卿商订类似日俄协定公约，上星期重新提议。国务卿以日屡次失信，例如门户开放等等，毁灭无遗，对日当局已无信用，婉词拒绝。又美驻日大使克鲁②报告，日海军不愿与美开战，社会名流亦多不满当局政策。此项消息，国务院密交纽约泰晤士报，于下星期登出，用意在表示日美间目前无重大变化。即如上月廿七日总统演说，未攻击日本一字，亦足见对日关系有不愿尖锐化之势。谨陈。文③支。六.四

144. 宋子文致蒋介石报告美与德意关系日益紧张电(1941 年 6 月 4 日)

S352 呈委员长电 六.四日 复 六.九

委座钧鉴：美与德义关系，日益紧张，太平洋舰队逐调大西洋。前陈概况，今已证实。于是两洋不便同时作战之说更盛，对日缓和派重新抬头。美著名律师陶纳文④，上届欧战上校军官，精于战略，为总统及海长之至友，因此在军事政治上具有势力。今春曾奉密令，赴欧、非两地调查，熟悉世界大势，深知我抗战对于国际之重要。文拟以钧座名义，请其赴我国一行，考察真象，据实报告，颇足打破海陆军中忽视我抗战者之心理。倘蒙俯允，彼再得总统同意后，即可首途，此君富于资财，完全自费。如何之处，乞示饬遵。○豪。文。六.四

145. 宋子文致蒋介石报告詹森回国谈国共关系甚详电(1941 年 6 月 5 日)

呈委员长电 六.五日

委座钧鉴：詹森⑤回国，谈国共问题甚详，共党诡谋，知之甚深。又称，留港时所得消息，敌人训练跳伞部队甚勤，将来用于滇缅路，如云南驿等处，占据机场，阻碍交通，则一时不易恢复，应加注意。再，军事上危险，以滇为最，不可不预为防

---

① 即野村吉三郎，时任日本驻美大使。
② 克鲁(Joseph C. Grew)，通常译作格鲁，时任美国驻日本大使。
③ 此处"文"字为拟稿者笔迹。
④ 陶纳文(William J. Donovan)，即多诺万，美国著名律师，后出任美国战略情报处处长。
⑤ 即美国驻华大使詹森(Nelson Johnson)，任期至 1941 年 5 月。

杜之计。等语。谨陈。○微。文。六.五

146. 宋子文致蒋介石报告美国人士咸望艾黎来美电(1941年6月5日)

S353　呈委员长电　六.五日　复　七.二

委座钧鉴：美国人士，对于合作事业有兴趣者，咸望ALLEY① 能来美一行，俾便筹助巨款。尚乞俯允饬遵为叩。○歌。文。六.五

147. 宋子文致蒋介石报告 P40 飞机已到仰光电(1941年6月6日)

S354　呈委员长电　六.六日　复　六.十九

委座钧鉴：P40飞机卅六架已到仰光，第二、三批亦已起运。周至柔主任②已派我队员准备接收。窃查此种飞机，速度甚高，性能特出。我队员未尝熟练，万一稍有疏虞，必为美方借口，与两国空军合作问题，不无关系。且该机之枪及弹随带在二、三批内，一时尚不能实用。愚见此百架新机统先交由美志愿军驾驶，并训练我方驾驶员，俟有相当经验之后，再由我队接收，以昭慎重。是否有当，伏乞分别饬遵为叩。鱼未。文。六.六

148. 宋子文致蒋介石孔祥熙提议对美所需军事有关物料办理办法电(1941年6月6日)

S355　呈委员长电　六.六日　复　六.十

委座钧鉴，孔部长勋鉴：据纽约世界公司接财政部五月九日代电，订购手枪四万五千枝，又军用器材一批，两共美金二百六十八万元，由中央银行拨付等语。窃查购运此项军械，原可并由贷借案内办理，毋须拨付现款。如贷借案内不能办者，该公司更不能办到。抗战期间，对美所需各种物料，多与军事有关，愚见应径先：(一)归贷借案内办理；(二)再动用进出口银行物资借款；不得已时，(三)始以现款购运。如此不但节省财力，抑且符合法案精神。惟以上三项办法运用之适当，须视物料种类及各方面情形而定，且美国局势紧张，厉行统制，即民用物品之购买输出，亦在统制之列，为申请优先购运起见，亦应有集中支配办法，

---

① 即路易·艾黎(Louis Alley)，新西兰人，当时在中国组织领导工业合作运动。
② 周至柔，浙江临海人，时任国民政府航空委员会主任。

用特电陈鄙见。嗣后对美需用一切物料,由国内主管机关审定开单电知,由文酌定究宜适用以上何项办法,呈核遵办。是否有当,伏乞示遵。○鱼申。文。六.六

149. 宋子文致蒋介石报告居里谈拉铁摩尔情形电(1941年6月11日)

S356　呈复委员长电　六.十一日

委座钧鉴:鱼电敬悉。遵谕面询居里。据云,麦克猷亦奉钧电转询,又称拉特摩尔①与总统确无深交,唯因其学识声望,颇加器重,故以推荐等语。谨陈。○真。文。六.十一

150. 宋子文致蒋介石报告拉铁摩尔飞华电(1941年6月12日)②

S357　呈复委员长真电　六.十二日

真电敬悉。拉铁马尔君定于七月一日飞华。○震。六.十二

151. 宋子文致蒋介石报告我最迫切需要之飞机尚无确实把握电(1941年6月13日)③

S358　呈委员长电　六.十三日　复　六.十六

委座钧鉴:军货贷借案各事虽有端倪,唯我最迫切需要之飞机,迄今尚无确实把握,焦灼何似。前与沈德燮等拟定一千架之计划,第一步五百架,内分战斗机三百五十架、轰炸机一百五十架,屡向美方反复申诉理由,尽力交涉。战斗机似有拨交希望,轰炸机则尚无着落。居里亦谓智穷力竭,无计可施。究其所由,固因英美各有急需,以致供不应求,而我申述之理由,或有未能动其观感之处。再四筹维,唯有以我国所处之险境、军事之危机,例如最近山西战况失利,非我官兵不忠勇,飞机缺乏实为最大原因,历举事实,率直密告,进以危言,晓以利害,用政治方法促动总统之决心,或可于英美需要之中,抽让若干。唯关系恭重,未敢擅专,焦虑之余,谨陈末见。伏乞指示机宜,俾有遵循,不致贻误大局。毋任叩祷。○

---

① 即拉铁摩尔。
② 该电文已收入《中华民国重要史料初编》第三编战时外交(一),第726页。
③ 同上书,第456页。

元。文。六.十三

152. 宋子文致蒋介石请示聘拉铁摩尔为政治顾问应否宣传电(1941 年 6 月 16 日)

S359　呈委员长电　六.十六日　复六.十九

委座钧鉴:钧座聘请拉特摩尔为政治顾问,中美合作更形密切,应否在美广事宣传,伏乞示遵。○谏。文。六.十六

153. 宋子文致蒋介石报告仰光运输情形紊乱电(1941 年 6 月 17 日)

S360　呈委员长电　六.十七日　复　六.十九

委座钧鉴:据美武官报告其政府,仰光运输情形,甚为紊乱,云云。谨闻。○篠。六.十七

154. 宋子文致蒋介石何应钦请示军政部通信器材可否在借款项下动用电 (1941 年 6 月 18 日)

委员长蒋并转何总长

委座钧鉴,何部长①勋鉴:军政部通信器材原拟两年之用,曾照原册六折提交美国陆军部。因该部程式过高,且有二十余项非美军所有,全部估计约需美金三千余万元,难于办到。查租借法案有源源供应之望,为争取时间,已择美军所有程式较为接近之卅项,估计最急数量约占原册三分之一,约值四百万元,先请供给,其余归纳二十余项,必须另购,亦以最急数量估计,约需美金一百万元。可否在借款项下动用,乞电示。○啸。文。六.十八

155. 宋子文致蒋介石报告已向总统设法促进飞机供给电(1941 年 6 月 18 日)

委座钧鉴:删电奉悉。已用钧电向总统设法促进飞机之供给,容当续陈。○巧。文。六.十八

---

① 即国民政府军政部部长何应钦。

156. 宋子文致蒋介石报告美志愿军已启程来华电(1941年6月19日)

S361

委座钧鉴：巧电敬悉。志愿军三十一人已启程来华，另九十人将于本月卅日离美，余视船位情形而定。又陈纳德将于七月八日乘机返华。敬复。文①。皓。文。六.十九

157. 宋子文致蒋介石告以滇缅路运输确为美国协助我国之唯一关键电 (1941年6月20日)

S362　呈委员长电　六.廿日

委座钧鉴：奉效电。经详细探询，前电所陈美武官报告仰光滇缅路运输情形紊乱，并非麦寇。麦寇最近由美大使转电居里，报告该路五月份运量为一万九千五百吨，内三分之二直达昆明，其余沿途卸交各站，超过以前纪录甚巨。同时居里所接陆军部报告，则上月只运四千吨，且仰光情形紊乱。居里以两不相符，前来询文，故所知真象如此。此事虽非麦寇报告，但钧座对于海长②之诚感，当于便中婉达，使其了解。再，滇缅路运输，确为美国协助我国之唯一关键，其协助之程度，胥视该路之运量如何。顷据政府中至友密告，如运输畅通无阻，钧座要求之五万万元军货，固不成问题。按其秘密预算，准备两年之中，接济十万万元之军货。彼以私人友谊见告，不愿形诸笔墨，但绝对可靠。谨电密陈。○智。文。六.廿

158. 宋子文致蒋介石报告聘拉铁摩尔为顾问事总统同意宣传电(1941年6月23日)

S363　呈复委员长皓电　六.廿三日

委座钧鉴：对聘拉特摩尔为顾问事，总统同意宣传，声明该氏为总统介绍于钧座，以示两国之密切合作。公布原文，系经总统亲自改正，已电霍亚民译呈钧览。如蒙核准，请照原文在渝公布，并迅电谕知，此间亦当同时发表。○梗申。文。六.廿三

---

① 此处"文"系宋子文本人的手迹。
② 即美国海军部长诺克斯(Frank Knox)。

159. 宋子文致蒋介石报告美国政府向议院要求增加租借法案数量电(1941年6月23日)

S364　呈委员长电　六.廿三日

委座钧鉴：美国政府向议院要求增加军货租借法案之数量,并询中英两国之需要。窃查我方初次办理此案,时间匆促,遗漏必多。今有此良机,恳饬各主管机关,统盘筹划,缜密研究,开单飞寄,以便答复。毋任企盼。○漾酉。文。六.廿三

160. 宋子文致蒋介石密告此间人士推测日本或实行南进电(1941年6月23日)

S366　呈委员长电　六.廿三日　复　七.五

委座钧鉴：德苏战事①起后,总统急欲获知希特拉②、松冈间有无秘密协定。此间人士推测,如有协定,日本或趁此机会,实行南进。鄙见日本或以全力对我攻击,俟苏联有失败模样,即向西伯利亚进兵,不知当否。德宣战以后,苏联对我有何表示,亦为此间人士急待明了者,并恳赐复。钧座复电,由文直接转呈总统,不经他人过目。再,美国因舆论关系,难以如英国之坚切表示援苏。并以奉闻。○漾。文。六.廿三

161. 宋子文致蒋介石报告已批准驱逐机数量电(1941年6月25日)

S367　呈委员长电　六.廿五　复　七.十五

委座钧鉴：总统已批准二百六十九架驱逐机,连同以前P40百架,可达原定三百五十架之计划。轰炸机继续催请,亦渐有端倪。前奉震电,拟派空军各种人员来美训练。文等商酌之下,觉人数过少,拟要求美方许可派来五百名,正进行中。谨陈。○有。文。六.廿五

162. 宋子文致蒋介石请示龙云托购卡车等是否可行电(1941年6月25日)

呈委员长电　六.廿五　复　七.十四

委座钧鉴：顷接缪云台③电称,龙主席志舟④托购卡车一百辆、机器脚踏车五百

---

① 指1941年6月22日德国向苏联发动大规模进攻,苏德战争爆发。
② 即希特勒(Adolf Hitler),时任德国总理,纳粹党领袖。
③ 即缪嘉铭,字云台,云南昆明人,时任经济部资源委员会顾问、云南省经济委员会主任。
④ 即龙云,字志舟,时任云南省政府主席。

部,为军事运输及警察等用,自备价款,云云。因未奉钧谕,尚未置答。是否可行,伏乞核夺示遵。〇径。文。六.廿五

163. 宋子文致蒋介石请示战车防御炮及炮弹拟向加拿大商购电(1941年7月1日)

S370　呈复委员长艳电　七.一日

委座钧鉴:艳电敬悉。三七战车防御炮及炮弹,因美国交货迟缓,拟向加拿大商购,仍归贷借案内办理,谨复东申。文。七.一

164. 宋子文致蒋介石报告代拟转呈总统申请飞机电稿内容电(1941年7月1日)①

S371　呈委员长电　七.一日

委座钧鉴:我国申请之飞机,原则上美方虽允供给,但进行极为迟缓,焦灼莫名。本日谨遵钧座删电意旨,代拟一电,已交居里转呈总统,其内容胪陈如下:(一)遵删电所示,告以入夏以来,敌机肆虐更甚,任意轰炸,我军民无法抬头反击。中条山失利②原因,即在飞机缺乏。(二)苏德战况未定之前,日本或利用驻东三省陆空军以全力攻我。苏若失败,日进占西伯利亚得手后,力量更大,益将尽力收拾战事,我国军事上危险将益甚。(三)敌机之不断轰炸、苏德开战、日本对我之实力加强,均为我士气颓丧之原因。钧座抗战四年,今始对于此层最为顾虑。只有加增空军之实力可以振作鼓励。(四)我方提出之五百架飞机,为数极微。闻克拉克③少将来我国视察后,完全赞成我方计划。(五)驱逐机一项,经过十二个月,仅得百架,其他二百五十架,虽允供给,交货迟缓。据闻英方所有驱逐机目前已可敷用,希望迅予提前拨给。(六)轰炸机问题,至今尚未解决,仅有驱逐机,焉能成军。轰炸机不但可以破坏敌人机场,即所以抵抗敌机轰炸,进一步尚可攻击敌人城市。(七)钧座以为美方给我一百五十架轰炸机,对于大西洋战局无大关系,而我方则影响极大。经过四年苦战之军民,可以吐气,战况必可逆转。以上所述,尤其士气颓丧之顾虑,只可为总统实告之,其他人员均请秘而

---

① 该电文已收入《中华民国重要史料初编》第三编战时外交(一),第458页。
② 即1941年5月日军在山西南部发动的中条山战役,此役国民党军失利,日军占领中条山地区。
③ 克拉克(Mark Wayne Clark),时任美国陆军总司令部副参谋长。

不宣。等语。谨电奉陈。〇东戌。文。七.一

165. 宋子文致蒋介石报告通信器材须另购电(1941年7月1日)

委座钧鉴:啸电计蒙钧察。军政部通信器材,除卅项由贷借案内办理外,其余廿余项必须另购,约美金一百万元。可否在借款项下拨支,乞电示遵。〇先。文。七.一

166. 宋子文致蒋介石关于商请英国于美所供飞机抽让部分予我电(1941年7月2日)

S372　呈委员长电

委座钧鉴:美国最近因我需要轰炸机,商英国于所供给飞机之中,抽让一部份予我,英尚未首肯。现苏俄军队,溃败在即,国际情势突变,英若有远大眼光,应与美彻底合作,尽量协助我飞机。最近渝英大使馆被炸,已可使其猛省。可否请钧座向英大使力述利害,嘱其电邱吉尔即与罗总统切实洽商。此亦无可奈何之中。作万一之想,伏乞裁夺为叩。〇冬申。文。七.二

167. 宋子文致蒋介石报告苏俄军队恐即不能支持电(1941年7月2日)

S373　呈委员长电　七.二日

委座钧鉴:伦敦消息,苏俄军队,四五日内,恐即不能支持。谨闻。〇冬。文。七.二

168. 宋子文致蒋介石孔祥熙报告中美平衡基金协约展期事宜电(1941年7月2日)

S374　呈委员长及致孔院长电　七.二日　孔复　七.九

委座钧鉴,孔院长勋鉴:中美平衡基金协约,原定本年六月满期,现因美国平衡基金法案展期,故中美协约①亦可先展期至明年六月。经与美财部商定,惟须经过签字手续,拟恳电饬驻美大使馆转知美方,仍由原约签字人员代表我政府及中央银行签字。至所叩祷。〇冬午。文。七.二

---

①　即1941年4月由宋子文代表中国国民政府与美国财政部长摩根索签订的《中美平准基金协定》。

169. 宋子文致蒋介石提出非有外交使节同心协力不足以求事功电(1941年7月6日)

S375　呈委员长电　卅.七.六日　复　七.十一

密急译呈委座钧鉴：前托石曾先生带呈一札，计邀钧察。窃文到美年余，一切秉承钧命，黾勉从公，幸免颠踬。惟各事进行之中，尤以特别之对外工作，非无困难波折，有时不得不避免手续问题，向美方军政最高当局直接商洽，以致引起各方对文越轨之责难，而使事务进行阻滞。高斯前有以后凡与其政府有关各电，皆请用正式手续之表示，即其明证。是以反复思维。四月艳电有副院长名义之渎请，当时为公心切，冒昧陈词，未能顾及立法手续问题，致烦厪虑，委曲成全，尤深感激。副院长名义提出困难，惟冀有精明干练之驻美使节，彻底合作，以便各事之顺利进行。目今施植之①在美，人地最为相宜。当此国际风云，瞬息万变，中美外交所关益巨。如文仅负责办理借贷事宜，外交上之关系尚浅，如兼顾国际特别工作，则非有外交使节同心协力，不足以求事功。文久历艰懔，深荷知遇，钧座必不以文为个人利禄之谋，私人恩怨之故，有此于渎。是否可行，伏乞裁夺，无任急切待命之至。○鱼亥。文。七.六

170. 宋子文致蒋介石转宋子良辞职电(1941年7月7日)

呈委座电　七.七

委座钧鉴：致安弟②马电敬悉。蒙允留美就医，无任感激。西南事务，关系重要，务恳准予辞职，以便负责有人，而免贻误。滇昆段运输已遵钧命电告，迅即移交贝克，并协助新任，安心服务。弟驻华府，一面就医，以求速愈，并备大哥咨询办理此间运输购料事宜。谨电奉陈，伏乞垂察。子良。阳。良。文。七.七

171. 宋子文致蒋介石告以宋子良辞意更坚电(1941年7月7日)

S376　呈委员长电　七.七

委座钧鉴：国务部友人密告，该部接高斯情报，西南运输处樵峰③兄恐开罪于宋家，未敢彻底改组。此项情报文决不置信。但良弟辞职未蒙批准之前，自难免种种揣测。

---

① 即施肇基，1931年曾任国民政府外交部长，1935年曾任驻美大使。当时宋子文聘请施肇基负责处理国防供应公司的日常事务，并且向蒋介石推荐施肇基取代胡适出任驻美大使。
② 即宋子文幼弟宋子安。
③ 即俞飞鹏。

良弟闻此消息,辞意更坚。公义私情,俱恳俯如所请,无任企叩。〇虞。文。七.七

172. 宋子文致蒋介石关于赶筑康印公路实为急务电(1941年7月9日)

S377　呈委员长电　七.八日　复　七.十五

委座钧鉴:由各方面观测,日寇进占泰越,为期不远。我滇缅路如被敌机集中轰炸,破坏必甚,赶筑康印公路,实为急务。文屡电陈请,谅蒙垂察。前向哈利法克斯探询意见,已表赞同。应请政府速向英大使磋商合作赶工办法。先事完成测量,材料工具则由贷借案内申请,美方当可供给。即恳钧座分别饬令外交、财政、交通各机关妥为筹备,一致进行,以期速成。再,塞地亚西昌航线机场亦应赶筑。并乞裁定,无任叩祷。〇佳。文。七.九

173. 宋子文致蒋介石请示龙云购车辆事应如何办理电(1941年7月10日)

呈委员长电　七.十日　复　七.十四

委座钧鉴:前呈经电,为龙主席志舟托购车辆事,未蒙赐复。应如何办理,乞示祗遵。〇灰。文。七.十

174. 宋子文致蒋介石报告兵工署研究爆炸枪弹美军亟需参考电(1941年7月11日)

S379　呈委座电　复　七.十九

委座钧鉴:据闻兵工署研究爆炸枪弹已有成效,美军亟需参考。拟请转饬将该项图说交美武官转赠美国军部,以示友谊。伏乞察裁。〇真。职江杓谨拟。七.十。文。七.十一

175. 宋子文致蒋介石报告总统对中英苏订立共同军事协定感想电(1941年7月12日)①

S378　呈委员长电　卅.七.十二日

委座钧鉴:支、微、真各电敬悉。谨复如下:甲、尊□转陈总统,经与军政各要人

---

① 该电文已收入《中华民国重要史料初编》第三编战时外交(一),第144页。

会商后答复：(一)总统对中俄订立军事协定,认于中国确切有利,中英苏订立共同军事协定亦具同样之感想,但美国不能参加或保证;(二)总统谓中国对俄如有军事上协商,希望随时密告。乙、(一)文见哈利法克斯,谈及英苏关系,据谓英方当然助俄抗德,惟两国政治观念不同,不能有军事同盟。但文闻之总统左右言,邱吉尔与哈利法克斯对于此点意见不同。(二)哈利法克斯接伦敦消息,日对越南将有举动。(三)海长接情报,日敌将于八月一日攻俄。(四)毛根蹈①顷密告,两星期来日无轮船开美。并接情报,驻美日轮公司经理秘密遣送眷属及用具回国,本身亦有退出模样。据以上消息观察,愚见日敌必有关系美国之举动,恐将实行南进。其第一步在完全占领越南及扩充泰国飞机场,准备袭击新加坡、荷印等地。丙、真电体谅周至,益增钦感。植之②使美,仰蒙俯允,尤佩荩筹。国际风云日亟,更非有外交方面之协助,不能相与有成。此次向总统商陈各要务,经过几许周折,始得其切实答复,处境困难,可想而知。长此以往,不但文不能尽责,有负委任,适之③亦属难堪。惟有恳请毅然处置,迅予发表。钧座如一时以为未便,文在此期间,谨当循分株守贷借案之职责。钧座必能鉴谅苦衷,曲予宽容。谨电奉陈,伏乞垂审。弟子文叩。震。

176. 宋子文致蒋介石密告日本陆续调回存美款项电(1941 年 7 月 14 日)

S380 　呈委员长电　七.十四

委座钧鉴:顷毛根韬④密告,日本陆续调回存美款项。○寒。七.十四

177. 宋子文致蒋介石呈报新批准驱逐机种类数量电(1941 年 7 月 15 日)

S381 　呈委员长电　七.十五

委座钧鉴:寒电敬悉。此次批准之驱逐机为:(一) REPUBLIC P43 一百廿五架;(二) VULTEE P48 C 九十二架、D 五十二架。两项合计二百六十九架。钧座谢意,遵即转达。文⑤。删。七.十五

---

①④　即摩根索(Henry Morgenthau Jr.),时任美国财政部部长。

②　即施肇基,字植之,宋子文曾推荐其取代胡适出任驻美国大使。此处《中华民国重要史料初编》第三编战时外交(一)为"适之",现据原拟电稿改为"植之"。

③　即胡适,时任中国驻美国大使。

⑤　此处"文"字为拟稿者笔迹。

178. 宋子文致蒋介石表示柏林商专处人员来美至为欢迎电(1941 年 7 月 16 日)

复呈委员长感电   七.十六

委座钧鉴：感电敬悉。(一)柏林商专处①人员来美，至为欢迎，谨当遵令酌留。(二)日内阁辞职，内容如何，乞示。(三)俄大使②言，列宁格勒及凯雅夫，确甚危急，莫斯科可支持。谨陈。○谏。七.十六

179. 宋子文致蒋介石密告美方判断日敌拟向西伯利亚进攻电(1941 年 7 月 17 日)

S382   呈委员长电   七.十七   复   七.廿一

委座钧鉴：此间接东京消息及海长与毛根韬判断，日敌目的似向西比利亚。又，铣电敬悉，谨当妥为照料。○洽午。文   七.十七

180. 宋子文致蒋介石关于塞地亚修机场请交涉疏通电(1941 年 7 月 21 日)

S383   呈委员长电   七.廿一日   复   七.廿七

委座钧鉴：闻塞地亚修机场事，恐印度各小邦反对。窃查前任英宣传部长达古柏现任内阁驻远东代表，似可请复初兄向其交涉疏通。○马。文。七.廿一

181. 宋子文致蒋介石请示承办租借法案各事仍送呈钧座批饬电(1941 年 7 月 22 日)

S384   呈复委员长电   七.廿二日   复   七.卅一

委座钧鉴：马二电敬悉。联系办法，自关重要。惟文承办军货租借法案以来，因事关军务，向受军委会指挥，秉承钧命处理一切。今四项办法，系似有变更，所有购运事宜、借款支配，财部总其大成，深觉在军事紧急期内，对内对外诸多窒

---

① 即位于柏林的中国驻德使馆商务专员处。
② 即苏联驻华大使潘友新(Alexander Semenovich Paniushkin)。

碍。反复思维，拟请仍照现行办法，各事进行，径呈钧座批饬主管机关存查办理，或集中军事委员会，另定联系办法。如何之处，恳请迅电示遵。○养。文。七·廿二

182. 宋子文致蒋介石报告法方业已应允日本占领越南电（1941 年 7 月 23 日）

S385　呈委员长电　七·廿三日

委座钧鉴：美国务院接驻法美大使①电称，据法海长达伦②见告，日本要求于廿四日以武力完全占领越南，法方无可奈何，业已应允，等语。大约英美对日经济制裁即将开始。○梗。文。七·廿三

183. 蒋介石致宋子文请向美建议与苏开诚相谈电（1941 年 7 月 23 日）

委员长来电

耀密。接邵大使③皓（十九）电称：月来观察所得，苏美取同一步骤之说，非苏所愿闻。以此与谈，势或愈□。若美先有切实表示，则情势自当不同。美驻苏大使不久回任，甚盼其受命与苏开诚相谈，乞电子文先生设法。等语。请兄向美建议何如？中正。漾（廿三日）。

184. 宋子文致蒋介石报告总统已批准轰炸机情形电（1941 年 7 月 23 日）

S386　呈委员长电　七·廿三日

委座钧鉴：总统已批准轰炸机六十六架，计 LOCKHEED HUDSONS 卅三架，DB7 卅三架，均为向英方商让者。谨陈。梗申。文。七·廿三

---

① 即美国海军上将李海（William Leahy），1941 年 1 月起出任美国驻法国维希政府大使。
② 即时任法国维希政府海军部长的弗兰索瓦·达尔朗（Admiral François Darlan）。
③ 即时任中国驻苏联大使的邵力子。

185. 宋子文致蒋介石报告美海长拟派记者由渝飞经新疆至莫斯科电(1941年7月23日)

S388　呈委员长电　七.廿三日　复　七.廿八

委座钧鉴：美海长诺斯①所办之芝加哥报纸,拟派 STEELE② 为苏俄战地记者。海长托文代恳钧座,赐予协助,俾得由渝飞经新疆至莫斯科。海长对我国素极热心,可否俯允,乞电示遵。○漾申。文。七.廿三

186. 宋子文致蒋介石请示有法国航空员可否飞渝与航委会接洽电(1941年7月23日)

S389　呈委员长电　七.廿三日　复　七.廿八

委座钧鉴：顷有法国航空员,由越南来美,愿从该地招募同人抗日作战。可否恳即电示,再令飞渝与航委会接洽。○漾。文。七.廿三

187. 宋子文拟复蒋介石在加拿大及美国订购火炮情形电(1941年7月24日)

S390　拟复委员长巧电

巧电奉悉。三七炮遵命在加拿大及美国各订购三百六十门,新七五山炮交货期迄未确定。拟待交货开始时相机增加,原则可无问题。○敬未。职江杓谨拟。七.廿四　文。七.廿四

188. 宋子文致蒋介石呈报向加拿大订购军械种类数量及交货时间电(1941年7月24日)

S391　拟将已向加拿大订购械弹详情电呈

委座钧鉴：我方向加拿大订购军械五种之申请书,经商妥后,于今日送致美军部,计：(一) 英式轻机枪一万五千枝,八月开始交货,明年九月交清；(二) 点五五枪三千枝,明年一至六月交清；(三) 三七炮三百六十门,八月开始,分十二个月交齐；(四) 四公

---

① 即美国海军部长诺克斯(Frank Knox)。
② 即 Archibald T. Steele,时为《芝加哥每日新闻》记者。

分高射炮一百八十门,十月开始,明年六月交清;(五)三英吋七高射炮四十八门,明年正月始至九月〈交〉清。各炮均附弹药。文①。迴酉。职江杓谨拟。七·廿四

189. 宋子文致蒋介石报告美国决定冻结日本财产电(1941年7月24日)

S392　呈委员长电　七·廿四

委座钧鉴:美国决定:(一)冻结日本在美约一万五千万元财产。(二)停止购日本金银。以上两项,即日宣布。再拟(三)扣留日本在美船只,(四)禁止汽油机油运日。谨闻。○敬申。七·廿四

190. 宋子文致蒋介石密告阎锡山与敌代表会议电(1941年7月31日)

S393　呈委员长电　七·卅一日

急呈委座钧鉴:此间某要人见告,据上海极可靠消息:(一)阎锡山②之代表与敌代表田中,于六月卅日在太原会议,晋军增至卅万人,军械给养,由日敌交南京伪组织③转拨。(二)阎之代表阎某,要求:甲、发行三千万纸币,日敌为后盾,供给准备金;乙、发还阎财产;丙、晋北十三县,归还山西。田中允就甲、乙两项商量,丙项因日敌与伪蒙政府④已有协定,不能洽商。(三)大约八月一日敌阎协约在太原签字后,双方停战,阎宣布反共及脱离中央,加入所谓东亚新秩序。签字代表,日方为第一军司令官或其参谋长,阎代表为赵景初(Cho Kyo Su)、王西国(O Sei Koku)(译音)。再,阎在西安之兵工厂及留川眷属,现正迁回太原,并在山东、山西实行征兵,为欺骗政府,故意放出会议已经失效之烟幕,云云。谨此密陈。○世。文。七·卅一

191. 宋子文致蒋介石恳转饬各机关请购贷借案物料注意说明用途电(1941年8月5日)

S394　呈委员长电　八·五　复　八·十四

委座钧鉴:窃查各机关请购贷借案内物料,对于用途,多无事实说明。美方查核,详细认真,每次必费周折,始得就绪。务恳转饬各请购机关注意,以免往返查

---

① 此处"文"字为拟稿者笔迹。
② 阎锡山,字百川,任军事委员会第二战区司令长官。是时阎正派人与日军代表进行妥协谈判。
③ 即1940年3月在日本扶植下在南京成立的汪精卫傀儡政权。
④ 即1939年9月在日本当局扶植下成立的伪蒙疆联合自治政府。

询延误时期为叩。○微。文。八.五

192. 宋子文致蒋介石请遴派高级电信专门人员来美电(1941 年 8 月 6 日)

呈委员长电　八.六日　复　八.十四

委座钧鉴：文处关于电信器材事务，因一时无人，暂交温毓庆①办理。今该员因病，不时请假。文恐有延误，敬恳钧座遴派精通英文、熟悉此间情形之高级电信专门人员，来美服务。无任企盼。○鱼。文。八.六

193. 宋子文致蒋介石询问川滇两省能否设法出口电(1941 年 8 月 6 日)

S396　呈委员长电　八.六　复九.十七

美国禁止日丝进口，但需要甚殷。我国川滇两省能否设法出口？可供给若干？沿海沦陷各省，有无方法私运？敬乞电示。○麻未。文。八.六已发

194. 宋子文致蒋介石说明康印公路南线须有航测电(1941 年 8 月 7 日)

S395　呈委员长电　八.六日

委座钧鉴：冬西电敬悉。关于康印公路，本拟定自西昌西行，至金沙江分两线：一、北线经阿敦子、盐井、察隅入印度，长约一五零零公里；一、南线经云南之贡山、江心坡，由缅北部入印，长约一二零零公里，此即美大使馆复文希望同时测量另一经过缅甸北底之比较线也。南线路程既短，且不经过康藏界限缪辖之地带，外交方面只须英缅同意协助，无其他困难。即恳转饬交部，同时勘测南线。如能航测，收效尤速。且为中印航运计，无论如何须有航测。如交通部无测量机，或可商中航公司办理。英派驻新加坡之内阁代表古拔君，不日到美，文当与商谈，托其协助。谨复。○阳。文。八.七

195. 宋子文致蒋介石强调红会物品须有优先运送之权电(1941 年 8 月 7 日)

S397　呈委员长电　八.七日

委座钧鉴：美红会前经文说明滇缅路运量增加，始允于原送救济物品外，增送

---

①　温毓庆，广东台山人，曾任国民政府交通部电政司司长，时任军事委员会技术研究室主任。

其他医药用品,业经五月盐日电陈。今查六月份仅运廿二吨半,积存仰光七百八十吨,运仰途中尚有七百八十吨。该会以运输迟缓,缅地酷热,药物易于腐坏,拟俟积存物品运尽,再定总续接济。滇缅路目前虽已改进,所有内运物品,似应有分别缓急、统盘筹划之办法,或另设机关,专司其事。尤以红会物品,须有优先输送之权,以免延误急需,而为友邦借口。尚乞钧裁。○虞。文。八·七

196. 宋子文致蒋介石报告美方允抽拨 DC3 飞机电(1941 年 8 月 7 日)

S398　八·七日　复　八·十五

委座钧鉴:宥电敬悉。美方允于一二月内,由其航运机中,抽拨 DC3 机十架。将来如何支配,请饬交部与中航公司商定。○阳。文。八·七

197. 宋子文致蒋介石报告购定军服用棉布交货日期电(1941 年 8 月 8 日)

复　八·十四

委座钧鉴:贷借案内购定军服用棉布一千万码,交货日期计八月约四十万,九月一百万,十月二百万,十一月三百四十万,十二月三百十万码。乞饬军政部知照。详单另寄。○庚。文。八·八

198. 宋子文致蒋介石恳拨冗赐见安司丹电(1941 年 8 月 8 日)

S399　呈委员长电　八·八日　复　八·十四

委座钧鉴:一、安司丹视察滇缅路已毕,真(十一)返渝。恳拨冗赐见,听取报告,以备钧座主持改革之参考。二、驻仰光陈质平①、陈长桐两员,建议设立委员会,分别所有内运物料之缓急,定起运先后之程序,似有见地。此委会或可由樵峰兄主持,尚乞核夺。三、陈质平等所请由仰内运物料之运费,不在贷借法案之内,所有申请物料,文仅负责运至仰光,请饬财部拨给。谨陈。○齐。文。八·八

---

① 陈质平,广东文昌人,时任中缅运输管理处处长,兼任国民政府行政院驻缅甸代表。

199. 宋子文致蒋介石吁恳饬属查明运输停滞真相电(1941 年 8 月 12 日)

S400   呈委员长电   八.十二日

委座钧鉴:顷据美方报告,卡车数百辆及其他贷借物资抵仰,因运费关税均无着落,输运停滞等语。钧座虽已派曾次长①、陈质平驻仰,但因经费及其他关系,亦有力不从心之势。美军官团即将来华②,见此情形,对于将来之供给,难免借口延宕。焦虑之余,惟有吁恳钧座饬属查明真象,妥筹改进方法,以资补救,无任企祷。○震。文。

200. 宋子文致蒋介石报告美希望我国遴派海军官员来美电(1941 年 8 月 12 日)

S401   呈委员长电   八.十二日

委座钧鉴:美总统情报部,因太平洋风云日亟,希望我国遴派海军官员来美驻华府,惟必须通晓英文、熟悉日本情势者。即乞裁定,赐复为叩。○侵。文。八.十二

201. 宋子文致蒋介石报告会晤英派驻新加坡代表情形电(1941 年 8 月 14 日)

S402   呈委员长电   八.十四日

委座钧鉴:顷晤英内阁派驻新加坡代表古拔君,一、代表钧座欢迎赴渝;二、申述中英美荷有在新加坡举行会议商讨抗敌之必要;三、贷借物资经缅纳税问题,古拔君允于即日电美要求免税。古君定下星期飞新加坡。谨陈。○寒。文。八.十四

202. 宋子文致蒋介石报告美政府对滇缅路运输情形不满电(1941 年 8 月 21 日)

S404   呈委员长电   八.廿一日   复   八.廿五

委座钧鉴:安斯丹③电请回国,居里嘱询钧座意见。安视察滇缅路报告,内容尚充实否? 美政府迭接各方消息,对我滇缅路运输情形,深致不满。我方要求贷借

---

① 即曾任国民政府外交部常务次长的曾镕甫,时任中国驻缅甸代表。
② 即美国军事代表团,于 1941 年 9 月赴中国访问。
③ 即安司丹(Daniel G. Arnstein)。

物料,达九万万元。如该路不能急速改善,美方势必逶延,事实上亦无法输送。瞻念前途,焦灼曷任。钧座烛照无遗,必能洞见症结。是否因权责未能专一,主其事者,不克尽全力彻底痛加改革,或另有其他原因? 仍烦尽虑察酌主持,不胜企祷之至。○马。文。八.廿一

203. 宋子文致蒋介石报告美军官团最近期内即可赴渝电(1941 年 8 月 22 日)[①]

S406　呈委员长电　八.廿二日

委座钧鉴:删电敬悉。美派军官团事,因国务部之慎重,进行迟缓。文乃径函总统催询,顷接复函,略谓:嘱派军官团一节,极愿接纳,陆军部长已选定麦克罗达[②]少将。彼正调集人员,于最近期内,即可赴渝。余切望该团在中国抗战之期间,能尽力为有效之协助等语。麦君及一部人员约两三星期内先行。确实行期,另电呈报。所率其他人员,以后分批起程。请饬准备住所,南岸北岸,何处为宜,并恳酌定。○祸。文。八.廿二

204. 宋子文致蒋介石报告阎锡山之代表与敌方代表会议情报电(1941 年 8 月 22 日)

S407　呈委员长电　八.廿二日

委座钧鉴:世电计邀钧览。美方于八月七日又获一消息:晋阎之代表与晋主席代表(或系伪组织)商定,先移调赵某军队于孝义,以便与敌军连络,即于八月六日,在孝义会议。敌方参加者为其第一军参谋长及太原特务机关长,结果已报告南京伪组织等语。窃查合众社(十五)日渝电称,日军占领三年半之孝义,本日已被华军规复,云云。未稔与上述消息有无关连耳。谨陈。文[③]。养。八.廿二

205. 宋子文致蒋介石报告贷借案内飞机已申请情形电(1941 年 8 月 22 日)

S408

委座钧鉴:马电奉悉。贷借案内,我方原按千架机计划进行,嗣以易于申请,改

---

①　该电文已收入《中华民国重要史料初编》第三编战时外交(一),第 463~464 页。

②　即 1941 年率美国军事代表团访问重庆的马格鲁德(John Magruder)。

③　此处"文"字为拟稿者笔迹。

先借贷五百架。兹已申请者,有驱逐机 P-43 125 架、P-48 144 架,轰炸机有 Hudson 33 架、DB-7 33 架、B-25C 138 架,初级教练机 70 架,另加前已购运之 P-40 100 架,尚可符合我空军驱逐机 350 与轰炸机 150 之企望。以上申请机数,美方俱已接受,惟生产所限,美机又供不应求,将来实交机数有无变动,甚难逆料。现正多方设法切催,早日交货。谨先电陈。养午。文。八.廿二

206. 宋子文致蒋介石密告美军事团内部组织电(1941 年 8 月 26 日)①

S409　拟呈委员长电

钧鉴:美政府派华军事团已明令公布,约于九月中启程。其内部组织如下:团长一人,团部分一处五科:(一)参谋处内置财务、经理、医务及专员等四课;(二)人事行政;(三)情报联络;(四)组织训练;(五)供应;(六)作战计划等科。第二至五科之下,按需要联合设股,计分空军、步兵、工兵、通信、交辎、兵工、化学兵、野炮兵、高射炮兵、装甲车队及杂项等十一股。供应科内另附四组,为运输组、滇缅公路组、需要分配组及铁路组。团部驻渝,贵阳、昆明、腊戍各设办事处。此外,有连络员五人,分驻上海、马尼拉、新加坡、香港、仰光各埠。在华盛顿设办事处,由主任一人主持,下设行政科,科分空军、军需、兵工、通信、工兵、运输及杂项等七股,管理我国租借案中与军部有关之事项。团员约四十名,刻在选择中。吾方招待及相对之连络组织,似应预筹。除组织表另函寄呈外,余待查明续报。文。宥。八.廿六

207. 宋子文致蒋介石报告拉铁摩尔对蒙古新疆素有研究电(1941 年 8 月 26 日)

S410　呈委员长电　八.廿六日

委座钧鉴:马二电敬悉。遵即试探美方意向,容续陈报。拉特摩尔顾问对蒙古、新疆素有研究,请垂询,上贡参考。窃以兹事不仅技术问题,政治、外交均有关连,中苏美之间必须有一整个办法。欧苏油田,或将被德侵占,新油开发,固可解决中苏之困难,苏联亦获益匪浅。惟苏对新疆,向来视同禁脔,闻早已助盛②经营。美国因援苏物资有限,未必能直接对苏为坚决有效之表示。是以政治问题,

---

①　该电文已收入《中华民国重要史料初编》第三编战时外交(一),第 464 页。
②　即盛世才,时任新疆省政府主席。

实为此事之关键。如得解决,一切自可迎刃而解。拙见不知有当钧意否? ○宥。
文。八.廿六。

208. 宋子文致蒋介石报告军货贷借案经过概略及款项支配数额函稿(1941 年 8 月 27 日)

呈委员长函稿　八月二十七日

委座钧鉴:窃查美政府为援助被侵略各民主国,曾于今春由国会通过"军货贷借案"。自开始迄今,屡有变更。兹将经过概略及款项支配数额,恭呈鉴察。

甲、今春三月二十七日,美国会通过贷借案,吾国所得之款项,分列如下:

(1) 军械	四七,八七六,一八一元	
(2) 飞机	五十,○○○,○○○元	
(3) 战车及军用车辆	六七,二八二,五八五元	
(4) 运输费用	五,○○○,○○○元	
(5) 军用杂项	九,八四一,二三四元	
(6) 国防工业	(未得分配)	
(7) 农工商品	五十,○○○,○○○元	
	(内有一五,○○○,○○○元系铁路材料)	

以上七项共计美金二三○,○○○,○○○元。

乙、美政府于一九四一年三月以前,购入之军用品及械弹等,经总统批准,可以转让于各民主国,我国分得美金二五,一○三,一○○元。

丙、七月九日得美政府通知,为备总统向国会申请第二批贷借案款项起见,限于二日内,将吾国所需军械器材至明年年底止之总额,列表送核。因事出仓卒,权由文与兵工署、航空委员会等机关派来人员,参酌国情,编列各项需要清册,其清册于七月二十一日航邮呈阅。其预算总值,约为美金一,五○○,○○○,○○○元。兹将各项分列如下:

(1) 军械等项	二九六,八六五,○○○元	
(2) 飞机等项	六七六,四五○,○○○元	
(3) 军用车辆等项	一六七,二○○,○○○元	
(4) 运输等项	五○,○○○,○○○元	
(5) 军用杂项	八三,八○○,○○○元	
(6) 国防工业等设备	二五,一○○,○○○元	
(7) 农工商品	一九一,七○○,○○○元	

(8) 其他管理检验等费   八,四〇〇元

美政府于八月十五日将上项预算加以审核,并将我方申请总额,在本年年底以前先拨美金六〇〇,〇〇〇,〇〇〇元。此案不久将由美政府提请国会通过。兹将该款各分配细目,条列如下:

(1) 军械等项   一七九,一二八,五〇〇元
(2) 飞机等项   二〇一,〇〇〇,〇〇〇元
(3) 军用车辆等项   七六,〇二〇,〇〇〇元
(4) 运输等项   三五,〇〇〇,〇〇〇元
(5) 军用杂粮(大部分为通讯器材)   二七,八三六,〇〇〇元
(6) 国防工业设备   六,〇〇〇,〇〇〇元
(7) 农工商品   七五,〇〇〇,〇〇〇元

上项数目,经文向美政府声明,各项内部,按事实需要,可有少数之变动,或各项互相通融。此点业已获得美政府之同意。

以上甲、乙、丙三项,为五个月内美政府由贷借案给予我国之援助。甲、乙、丙三项核准之数额,为美金八五五,一〇三,一〇〇元,来年度可拨到之款,尚不在内。综观以上所陈,美国援华物资之数额,在彼已觉尽力,其为生产迟缓,求过于供,亦属实情。据闻全部南美拉丁各国所得数目,尚不及此数也。专此。敬请钧安。〇〇〇谨上。八月二十七日

209. 宋子文致蒋介石报告罗斯福丘吉尔会谈情形电(1941年8月28日)①

呈委员长电 八.廿八日

委座钧鉴,罗邱海上会议②处所得消息,汇陈如下:(一)苏联节节败退,或有再蹈上次欧战之故辙,单独与德媾和。英美虽愿积极援助,但军械产量太少。例如苏联要求飞机六千架,英美只拨给二百零五架,内驱逐机英拨一百四十架,美拨六十架,轰炸机只给五架。因恐苏联失望,故有英美苏莫斯科会议之举,以示援助之决心,藉以延宕时日。(二)罗主张英对泰国问题取强硬态度,但罗不肯切实表示英日如因此发生战争,美当参加。故上星期邱吉尔演说,关于南太平洋问题反宾为主,牵连美国,使其不能置身事外。美方对邱之手段,颇

---

① 本电稿与下电稿内容大体相同,但部分文句有差别,故一并收入。
② 指1941年8月14日,美国总统罗斯福和英国首相丘吉尔在英国皇家海军舰艇威尔士亲王号上签署《大西洋宪章》,提出维护国际和平与安全的原则。

为愤懑。霍尔①向报界声称,余对邱首相一般演说文字之雄壮,备极钦佩,惟余对此演说,不愿有所评论,云云。(三)英国对于美军械产量,表示关心。英美决定两国军械生产切实合作,以期来年下半年飞机坦克枪炮产量超过德国。至美国参战问题,罗表示时间尚未到,惟允不久向议会提出派军舰保护英国运输。再,文等对于海上会议不提中国,莫斯科会议中国不能加入,屡向朝野透露不满之意,是以原来反对派遣军官团之国务部,请总统正式发表该团之派遣。是否恐我向苏要求,使美方独为其难,故先自行表示②,抑或另有其他深意。盖苏方明知,如日本继续南进,美参战之成分较多,如攻西伯利亚,美未必参战,而日攻西伯利亚,大有箭在弦上之势,故苏极力牵连美国,一如邱吉尔演说之用意耳。(四)文等对海上会议不提中国,莫斯科会议中国又不能参加,屡向此间朝野透露不满之意,是以原来反对派遣军事顾问,□□③以示不忘中国。文。

210. 宋子文致蒋介石报告美英苏莫斯科会议情形电(1941年8月29日)

呈委员长电　八.廿九

委座钧鉴:支电奉悉。莫斯科会议〈产〉生于罗邱海上会议。苏联节节败退,损失极巨。英美恐其再蹈上次欧战覆辙,单独与德媾和,惟虽愿积极援助,但军需产量太少。例如苏联要求飞机六千架,英美只拨二百零五架,内英拨驱逐机一百四十架,美拨六十架,轰炸机只给五架。因恐苏联失望,故有英美苏莫斯科会议之举,以示竭诚援助。故此次出发点,绝不如外人宣传之盛。至美国方面因尚想与日方延宕时期,故不愿中国参加。适之前向国务部提出,彼表示中国不必参加。目前情形,罗因向邱主张英对泰国问题取强硬态度,但罗不肯切实表示英日如因此发生战事,美当参加,故两星期前邱吉尔演说关于太平洋泰荷星加波④问题,反以美为主,英为援助者,牵连美国,使其不能置身事外。美方对邱之手段,颇为愤懑。霍尔向报界声称,余对邱首相一般演说文字之雄壮,备极钦佩,惟余对其各个演说,不愿有所评论,云云。查莫斯干会议⑤苏外次公开及向力子表示,会议苏英美开会对付德国之军械,故中国当然不参入□□。今苏顾问忽向钧

① 即时任美国国务卿的赫尔(Cordell Hull)。
② 原稿为"故先自行表示,使美方独为其难",现根据前后文加以调整。
③ 以下脱字若干。
④ 即泰国、荷属东印度(印尼)、新加坡。
⑤ 即莫斯科会议。

座表示欢迎中国参加,是否推□之辞,抑或有更深用意。因苏方明知,如日继续南进,美可参战成分多,惟如攻西比利亚,美并不一定参战,而日本对西比利亚大有箭在弦上,故苏方欲牵入美国,犹邱吉而对日发表谈话之用意。文等对于海上会议不提中国,莫斯科会议中国又不能加入,屡向此间朝野透露不满之意,是以原来反对派遣军官团之国务部,于事后特请总统正式发表该团之使命,以示不忘中国。谨陈。

211. 宋子文致蒋介石报告卡车运出情形电(1941年8月29日)

S412　呈委员长　八. 廿九日

委座钧鉴:沁电敬悉。十轮军用卡车,于九月十八日以前,可再运出一千五百辆。又,滇缅路、甘肃油矿、滇缅铁路需用卡车4×2式共两千五百辆,顷已装运七百卅三辆;九月八日以前,装运一千一百卅一辆;余六百卅六辆,可于十月初旬运出。除装船详单另寄何部长、俞总监①外,乞先饬知照。○艳。文。八. 廿九

212. 宋子文致蒋介石密告近卫致罗斯福函内容电(1941年9月3日)

S414　呈委员长电　九. 三日

极密。委座钧鉴:近卫②致总统函内容如下:(一)欧战期间,日本应允不再向外有军事上发展;(二)日驻越军队减至一万人,越军港不建筑工事;(三)中国本部及东三省维持现状,希望美国劝告中国长期停战;(四)日本希望美国恢复经济关系,解除冻结,另订通商条约,及劝告英荷同样与日恢复邦交。以上消息,美政府严守秘密,钧座如有运用是项消息之处,务使外间勿知由文传来。再,美政府之感想,以为近卫所提各节,无非延宕手段,德胜,日自可无往不利;德败,日仍有与民主国家洽商之余地。而在此胜负未确定期间,日军事经济之地位更可增强,已经吞食之物可以消化。美政府对此种种,绝对明了,不愿对外公开发表,恐竟因此惹起军人对近卫内阁之暴行,但认定无论如何,一二月内近卫亦难支持,届时即为太平洋战事发动之时期。美方因不愿日军人借口此次向美协商而推倒近卫,故绝对不愿丝毫有所泄漏也。谨电密陈。文③。江。九. 三

---

① 即俞飞鹏,时任军事委员会运输统制局参谋长。
② 即时任日本首相的近卫文麿。
③ 该"文"字系宋子文笔迹。

213. 宋子文致蒋介石报告与马格鲁德谈话情形函稿(1941年9月4日)

最密

呈委员长函稿　九.四日

委座钧鉴：美军事顾问团麦克罗达将军,率一部份人员,即将于本月中旬飞渝。谨将拙见所及与洽谈经过,胪陈于左,伏希垂察。

(一) 文嘱齐焌①,将以前德顾问团之组织、高级官长之阶级及其对我军队之好评,一一译告该团,以资参考。

(二) 嘱兵工署专员江杓,告知该团以前德国所供给之精良武器,便其有所观摩。

(三) 本年春季,鲁斯 LUCE 夫妇参观驻潼关部队,感想极佳。麦君于民国十四五年,曾充驻华武官,现在抗战军队,自与当时情形不可同日而语。我国军队之飞速进步,已为各界所公认。该团到后,应使其参观我最优良之部队,俾先获一良好之印象,而不敢稍存轻视之心。

(四) 文向麦君坦率言之,我军队之质量俱不成问题,所缺乏者,惟飞机及军械耳。将此种情形,报告美国政府,俾得尽量供给武器,迅速运到中国,即为该团最重要工作之一。该团之成功与失败,胥视此节能否办到。美国供给武器过于迟缓,所持理由不过两端：一、美军火飞机生产量少,二、中国运输不能通畅。固非尽属托词,亦应设法多加辩解,尤以我方集中权力,改善滇缅路运输情形,使其了解,并予以事实上之证明。

(五) 麦克罗达虽属军人,亦娴政治,故不能以纯粹军人视之。

钧座声威所播,中外翕服,该团必可顺令承教,毋待晓渎也。专肃。敬请钧安。

谨呈　九月　日②

214. 宋子文致蒋介石报告滇缅铁路材料开始起运电(1941年9月4日)

S413　呈委员长电　九.三日

委座钧鉴：滇缅铁路材料已于八月廿九日开始起运,计黄炸药及附属品约六百吨,测绘仪器、修造路基工具及药品等约一百吨,共两万五千余件。装船详单另寄交通部。特此电陈,并恳特饬该部知照。○支。文。九.四

---

① 齐焌,时任国民政府军事委员会秘书。

② 原稿纸末注有"九月二日发出 C.S.Liu"字样,C.S.Liu,即宋子文的秘书刘景山。

215. 宋子文致蒋介石请示拟聘美国技术顾问电(1941年9月4日)

S415　呈委员长电　九.三日

委座钧鉴:航委会一时不能派技术专员多人来美,关于技术问题,无法解决。拟聘美国技术顾问一二员,襄助办理,惟薪金较高。可否乞示遵照。○豪。文九.四

216. 宋子文致蒋介石请召见垂询杨格电(1941年9月4日)

呈委员长电　九.四日

委座钧鉴:财部杨格顾问,对于滇缅路情形颇为熟悉,暇中请召见垂询一切,并令将其视察该路报告译呈钧览,以供采择。○支酉。文　九.四

217. 宋子文致蒋介石报告美国军事顾问团所需电(1941年9月5日)

致委员长电

美国军事顾问团官员约廿八人,随员十四人,现正陆续出发。其主要团员约十月七八日齐集香港飞渝,余随员乘船赴仰光。所有在渝办公处住所及港仰招待问题,亟宜早日筹备。兹将该团所需电陈如下:(一)在渝需要团员廿五人、随员十四人住所及办公所三处,拟将成渝铁路嘉陵村住所,全部拨给应用。此外尚须于左近觅住所一处,需客廿五人住宿。另在江北岸觅住所一处,客十余人住宿,并须有停车十余辆地段。(二)所有应需床枕、被单、毛毯,以及起居日用必须物件,祈饬早为购备。(三)祈指派干员在港会同中国银行秘书陈康齐,在仰光会同中国银行行长陈长桐,与该团洽办筹备及招待。祈电复。○○①

218. 宋子文致蒋介石报告英政府决定我贷借物品通过缅境不再征税电 (1941年9月8日)

S417　呈委员长电　九.八日

委座钧鉴:据英大使馆密告,英政府决定我贷借物品通过缅境,不再征税,由英补偿缅政府每吨十卢比。明日公布此项消息。查英内阁驻新代表古拔,过美时

---

① 稿纸末写有"CSLiu 9/5"。

对于此事出力最多,请钧座电谢,并欢迎赴渝。○齐。文。九.八

219. 宋子文致蒋介石报告军械起运情形电(1941年9月9日)

S418　呈委员长电　九.八日

委座钧鉴:鱼电敬悉。(一)美国正赶造自用枪弹,年内不能让售。南美仅厄瓜多有七九子弹,因量少作罢。据闻我兵工厂因子弹制造材料缺乏,以致减工,现已由此间陆续接济大批材料到仰,应请饬令速运加工自制。(二)加拿大轻机枪本月内先运一千挺。(三)山炮廿门,七五榴弹炮五十门,亦可于本月内起运,步枪正设法中。○佳。文。九.九

220. 宋子文致蒋介石报告滇缅铁路能否完成缅方赶工衔接确为关键电 (1941年9月9日)

呈委员长电　九.九日

委座钧鉴:江电敬悉。滇缅铁路能否如期完成,缅方赶工衔接,确为重要关键。已告美顾问团注意,当能协助促进缅方赶工。乞特饬曾督办①知照。○佳酉。文。九.九

221. 宋子文致蒋介石报告英方希密支那机场房屋我方出资构造电(1941年 9月9日)

S419　呈委员长电　九.九日　复　九.十五

委座钧鉴:密芝那机场,英方已允出资兴筑,备与滇西各站联航运输,但场上房屋希望我方按照中航公司需要之格式,出资构造。即恳径饬曾次长镕甫,商承钧命办理。○青申。文。九.九

222. 宋子文致蒋介石建议顾问团拟经过相当时期再提聘约电(1941年9月 9日)

S420　呈委员长电　九.九日　复　九.十二

委座钧鉴:虞电敬悉。总统派遣顾问团,除备咨询外,兼有贷借案内任务。官兵

---

① 即曾养甫,时任滇缅公路督办。

薪饷,均由美陆军部发给。似以经过相当时期服务察看情形,再提聘约为宜。仍候钧裁。○青。文。九.九

223. 宋子文致蒋介石报告顾问团将分批到渝情形电(1941 年 9 月 11 日)

呈委员长电　九.十一日

委座钧鉴:蒸电敬悉。顾问团因分配机位,稍有变更,第一批三人,定九月十四日,第二批五人,内有麦克罗达将军等四人及江专员①杓,定九月廿一日均自旧金山起飞,其余陆续启程。到渝日期江杓随时呈报。谨陈。○真。文。九.十一

224. 宋子文致蒋介石报告顾问团任务电(1941 年 9 月 12 日)

S421　复委员长电　九.十二日

委座钧鉴:真电敬悉。总统派遣顾问团,曾向国会声明,其任务:(一)视察贷借案运用情形,与派遣驻英军官团任务相同;(二)备中国咨询,又定名军事顾问团,即属阐明此义,当然应受钧座之指挥。详情嘱江杓面秉。至纳德②,系非正式介绍,与该团派遣情形不甚相同也。谨复。○侵。文。九.十二

225. 宋子文致蒋介石报告驻美英机关拨让军械情形电(1941 年 9 月 12 日)

S422　呈委员长电　九.十二日　复　九.十七

委座钧鉴:驻美英机关拨让轻机枪千挺,燃烧弹百吨,及总统应允我之轰炸机六十六架。种种协助,可否请钧座向卡尔大使表示谢意之处。敬求酌夺。○震申。文　九.十二

226. 宋子文致蒋介石请示腊戍昆明间设输油管是否可行电(1941 年 9 月 17 日)

S423　呈委员长电　九.十七日　复　九.廿五

委座钧鉴:援亚细亚油公司③建议,腊戍昆明之间沿路设轻便输油管,以替代卡

---

① 即江杓,时任国民政府军政部兵工署驻美国代表。
② 即中国空军美国志愿队队长陈纳德。
③ 即亚细亚火油公司(Asiatic Petroleum Co.),为英国壳牌公司与荷兰皇家石油公司合设的子公司,总部位于英国伦敦。

车运送汽油,滇缅路上每月可节省汽油运量四千吨,先须派专家调查,经费由我方发给,并称德国行军应采用此法。是否可行,乞电示遵。○篠。文。九.十七

227. 宋子文致蒋介石报告此间各事函稿(1941年9月18日)

函稿　卅.九.十八日　江枬带呈

委座钧鉴:江专员枬,伴同美军事顾问团赴渝。此间各事,函电所不能详尽者,除嘱其面禀外,谨再胪陈如左:

(一)美国目前军火产量尚少,文数月来工作,仅能就其产量供给之可能,为我需求之标准,不能满意,无可讳言。此后产量日渐增强,我方之需求,亦应改变方式。

(二)美国现在供给我方物资,似出乎情义居多,此后应使其更加明了中国之抗战,在国际上有莫大关系,尤其中美两国之间,利害与共,不可分离,供给我军械,系为我达到一种任务,非关于情面交谊,否则我永久处于请求之地位,焉得谓之平等合作。

(三)是以愚见所及,拟照钧座于一二月内规定反攻计划,说明先后目标、预示步骤,为我国独自达到肃清敌寇之目的,共需要新组织精强军队三四十万人,共应配备若干坦克车、重炮、高射炮等新式武器,以及若干飞机,掩护出击,一一规划周详,切实可行。

(四)完善之反攻计划做成后,请咨询美军事顾问马古德①将军,得其赞助,再由文提交美方,要求供给,收效必宏。届时特派高级参谋人员,专来华府助文与美国陆海军最高级人员商洽。谨抒管见,伏乞决择,不胜待命之至。

(五)今日接复初兄来电,英使卡尔提议在美京设中英美联合委员会,在渝设分会,已蒙钧座赞同。窃查此事为文一向所希望,有此机构,三国之合作,更见切实。前托石曾先生代呈钧座禀中,亦曾提及。目前美国对于大西洋战事,不久即有更进一步之趋势,太平洋中英美三国之合作,更有急切之需要。文俟英使哈利法克斯返美,即当详细洽商,再行呈报。敬请钧安。谨上。月　日

228. 宋子文致蒋介石答复垂询聘美技术团事宜电(1941年9月18日)

S424　呈委员长电　九.十八日　已复　十.六

委座钧鉴:(一)元电垂询聘美技术团一事,仰见高掌【瞻】远蹠【瞩】之怀。上次

---

①　马古德(John Magruder),即马格鲁德,时任访华的美国军事代表团团长。

欧战之后,美国过剩机械,颇多当废铁出售,此届战后,必有大批可为我利用,总统对我关怀素切,当能用特别方式给予。适当美朝野专注重目前战争,但此时提议聘请技术团,窃恐美方不日滇缅路运量尚不易输送笨重机件,则曰正在扩充军备,专门人才不敷应用,或我沦陷区尚未克复,整个国防建设计划,不易着手。再四思维,目前提请,似非其时。美顾问团中,不乏各种技术人员,拟恳先与开始讨论,一面交与美国国防建设委员会从长计议,俟时机成熟,再请正式向美方提出。是否有当,仍候钧裁。(二) 前奉马二电,遵向美方商洽,允派专家调查研究新疆油矿产量,但政治问题,殊关重要,苏联是否完全谅解,及矿区所在地点,均乞电示。(三) 谏电敬悉,刘参谋田蒲①来美工作,美方业已同意,英语稍差,此间可以协助也。○巧。文。九.一八

229. 宋子文致蒋介石报告往访史汀生情形电(1941年9月25日)②

S425　呈委员长电　九.廿五日

委座钧鉴:苏俄战况危急,闻此间有人主张,应尽量尽先接济苏俄军械。文今日特往访晤陆长史汀生③,告以苏俄战事固属重要,但中国抗战四年余,军械消耗殆尽,美方应给中国之军械,望勿抽让苏俄。史允竭力协助,并请文密陈钧座,美在菲列滨④积极扩充军备,派遣多数重轰炸机队,以冀牵掣日敌海军,毋使南进,此亦间接帮助中国。文谓盛意至为感谢,惟目前敌攻华中甚为激烈,美国充量接济军火,直接援我更属刻不容缓耳。谨陈。○有。文。九.廿五

230. 宋子文致蒋介石建议直接电请居里向军部催提高射机枪电(1941年9月26日)⑤

S426　呈委员长电　九.廿六日

委座钧鉴:本月内美方应给我之半寸径高射机关枪,闻因苏俄战况紧急,有转给苏俄之说。请钧座作为不知此事,直接电致居里,告以华中战事激烈,军队急需

---

① 刘田蒲,即刘田甫,字仲超,时任国民政府军令部高级参谋。
② 该电文已收入《中华民国重要史料初编》第三编战时外交(一),第466页。
③ 史汀生(Henry L. Stimson),时任美国陆军部部长。
④ 即菲律宾(Philippines)。
⑤ 该电文已收入《中华民国重要史料初编》第三编战时外交(一),第466~467页。

防空武器,请其向军部催请提议速拨一千枝,电交麦寇由①转拍。当否仍候钧裁。○宥。文。九·廿六

231. 宋子文致蒋介石报告急需机器工具及电信交通材料正催提前运购电 (1941 年 9 月 30 日)

呈委员长电　九·卅

委座钧鉴:敬电承示曾督办所陈各节,谨聆一是。建筑路基,急需机器工具及电信交通材料,现正切催提前运购,除随时与曾督办洽办外,谨电附陈。○卅。文。九·卅

232. 宋子文致蒋介石报告滇缅公路运输机关及人员情形电(1941 年 9 月 30 日)

呈　委员长电　九·卅

委座钧鉴:寝电敬悉。(一)居里前因滇缅公路运输机关繁杂、权责纷歧,以为威尔逊退伍加入服务,亦无能为力,今该路切实整顿,各机关正在分别归并中,事权逐渐统一,故已不持异议。但威尔逊隶属于军事顾问团,为尊重其统属起见,退伍手续及聘充副局长各节,应请钧座径商马古德将军,较为适当。(二)滇缅路装置修理汽车人员卅三人,及车辆调度专门人员六人,川资薪金,均由美方供给。正考验选择,约十月十日分批起程。(三)拉丁率领之另一批装置车辆人员,系通用汽车公司自派协助,装配车辆,亦正严催赶速赴华。谨陈,并恳转饬俞樵峰总监知照。○卅。文。九·卅

233. 宋子文致蒋介石请令饬新闻检查人员特加注意电(1941 年 10 月 1 日)

S427　复　十·六

委座钧鉴:美合众社卅日重庆电讯,潘某在渝谈话,述及美飞机师来华与美舰护航等事。美政府对露布此项消息,深感不满。乞令饬新闻检查人员特加注意,勿使军事秘密泄漏为祷。○先。文。十·一

---

① 麦寇由,即麦寇猷(James M. McHugh)。

234. 宋子文致蒋介石报告美方函询我三年内原料究需多少电(1941 年 10 月 1 日)

S428　十一.十八由政院复

委座钧鉴：美副总统①主持之国防优先分配局，对于国防及援助中英俄所需物资主要原料，计一百十二种，拟作三年计划。顷军货贷借事务处长斯的铁尼②函询我国在三年内各项原料究需多少，请估示数字，以便统筹，等情。查：(一) 我国所需各项物资，尚无详细统计，原料数量，更难估算。(二) 即就我向美贷借及购办物资而言，亦以制品为多，其中所含各种主要原料成分，究有多少，分析不易。(三) 我在美采办物资，除军货贷借案尚能有计划的整批提出外，其余每分批办理，零星琐碎，随需随购，提出整个计划，自有其事实上之困难。惟美政府此项调查，为将来生产计划之蓝本。我国之需要如不及时列入，此后我方需美供给货品之原料，在美全国生产计划之中，将无着落，即有现款，亦恐无货可购。现拟与该局交涉，先提出此间现有之军货贷借及请求采购货品清单，由该局助我估算原料数量。惟此系应付办法，实不能包括我方一切需要。为特电恳钧座令饬主管机关：(一) 在可能范围内，估计我国三年以内每年所需(甲) 军用、(乙) 民用、(丙) 输出用之物资所需主要原料，暂以钢铁、铬、镍、铝、矾土矿、钴、钒、铜、黄铜、钼为限，分列(甲) 自产、(乙) 由英苏荷供给、(丙) 由美国供给等三类。此项数字，宜于从宽估计，惟不可过涉广诞。(二) 火速编寄一九四三年度军货贷借案内拟向美方申请货品详单。(三) 电示我国锡、钨、桐油、丝三年分年产量及运美数量估计。又，九月十七航函，附主要原料清单，与本电所述，系属一事，并以附陈。○东。文。十.一

235. 宋子文致蒋介石呈请转知交部派孙正前来甚属相宜电(1941 年 10 月 4 日)

呈委员长电　十.四日

委座钧鉴：冬电敬悉。交部拟派孙正前来，甚属相宜，请转饬知照。○支午。文。十.四

---

①　即时任美国副总统的亨利·A·华莱士(Henry Agard Wallace)。
②　斯的铁尼，即斯退汀纽斯(Edward R. Stettinius)，时任美国军货贷借事务处处长。

236. 宋子文致蒋介石报告陈长桐请辞西南运输公司经理电(1941年10月6日)

S430　呈委员长电　十.六日

委座钧鉴:江电敬悉。顷接陈长桐电称:奉命派充西南运输公司经理,惶恐万状,因向在银行服务,对于运输事宜,毫无经验,特请代为恳辞,俾免遗【贻】误军运等语。所称确属实情,并查贷借物资,业已源源起运。美方遣派来华各项专门人员,日见增多,所有接收、照料、调查、接洽事务,极形复杂,应请另派熟练运输车务干员接替,以资各方兼顾。再,陈质平不谙外交,以致美缅不满,惟该员对沿线警卫,异常努力,可否仍命担负保卫责任之处,统祷钧裁示遵。〇麻。文。十.六

237. 宋子文致蒋介石建议波兰前政府驻日大使可任为驻华大使电(1941年10月6日,附原加注)

S431　呈委员长电　十.六日　复　十.十三

委座钧鉴:波兰前政府驻日大使①,因归附反对轴心之新政府,为日本勒令出境。据闻此人在日八年,熟悉军政内幕,如我国同意,波政府可任为驻华大使,或有利用之处。敬祷钧夺。〇鱼。文。十.六

[原稿另注:当时波兰仇俄,日极力表示合作,故所得日方军事消息甚多。]

238. 宋子文致蒋介石建议由资委会招集各机关筹拟在美采办计划函稿(1941年10月7日)

呈委员长函稿　十.七日　付邮霍②转

委座钧鉴:本月东电,计达钧览。兹再将军货贷借事务处长斯的铁尼九月廿四日来函译呈察阅。美国为放大眼光,策划将来起见,决定将本年及一九四二年、一九四三年所拟供给中英俄各国军用民用物资之原料,配合本国之生产,作全盘之计算,要求我方对于三年所需物资之主要原料,从速估计数字,列表汇交,以凭审核。窃以此事至关重要,将来我国之需求,如未有事先估计之根据,难免美方借词搪塞,

---

① 即塔德·德·罗梅(Romer),1937年11月2日起任波兰驻日本大使。
② 即时在重庆的中国银行副总稽核霍宝树。

应请迅饬各主管机关,会同集中筹划,妥慎办理。我国历来对外采购物资,向无整
个办法,或由世界公司,或由华昌公司,或由私人公司,各机关各自为政,漫无标准,
互不关连,以致不能配合全部国防需要及生产。无形之损失,可想而知。今乘此时
机,为统筹全局之计,不独有益于我,即美国将来之供应,亦同时感到便利也。美方
此项计划,非仅限于贷借法案,其他各种民用物资之原料,亦均包括在内。我国贷
借法案今年及明年之需要,归并十五万万计划之内,已估计概数,于本月十日以前,
提交美方,作初步之核计。江专员杓带呈钧座禀〈函〉中所述组织精强军队三四十
万人,配备各项武器之反攻计划,因须审慎周详,并咨询美军事顾问马古德将军,自
需相当时日,拟作为一九四三年贷借法案之要求。文①在国外所能举办者,仅限于
贷借法案而已,且资料搜集不易,未能完备精确,其他应赖国内各主管机关之调查
统计。窃查资源委员会,对于国内外之资源,研究有素,可否饬令召集各主管机关,
共同筹划。其应召集者:一、兵工署,关于各兵工厂所需之原料及所需美国供给制
成品之原料;二、航空委员会;关于飞机及其附件,及修理厂之需要;三、贸易委
员会,关于我国原料之生产量及进出口之原料;四、卫生署、军医署,关于各种药品
卫生器材;五、交通部,关于通信器材及运输工具;六、经济部,关于工矿器材。
除此各机关以外,所有其他有关之机构,一并召集、查照斯的铁尼来函,不厌求
详,迅予调查估计,务于十一月十五日以前,编制完竣,航邮寄美,由文整理后,提
交美方。事关国防大计,伏乞鼎力主持。毋任企祷,敬颂钧安。

239. 宋子文致蒋介石报告美政府对苏之继续抗战甚为悲观电(1941年10月9日)

S432 呈委员长电 十.九日

委座钧鉴:据各方消息,苏联军队有总崩溃模样。美政府对苏联之继续抗战,甚为悲
观。谨闻。○佳。文。十.九

240. 宋子文致蒋介石请饬江杓速回电(1941年10月14日)

呈委员长电 十.十四日

委座钧鉴:江专员杓在此办理兵工器材事宜,本极繁冗,马古德将军飞渝,临时派其
随同照料。接洽事毕,请饬日内速回为祷。○寒。文。十.十四

---

① 此处原稿为○。

241. 宋子文致蒋介石提议贷借案申请之汽油应核发机关电(1941年10月17日)

呈委员长电　十.十五

委座钧鉴:贷借案申请之卡车汽油一千三百万加伦,业经美政府核令煤油公司供给,即由新加坡装桶,约本月底开始运达仰光,交陈长桐。为统筹支配起见,应请军委会核发下列各机关:一、军政部,二、航空委员会,三、滇缅公路局,四、前西南运输公司,五、滇缅铁路局(以上均在贷借案内申请者),六、液体燃料委员会。本托世界公司代购,因贷借案油料,即将起运,故暂缓办,亦请酌量分发。再,何部长敬之①东电所购油料,已嘱世界公司另购一百万加伦。谨此电陈,并恳分饬何部长敬之、俞总监樵峰查照为祷。○洽。文。十.十七

242. 宋子文致蒋介石报告油管问题电(1941年10月17日)

S433　呈委员长电　十.十七日

委座钧鉴:佳已电敬悉。油管问题,安司丹长于公路运输,其他工程技术,未能谙悉。且即使滇缅铁路两年如期完成,运量亦不能满足抗战需要。安设油管,每月可运油一万六千吨,油料问题得以完全解决。文研讨之余,为审慎起见,决派油管专家霍尔于廿一日起程飞仰,勘测路线,研究利弊。川资等项,所费不过数千元。其最后报告,如认为事属可行,拟嘱其迳呈钧座,敬候决择。除函俞局长樵峰查照外,谨此奉陈。○篠。文。十.十七

243. 宋子文致蒋介石报告苏俄可能向东南迁都电(1941年10月20日)

S434　呈委员长电　十.廿日

委座钧鉴:苏俄向东南迁都,将来有迁至伊朗模样,似非向西比利亚一带撤退。敬请注意。○廿。文。十.廿

244. 宋子文致蒋介石报告最近期内拟向美当局提议武器电(1941年10月23日)

S435　呈委员长电　最新密码　十.廿三日

委座钧鉴:(一)昨美军部开始最秘密会议,讨论新自莫斯科回美军械会议代表

---

①　即何应钦,字敬之,时任国民政府军政部部长。

之报告,备极重视红军战斗成绩,谓德军攻苏之部队,已损失三分之一,苏西方各工厂虽为德所占,但其余工厂,仍足维持一百师团之军需;对苏空军,尤为赞美,技能勇敢,均在英国以上。历来美对红军之观察,每趋极端,不求甚解,每犯过分不平衡客观之迷梦。会议结果,以为大战关键全在苏联,美国更应加紧物质上之援助,英次之,至于中国,则只视所余物质之盈绌为点缀。文闻悉之余,异常焦虑。无论美方观察是否准确,拟于最近期内向美当局提议,惟有中国抗战反攻,始能牵掣日敌之进攻苏联,关系世界局势,非常重大,美应积极助我完成任务。乘日敌未动以前,钧座急需之各项武器如下:甲、飞机,原申请驱逐机三百五十架,已给一百架,年内允再给八十三架,要求即时供给一百七十七架,全数由英美已有之飞机内抽让;轰炸机本申请一百五十架,允拨六十六架,年内交廿四架,要求同时拨给一百六十架。乙、半寸径高射机枪,允年内交二百八十五挺,要求即时再拨七百五十挺。丙、三七战车防御炮,年内拨六十门,要求即时再拨三百门。丁、七五山炮,本申请六百门,年内允拨一百七十八门,要求即时再拨三百门。戊、十三吨轻坦克车,申请一百廿辆,要求全拨。己、九零公分高射炮,允拨九十六门,要求至少先拨廿四门。庚、要求速拨枪药八百吨。以上各项,要求即予答复,以便电呈钧座。(二)上列各项,俱为目前急需,以美国产量估计,并非奢望。请钧座同时向马古德将军郑重提出。(三)马古德电军部,有滇缅公路运量太小,非最急品勿起运等语。请予注意,勿使借词推诿。是所至祷,谨电缕陈,伏候钧夺。○漾。十·廿三

245. 宋子文致蒋介石报告美援俄军火改航线问题电(1941 年 10 月 24 日)

呈委员长电　十·廿四日

委座钧鉴:美航政会公布,援俄军火,不由海参崴,改由大西洋至白海阿安界口岸登陆。此举本为航线问题,无政治意义。总统对公布深为不满,因恐引起外间疑虑美有缓和日本之意。○敬。文。十·廿四

246. 宋子文致蒋介石可否请饬江杓酌办礼物带美电(1941 年 10 月 25 日)

呈委员长电　最新密码　十·廿五日　复　十·卅

委座钧鉴:美陆海军与我有关人员,素日热忱相助,除有时欢宴联络外,今圣诞节近,可否请饬江杓酌办礼物带美,分赠各员,以示慰勉。尚祷钧裁。○有。文。十·廿五

247. 宋子文致蒋介石报告马格鲁德致史汀生最密电内容电(1941年10月27日)

S436　呈委员长电　最新密码　十.廿七日　已发誊清

委座钧鉴：顷获阅马古德致陆长①最密电，内容如下：

（一）华军因策应长沙，反攻宜昌，任务完成而退，不背战略。

（二）华军非增添炮队，无大规模反攻能力。

（三）中国目前最需要者，甲、兵工厂原料，乙、子弹，丙、轻机枪及步兵炮，非此不足维持现状。榴弹炮、防御唐【坦】克车炮，亦属需要。空军事另电报告。

（四）以后供给中国军械之质量程序等等，均请凭其迳电军部核办。居里及中国驻美京机关，要求过奢，可置之不问。

（五）美政府凡关于英俄各项问题之宣布，不妨将中国一并提及，于美无损，而可使中国人心益加感奋。

（六）较大计划，俟见钧座后续告。

等语。窃查此电所述，虽亦不为无见，惟军火一项，与我所期太远。文漾电列举如唐【坦】克车，高射机枪，高射炮，十生的五、十五生的榴弹炮及野战炮等等，均未提及。再第四项关于事权问题，未免非分越俎，一切将听其个人支配，钧座无直接要求之余地。再，美国内部，党派甚多，非但马古德与居里意见分歧，即马古德与军部供应租借案武器机关，亦不能合作。马将军如能包揽一切，实心援我，亦未尝不可，但彼绝无包办能力，是以应请钧座向马古德及高斯表示：（一）关于申请供给等事，一切照旧办理。盖代表团仅备咨询及从旁协助，不便代表我政府之要求。美驻英代表团，亦非有支配之权，凡英方要求，亦直接由英国驻华府代表与政府商洽。（二）美方供给军械过缓，应请向其表示不满。谨电密陈，乞勿宣泄。是否有当，仍候钧裁，并盼赐复。○感酉。十.廿七日午后八时拍发。文。

248. 宋子文致蒋介石请示财部顾问可否再留美两月电(1941年10月28日)

呈委员长电　十.廿八日　复　十.廿八

委座钧鉴：财部顾问麦易斯②，前奉钧令来美，遵派协助筹办各处修理厂事宜。该员顷奉孔部长电令返华，可否再留两月，以资准备交替经手各事。尚祷饬遵。○俭。文。十.廿八

---

① 即时任美国陆军部部长的史汀生(Henry L. Stimson)。
② 麦易斯(D. F. Myers)，时任国民政府财政部顾问。

249. 宋子文致蒋介石报告中印路问题印政府颇有隔膜电(1941 年 10 月 30 日)

S437 呈委员长电　十.卅日　复　十一.廿

委座钧鉴:英政府某君私相密告,中印路问题,印政府颇有隔膜,因一、印方愿代我航空测量路线,经费自备,我方无意接受;二、我行政院派海关关员那布罗特私往印度军事区域内调查路线,并未通知印方;三、我方对美国所称西藏之态度不甚确实。等语。所言如是,谨以奉陈。〇陷。文。十.卅

250. 宋子文致蒋介石关于空军学生来美训练电(1941 年 10 月 30 日)

S438　民国卅年十月卅日　电渝(七)　复　十一.五

委座钧鉴:关于空军学生来美训练事,因美国轮船航期更改无定,船名及确期尤难预知,请饬按每五星期一批,先期赴港待船,以免临时运输不及,如能一次送二百至二百五十名来美候训则更佳。如何,乞示。〇卅。文。十.卅

251. 宋子文致蒋介石报告与罗斯福会谈情形电(1941 年 10 月 31 日)①

S439　呈委员长电　最新密码　十.卅一日

委座钧鉴:接三妹②电,得悉钧座接见马古德,并日敌有侵滇模样。文今早特往谒见总统,转达钧座意见,密谈四十五分钟。

总统云:据陆军意见,日本非再添四师团,无法攻滇,且战区山岭重叠,交通阻碍,即使占领滇缅路,亦恐不能持久。

文云:地势困难,固于作战不便,组织完善而有飞机掩护之机械化部队,无险不可克。德人之迅速占领南斯拉夫③,即其明证。日军中不乏德国专门技术人才,殊未可轻视。

总统云:中国已英勇抗战四年余,即使滇缅路被占,再打年余,亦当可支持。

文云:继续抗战为钧座不移之决心,但如无外间接济军火,人心能否维持,是一疑问。万一滇缅路被占,军队不能支持,日敌至少可在驻华军队中抽出一百万

---

① 该电文已收入《中华民国重要史料初编》第三编战时外交(一),第478~479 页。
② 即蒋介石夫人、宋子文三妹宋美龄。
③ 南斯拉夫,国家名,位于东欧巴尔干半岛上,当时已为德军占领。

人,攻苏或南进。

总统云:一,美国对于此事警告日本,尚未至哀的美敦书时期,但下午与赫尔一商,拟告日本如进攻滇缅路,即系危害美国权利。二,英人不便由新加坡派飞机与我会同作战,否则英日战事,即行爆发,日本可以切断澳洲苏彝士间之交通。

据总统之意,英人应可将飞机改我徽号,英空军改充义勇队,一同作战。

文谓:如此办法,恐须相当时期。

总统云,彼愿提议,二三日内可得英方答复。

文云:盛意至为感谢,今日敌侵滇,即在旦夕,美国已允供给之军械,交货过于迟缓,恐不济急。务请于最短期内,由美陆军所用制成品中,抽让运华。文并面递清单,即文漾电所列者。

总统逐项与文讨论后,即在单上加批,交霍布金斯①赶办。

文云:军械如能迅速供给中国,非仅我获其利,且为间接援苏,即系予德国一重大打击。如苏退至乌拉尔以东,仅有五千一百万人口,恐难与德作战。至中国则有四万万五千万之人民,为民主国中最大之后备队。

总统对此点极为注意,并云:本年冬苏俄或不致退至乌拉尔以东。又详问中俄交通,如西比利亚阻断,能否由我国西境派兵援俄。

文云:新疆路线,苏援华军火,即由此而来。

总统云:无论如何,钧座应具坚决之信心。须知德日联合,不过一万万五千万人,而全世界反侵略之国家,加以中国广土众民之力量,何止超过数倍。

最后总统暗示,即便滇缅路被占,日本亦无办法,因国际战事区域,将蔓延愈广也。此语意在言外。其余谈话尚多,谨择最重要者,奉陈钧察。嗣总统派副官陪同往见霍布金斯。关于军火供给问题,霍即与军部洽商,并云数日内当有切实答复。并陈。○世酉。卅.十.卅一午后七时拍出。文。

252. 宋子文致蒋介石请饬查液体燃料委员会售卖柴油原因电(1941年11月3日)

S440　致委员长电　十一月三日

顷美军部接报告,液体燃料委员会于九月廿二日在仰②托德士古③运印售卖轻柴

---

① 即霍普金斯(Harry L. Hopkins)。
② 即英属缅甸首府仰光。
③ 即美国德士古石油公司(Texaco Inc.)。

油一万余桶、重柴油四千余桶,甚为诧异,并责问我方,中国政府有油存仰出售,何以仍向美方催购同样油料,等语。事关贷借案我国信用,并影响我国申请物料前途,务祈严饬查明出售原因赐复,俾向美方解释。并请通令各机关嗣后不得再有此项情事为祷。○○○江未。文。十一.三

253. 宋子文致蒋介石提议西南运输公司经理仍遴派他人电(1941 年 11 月 3 日)

S441　呈委员长电　十一.三日

委座钧鉴:柬电敬悉。陈长桐对于运输确无经验,深虞险越贷借法案。仰光事务繁忙,文特调该员驻仰,接洽一切,人地渐习,一时难觅要员接替。西南经理,较易物色,仍恳遴派他员为祷。○肴。十一.三

254. 宋子文致蒋介石报告与罗斯福谈日美交涉情形电(1941 年 11 月 3 日)

S442　最新密码　呈委员长电　十一.三日

世酉电计达钧览。是日见总统时,并谈及日美交涉。总统云:日本徒以空言,妄想交换恢复经济关系,余真意非待中日问题圆满解决,谈不到其他问题。日方要求余与近卫海上会面,余虚与委蛇。最后日本发觉我故意延缓,近卫内阁遂倒。但此次交涉延宕时间,非无裨益。六个月前,认为菲律宾不可守,毫无防御设备,现在炮台工事,俱已坚固,飞机足以控制菲律宾华南间之航线矣。等语。谨此续陈。○江。十一.三

255. 宋子文致蒋介石密告美军部拟采侧击日敌攻滇之计划电(1941 年 11 月 4 日)①

呈委员长电　十一.四日

委座钧鉴:(一)文世日见总统后,总统即与赫尔讨论。东②外部告军部,应准备侧击日敌攻滇之计划。据军部中人密告,拟采两种办法:甲、菲律宾飞机轰炸日越交通线,乙、派一部份驻菲飞行堡垒,助华作战。但俱未决定,容续

---

① 该电文已收入《中华民国重要史料初编》第三编战时外交(一),第 482～483 页。
② 此处"东"为韵目代日字,即"一日"。

探陈,请守秘密。（二）昨美航空署开会,决定改变以前对华之态度,不再以剩余之有无为供给之标准,应维持我五百架最新式飞机之计划,以迅速改良之手段供给员机,实行方法热烈讨论中。（三）美方已允拨给之六十六架飞机,因转动炮位及其他武器来自英国,非数月之久不能装竣,拟要求由航空母舰上飞机,抽让若干,以济急需。现竭力进行,不能谓有把握,先此密陈钧察。再,本日见澳洲公使,请其电政府促动邱吉耳①援我空军,并附陈。文。支申。文。十一.四

256. 宋子文致蒋介石报告美方要求将德造榴弹炮及炮弹运美试验电(1941年11月4日)

谨代拟呈委员长电　复　十一.十二

委座钧鉴:窃查我方在租借案内向美国订购炮药,美方要求将德造十公分五榴弹炮及炮弹运美试验,曾电江委员②面请俞署长③设法。据复称,该炮散布前线,一时无法抽调。查美方态度,虽借口试验,实欲研究该炮性能及构造,曾一再催询。为顾全两国关系起见,拟请准予设法抽运,对本处办事前途亦可增加便利。是否可行,恳电示遵。○豪。文。十一.四

257. 宋子文致蒋介石报告与史汀生谈话情形电(1941年11月6日)④

S445　最密　五种密本加数字　呈委员长电　十一.六日

委座钧鉴:军部友人密告,昨晚该部会议,关于钧座要求即拨飞机军械以御日敌攻滇,其结论美国现正积极备战,除已允照单分期拨给者外,若由陆军现用成品中抽让,势必打破其预定军事计划。文遂要求见陆长史汀生。承其约今日午餐,密谈良久。史云,钧座致总统电,及文与总统世日谈话,俱已获悉,继谓,上届欧战彼为军官,曾一度认为美国兵士渗入英法军队,混合组织,必较优良而迅捷,乃潘兴大将⑤较我聪敏,仍决定美军单独组织,由美军官统率作战,始获最后之胜利。又云,今

---

① 即时任英国首相的丘吉尔(Winston S. Churchill)。
② 即军政部兵工署驻美代表江杓。
③ 即时任国民政府军政部兵工署署长俞大维。
④ 该电文已收入《中华民国重要史料初编》第三编战时外交(一),第483~484页。
⑤ 即约翰·J·潘兴(John J. Pershing),美国著名军事家,第一次世界大战中任协约国美军部队总司令。

密告足下,美对菲律滨军事上计划,已九成成功,幸日本尚未发觉,该地海陆空军乃专以对付日本,尤以空军力量,足以控制日舰队南进企图无疑,但如抽派机队援助中国,分散力量,是违背军事原则矣。文云,日敌攻击荷印、新加坡,美国不能袖手,但如攻滇,是否亦取同一态度,假使不能,我方需要飞机军械,更属万分急迫。史云,日本攻滇,因地势关系,恐甚困难。文云,以机械化之部队,加飞机之掩护,何险可守。史问,攻滇约需若干时期可达昆明。文云,若无充分之飞机军械,或在数星期之内,亦未可知。史谓,我已告赫尔,五星期最多六星期之内,军事准备即可告成,如以日期计算,下月十日为最重要之关键,一过此日,美国可以最强硬之手段对待日本,即使日军开始由越南攻滇,未到昆明以前,美国可有制裁之方法。文追问,此事关系我国太大,是否十二月十日以后,美可制裁日敌侵滇,与攻击新加坡、荷印取同一动作。史云,余为陆长,此事涉及外交,不便越位;不过以余观察,滇缅路关系全世界局势至为重大,甚于援俄问题;或有以为援俄重于援华,应迅速供给苏俄轰炸机等军事利器,即贵方亦有人作此论调;余以为接济苏俄,因时间问题,恐无大效,中国在蒋委员长领导之下已抗战四年余,今滇缅路为生命线关系,焉可不加以支援。文云,有此决心,甚为感谢,惟军情瞬幻,务盼以迅速方法供给我飞机军械,俾中国于艰难之中为万全之计。史云,飞机甚难,军械已饬切实筹办。等语。史陆长为人深练稳重,道德甚高,所言自无掩饰,并谆嘱事关军事动作,钧座以外,切务宣泄。谨陈。文。鱼戌。文。

258. 宋子文致蒋介石报告与美海军部长会谈情形电(1941年11月7日)

最密　呈委员长电　十一.七日

委座钧鉴:今日总统宣布拟撤退美国驻平津沪海军陆军队。文顷赴海长诺斯午餐之约,在座有参谋长及其他人员。文首先说明日敌攻滇之企图,中国军队缺乏飞机军械,万一不能支持,国际情势更增危险。诺云,在越日军仅三个半师团,据海军方面观察,非二个月期间,不能进行攻滇。文云,琼崖、台湾距越南甚近,军队可朝发夕至,日军侵犯亦可由越入桂转滇,数路进攻,故中国盼望美国飞机军械之接济日益急迫。嗣谈美陆战队撤退事。文提及上海为金融重心,此举关系太巨。诺谓,中国应认此举为好现象,表示美国积极布置一切,两月内美国远东政策可切实表现。并云,麦克猷来电,极力主张美派一部份飞机助华作战。等语。因同座人多,所谈不能如日昨史汀生之透彻。谨撮要电达钧听。

259. 宋子文致蒋介石补述与美海军部长会谈情形电(1941 年 11 月 7 日)①

S446　已发誊清　最密

呈委员长电　十一.七日

委座钧鉴:本午海长诺斯约文及其参谋长②午餐。文先表示,美国撤退驻沪陆战队,上海经济重心行将失却保障。诺谓,前拟必要时陆战队冲入内地,惟再三研究,此举不能办到,撤退陆战队为予日本最后警告,使其知我已有决心,或对租界不敢有所举动,况两月内,美国远东政策,即可有有效之表现。文谓,在此期间,恐我国受莫大打击。嗣讨论日敌攻滇。文再三提出美国须即补充我飞机军械。诺谓,麦克猷有来电,极力主张美国派一部份飞机协助作战,但难题甚多。等语。再,诺斯与史汀生虽云十二月十日以后美国可以最大力量援助中国,但军事政治情形,千变万化,我急需之飞机等项,不能坐待时机,已切托总统左右,极力催请速拨。并陈。○虞(七日)。文。

260. 宋子文致蒋介石呈询美联社消息有否阻碍与英美交涉电(1941 年 11 月 7 日)

呈委员长电　十一.七日

委座钧鉴:美联社六日渝电,略谓,据中国方面消息,中英军事合作已告完成,为应付日本切断滇缅路情事之发生,美国亦将全力援助中国,如日本再有大规模攻击中国之企图,云云。此类消息未悉于钧座与英美方面交涉有阻碍否。虞。文。十一.七

261. 宋子文致蒋介石报告胡适在匹兹堡对记者谈话情形电(1941 年 11 月 7 日)

S447　最密

呈委员长电　十一.七日

委座钧鉴:适之最近在毕次堡③对记者宣称,美国应尽先以飞机军火供给苏联,

---

① 该电文已收入《中华民国重要史料初编》第三编战时外交(一),第 484～485 页。
② 应指时任美国海军作战部长的斯塔克(Harold R. Stark)海军上将。
③ 即匹兹堡(Pittsburgh),美国宾夕法尼亚州西南部城市。

中国已抗战四年余,虽无新式武器,亦可支持,云云。昨史汀生谈话中,曾暗示此语。居里亦引以为异,并谓中国步骤未能一致,愿助中国之友人实感困难,等语。谨闻。○阳。文。十一.七

262. 宋子文致蒋介石报告为胡适所准备之军事及美贷问题说帖电(1941 年 11 月 10 日)①

S448 最密 呈委员长电 十一.十

密呈委座钧鉴:适之今午将见总统,文恐询及军事及美贷问题,适之不甚熟悉,备一说帖,交其代递,择要条列如下:

一、先声述文见总统后,复与陆海财长、霍布金斯、贷借事务处长斯但铁尼②、彭斯中将及陆军各要员,分别讨论各项问题,诸君俱能协力同心,态度甚为诚恳。

二、至今日止,委员长要求之飞机军械以资捍卫滇缅路,尚无答复,惟有请总统毅然决定济我急需。

三、日敌攻滇,一方面可由越而北,直犯昆明,他方面可由越入桂攻滇,此路地形,比较开阔,可以使用坦克,并为历史上行军大道。

四、日敌攻滇,与美国有直接之关系。现在持以保卫滇缅路之空军,为陈纳德所指挥之美籍飞机队。马古德将军来电,该队只有机员八九十人、飞机百架,决不足以抗敌,万一被敌摧残,影响至为重大。若因漫无把握,暂时不参加作战,则中国内部人心作何感想,国际信誉何以维持。等语。是以马将军及麦克猷俱有电来,极力主张美国应增飞机协助陈纳德队,因时间急迫,并请派航空母舰输送。

五、世日见总统时,曾蒙拟商英国由新加坡抽派飞机助华作战,但中美所得消息,美国如不能遣派,英方亦不愿参加。

六、末述文与陆、海军各员熟商后,文认为下列飞机军械,似可立即供给中国,因俱系美陆海军现用品,惟有总统始能加以裁决耳。飞机一项,拟请拨给 SBD 八十架,为航空母舰所用。飞机可由母舰运菲律滨或星加坡、仰光后,直飞中国,驾驶甚易。上次美国卢西阿那省③演习结果,证明如用以轰炸行军,成绩必甚为优良。每机可带一二七五磅炸弹,长行距离一千四百五十里,每小时二百十英里。至其他军械,已详另单(即漾电所列各项略加修改)。等情,谨呈察核。○灰。文。十一.十

---

① 该电文已收入《中华民国重要史料初编》第三编战时外交(一),第 485~486 页。
② 即斯退汀纽斯(Edward R. Stettinius),时任美国军贷贷借事务处处长。
③ 即美国路易斯安那州(Louisiana)。

263. 宋子文致蒋介石报告日敌攻滇尚无特别军事准备电（1941 年 11 月 12 日）

S449　呈委员长电　十一.十二日

委座钧鉴：据此间各方消息及最近联合社电，日敌攻滇，尚无特别军事准备模样，军队集中，似对泰国，越境谅山、同登、高平一带，并无军事布置。法大使馆所得消息亦同。因此我方要求飞机军械，颇受阻难，总统及陆海外长，多以此为词。文惟有答以日敌攻滇计划，业已秘密完成，海南台湾大军，朝发夕至。钧座所得情况如何，务恳随时电示，俾得阐明真象，积极进行。再，感酉、世江、支申、奂戍、虞灰各电，计已早邀钧览，一切举措，未悉有当尊意否，不胜悚念。○震。文。十一.十二

264. 宋子文致蒋介石密告来栖来美情形备忘录稿（1941 年 11 月 14 日）

S450　最密

据某要人密告，此次敌使来栖①○○来美，携有根本让步条件，惟与中日事无直接关系，其内容不愿见告，并谓似非如外间臆测毫无成功希望，等语。鄙意推想，或与海参卫运道及不侵犯西比利亚有关。但如不妥协，则日敌攻占滇缅路，事在必行，美方屡传日敌攻滇并无准备，务恳钧座急电示知敌方一切准备情报，俾得向美方说明，尽速供给我飞机军械，不胜迫切之至。○寒戍。文。十一.十四

265. 宋子文致蒋介石报告与霍普金斯谈美日谈判情形电（1941 年 11 月 22 日）

最密　呈委员长电　十一.廿一日

委座钧鉴：（一）霍布金斯因病入院，文昨往探视，提及美日谈判问题。据云，美海军对日主战，陆军则以为美德战事终不可免，希望太平洋无事（此点与史汀生谈话不同）。国务部一部份人士亦有同样理想。来栖深知美方意见纷歧。（二）日前中央社记者卢祺新②往见上议院外交委员会主席克诺来，据谓，尽驱日人于中土之外，固吾人所愿，但亦不能不迁就事实，例如东北问题，云云。

---

① 来栖，即来栖三郎，日本资深外交官，时任日本赴美谈判特使。
② 卢祺新，时任国民党中央通讯社驻美国办事处主任。

(三)昨与报界领袖鲁斯①晤谈,彼曾于上春与其夫人面谒钧座,对我国感情极佳。据云:日方希冀恢复美日经济关系,不提中日问题,美方绝办不到,舆论亦不许可,且亦不能容许再以油铁供给日本,俾得蹂躏中国。惟东北问题,舆论以为日本如以承认伪满为交还其他全部占领区域之条件,不无赞同之可能。美国人民颇多以为东北问题中日双方均俱有坚持之理由。等语。综合以上所陈各方之论调,我国在美国关于东北之宣传,为刻不容缓之急务,俾知东北于中国有不可分离之关系。钧座九一八告国民书,已有详尽深切之宣示矣。此时惟有不惜耗费,在此扩大宣传,对于将来最后之和平条约,必有莫大之裨益。又云:日代表仅希望商谈恢复美日经济关系,以不侵犯海参崴、西比利亚为交换条件,而对中日战事不愿讨论。但美方以为,舍解决中日问题,日本无代价可以供献,故谈判最后预料日方必请美方调停。霍续云,足下以为日方将提出承认伪满否。文答,美如承认伪满,是违背既定之基本国策,且中国如此重大牺牲,绝不能置三千五百万人民于日本奴役之下。等语。霍为总统最亲信人物,居于白宫,虽随意谈话,亦堪注意。是否可行,敬候示遵。(四)总统友人《纽约时报》主人苏资贝②密告:上星期五谒总统云,余向来拥护总统强硬外交政策,但事实上尚未尽量表现,本报地位,不无困难,余驻伦敦代表报告,邱吉尔对总统之积极主张,亦怀疑虑。总统稍息答云,君不察事实上美国已在大西洋、太平洋作战矣。等语。谨据所闻备贡【供】参考。〇养。十一.廿二

266. 宋子文致蒋介石报告美航空志愿队开支浩大电(1941年11月22日)

S451　最密

呈委员长电　十一.廿二日

委座钧鉴:马电敬悉。美航空志愿队,开支浩大,招募困难,俱系事实,但英国现由星加坡拨两队参加,不能不归功该队之成立。将来作战成绩,虽未可逆料,然国际视听、政治影响,则所关重大。麦克猷、马古德等,屡言该队失败与美国威望感受打击,足征彼方之重视。至新到飞机,本应交由航委会全权处置,因恐人机损失,归罪于中国飞机师之无能,文乃极力主张另组一队,俾无遁辞。而美政府避免此时与敌冲突,不愿居直接指挥派遣之名,该队经费,故不

①　即亨利·卢斯(Henry Luce),美国《时代》(Time)杂志所有人。
②　即哈里森·索尔兹伯里(Harrison Salisbury),《纽约时报》副主编,晚年著有《长征——闻所未闻的故事》(The Long March, The Untold Story)一书,1985年在美国出版,中译本1986年由解放军出版社出版。

得不仍由我方担任,惟有俟情势发展,再作进一步之办法。复呈钧察。○祃。文。十一.廿二

267. 宋子文致蒋介石请速电示滇边敌军行动情报电(1941年11月24日)

S450　呈委员长电　十一.廿四日　复　十一.廿七

委座钧鉴:滇边敌军行动最近情报,请速电示。又,箇电敬悉,甘肃油矿续订机件,谨遵洽办。○敬。文。十一.廿四

268. 宋子文致蒋介石报告与美海军部长会谈情形电(1941年11月25日)

S452　极密　呈委员长电　十一.廿五日

委座钧鉴:有电敬悉。昨致胡大使电,尚未译出,文顷往见海长诺斯,遵将钧意面达。诺云,词意极为动听,但请信我为中国忠实友人,今以友人地位奉告,中国绝对无须顾虑,不过以政府立场,有许多话恕不能奉达以慰蒋委员长耳。文曰:足下之言,我无不信之理,但委员长为中国军事领袖,责任綦重,值此危急存亡之际,凡不以事实根据之安慰,恐无裨补。据胡大使闻霍尔之言,要求日本停止南进或北进,不题【提】中国,是日本更将全力进攻中国。如有此种情形,中国军民心理必将崩溃。诺云:可告足下,霍尔并未将全部条件告胡大使。据我所知,美国种种条件,要求日本必须彻底改变其政策,假使日政府接受,必被推倒,绝不能维持廿四小时。依我推测,日美战事,时期已到,战事发生,各事皆易解决矣。文用种种方法探询之后,诺续云,此次主要条件之一,即为日本脱离轴心国家,日本今日方与轴心续订五年之约,焉能立即取消,总之日本剖腹之时,已非远矣。文云,据胡大使转告霍尔谈话,此次不得不商拟暂时办法,因海陆军参谋本部要求最好再有三个月之期间,以资准备。诺云,任何海陆军,均无准备完全之终期,时间充裕,自属更佳,但在今日已有之准备,我等固不必再因准备之故,而有任何牺牲,处置日本,易如反掌。文问,据胡大使见告,霍尔于星期一谈判之后,颇现惊慌之色,澳洲公使①告文亦有同样之感想。诺云,霍尔年高体弱,乃紧张状态,非惊慌也,日本已到绝地,中国应感觉欣幸,无须顾虑。文问,谣传德国攫夺全部法国海军,对于美国计划,是否有碍。诺云,即使如此,因训练等事,德在六个月内,亦不能使用。等语。诺为人

---

① 即澳大利亚驻美公使。

甚为积极,向来主战,恰与国务部相反,所言是否能代表美国政府全体意见,及美方确未将所有条件尽告适之,尚待事实证明。再,诺又言,英国无胜德之武力,美国必须在大西洋、太平洋即行参战。诺并要求谈话内容勿向任何人泄漏。谨陈。○径戊。

269. 蒋介石致宋子文请设法把昨致胡适原电之意转告美陆海两长电(1941年11月25日)

委员长渝来电　卅.十一.廿五

昨致胡大使电,谅已由其抄阅。请兄设法将中原电之意转告其陆海两长,并译送居里一份,再望口头说明此事严重之程度。如美对日经济封锁或资产冻结果有一点放松之情况,华盛顿或有此种消息之泄露,则我国军心必立受影响。因两月以来,日本在华宣传,多以本月内美日谈话必可如计完成,故我南北各方动摇分子,确有默契。只要美日一旦妥协,或美国经济封锁略有一点放松,则中日两国人民观感,即视为美日妥协已成,中国全被美国牺牲。如此全国人心不仅离散,而亚洲各国失望之余,因其心理之激变,必造成世界上不可想像之惨史。从此中国抗战崩溃故不待言,日本计划乃可完全告成。若此美国虽欲挽救,亦不可能。此岂只中国一国失败而已哉? 此时惟有请美国政府立即宣明与日本决不妥协之态度,并声明,如日本在华侵略之军队撤退问题未有根本解决以前,美国对日经济封锁政策决不有丝毫之改变或放松,则中国军民心理方可安定,大局方有补救。否则美国态度暧昧,延宕不决,而日本对华之宣传必更日甚一日,则中国四年以前之抗战,死伤无穷之生命,遭受历史以来空前未有之牺牲,乃由美政府态度之暧昧游移,而与再三毫不费力之宣传,以致中国抗战功败垂成,世界祸乱迄无底止,不知千秋历史将作如何记载矣。中正手启。有(廿五)。

270. 蒋介石致宋子文请与胡适切商对美有效之交涉方法电(1941年11月25日)

委员长渝来电　卅.十一.廿六

刻电请抄送适之一份,并与之切商对美有效之交涉方法,总使美政府能迅速明白表示其对日决不妥协之态度。关系重大,务请协力以赴之。中正手启。径(廿五)。

271. 宋子文致蒋介石报告与罗斯福谈话可注意各点电(1941 年 11 月 26 日)

极密　呈委员长电　十一.廿六日

委座钧鉴：本日文与适之联名电，计邀钧览。文昨晨奉有①电，因时机急迫，当日即将钧座意旨托总统亲信高可任②君代达。总统乃约文与适之今日进谒。谈话情形，可注意各点，谨陈如下：

(一) 总统首谓，钧座或因所闻不实似有误会，云云。实则钧座有电之动机，乃根据适之廿二、廿四日两电(该两电附后)报告霍尔、美澳荷各使谈话之事实。

(二) 适之两电，颇有美国原则已定，事在必行之意，故不能再事商量。但总统云，向来主张美方之提议，先向关系友邦征求同意，再向日本提出。

(三) 霍尔前所持主要理由，为美陆海军不得不要求三数月之时间，俾得充分准备。总统则只字不提。

(四) 总统云，昨日据报，日本由山东海上运输二三万军队南下，正值两国谈判之时，而有如此行动，是无诚意，谈判似难继续，等语。总统是否藉此转圜，未可妄测。

(五) 总统以美方提案乃完全注重保护滇缅路，经文一再申述，按照提案，该路仍不能避免威胁，各地仍不免蹂躏，则中国毋宁因抵抗攻击而牺牲，不愿因日美妥协之故而崩溃。总统无词可答，态度似露窘促。

(六) 适之过信国务部，以为霍尔之方案，为循守美国已定之政策，不可变更，故不愿在原则上力争，仅断之于驻越北日军多寡之问题。舍本逐末，何济于事。此次若能挽回牺牲中国之厄运，实由钧座义正词严之一电。适之对于美政府权要素少接洽，仅与英澳各使约略商谈，真象不明，几致贻误事机。

(七) 文昨晚特邀财长摩根韬③晚餐，据摩云：国务部态度，向来懦怯。两年前中国借款，乃特候霍尔赴南美洲时进行，始得告成。冻结日本资产，我已费两年心力，艰难可知。美日谈判，何等重要，事前亦未与我相商，殊不免令人发生反感。惟渠深信，日美妥协，不易实现，对于日本，只有以武力制裁。

(八) 文在此极力连络各方，反对妥协，国务部自不免非难，只有听其日怨，但一般舆论均属同情。惟当此千钧一发之际，适之不能胜任，殊可危虑矣。文。寝亥。

---

①　此处"有"系韵目代日字，即"二十五日"。
②　即科克伦(Thomas Cochran)，亦作郭可仁，当时被中国国防供应公司聘为法律顾问。
③　即摩根索(Henry Morgenthau Jr.)，时任美国财政部部长。

272. 宋子文胡适致郭泰祺转蒋介石报告与罗斯福会谈情形电(1941 年 11 月 26 日)

电郭外长①　　三十年十一月廿六日

极密,并乞速陈介公②

今日下午两点半总统约适、文二人谈话,约一点钟。总统先说:蒋先生因滇缅路危急,叠电见商救急之方,其后日使来栖等来谈,曾表示不欲美国调解中日和议,故中日整个问题无从谈及。其后彼方提出临时过渡办法中,有不再增加南越军队一项。余等因念此中或有帮助中国解决滇缅路危急之途径,故外长曾与 ABCD 各国③讨论一个临时过渡办法,其中即注重安南全境日军减至不能危害之数目,其意即有借此帮助蒋先生解救滇缅路之危急。本意欲求得中英荷澳四国大致同意,然后与彼方开谈。此案迄今未提出,但昨夜我方得报告,谓日本军舰三十余艘由山东南驶,已过台湾南下,其所运军队数目有三万至五万之估计。此可见彼方毫无信义,在谈话时已增加南面兵力。似此情形,恐谈话根本即无继续可能,而太平洋上之大爆发恐已不在远,故此案不但未交去,谈话或亦即有中止之可能。闻蒋先生对此事颇有误会,甚感焦急,请代为解释。云云。

适因陈说:我政府之意旨,侧重两点:一则经济封锁之放松,可以增加敌人持久力量,更可以使我抗战士民十分失望灰心;二则敌人既不能南进与北侵,必将集中力量攻我国,是我独蒙其害,而所谓过渡办法,对此全无救济。

总统云:外长所拟办法,只限于局部的临时救急,其中确不能顾到全部中日战事。譬如当前有两个强盗由两面攻入,若能给五元钱使其一人多湾【弯】几十里山路,以便全力以抗其他一人。我方用意不过如此。

文因陈说云:美国以日本不侵犯西比利亚及荷属东印度④、泰国、星加坡为恢复有限制的经济关系之交换条件,我国一般军民心理必以为无异表示日本对华可以进攻。日本军事布置有三点:一、攻西比利亚,二、南进,三、全力侵略中国。前两者既不可行,中国势必独受其祸。至滇缅路之保护问题,因属重要,但仅限制日本越北驻军亦属无济于事,日方仍可以越南为运输根据,调遣大军,由桂入滇,且此者为历史上战争必经之路。即便滇缅路暂时不受攻击,其他区域

---

① 即时任国民政府外交部长的郭泰祺。
② 即蒋中正,字介石,时任中国国民党总裁、国民政府军事委员会委员长。
③ 即澳大利亚(Australia)、英国(Britain)、中国(China)、荷兰(Dutch)四国。
④ 即荷属东印度群岛,原荷兰的海外领地之一,现为印度尼西亚。

仍不免于蹂躏,滇缅路仍旧感受威胁也。故有限制的恢复经济关系,殊不能使中国军民了解。中国军民只知解除封锁,日本即可获得油料,以供飞机轰炸。是以蒋委员长深为焦虑,认为日美一旦妥协,即是中国被牺牲,中国军民抗战之心理,势不能维持。是以余敢谓,如因欲保护滇缅路而放松经济制裁,中国宁愿抵抗敌军之攻击,盖放松经济封锁,影响中国军民心理至大,抗战前途,不堪设想也。总统对文所说各点,未加直截答复,但云,现时局势变化多端,难以逆料,一两星期后,太平洋上极有大战祸,亦未可知,余只盼望蒋先生对余等勿遽生误会,则幸甚已。

　　文等辞出后,追思总统所谈,大致有三点:(一)所谓临时过渡办法,尚未提交日方,此一点适在外部已得证实。(二)在未得四国同意之前,或不致开谈,只此一点当再向外部方面证实后续报。(三)若日方此时增加南面军力,则谈话即可决裂,而战事或将不免。子文　适①。

273. 宋子文致蒋介石报告赫尔因钧座有电分达陆海两长深为不满电(1941年11月27日)

极密　呈委员长电　十一.廿七日

委座钧鉴:居里来言,霍尔因文将钧座有电意旨,分达陆海两长,两长并有所表示,故深为不满,居里不得不电致拉铁马②顾问。又云,有电办法效力极大,彼电虽发出,钧座置之不问可也。等语。○感酉。文。十一.廿七

274. 宋子文致蒋介石报告摩根索谓中国应取坚决之态度电(1941年11月27日)

极密　呈委员长电　十一.廿七日

委座钧鉴:摩根韬今午约文密谈。据谓:中国应取坚决之态度,内阁除霍尔外均同情于我。彼已准备一最恳切之信呈总统。因美日妥协告成,则民主主义、世界公道必将崩溃。即使总统因此命其去职,亦所不辞。文答,盛意已感,目前局势好转,尚请继续援助。等情。谨闻。○感。文。十一.廿七

---

① 此处"子文　适"为拟稿者笔迹。
② 即拉铁摩尔。

275. 宋子文致蒋介石对日美谈判内幕分析详陈电(1941年11月28日)

极密　呈委员长电　十一.廿八日

委座钧鉴：日美谈判内幕,逐渐揭开,谨分析详陈如下：

一、霍尔为一纯正君子,秉性和平,复为国务部缓和派包围。该派亟欲与日本妥协,虽牺牲中国,亦所不惜。东方司长汉密登①,为该派首领。顾问霍贝克②虽同情于我,亦不免随声附和。文敬酉电陈霍贝克与田本烈之谈话可以想见。霍尔本意,原拟延宕时间,但因来栖告以为压制日本国内激烈派,须于廿六日嗣致廿九日以前有一办法,无异哀的美敦书。霍尔焦灼之余,不得不顺从缓和派之意见进行矣。

二、美海、陆军,固已有相当准备,观文鱼径电陈海陆两长谈话可知。惟国务部用巧妙方法,征询海陆参谋长是否需要延长时间,以利准备。准备本无终期,军人坦直,无不同意之理。霍尔遂先与英、澳、荷三使洽商所拟过渡办法。英、荷趋于反对,澳赞同。因关系中国最大,并邀适之参加。适之柔懦,不忍探本追源,仅集中力量于过渡办法之修改。霍尔遂以过渡办法可以推进告知总统。

三、总统明知日美战争不可避免,但政治家素喜运用手腕,又以为过渡办法于中国无多大损害,故加赞同。此时若无钧座有电,并迅速转达各方,表示坚决正当之立场,则此过渡办法,即预备廿五或廿六日正式提交来栖。

四、昨居里言,总统于廿四日主张过渡办法,语气甚为坚决,身为部属,人微言轻,不敢表示反对。文严责其有负总统及中国。居云,总统向来主见甚强,孰知亦可变易,此后对其心理,更多一层明了,并请见谅。等语。

五、总统获知钧座态度坚决,知过渡办法之不妥,且政府一部分要人得悉中国之立场后,认为此种过渡办法不过亚洲"明舆"协定之重演,对总统有所陈述。但总统尚欲试探,故于廿六日午后召见文与适之,三人密谈。文个人之判断,已于寝亥电陈。电中第一、二两项所述总统之言,不尽符合事实,可知其动摇之心理。第三项今已证实确系藉此转图。

六、总统见文等后,即召见霍尔,决定放弃过渡办法,并决定提出准备决裂时美方所定之基本原则。窃查过渡办法,虽未正式提交日方,而各报已将概略登载,来栖亦必获知其内容,即廿五六日可以正式提交之消息,来栖亦必已得到,故各

---

① 即汉密尔顿(Maxwell M. Hamilton),时任美国国务院远东司司长。
② 即贺恩贝克(Stanley K. Hornbeck),时任美国国务院政治顾问。

报访员见来栖赴国务部时满面笑容,及收到负面答复后,懊丧而返。

七、此次挽回危局,全仗钧座刚明沉毅之决心,非惟救中国,亦救美国,而正义公道亦赖以维持。历史运命往往决于片刻,追述经过之余,益增钦服。○俭申。文。十一.廿八

276. 蒋介石致宋子文告以国务院不满何足悬怀电(1941年11月29日)

委员长渝来电　加码　卅.十一.廿九

寝(廿六)亥、沁(廿七)、感(廿七)、感(廿七)酉各电均悉。此次幸赖兄在各方努力呼吁,乃得转败为胜。国务院不满一节,何足悬怀。当望以后不断注意,能收更大功效也。中正手启。艳(廿九)。

277. 宋子文拟致蒋介石关于开发甘新油井电稿(1941年12月1日)

拟上委员长电稿

委座钧鉴:关于开发甘新油井事,美当局现介绍著名油井地质专家克拉普来华探勘石油储藏量,以一年为期,连同助手三人薪旅、仪器等费,约需美金六万元,如需探井钻机等,另加美金九万元。此人探井经验丰富,又为美当局介绍,对保守秘密,可无问题。如能得其来华,于我国开发油井,不无裨益。应否照聘,祈电示遵。○○叩。东。文。十二.一

278. 宋子文致蒋介石请随时电示敌在越军事情况电(1941年12月1日)

呈委员长电　十二.一日

委座钧鉴:敌在越军事情况,关系我方对美交涉,异常重要,乞随时电示。○先。文。十二.一

279. 宋子文致蒋介石报告与史汀生会谈情形电(1941年12月2日)

极密　呈委员长电　十二.二日

委座钧鉴:顷见史汀生。彼首谓:余非外长,谈话自有不便,但蒋委员长困难情形,可想而知。同情之余,应有数言,略表慰藉。目前请委员长只须稍稍忍耐,美国立场及其政策,一如十一月六日(文奂戌电)与君所谈,不稍更改。今日陆军已

准备妥当,虽一月后更有把握,亦可毋须等待。余以友谊据实奉告,务请严守秘密,泄露反于中国不利。文谓,中国最顾虑者,为一切不适当之暂时办法,是使中国军民抗战心理不可收拾。史答,中国不必,云云。语未毕即止,其意即此一点,亦不必虑及也。史末谓,敌目前决不攻滇缅。文辞出时,又再三请守秘密。再,此间昨日各报,因觉美日战事,可暂时避免,尤因外部暗中宣传,故对日论调,语气略松,今日已转变,一致反对日本之假意和平矣。谨闻。○冬。文。

280. 宋子文致蒋介石关于派飞机师赴英印受训练电(1941年12月5日)

S454　电蒋委员长

英大使馆友人某密告,如我政府有意派飞机师赴印受训练,印度政府似有允意。特此奉达。文①。微。十二.五

281. 宋子文致蒋介石建议东北问题拟在美扩大宣传电(1941年12月6日)

极密　**呈委员长电　十二.六日**

委座钧鉴:养电所陈关于东北问题,拟在美作有组织的扩大宣传,不惜相当耗费。是否可行,乞电示遵。○鱼。文。十二.六

282. 宋子文致蒋介石密告罗斯福与日妥协不可能电(1941年12月6日)

极密　**呈委员长电　十二.六日**

委座钧鉴:纽约时报馆主,见总统后,密告文,总统云,与日妥协不可能,和平无望,圣诞节后恐有动作,又谓不愿东条内阁②即倒,等语。谨闻。○麻。文。十二.六

283. 宋子文致蒋介石报告太平洋航空线可置新线电(1941年12月8日)

S455　*极密*　呈委员长电　十二.八日

委座钧鉴:太平洋原来航空线已阻断,此后可置两条新线:一由檀香山趋南,经

---

① 此处"文"字为拟稿者笔迹。
② 即1941年10月成立的以东条英机为首相的日本新内阁。

东荷印①、新加坡；一由北美，经南美及非洲、印度、仰光。可否请钧座正式向美使②提议开辟，乞酌。〇齐。文。十二.八

284. 宋子文致蒋介石告以如需用大票面券当托美政府空运电（1941 年 12 月 12 日）

S456　呈委员长电　十二.十二日

委座钧鉴：仰光海运，或将梗阻。国内钞票共存若干，敷用几月，内地可印若干？如需用大票面券，文当尽力托美政府空运，经非【非】洲转送内地，以资接济。请裁示，并将需用详数电知。〇震。文。十二.十二

285. 宋子文致蒋介石关于太平洋战局突变中贷借事务近况电（1941 年 12 月 12 日）③

S457　极密　拟致委座电稿　十二.十二

委座钧鉴：在太平洋战局突变之中，贷借事务近况如下：（一）总统已明白宣布，贷借政策不加变更；（二）但美军事当局，对于多种重要军用贷借物资，已暂时停止交货，此次战事发生过骤，美物资分配须加整理之后，方可继续进行贷借；（三）太平洋各航线现已全停，惟护航制度，已在计划之中，经由南美、非【非】洲直通印度、加尔加搭④及仰光之航空线亦将实现。此最近关于贷借政策与交货及运输情形之大概也。查此后贷借计划，或将依据全部作战计划及各战区分区需要而定，视战局进行之情况，定各战区需要物资之数量。整批贷借，不如以前之零碎点缀办法。如以飞机为例，某区需要飞机单位，则（甲）飞机、（乙）零件配件、（丙）机师、（丁）机场员司等，均应同时供给。但此项计划须待珍珠港等处损失补充后，方有实现之可能。现时所能确定者，不过贷借计划有此种新趋势而已。再，运华物资与远东军事局势直接有关，滇缅及香港最近军情，尚祈随时详细赐示，俾得相机因应。〇侵亥。文。

---

① 即荷属东印度群岛。
② 即时任美国驻华大使的高斯（Clarence E. Gauss）。
③ 该电文已收入《中华民国重要史料初编》第三编战时外交（一），第 493 页。
④ 即加尔各答（Calcutta），印度东部城市，位于恒河三角洲地区。

286. 宋子文致蒋介石报告美军部已可如期交货电(1941 年 12 月 13 日)

S458

委座钧鉴：侵亥文①电陈美军部暂停交货一节,今日该部通知,本年内应交各种炮械,已可如期交货,余正磋商中。谨闻。○元□。文。十二.十三

287. 宋子文致蒋介石提出订印钞券应有整个办法电(1941 年 12 月 13 日)

呈委员长电

委座钧鉴：此后运输困难,订印钞券,似应有整个办法。沪平准会②存钞,想为数不少,恐已为敌所掠。今后施用大票面券,势难避免,或大小票面券即刻搭用,请裁夺。○覃未。文。十二.十三

288. 宋子文致蒋介石报告拟向美方提出军械弹药货单电(1941 年 12 月 16 日)③

S461　极密　呈委员长电　十二.十六日

委座钧鉴：美日开战后,美方更应格外注重供给我国军械。兹与江杓商酌,参照国内需要及美国供给能力,拟定一单,向美方提出,计(照江杓稿甲至庚七项)：甲、轻机枪一万挺、子弹一万万发；乙、七五山炮三百六十门、弹十八万发；丙、一○五或一五五榴弹炮三百六十门、弹十八万发；丁、三七平射炮三百六十门、弹三十六万发；戊、半吋高射机枪七百二十挺、弹一百四十四万发；已、四公分高射炮一百八十门、弹二十七万发；庚、六公分迫击炮二千门、弹一百万发。上列械弹,请其务于三个月内全部起运。炮弹须陆续补充。七九枪弹五万万发,盼明年三月前出品,十二月前交清。并请钧座于此次四国军事会议④中提出,当更有力量。乞核夺。○谏申。文。十二.十六

---

① 此处原稿为○。
② 即中英美平准基金委员会,总部设香港,在上海设有办事处。
③ 该电文已收入《中华民国重要史料初编》第三编战时外交(一),第493~494 页。
④ 即拟在重庆召开的中、美、英、荷四国军事代表会议。

289. 宋子文致蒋介石报告美空军飞行学校正筹备电(1941年12月23日)

S462　极密　呈委员长电　十二.廿三日

委座钧鉴：啸电敬悉。美空军双发动机飞行学校正在筹备，约明春或夏季始能开学。前向军部交涉训练我国学生，据称，该项训练机缺少，训练美生，尚感不足，等语。足见美空军准备之不充足。惟目前情形不同，自必尽力扩充训练。拟再要求多量收容我国学生，俟有端倪，再电奉陈。○梗。文。十二.廿三

290. 宋子文致蒋介石请取消国际新闻电费加价电(1941年12月23日)

呈委员长电　十二.廿三日

委座钧鉴：顷闻我国国际新闻电费加价数倍，值此抗战紧急时期，势必妨碍新闻来源，影响国际宣传，殊属得不偿失。可否请饬主管机关取消，乞酌。○漾午。文。

291. 宋子文致蒋介石报告已饬将三行钞券在菲同时焚毁电(1941年12月24日)

S463　极密　呈委员长电　十二.廿四日　复　十二.卅一

委座钧鉴：昨已饬美钞公司，并请菲律滨杨总领事光泩[1]监视，将中国银行运华钞券焚毁。前曾电中央、交通两行遇必要时同样办理，迄未得复。今情势危迫，已饬美钞将三行钞券在菲同时焚毁，请备案。○敬未。十二.廿四

292. 宋子文致蒋介石询陈纳德指挥问题电(1941年12月26日)

委座钧鉴：据陈纳德电告，两队驻昆明，一队留仰光，助英作战。此后陈纳德指挥问题与英美将领商洽否，乞示。○寝。十二.廿六

---

① 杨光泩,时为中国驻菲律宾总领事。

293. 宋子文致蒋介石请示萧勃调充中校副武官电(1941年12月26日)

次要　呈委员长电　十二.廿六日　复　R.159
S464
委座钧鉴:朱武官①在此颇资臂助。嗣后武官处事更繁冗,人员似嫌不敷,查大使馆三等秘书萧勃,原任少校副武官,熟悉此间情形,可否调充中校副武官,以资佐理。国内虽已另派一副武官,惟各国惯例,副武官不限一人,必要时可加派也。伏乞钧裁。○宥。文。十二.廿六

294. 宋子文致蒋介石报告印度可代造子弹电(1941年12月29日)

S465　极密　呈委员长电　十二.廿八日
委座钧鉴:俞署长大维电告,印度可代造七点九二子弹。窃以在此间进行,必展转延缓,可否请直接与魏佛尔②商办,价款由美拨付,或可办到。乞示。○艳。文。十二.廿九

295. 宋子文致蒋介石提议东北情势及早扩大宣传函(1942年1月5日)

委座钧鉴:敌方向以人口过剩、中国地广人稀,应为尾闾,妄肆宣传。欧美人士受其鼓惑已久,尤其关于东北情势不甚明了,如此次对日宣战,总统演词中尚且直称满洲国,其他人士可知。文危虑之余,故有前电之请,将来最后和平,美缓和派难免迁就穷寇,牺牲东北,以免压迫过甚,结永世之仇,故不如及早扩大宣传,纠正美人士心理之错误。仍候钧裁。专肃。敬请钧安。谨上。一月五日。

296. 宋子文致蒋介石译呈美陆军部向英方提出秘密说帖电(1942年1月19日)③

极密　呈委员长电　卅一.一.十九日
委座钧鉴:今日史汀生约谈,面称鉴于魏佛尔、勃兰特④上次赴渝,结果毫无成

---

① 即朱世明,时任中国驻美国大使馆武官。
② 魏佛尔(Archibald P. Wavell),时任驻印英军司令。
③ 该电文已收入《中华民国重要史料初编》第三编战时外交(三),第109~111页。
④ 勃兰特(George H. Brett),亦作布雷特,美国将领,时任驻澳盟国空军指挥官。1941年12月下旬,他应蒋介石邀请,作为美军高级代表抵达重庆,出席中美英军事会议。

绩,又因仰光扣留军械及钧座请总统介绍中国战区联军参谋长种种情事,故本人尽其心力向英方提出秘密说帖,并请求我方同意,促成英与中、美在中国区切实合作。译意如下:

(子) 原则:

　　(一) 英、美均应深切了解,非与蒋委员长彻底合作,无裨战局;

　　(二) 英、美在军事上、政治上观点,俱应尽力扩充中国武力;

　　(三) 目前最大问题,为中国与英、美运输上之困难及心理上之隔阂种种。

(丑) 目的:基于以上原则,应共同做到下列各点:

　　(一) 完成与蒋委员长切实联络之办法及其工具;

　　(二) 保卫滇缅路及缅甸之安全;

　　(三) 改良滇缅路运输管理;

　　(四) 扩张陆、空军据点,充实技术上援助;

　　(五) 增强中国抗战力量;

　　(六) 规定中国战区与魏佛尔所辖战区切实联络方法。

(寅) 实施计划:为实现以上目的,陆军部拟施行下列计划:

　　(一) 商请蒋委员长允准接受美国高级军官为驻华代表,并同意其具有下列职权:

　　　　(甲) 办理所有在中国之美军货援华事宜①;

　　　　(乙) 在蒋委员长统辖之下,指挥所有在华之美国军队,及委员长自愿交与指挥之某部中国军队,如遇此项军队有在缅甸参加作战之必要时,其作战总计划应受魏佛尔之指示,但实行作战则由美军官指挥;

　　　　(丙) 代表美国参加在华之一切国际军事会议;

　　　　(丁) 维持及管理中国境内滇缅公路运输。

　　(二) 蒋委员长如同意寅项第一款所列各点,陆军部拟即:

　　　　(甲) 增加华南、缅甸区域之空军力量,先由增加及补充志愿军飞机及人员入手,对于蒋委员长所拨交指挥之中国军队若干师,供给全□军械器材,亦属可能;

　　　　(乙) 在英国同意之下,设立兵站,供应中国在缅甸或印度方面之陆、空军,并供给专门器材及军队,以维持仰光港口货运与设备,及协助维持滇缅公路;

　　　　(丙) 为便利计划之施行,英国对下开各点之合作及允诺,实有必要,但英国之合作与允诺,以委员长全面接受寅项第一款所开各点为

_____

① 即 1941 年 5 月美国政府宣布以租借形式向中国援助武器及其他军用物资。

前提：

（一）美国代表在缅甸及缅甸以北地域有所经营时，须与邻区指挥官合作设立及利用印度及缅甸之一切军事据点、路线、站所；

（二）美国代表得用全力设法增加滇缅路之运量，由仰光以迄昆明，为达此目的，中国政府将授美代表以滇缅路华段之管理权，滇缅路英段仍由英国军政当局负责，但英国当局应接受所有美代表对改进路务之建议，并接受改进仰光港务及滇缅路务所需之美国专家及器材；

（三）美代表与英指挥官接洽之后，得在缅甸利用各航空站及建设新飞机场；

（四）接受美代表魏佛尔即将【蒋】委员长间之主要联络员。

以上为史汀生说帖译意，据谓确系根据事实，苦心研究之结果。文答，据以转陈钧座，恭候训示，即请详加考虑，迅予指示机宜。其中有应补充陈明者：

（一）所谓高级军官，即以之兼充中国战区联军参谋长，拟推荐 Stillwell ①中将，此人公认为美陆军中最优秀之将材，现充军团长，曾任 Marshall② 参谋长之作战局长，通华语，未发表前，请暂守秘密；

（二）星期六文英文电所陈各节，意义现已明了，乃为避免中英隔阂，故拟将入缅华军归此君指挥，不直接受英方统辖；

（三）钧座对于魏佛尔及缅军政当局之应付，可使此君负责，至中国军队如进驻越南及泰国，固与派遣缅甸协助作战之军队不同，应由钧座直接统辖指挥；

（四）史汀生或因新加坡危急，亟欲中国战区与缅甸方面军事有切实合作办法，故切催转请钧座示复。

谨陈。文。效亥。卅一·一·十九

297. 宋子文致蒋介石提议向美方速商议大借款等三事电(1942 年 1 月 26 日)

极密　呈委员长电　卅一·一·廿六日

委座钧鉴：星缅危急，我国际交通有断绝之虞，影响军民心理，尤非浅鲜。为补救计，此际似可速向美方商办三事：（一）大借款③从速决定；（二）以大批飞机

---

① 即史迪威(Joseph W. Stilwell)，美国陆军中将，后出任中国战区最高统帅蒋介石的参谋长。
② 即马歇尔(George C. Marshall)，时任美国陆军参谋长，四星上将。
③ 即 1942 年初美国政府承诺向中国国民政府提供的 5 亿美元借款。

由加尔加答①、米芝那转云南驿,输送物资;(三)中美军事同盟。前两项已在进行;第三项,美国虽向来不与他国订立军事同盟,但一九四零年夏,法国危急,英国且有英法并为一国之提议,况军事同盟,本非新奇之举,美方或在此时有破除成例之可能。三事如能告成,颇足振奋人心,实际上裨益战局,更无论矣。钧意若何,及对于条件磋商应加注意之点,尚乞裁量指示。再,国内舆论,不满英美军事之表示,配合我此间行动,□□无益耳。文。

298. 宋子文致蒋介石密告美方嘱意俾索威担任联军最高空军职位电(1942年2月5日)

耀密　呈委员长电　卅一.二.五日

委座钧鉴:美方晋升陈纳德为少将,不另派高级空军人员各节,已于卅酉电陈,计邀垂览。惟美参谋长及史梯威②本意以为:反攻日本时,空军根据地必在中国,不但义勇队及中国空军须指挥得人,并积极准备调遣大队空军赴华共同作战。指挥人物之重要,可以想见。以陈纳德之技能、经验、资望,及与美空军之关系,能否胜任,殊未可必。故属意于俾索威③少将担任联军总部最高级空军职位,主持一切。义勇军自当仍由陈纳德少将率领,并兼管组训中国空军。文以此事甫定,似未便变更,不过,俾索威确与美空军各高级将领关系极深,声望素著,为将来种种着想,失此机会,此人不能赴华,殊觉可惜。究应如何处置,敬候裁夺速示。〇微西。文。卅一.二.五

299. 宋子文致蒋介石提议我国授予外人勋章可予酌改电(1942年3月9日)

呈委员长电　卅一.三.九日

委座钧鉴:现今中外接触益频,我国授予外人勋章,质地既恶,式样亦不美观,且等级甚多,如七级、八级,受者每嫌太低。各国勋章新办法虽有高下,但各有名称,不明列等级。我国是否可予酌改之处,乞饬主管机关,另定式样办法,或在美设计,绘图呈核。当祈钧裁。文。

---

① 即加尔各答(Calcutta),印度东部城市,位于恒河三角洲地区。
② 即史迪威(Joseph W. Stilwell),时任中国战区联军参谋长。
③ 俾索威(Clayton L. Bissell),美国第十航空队司令。

300. 宋子文致蒋介石孔祥熙报告与美代理国务卿商谈借款条款电(1942 年 3 月 21 日)[①]

急　加码　呈委员长致孔部长电　卅一.三.廿日

委座钧鉴,孔部长勋鉴:庸兄篠巧电奉悉。委座意见,除最低限度一节因稍有放松口气未译转外,余均转达财长。经国务、财政两部开会讨论,颇费斟酌,以为此次借款条件,较之任何借款皆优,毫未述及苛细,云云。文闻悉之下,即向最高当局及有关主官,作私人之疏解。本晨代理国务卿[②]约谈,重行声明美政府之立场,表示第二条[③]可删除,但要求由文另具函证明:(一)中国政府愿与美财政部长对于借款用途,随时交换意见,磋商有效之办法;(二)中国政府愿将此项借款用途,随时详细通告美方。文谓,中国政府关于此项借款用途,绝无对美国政府守秘密之意,且愿得美方技术之援助,但不能有任何表示中国政府负有交换意见及磋商之义务。极力坚持之结果,经代理国务卿以电话与各方商洽,始决定第二条全条删除,协约签字后,仅由文函致财长,声明中国政府愿以本约借款详细用途,不时告知美方。全文如下:关于今日中美两国政府订立之借款协约,为表现中美两国协力抗战之精神,鄙人谨奉告阁下,中国政府愿以此项借款之详细用途,不时由财政部长详告贵财长,云云。此为美国最后让步,且不悖委座屡次指示之方针,借款协约遂于本日午刻双方签字,并约定协约条文公布,文致财长函不发表。谨陈鉴察。○马未。文。卅一.三.廿一

301. 宋子文致蒋介石提议请克利普斯来渝一叙电(1942 年 4 月)

设法转呈委座

委座钧鉴:克利普斯[④]为人颇识大体,不为一般英国官吏之陈旧不改,且对钧座备极尊崇。此次印度事顺利回国,声誉大增,不久之将来,颇有代邱吉尔之可能。谨为提议,请钧座电请其来渝一叙。英国朝野对强征军械及缅甸统率问题不明真相,钧座可乘此明告内容。英国无论胜负,帝国制度必瓦解,但在此共同危急

---

　　①　该电文已收入《中华民国重要史料初编》第三编战时外交(一),第 342~343 页。
　　②　即韦尔思(Sumner Welles),时任美国副国务卿、代理国务卿。
　　③　即 1942 年 2 月由美方拟订的 5 亿美元借款协定草案第二条:"中国愿将本约中所列资金之用途,通知美国财政部长,并愿对该项用途随时征询其意见,美国财政部长愿就此项资金之有效运用方面,向中国政府提供技术上及其他适当之建议,以期完成本约中所述之目的。其因履行本约中所定财政协助而随时发生之技术问题,由美国财政部长及中国政府讨论之。"
　　④　克利普斯(Stafford Cripps),英国爵士,曾任英国驻苏联大使。

之际,不妨与之联络,免为敌所乘。

302. 宋子文致蒋介石报告今日太平洋战时会议情形电(1942年4月1日)

加码　呈委员长电　卅一.四.一日

委座钧鉴:今日开太平洋战时会议,总统主席。因系预备性质,总统仅解释划分战区制度,大致如文侵亥电所陈,并决定下星期二讨论:

(甲)澳、新西兰提出之抗日军事计划;

(乙)朝鲜问题。

总统嘱文下次提出,如何运用朝鲜人民扰乱日敌计划,并附带东北义勇军组织问题。此两事,应请指示者:

(一)钧座是否赞成由参加太平洋战事会议各国,或仅由中美两国,发表宣言,主张朝鲜独立,由此而决定分散日本帝国之政策,是否须在苏联未能参加表示以前公布之;

(二)朝鲜国内秘密工作团体,有无确实力量,是否与苏联有关,我政府是否有意在渝指导其革命,并派员赴朝鲜秘密活动;

(三)美国显欲以械款助朝鲜革命及东北反抗,牵制日敌,请即电示详细应如何进行;

(四)东北义勇军最近之情况及其组织如何。

统乞迅予赐复。○东酉。文。三十一.四.一

303. 宋子文致蒋介石提议派员到美说明动用借款用途电(1942年4月12日)①

D441　加码　呈委员长电　卅一.四.十一日

密呈委座钧鉴:本午毛根道②密约谈话。据云:福克斯回国面称,中国当局嘱声明此次借款成功后,必先与余商洽,再行动用。余素极信仰中国,故协约上并不坚持注明此点。今协约甫于廿一日签字,廿四日孔部长即发表二万万施用方法③,廿七日始电告该款用途,并请拨款,事先毫未洽商。但为遵守协约,勉于下

---

① 该电文已收入《中华民国重要史料初编》第三编战时外交(一),第346页。

② 即摩根索。

③ 孔祥熙于1942年3月24日在重庆宣布,中国计划发行1亿美元4厘联盟胜利公债与1亿美元储蓄券,并指定中央银行代表中国政府在美国联邦储备银行开户。

星期四即十六日以前,将二万万元全数拨交准备银行中国户备用。不过中国此举未能表示互信精神,引以为憾,且所定办法罅隙极多,恐难见效。万一中国金融方面失败,即美国失败,亦余本身失败,不知阁下何以教我。云云。

文答:商议借款经过时期较久,而中国金融状况危急万分,救急如救火,孔部长抱病,财部人员容有不周到之处,亦非故意。所谈各节,当特陈委员长。等语。

查协约并无征求美方意见之明文规定,但我方如确有此种表示于前,似宜先作友谊上之协商,若意见不合,即行根据协约,请其拨款,彼自不得拒绝,而我方则人情已尽。今毛氏虽遵约交款,然误会滋深。来日方长,从大处着想,中美连系关乎全局,美方经济援助,亦非至此而止。

文离国已两年,国内经济金融生疏已久,复杂情形又非电报所能详尽,自不能作深切尽情之解释。为补救起见,可否请钧座嘱庸兄派熟悉国内金融财政情形者,如贝淞孙①或顾季高②来美,与财长说明,费时不过一二星期。文意此事成为毛氏及政府人员对中国信仰及情感问题,派人到此稍稍交换意见,误会自可冰释无疑,庸兄与毛之友谊亦可以无损。如何之处,敬请钧裁,并盼示复。○震子。文。卅一.四.十二日晨一时发。

304. 宋子文致蒋介石请切催加派明了财政经济一般状况者来美电（1942 年 4 月 17 日）③

加码　呈委员长电　卅一.四.十七日

委座钧鉴:震子电计达钧览。际兹军事紧急,本不应以琐事烦渎,惟此次大借款成功,实赖美方对于钧座之信仰所致。今因福克斯来美时曾告毛财长④,一月十五日钧座面嘱转达毛财长,借款成功后,愿先与美方洽商有效之实施。据毛财长谓,我财部措施未顾及此点,故似有误会,并对我方宣布之办法,颇有批评。文离国日久,国内财政金融状况甚为隔膜,又不能作透切之解释,是以电请庸兄速派人来美,主持此类交涉及连络,文以外长地位,从旁帮助。顷接庸兄电,拟派席德懋⑤。文又电请除派一熟悉金融情形者外,加派明了财政经济一般状况者一人,如顾季高等同来布置,以后由席德懋驻此主持。即恳切催庸兄照办,并盼赐复。

---

① 即贝淞荪。
② 即顾翊群,字季高,时为国民政府财政部代理常务次长、外汇管理委员会委员。
③ 该电文已收入《中华民国重要史料初编》第三编战时外交(一),第347页。
④ 即摩根索,时任美国财政部部长。
⑤ 席德懋,字建侯,江苏吴县人,曾任财政部业务局、汇兑局总经理,时任财政部外汇管理委员会常务委员。

文。篠亥。

305．宋子文致蒋介石报告与霍普金斯会谈情形电(1942 年 4 月 22 日)

加码　呈委员长电　卅一．四．廿二日

委座钧鉴：顷晤霍布金①。据云，英国防卫印度之主力舰、飞机甚多，日似不致进犯，伦敦方面观察，敌如不侵印、澳，必以全力由缅、越攻华，应作充分准备。文答，最急最需要准备者为军械飞机，请美方赶速起运。霍又谓，关系中英苏美间各要事，急待商决者甚多，切望文能偕其赴渝，当面请示一切，再至英、苏。文意霍为总统最亲信之人，此举固甚重要，但文在此所洽办各事，无人继续进行，势恐停顿，故未肯定答复，但伊仍一再声述此行之必要。再，英国前拟借用运华飞机事，总统已径电钧座，并承抄阅。〇祃酉。文。三一．四．廿二

306．宋子文致蒋介石说明请派顾翊群等来美缘由电(1942 年 4 月 23 日)

加码　呈委员长电　卅一．四．廿三日

委座钧鉴：前奉□电，本拟遵达毛财长，因思毛为当局中最热心帮助中国者之一，如陈纳德义勇队之飞机，即由彼设法而来，此次借款，亦异常出力。筹思至再，似以不提为宜。且二万万元提用后，万一通货膨胀，未能收抑止之效，不久之将来我方或再有需彼援助之处。至文之请派顾季高等来美，完全欲使双方财部将复杂之内容，作彻底之了解，谅蒙钧察。文。

307．宋子文致蒋介石说明亟需得知缅战不利之因素电(1942 年 4 月 28 日)

D481　加码　呈委员长电　卅一．四．廿八日

委座钧鉴：缅战不利，深虑减低我国际地位，影响租借案及其他在美工作。是以文亟须得知战事不利之各重要因素，例如联军不能统一指挥，无空军掩护，缺少重炮及唐克车，运输困难给养不足，缅人倾向日敌，凡此种种，虽知其然，但无具体事实，以备做成合乎理智之报告，向美方当局声述。史梯威亲历其境，利害相阅，所知当更透彻，此事必能与我合作，设法使联合国间明了真象。即乞饬商赐复为祷。〇俭酉。文。卅一．四．二八

---

① 即霍普金斯(Harry L. Hopkins)，美国总统罗斯福的政治顾问。

308. 宋子文致蒋介石报告军械贷款效果极小请派人接各职务电(1942年4月)

呈委员长电

介兄赐鉴：自弟办理军械贷款，已满一年，而效果极小，只有六千万元之物品，推其原〈因〉：(一)去年初产量小求者多，大有僧多粥少之患。(二)马古德等美军官轻视中国抗战能力者甚多，时时有报告来此。(三)美国种种关系重视英俄战场，忽视我战场。(四)仰光未失以前，滇缅运量太小，加之奸人造谣，谓西南运输公司弊病极多，赖【例】如夹带私货等等，而污满【蔑】为弟暗中掌住该公司从中渔利。此弟屡次报告于兄。近来仰光已失，而交通更阻碍，新道路迟迟不进行，空运美方亦不得力，即缅甸印度亦有不保之虞，是以更有词可道。甚至有人提议已拨中国车械未装出，今欲提还。(五)美国船艘被沉者日多，海运日益困难。(六)国内以美国不能充分接济，而美方已谓美国帮忙不少，中国人尚有批评忘恩者，弟夹居其间，甚觉智尽力竭。至财政方面而言，弟初到四个月，因适之非但不能帮忙，种种不识大体，故弟坐冷班顿【板凳】四五个月，屡次有极危难之事，今大借款已成，而中国财部与美国财部应商洽之事仍不能上轨道。弟因种种无法解决各问题，故经夜不睡，常如此有误国家大事。弟来此已二年，自以为事事不能办通，只有呈请从速派人接各职务，是为至盼。

309. 宋子文致蒋介石坦陈美借款之运用未能尽善电(1942年5月2日)

加码　呈委员长电　卅一.五.二日

介兄赐鉴：近闻敌伪区经济状况，日有进步，华北伪钞比法币高八倍，华中亦高二三倍，我则物价有涨无已，情势蓄趋险恶。美借款之运用，未能尽善，效力等于画饼，以后如何得了。弟屡请派员来美，即欲使与美财部商定各项切实有效办法，以图挽救。顾季高为庸兄所信任，且熟悉国内财政金融情形，必能使中美财政关系更加密切，并互筹救急之方，立即见诸实行。席德懋来美国，固非无用，但其才具，恐不足应付。弟确因离国日久，深虑筹划不能周到，绝非避越位之嫌，遂涉推诿。力所能及，仍当竭诚相助。大局危矣，尤以财政关乎存亡，不容再瞻顾徘徊，因循度日，亦非空谈理论所能挽此颓波。弟为此激直之言，或不为人所谅，惟望兄鉴其赤忱，知我苦心耳。弟〇手稿。

310. 宋子文致蒋介石指出经济状况日趋危殆函(1942年5月2日)

委座钧鉴：我国经济状况，日趋危殆。闻沦陷区反较优于我，长此以往，对于军民抗战心理，影响殊匪浅鲜。瞻念前途，杞忧何极。美机此次轰炸东京，收效甚伟。不久空中炮垒来华后，应令先轰炸上海，尤以破坏电力厂为上着，使敌伪金融中心区域发生恐怖，停滞活动，并同时轰炸南京、广州等都市。此亦破坏敌伪金融中心之一策。较之轰炸东京，于我效力更大。愚意所及，谨此奉陈，当乞参酌。敬请钧安。文。

311. 宋子文致蒋介石报告福克斯来美一切颇为尽力函稿(1942年5月2日)

呈委员长函稿　卅一.五.二日　福克斯带渝

委座钧鉴：福克斯君来美，一切颇为尽力，多所协助，不愧为中国好友。回华后，对我国财政金融问题，贡献必多，当乞特赐咨询。托其带呈借款签字摄影一帧，伏希赐存。再，美国空中炮垒廿五架，定本月十五日分批起程飞往我国，六月间可开始工作。黄秉衡①同行。敬颂均安。○○○谨呈。

312. 宋子文致蒋介石报告本日太平洋军事会议情形电(1942年5月5日)

D503　加码　呈委员长电　卅一.五.五日

委座钧鉴：本日开太平洋军事会议，总统报告：

（一）英国占领法属麻达加斯加②岛经过；

（二）美海军在太平洋西南，近建奇功，详情尚未接报，云云。

文提以空运接济中国军械，为世界战事重要关键之一，无论如何牺牲，必须达到目的，拟请以空中炮垒改为运输机，由印度阿拉哈巴特③直达叙府④或成都。众一致赞成，并竭力鼓动。惟据美空军报告，技术问题，尚须研究。每次载重，恐不能多。总统命霍布金、航空署、空军司令与文共同讨论，结果续陈。微申。文。

卅一.五.五

---

① 黄秉衡，浙江余姚人，时任中国驻美大使馆空军武官。

② 即马达加斯加(Madagascar)，位于印度洋西南部，1896年沦为法国殖民地。1942年初，英军发动马达加斯加登陆战并占领该岛，以防止其为日军所利用。

③ 阿拉哈巴特(Allahabad)，印度北部城市，中印空中运输通道(驼峰航线)的印方起点之一。

④ 即今四川省宜宾市，抗战时期中印空中运输通道(驼峰航线)的中方起点之一。

313. 宋子文致蒋介石报告本日开会讨论飞机运输事项电(1942 年 5 月 6 日)①

加码　呈委员长电　卅一.五.六日

密呈委座钧鉴：微申电计达钧览。本日开会讨论飞机运输事，结果拟即拨空中炮垒五十架，专为输送援华军货之用。惟因塞地亚机场不久或为敌轰炸，故须由阿拉哈巴特直飞叙府，途程来往二千八百英里，每次只能装运三吨，每月只能运一千五百吨。原定拨定之一百架马达机，拟仍照拨，或可运一千五百吨。共计三千吨。如一切无阻碍，六、七月间运量可达到此数。最紧要者为加强叙府飞机场，俾四马达飞机可随时起落。到叙府后，可沿江运至重庆，较成都为便利也。再，据由缅退至加尔各答之美军官告陈长桐谓，曾派飞机接史梯威赴印，史不愿擅离，仍率副官数人居重围中云云。史氏临难不苟，不失军人本色，惟思史氏其他更重要任务尚多，如空军援华、中印空运、军货接济等等，均赖其筹维，虽有马古德等可代，必不能为力。钧座可否以命令着其回渝，尚乞权衡轻重，赐予考虑。此并非美方授意，合并陈明。叙府机场现状，仍乞速示。○麻戌。卅一.五.六

314. 宋子文致蒋介石提议以命令着史迪威回渝电(1942 年 5 月 6 日)

加码　呈委员长电　卅一.五.六日

据由缅退至加尔加答之美军官告陈长桐谓，曾派飞机接史梯威赴印，史不愿擅离，仍率副官数人居重围中，云云。史氏临难不苟，不失军人本色，惟思史氏其他更重要任务尚多，如空军援华、中印空运、军货接济等，均赖其筹维。虽有马古德等可代，必不能为力。钧座可否以命令著其回渝，尚乞权衡轻重，赐予考虑。此并非美方授意，合并陈明。叙府机场现状，仍乞速示。○麻戌。卅一.五.六

315. 宋子文致蒋介石请查明罗卓英离军队遁宝山事实电(1942 年 5 月 9 日)

急

军部密告，接史梯威电，罗卓英②离军队遁宝山。余谓难以置信云云。事实请钧

---

① 该电文已收入《中华民国重要史料初编》第三编战时外交(一)，第 496～497 页。

② 罗卓英，字尤青、幼青，广东大埔人，时任中国入缅甸远征军第一路军司令长官。

座查明指示。

316. 宋子文致蒋介石报告美驻华大使致海军总司令密呈内容函稿(1942 年 5 月 15 日)

黄秉衡带呈

呈委员长函稿　卅一.五.十五

委座钧鉴：天翼①兄抵美后,文特向总统及各重要当局介绍,并竭力推动,参加英美联合参谋团会议。迄今尚无端倪,百思不得其故。项由至友秘密交阅海军情报处将美驻华大使高斯电酌要呈海军总司令,对于天翼兄及其随员语多误解,进行不能顺利或由于此。兹将英文抄件及译文随函附呈,伏乞垂察。至如何应付之处,并恳训示祗遵。敬请钧安。

译文

密呈海军总司令

事由：中国陆海军军官团(摘录高斯大使一九四二年三月十一日第二一七号来文)

我驻华大使来文,闻于中国驻华盛顿陆海军军官团之预示,对该团与我海军部磋商重要问题之时,颇有参考价值,兹摘录要点如下：

中国方面消息,据私人意见,以为该团人选,有辱使命,殊属不幸。

军官团团长熊式辉中将,昔受训练于日本,在中国陆军中资望亦不高,并未切实参加中国抗战。彼政务官及政客之成份,较多于军人。传闻一九三七以前,彼已偏向与日本妥协,并极力反共。军官团参谋长徐培根②少将,过去有倾向法西斯嫌疑,且于一九三五年购买飞机时,有处置不当之嫌。金镇③少将、蔡文治④上校,均无资望,碌碌无闻。

我驻华陆军参赞认为,如重庆所传,该团来美为参加重要军事计划之讨论,但以蒋委员长所派人选之性质资格观之,显见对于该团,并未重视,即在中国人方面,亦作如是观也。

---

① 即熊式辉,字天翼,江西安义人,时任中国驻美军事代表团团长。
② 徐培根,字石城,浙江象山人,时任中国驻美军事代表团参谋长。
③ 金镇,又名岱峰,辽宁辽阳人,军训部炮兵副监,时为中国驻美军事代表团成员。
④ 蔡文治,字定武,湖北黄冈人,时为中国驻美军事代表团成员,同年秋升任代理团长。

317. 宋子文致蒋介石提议务请命史迪威来渝详商各点电(1942 年 5 月 19 日)

加码　呈委员长电　卅一.五.十九

委座钧鉴：本日午后见空军参长亚诺①，告以既谓双马达运输机足可应用，今以两星期为试办，期间如成绩不佳，仍须照拨四马达飞机，等语。

史梯威不久抵印，务请命其来渝详商：

(一)中印空运每月最少吨位及运输机种类；

(二)我需要之驱逐机及轰炸机；

(三)中国派军入印训练及军械配备详细计划等等。

盖美军部以史梯威有全权，每有所商请，辄以史梯威并未要求，为不负责任推诿之词，谈及空运亦然。是以此后史梯威应令常依左右，遇事随时饬办，勿使远驻印度，否则种种计划进行愈感延滞。伏乞钧裁。○皓申。卅一.五.十九

318. 宋子文致蒋介石报告美情报局人员拟前往我内地以婉词拒绝为宜函稿(1942 年 5 月 20 日)

黄秉衡带呈　呈委员长函稿　卅一.五.廿日

委座钧鉴：美情报局近拟酌派人员，前往我国内地青海、甘肃、西康、陕西、四川一带旅行考察，归史梯威将军节制指挥，请文准予发给许可证。惟推想，此类人员，名为考察农村，实为政治侦探性质，若任其深入腹地，滋弊滋多，将来报告，难免不实不尽，淆乱听闻，于我对美工作，必多窒碍。中美各事往还，向来开诚布公，互无猜疑，惟所派此项人员，是否适当，无法证明，亦无从查考。与其日后发生枝节，莫若先事防维。文已告以既归史将军指挥，应由史氏在渝直接办理。如有人向钧座请求，亦以婉词拒绝为宜，尚乞垂察。敬颂钧安。谨上。附呈美情报局节略译文。

319. 宋子文致蒋介石密陈轰炸上海电力公司及仿制敌伪纸币函稿(1942 年5 月 20 日)

致委员长函稿　卅一.五.廿日

委座钧鉴：敌寇在南太平洋地区，一时获得胜利，自东北四省至荷属，丰富资源，

---

① 亚诺(Henry H. Arnold)，亦译作安诺得、安诺德，时任美国空军(隶属于陆军)司令。

尽归掌握,帝国经济主义势力,日见膨胀。若长此任其猖狂,为患更无底止,于我更为不利。昨谒总统时,曾熟商对付之策,在我国有两事可办:

一、上海为敌伪金融枢纽,故敌寇不加破坏,即英美技术人员,亦未多骚扰。而沪市工商业之维持,十之七八,赖有美国人所办之电力公司。若能设法摧毁,不独摇动敌伪人心,亦足破坏其经济重心。总统极为赞同,已电白赖顿①由印度派轰炸队,相机施行轰炸(或须在成都附近加油)。

二、敌伪纸币价值日高,拟于此间仿制,运回中国,援予游击队,至各沦陷区散发,亦足扰乱其金融。总统甚以为然。文俟贝淞孙寄来各种伪钞样本,即可进行。谨此密陈,钧察专承。敬请崇安。谨上。月　日

320. 宋子文拟呈蒋介石请电示各兵工厂急需材料电稿(1942年5月20日)

拟呈委员长电　另缮发5/20

观察日寇动态,最近或将在我国各处大举骚扰。各兵工厂需一方面积极开工,一方面将各厂自七月起最低限度之急需材料项目及数量电示,以资设法空运。文。职江杕谨拟。五.十八

321. 宋子文致蒋介石请告史迪威日军企图并派飞机来华助战电(1942年5月20日)②

皓申电计达钧鉴。近来美国运印度飞机及各种武器甚多。史抵印应与魏佛尔洽商雨季后恢复缅甸计划。同时,钧座派员告其日敌目前在中国企图,例如集中大量飞机于武汉。史一方面可训令Bereton③由印度派飞机轰炸汉口等机场及增派驱逐机来华助战。陈纳德队飞机到华数量尚少,如何策动军部多派,因军部每以在印度、中国运输及战斗机皆归史负责调遣。如何,盼复。

322. 宋子文致蒋介石报告本日太平洋会议情形电(1942年5月27日)

(一)本日太平洋会议,总统将三妹至【致】居里电诵读,谓,据电三师突围,惟兵

---

①　白赖顿(Lewis H. Bereton),即浦立顿,时任驻印度的美国空军第十航空队司令。
②　该电文已收入《中华民国重要史料初编》第三编战时外交(三),第594页。
③　Bereton,即同前注之白赖顿(Lewis H. Bereton)。

士饿死甚多,何以竟然为此。文谓,第五军经无人烟之道突围,日本广播缅甸作战,始终虏四百廿名,足证我军宁死不降。总统继谓:史梯威上星期五要求Bereton①之第十大队归其指挥。事出仓卒,未曾与英方协商,即已调动,惟此后当派其他飞机队至印度【增】防。此事昨已电蒋委员长。至此后第十大队如何调动,史梯威归蒋委员长节制,当无问题。再,第十大队不久可补充足数。(二)莫洛托夫大约明晚可到。(三)日海军集中,有攻 Aleutian Island② 或苏 Kam-chatka③ 模样。(四)荷大使谓,得报告,日本售树胶于苏联。(五)海军部报告,苏船每月有十艘左右装粮食等粗品由美西部至西比利亚,其不装军械,恐与日方有谅解。等语。文。

323. 宋子文致蒋介石代拟霍普金斯访华邀请函稿电(1942 年 5 月 27 日)

急

霍布金决愿来华一行,约文请钧座电总统邀请。兹敬代拟稿如下:缅甸被日敌占领,敌急攻滇浙及准备赣湘豫各处陆空军大举进攻。抗战已入最危险状态,其困难情形为五年所未有。余有极要事与阁下面商,若不能成行,可否请派霍布金来华,俾得转达阁下意见及明了余各种问题。如蒙赞成,文当面提总统。查总统每有极重要事,如首次帮英械资及苏德战争开始而美国各方对援苏多有反对者,总统派霍布金前赴。今抗战入最危险阶级,而利用寻常轨道不足以达到美方全力来帮中国时,兹有此举。当否。

324. 宋子文致蒋介石提议向美要求 DC4 式四马达运输机电(1942 年 5 月 28 日)④

沁电　5/28

委座钧鉴:昨电计达。得谢总统拨第十大队飞机来华助战时,可否告总统,两个马达飞机由印度运输至中国,其过去成绩量甚少,如不愿将空中炮垒改为运输机,闻美方自六月至九月间出 DC - 4 四个马达运输飞机十五架,请将此数全拨中印运输应急,等语。同时将此意告史梯威。据军部友人密告,此机英国及陆、

空军均竞索,惟在中国特殊情形之下,或可拨中国。

325. 宋子文致蒋介石报告史迪威诸项意见电(1942 年 5 月)

致委座电

史梯威昨告文在印度代表:

(一) 在中国境内为有效之利用租借案物品,须先整理军队之供应机关,及训练中国军队用新式武器。

(二) 空运能力几有限,是以当先尽力供给轰炸及驱逐队之需要。

(三) 空中炮垒改为运输机,彼视为太可惜。

(四) 美国驱逐队轰炸队已接命令加入中国战争。

(五) 渠反对英方借用原供中国飞机队之飞机,并已请军部【?】比较 P-43 更优之飞机。

(六) 应整备中英夹攻缅甸,重开运输大道。

(七) 钧座需要大运输机,抵渝后拨。

文现已电史:美方供给中国每月三千五百吨军械,系简单之炮,如山炮,及必须之七九子弹及兵工材料。此急不待迫,为钧座所噶望。且空运美国有能力扩充至四马达轰炸机,改为运输机当然可惜,惟过去二个马达运输机载量成绩不佳,且印度大雨季已到,在此时期两个马达机不能达到远距之飞行。为维持军民心,不得不用四个马达飞机。且据余所知,美方此牺牲,非不能负起。云云。

326. 宋子文致蒋介石报告太平洋会议讨论朝鲜问题情形电(1942 年 5 月)

本日太平洋会议,总统出席,不举开会形式。总统解释划分区域制,大致已前电报告,预备性质下星期二讨论:

(甲) 澳新防日军事计划。

(乙) 朝鲜问题。总统欲文提出计划,如何运用朝鲜人扰乱日敌,并附带东三省组织义勇军问题。

关于此事请示者钧座者。

(一) 钧座是否赞成由太平洋会议各国或中美两国发宣言,主张朝鲜独立,已决定瓜分日本帝国之政策,而在苏联未能参加表示前发表之。

(二) 朝鲜国内秘密工作团体有无确实力量,是否与苏联有关,钧座愿在渝指导,统制其革命力量,并派员秘密赴朝鲜活动。

　　(三) 美国愿以械款助其革命,牵制日军。应如何进行,统请速复。

　　(四) 东义美助,有何方法?

327. 宋子文致蒋介石报告与美商洽空运计划电(1942 年 5 月)

缅甸情形不妥。文拟与美方商洽,由其包办运用四个马达大飞机由 Allahabad① 直飞 Likiang②、叙府。每月开始运五千吨,第四个月每月运七千五百吨,第六个月每月运一万吨。顷已与 CDS③ 各组商洽。三千吨为大炮、炮弹及子弹,飞机用油及零件一千二百吨,药品三百吨,汽车零件二百吨,无线电机零件等等三百吨,兵工材料及普通汽油等一切无法用。此在无可办法中设法焉。至二个马达飞机一百架,如能航运,仍可继续运用,不在此计划中。请即设法扩大 Likiang 及叙府飞机场,为四个马达机即空中炮垒用,两个机场现状情形如何,请即告知。
内建四马达机场,二千五百万平方尺面积。四千尺长、二百尺宽之跑道,夜间起落设备、油库设备、一切维护必要设备

328. 宋子文致蒋介石提议就缅战失利向英美交涉电(1942 年 5 月)

致委座电

缅甸战事失利,主要毅因,英国不能彻底合作。但:(一)战后我尚须用印度为军械及飞机空中运输站;(二)英美两国生死有关,战后虽别道而驰,在战事时期不能分开。故我如公然向英国责难,反失美国当局之同情。文愚见,趁此时由钧座秘密电总统及邱吉尔,直说过去缅甸战事上之错误,其语词可严正而不带火气,并以中国之被累,要求:(甲)英美即派大批飞机来华助战;(乙)英美中即策划雨季后反攻缅甸,夺回仰光,恢复中国与国际交通线。史梯威将抵印,请总统与邱吉尔责任其与魏佛尔会商计划后,飞渝决定。文。

329. 宋子文致蒋介石请约史迪威来渝商洽诸事电(1942 年 5 月)④

午后见航空参谋总长。其试办两个星期,试用两个马达运输飞机。如成绩不佳,

---

①　Allahabad,即阿拉哈巴特,印度北部城市。

②　Likiang,即丽江,位于中国云南省。

③　CDS,即 1941 年 5 月宋子文在美国注册成立的中国国防物资供应公司(China Defense Supplies Inc.)。

④　本电稿与第 317 号原稿意思相近,日期和少量文字有不同,仍予收入。

仍须拨四个马达。

史梯威不久抵印,请钧座约其来渝详细商洽:

1. 中印空运事,每月最少吨位及运输飞机种类;

2. 我需要之驱逐机及轰炸机;

3. 中国在印度训练军队及配置军械详细计划。

因美军部方面每以史梯威有全权或史梯威并未要求,作为不负责推托之词,例如谈及空运,则谓此系史之责任。再,此后史梯威应长驻钧座左右,不可远驻印度,否则种种计划无法进行。

330. 宋子文致蒋介石报告与罗斯福会谈情形电(1942 年 6 月 1 日)

卅电奉悉,本日持钧座电谒总统。总统谓:亟欲派人来华,惟霍①素来有病,长期飞行必不能支持。除霍外,任何人蒋委员长愿其赴华可派往,陆②、外长③年老,副总统④、海长⑤等均无不可。文谓,霍为总统最忠实之友,且眼光远大,可贯彻总统对于我国盛意,舍霍君实难有适当人负此重任。继总统谓:莫洛托夫来此谈接济苏联各问题,余顺便告:(一)余对于战后中美英俄当负永久解除德意日武装,世界之治安由四国负担。(二)各弱小民族应自决自主,如有某国如越南、缅甸等民族不能即刻自主,亦当有集团 trustee⑥,不能再有殖民地。莫洛托夫颇以为是。蒋委员长有便可发表此主张,以获亚洲人民同情。盖中国作战非仅为中国本身作战。(三)日本主力舰队已向北开,接触期恐不远矣。

谒总统,见霍。彼谓,经大开刀后,体确甚弱,惟不致如总统所谈之险,此时极紧要,不能以个人之身命为问题,愿亲向总统陈述,惟坚欲文偕往。钧座前有电令勿离华府,欲适之偕来。彼谓,适之太空洞,此次愿牺牲其本人之健康安全,无非欲与钧座解决战事后中美诸大问题,且用包机来华,往返只需三个星期。文谓,本人极愿偕来,惟仍须请示钧座。查霍在美国为第二重要人,文来此经长时期方得其信仰,最近半年交谊极深兄弟,是以此次如其来华,当能多多在旁协助。盖美国军部对中国之见解,多不能明了,渝军官团⑦报告多有貌【藐】视我实力,此

① 即霍普金斯(Harry L. Hopkins),时任美国总统罗斯福的政治顾问。

② 即时任美国陆军部长的史汀生(Henry L. Stimson)。

③ 即时任美国国务卿的赫尔(Cordell Hull)。

④ 即时任美国副总统的华莱士(Henry Wallace)。

⑤ 即时任美国海军部长的诺克斯(Frank Knox)。

⑥ 即主张由四大国对尚不能进行民族自决的国家进行国际托管。

⑦ 指由马格鲁德(John Magruder)领衔前往中国考察的美国军事代表团。

次如有负政治重要地位人,能纠正其见解,否则对于械弹飞机及空中运输难有完满之解决。

331. 宋子文致蒋介石密告美军部接各种报告于我不利电(1942年6月2日)

致委座电

最密。托古达程亲交委座。

自缅甸失利后,美军部接各种报告,以中国军队无战斗力量,各军官各自打算。马古德对中国素为不佳,今据报告未得史梯威同意托病归国,必于我不利。史梯威本为陆军部推重中国派者,闻近亦不满意,故军部对中国似比较不如前热忱。文皓申电请钧座在史梯威回渝后与其决定各要点,分别详告,以便与军部接洽。再,本日关于通盘需要之飞机及巧电向军部提出之军械紧急空运之计划。①

332. 宋子文致蒋介石孔祥熙报告与摩根索会谈情形电(1942年6月2日)

加码　致委座孔部长电

顷毛财长约见。据云,斐列普②来述英新借款,因本身力量问题,只可以战事时期为限,希美方谅解等语。财长答以此乃中英两国关系,不表示意见。非【斐】复谓,平衡款项需要五百五十万镑,除平衡基金存有二百八十万镑外,缺二百七十万镑,该款不愿意在英新借款内提用,征求美方意见如何,毛财长欲征求文意见。文谓,英借款如限于战时用,中国方面当然希望用之,以补不足之二百八十万镑,如英不允,则只可由美国之平衡基金,但此事余不甚接头,当电钧座等指示。如何,盼复。

333. 宋子文致蒋介石报告美当局对中国战事情报有不可靠之评电(1942年6月3日)

致委座电

美国陆海空军当局对中国战事情报渐有不可靠之评,海军部有训令所属各机关,此后对重庆宣传式之情报,不必注意云云。文。

---

① 以下文稿断。
② 即菲利普(Sir Frederick Phillips),时为英国财政部次长,曾担任中英平准基金借款英方谈判代表。

334. 宋子文致蒋介石请饬各机关对于宣传敌施用毒气慎重注意电(1942年6月12日,附宋子文注)

D619　呈委员长电　卅一.六.十二

委座钧鉴:九日渝发言人称,敌用毒气八百次云。一般人多以为此类情报不近情理。总统对施用毒气已经切实严厉警告。嗣后敌如再用毒气,最好证据确实,或使友邦军官医士目睹死伤惨状,始足以激发友邦公愤;或实行报复手段,则反足使警告失其效力。尚乞饬各机关发言人对于宣传敌施用毒气万分慎重注意。〇震。卅一.六.十二

[宋子文在该电报开头加注:如常此报告敌施用毒气而不供给确实证据,友邦不能置信。]

335. 宋子文致蒋介石提议与史迪威商谈各点电(1942年6月12日)

D623　急　加码　呈委员长电　卅一.六.十二日

委座钧鉴:综合各方消息,中印空运,六、七、八三个月,每月只能运五百吨。质之美空军参谋长,则推诿为史梯威之责任。向总统陈说,亦谓史梯威为钧座参长,诸事可由钧座命令。文巧、效、卅、冬、蒸各电,请与史切实商决(甲)中印空运计划;(乙)中美在华空军计划;(丙)国内及赴印陆军计划及附带军械问题等等。始终未蒙详细示复与史梯威商办之结果。美方因缅路断绝,已将拨给中国之十余万吨械料大部分收回。故商定最低限度每个月紧急输运三千五百吨军械,已于巧电详陈。但中印空运,如每月只运五百吨,则此项计划亦必为取消。文追随钧座二十年,必知其素性憨直,绝非意存推诿,更不愿敷衍因循。事实如此,不得不一再哓渎。即请钧座明白示知,钧座对史梯威感想如何,文各电所列问题,是否已与其商洽,有何困难。美方认定接济中国,必须史梯威商承钧座之后,来电证实,始克有济。是以文必须明了钧座对史之感想及史对我之态度,始可设法相机应付也。〇震酉。文。卅一.六.十二

336. 蒋介石致宋子文指示下次太平洋会议提案电(1942年6月14日)

委员长来电　卅一.六.十四

下次太平洋作战会议提案如下:德国为陆军国家,英美欲以优势之海空军力,先击败德国,势必费力多成功少。反之,日本战斗力与其国家命脉所系者乃为海

军,英美海空军力量较强,两面作战应先击破其最弱环,亦为兵略上不易之原则。现苏德在欧陆相持,实力充足,英美在大西洋战局亦已稳定,且欧区开辟第二战场之时机尚早,大西洋战局已经巩固,则英美尤其美国宜乘此时机运用优势之海空军先击破日本,消灭其向东北太平洋急击之野心,以巩固美国西岸之防务。观于日本最近在中途岛、阿留申岛之举动,可见如不先解决日本,则日对美始终可取攻势。且英美不取主动,日本即可坐大,则整个作战期中,美国始终限于两洋作战被动。若日本扩张其在东北太平洋扰乱之范围,则美国西岸防务更蒙不利影响。现时美国实为整个反侵略阵营之枢纽,美国之安危利害即全体盟邦之安危利害所托。余实就全局观察,毫不为中国利害而作此主张。余意无论从盟国整个战略与政略上言,对日本日益扩张之海上行动均必集中全力,以主动攻势先予以制命打击不可。如照以往先解决德国则日本不成问题,或日本虽败德国仍能挽回形势之观念,证以最近战事经过,实非修正不可。盖必先击破轴心弱点之日本,以绝后患,而后可专心对德。反之,若予日本以坐大之势,且使之以弱小兵力牵制我盟邦中心势力之美国,不仅贻误解决德国日期,而徒陷于逐两兔者不能获得一兔之大害,且使战事无限延期,最后仍必循先击破弱点而后再图强者之途径。何不早日修正之? 为得计,切望同意余之建议,速收太平洋上主动之战略。

337. 宋子文致孔祥熙并抄呈蒋介石商讨中美平衡基金借款不再展期电 (1942 年 6 月 16 日)

孔部长勋鉴并抄呈委员长：文电奉悉。蒙示一九四一年五千万美金平衡基金借款协定拟不再展期,细绎各项理由,是有可商讨之处。呈询鄙见,择要胪陈。

一、中外外汇平衡基金,肇端于中英四银行协定①。当时上海金融市场仍占重要地位,而维持法币对外汇率,为安定金融主要之图。中英平衡基金之成立,于维持法币信用,功不可没,惟数目有限,不敷维持汇率之需要。弟抵美后,首即从事与美财部商讨平衡基金借款事宜,及一九四一年四月中美、中英两协定,始获同时成立。

二、中美平衡基金借款协约,自美总统宣布决定借款起,至协定签字止,历五阅月之久,其间讨论细目,煞费经营。又以美方坚持分期拨款,旁生枝节。蒙委座

---

① 指 1939 年 3 月签订的《设立中国国币平准汇兑基金合同》,该合同由中国银行、交通银行代表中国国民政府与英国汇丰银行、麦加利银行在伦敦签订。

电示机宜,幸得克服种种困难。其经过情形,均在兄洞鉴之中。尊电所称:(甲)随时可片面取消合同一点,系因美对我借款,其来源为美本国平衡基金之一部,美议会通过本国平衡基金原案时,附带期限,而展期之权,操之议会,故在法律立场上,美财部与我成立协定,不得不预订取消办法。(乙)我国所收外汇均须归入平准会尽先使用一点,原约似无此项规定。(丙)平衡会决议须有外人同意一点,谅系指该会决议案须有四人以上同意方得通过而言。平衡外汇,需专门智识、专门经验,利用美英专家技术上之协助,于我似亦不无裨益。

三、太平洋战事发生,沪港相继沦陷,局势丕变。我以交通阻塞,对外商务几全断绝,外汇需要不复存在,而法币价值与外汇汇率失去关联,平衡外汇,已非当务之急。中美、中英两借款之未充分动用,其理由即在于此。但将来战后建设,我需大量外资,而外汇之稳定,实为外国政府或人民向我投资之主要先决条件。且现时国内物价高度膨胀,战后货币之整顿,如须外力协助,则现有外汇平衡基金委员会之机构,或能任重要联络工作之使命。

四、国际平衡基金计划,此刻正由我代表与美方讨论之中,将来各国平衡外汇,或可由国际机构负协助之责任。其中美、中英两协定,是否能在国际机构之外继续存在,实有问题。但就国际立场言,我国仅为需要协助国家之一,而战后真能有羡余财力助我建设之国家,仅一美国。我国经济,已因历次借款与美发生特殊关系,如由我自动将已成之局一一推翻,以后再商单独援助,深恐不易为力。

五、弟对美折冲,竭尽棉薄,数年于兹,劳怨毁誉,无所容心,徒以兹事关系国家经济之前途,未敢缄默。

统希亮察。

338. 宋子文致蒋介石报告与史汀生专谈史迪威问题电(1942年6月16日)

急 加码 呈委员长电 卅一.六.十六日

委座钧鉴:删电敬悉。适陆长特约专谈史梯威问题。文谓:蒋委员长以入缅华军归史指挥,直为历史上空前之举,与美国以陆军交苏俄军官指挥,同其困难。君前亦告我,第一次欧战时,有人提议美军添入英军作战,几酿成两国间极大误会。史汀生急谓,蒋公有此非常果断,故美方更愿十二分尽力帮助。又云:余与参谋总长均认史梯威为第一流战将,美军官中无出其右,故特派充蒋公参谋长。但余等崇拜蒋委员长及爱护中国之热切,不能以对史个人感情为比例,如蒋公以为史不适当,务请直言无隐,俾得更换其他将领,决不因此发生丝毫意见。因余阅蒋公暨夫人来电语气,觉对史虽好,但无十分信任之表示,即请阁下转达余意,并盼蒋公诚恳之达【答】复。云云。

文意,钧座顾全大局之苦心,为中外所共见,但如史梯威确不能共事,不妨此时乘机直说。如鉴于马古德辈一般美军官之前例,恐仍换汤不换药,则钧座似可表示对史梯威因甚信任,但对其见解当然不能事事俯从。如此,一方面不伤感情,一方面可留他日地步。陆长等既自动有另调之意,且自总统以次,均认史为钧座部属地位,钧座尽可照部属指挥命令之,不必以上宾相待,但善为利用其地位,以推动美军部充量之接济。愚见谨陈备考。○铣酉。文。卅一.六.十六

339. 宋子文致蒋介石密陈中国战区需要飞机等五项建议电(1942年6月16日)

急　加码　呈委员长电　卅一.六.十六日

委座钧鉴:删电承示。与史梯威商议各点,谨陈管见如下:

(一)美方决在澳洲维持一千架飞机之美国空军,中国战区立刻需要五百架,确非奢望。

(二)中印运输,按美方能力,足可在三个月内即达到每月五千吨之数无疑,根据以往经验,如以六个月达成此数,其结果反恐遥遥无期。可否请钧座即饬史梯威速电军部,将一、二两项,提早在三个月内完成我所定标准之数,并须详细估计各式战斗机、驱逐机、轰炸机每月作战之平均损失,以便补充。再,逐月应拨之运输机,亦应一并声明。此项计划,请商定后速示。

(三)顷闻军部以目前空运能力,月只四百吨,故将商定七月起每月三千五百吨之紧急空运军械减为四百吨云。文拟严厉交涉。运输能力如此之劣,完全为美方责任。补救办法,在扩增空运能力,不能反减少我最低限度军械之数量。七月份装运之军械,九、十月间方能到印度东部。应照预定计划,逐月增加空运能力,务使足以载运此数。恳请钧座饬史亦电军部。

(四)文迄未与史梯威通电,以后有事商办,拟与其直接通电。由三妹转办,事或更迅捷顺利,但对于应付外卿,不知有无不便。请示遵。

(五)顷与陆长谈,彼对美军赴印助我克复缅甸,颇为心动。查打通缅甸,为我异日反攻之先决条件,此举且更能于战后应付英国及苏联,似有相当价值。乞考虑。

统祈赐复。○谏戌。文。卅一.六.十六

340. 宋子文致蒋介石报告本日太平洋会议情形电(1942 年 6 月 17 日)

致委座电

本日太平洋会议,菲律滨总统开始参加会议。总统谓:(一) 接史梯威电,二个马达飞机已开始,中印航运无阻。文谓,惜成绩不佳,数个月至今仅五百吨。总统闻之骇然,饬即查明报告确实吨位。可见美方向元首报告,亦不恳实。下次会议当再催询。(二) 日敌在东北增兵,彼已去电史丹林。美方所得消息,敌有攻海参威或 Kamchatka 模样。(三) 苏在积极进行商洽西比利亚运输道。(四) 德意对英美警告勿用毒气宣言,实为准备自己开始用毒气,故我联盟国对于敌施用毒气宣传最好谨慎。继谓,敌确对中国军队施用毒气。例如,在缅甸中国某师进攻时敌佯退而施用庇【砒】霜毒气,致中国军队有损失。(五) 参谋本部谓,文提出之轰炸上海电力厂,以其研究,并不如攻日本各兵工厂之紧要。文谓,攻上海电力厂之意义有二:(一) 上海目标,可由成都飞机场为根据地,日本之部因衢洲【州】机场被陷,不易工作;(二) 上海确为敌经济侵略重心,并为日敌对中国军需总站,上海摇动,足以影响其金融。结论此事,请蒋委员长考核,交史梯威执行。文。

341. 宋子文致蒋介石提议对英派空军来华表示欢迎电(1942 年 6 月 18 日)

英亚洲司长前来表示,中英间隔阂为患。文谓,此事非空言能补救,英方最好自动派轰炸机来华参战,等语,并电少川①授意艾登②。顷接少川电,英已决定派轰炸一队来参战。其数虽小,但英首次派空军来华,盼钧座表示欢迎。文。

342. 宋子文致蒋介石报告美军部询日准备攻西伯利亚有无确切消息电 (1942 年 6 月 19 日)

致委座电

军部询我方,关于日敌准备攻西比利亚模样有确实消息否。文。

---

① 即顾维钧,字少川,时任中国驻英国大使。
② 艾登(Anthony Eden),时任英国外交大臣。

343. 宋子文致蒋介石报告美方对中方加强空运要求处理情形电(1942 年 6 月 20 日)

加码　呈委员长电　卅一.六.廿日

委座钧鉴:

(一)顷得军部消息,钧座要求之四马达运输机十五架,另空中炮垒改为运输机十架,正考虑拨给时,接驻渝印人员报告目前状况,至多只能有效运用双马达机十七架,故决定只拨双马达机十七架,定七月一日飞华,云云。窃查此电与钧座意旨不符,或出于双方未接洽之故,步骤不一,致此结果。钧座已与史梯威商定数月内达到每月空运五千吨之计划,彼方何以尚有此报告,请直接探询史梯威,以明真象。

(二)钧座与史商定维持每月空运五千吨,及前线五百架战斗机,军部似亦未接史梯威切实之报告。

(三)奉钧电,始知白赖顿第十大队轰炸机只到华五架,而总统一个月前已饬令全部赴华。

以上三事均足证明美驻华军官团与我方缺乏联系。焦虑万分,应如何补救改善之处,恳即饬筹速办,并乞指示。〇号。文。卅一.六.廿

344. 宋子文致蒋介石宋美龄报告与居里谈对华空军援助情形电(1942 年 6 月 22 日)

新加码　致蒋委员长、蒋夫人电　卅一.六.廿二日

介兄、三妹惠鉴:昨日太平洋会议散会后,各报访员纷纷探询经过。各代表所答均抱乐观,文则独异其词,直告以本日会议我要求英美空军援助。记者问满意否,答以此则有关军事秘密,恕不奉告。斯言意在言外,颇堪寻味。总统果于昨晚召见居里,并命其赴华,意在解释。居里来晤,文告以此行殊可不必,中国所急切需要者,为实际行动之援助,至代美国向中国解释其困难之工作,余与阁下已努力一年余,空言何补,徒劳往返而已。今以空军一事而言,(一)黄秉衡同行之空中炮垒廿四架,原来赴华,中途应英人之请,改派地中海作战;(二)轻轰炸机六十二架,八个月前已允即行拨给,因珍珠港之变,减为卅三架,今亦决派往地中海;(三)原派担任中印运输之双马达运输机十七架,前电已奉告,顷亦改赴地中海;(四)白赖顿抵渝,蒋委员长召见,据称未奉史梯威之命,故不见,似系托词规避,此第十大队想亦有改派地中海之企图。事实如此,解释何益?为中美之关

系,总统应给余确切实施不移之空军援助方案,然后君再讨论赴中国之行,并许其将此意转告总统。等语。文今日致三妹英文电,转请介兄与史梯威商定空军援助及空运计划,务请俯准从速施行,急电示复,以便在此间严催照办。总统对文友谊,或与家人无异,无话不谈,不拘形迹,称名去姓,亲切可知。但国家危殆若此,绝不容以私人感情稍涉苟且因循。再,三妹此后勿与居里通电,以免彼方视机利用,在文急进之间,从事延宕。为国家计,一切由文代表相机交涉。我方步伐齐一,缓急轻重,权衡得宜,或可稍有实效。如何,即请核定示复。再,如美方有征求派居里之电,请答复与文就地商酌。文。

345. 宋子文致蒋介石报告本日太平洋会议情形电(1942年6月25日)①

本日太平洋会议,总统谓,日本有航空母舰十二,今已损失五艘,足见日敌空中力量渐减,至 Aleutian 群岛战事,无重要性,继请邱吉尔发表意见。邱谓:太平洋方面战局,已较上次来华府时好转:星加坡伦【沦】陷后,敌以海军及航空母舰五艘攻锡兰岛(Ceylon),卒失败而归;美海军在 Ceylon 汕湖岛(珊瑚岛)及中岛(中途岛)Midway 战胜,已将敌势大挫;印度方面已增加英军数师,海军极大力量。原规定七月间集中 Ceylon,业因有其他用,故集中期已改晚两个月,即九月准备完峻,然此于反攻缅甸援中国无妨,因在印度雨季无法开战。反攻以魏佛尔为总司令,亚力山打②为总指挥。援中国为吾与总统时刻不忘之事,南非【非】洲 Smuts③ 亦对此极注意,乃诵读 Smuts 电,注重中国之战事战后最重要地位。

邱继谓:日已增调四师,由日本本部至东三省,至共有二十四师。有种种模样,令人推测日将攻俄,俄方极不愿日攻。但此事如发现,日本在太平洋将多一敌人。继总统问中国战事情形。文具曰,敌人企图,及仍注重英、美空军及航空运输。总统谓,两国飞机产量有增,当可设法也。席散后即留总统府宴餐,餐后又召见苏大使。根据各方所得消息:(一)英美会议决定,一时无力辟第二战场;(二)讨论集中在保持近东;(三)邱不日内离华府。余续电。

---

① 该电文已收入《中华民国重要史料初编》第三编战时外交(三),第164~165页。
② 即亚历山大(Sir Harold Alexander),时任驻缅甸英军总司令。
③ 即史沫资(Jan Christiaan Smuts),为英国自治领之一的南非联邦领袖。

346. 宋子文致蒋介石报告与美军部商洽贷我运输机拟电稿(1942年6月)

拟电　委座　不发

委座钧鉴:借贷案内已运及待运之驱逐机二百六十架,又待飞印之轻轰炸机三十三架,暨史梯威将军所需之驱逐机一百五十架(另每月补充五十架)如全部运华,每月所需油弹器材约三千五百吨,自本年五月起至十月止约共二万一千吨。现正与美军部商洽,请贷我 B-24D 重轰炸机五十架,略加修改作运输机,将上述器材由印飞运内地以应急需。除详情续报外,谨先电奉闻。

347. 宋子文致蒋介石盼对史迪威万分忍耐以免耽搁时期电(1942年6月)

加密　致委座电

钧座侵亥寒电为一向主张,前已将该意口头与总统说明。惟总统意,英美开辟欧洲第二战场,并非为取胜于德耳。去冬德俄战争,德方死伤三百万以上,本夏德将倾全力攻苏南部,苏方万分危急,如苏军溃败,则大局动摇,是以英美允开辟第二战场以救苏。此项计划已定,无法更改。据文观察,美方对日除 Aleutian 阿留申群岛附近决与周旋或可削减其一部份海军外,并不取大规模攻势。本年九月起,航空母舰逐渐增加,明春可占绝对优势。自以日本海上利于速战速决,而美方则反之。昨日遇苏大使,问其土耳基【其】情形。彼谓,如 Sevastopol ①被陷,则土即倾向德方。其对于战事之悲观,可见于此。鄙见我国本年内不能盼望英美对日取攻势,如有此企图,费力而不能收效。我方应尽力于以下工作:(一) 中印空运;(二) 美空军多派数大队来华助战;(三) 美根据史梯威要求派陆军二三师赴印助我克复缅甸,以利我陆运。为贯彻此主张,恳盼钧座对史梯威万分忍耐,以免耽搁时期。文。

348. 宋子文致蒋介石报告与史汀生英大使会谈情形电(1942年7月1日)②

急　加码　呈委员长电　卅一.七.一日

委座钧鉴:(一) 今日晤史汀生,告文原拨中国飞机,因埃及情况危急,改调增援,深恐中国误会,乃荷谅解,引以为慰之。钧座于此事,或对史梯威已有表示。文答此为临时措置,蒋委员长告史梯威,中国目前急需之三项(即删电所示),仍请

---

① 即塞瓦斯托波尔,苏联港口、海军基地。
② 该电文已收入《中华民国重要史料初编》第三编战时外交(三),第175~176页。

速办。史谓已接史梯威电，俟克罗柏到美，即详细商讨，并暗示英美对日，不久即有大举，此可以解除日敌对于中国之压迫。又谓罗默尔①攻埃及促成英海军集中锡兰，但详情未肯明言。

(二) 文见英大使，日内即将返国，示以甘地②函及驻渝英使对钧座之言，并云，此为内政问题，蒋委员长不愿预问，但甘地如被拘捕，除印度内部纠纷外，必影响美国对英之舆论，不可不加慎重。反复力陈利害得失之余，英大使谓，此时英方如向甘地磋商，恐无效果，蒋委员长可否加以劝告，返英后，当向邱相③陈述解决方法，等语。其方法容续电闻。□□，此亦中国最好机会，为出面调停之先声，尚乞考虑。

(三) 顷国务部传出消息，日本在数小时内，即时进攻西比利亚。愚见英地中海失败，日敌攻苏引起英美急起对日，于我更为有利也。○东西。卅一.七.一

349. 宋子文致蒋介石提议由驻美专员统一办理所需武器事宜函稿(1942年7月1日)

呈委员长函稿　七.一日

委座钧鉴：据闻，美陆军部电驻渝武官，向余【俞】署长大维探询我国究竟急需何种武器。余【俞】署长答以步枪最急，机关枪次之，迫击炮又次之。陆军部以为与兵工署所派专员江杓在此所言不符。云云。余【俞】署长必为随意谈话，语出无心，孰知听者据以报告。关于军械等专门事项，各机关大都派有专员，务乞饬知各主管机关，嗣后如遇外人探询，可以已由驻美专员办理答之，以免纷岐，勿致应付困难。无往叩祷。专肃敬请钧安。文。

350. 宋子文致蒋介石报告罗斯福对印度问题之主张电(1942年7月5日)④

D673　急　加码　呈委员长电　卅一.七.五

委座钧鉴：顷白宫秘书长来见，奉总统命告文：甘地前发表宣言，印度非但欲驱逐英帝国主义，亦不愿美帝国主义侵入印度，殊不明其意何在。此君缺乏实际，虽与共事，然蒋公如有机会，当然希望能代余共同劝告甘地，勿走极端，以免为敌

---

① 即隆美尔(Erwin Rommel)，德国陆军元帅，时正在北非指挥德军作战。
② 甘地(M. K. Gandhi)，亦称"圣雄甘地"，印度民族主义运动和国大党领袖。
③ 即时任英国首相的丘吉尔。
④ 该电文已收入《中华民国重要史料初编》第三编战时外交(三)，第467页。

利用,危害中印数万万人民。等语。文推测总统之意,一、不愿于此近东危急之际,表面上有逼迫邱相之形迹,但又授意佛兰发出面,与英大使谈话,借探英方意向(请参阅支电);二、短时间内,印度事确有顾此失彼之虞,甘地如满意,现充印军骨干之数千万回教徒,势将失望,近东一带,回教徒势力最大,或亦被牵入,故总统不得不借故延宕也。○微。文。

351. 宋子文致蒋介石询问是否仍拟留史迪威在华供职电(1942年7月6日)①

急　加码　呈委员长电　卅一. 七. 六日

委座钧鉴:微电敬悉。史梯威态度殊属离奇,阅其原函,强词夺理,谬解职权,非神经错乱,不能狂妄至此。文日内即进谒当局,谅能加以纠正。但文丞欲知者,从【重】新明确规定参谋长职权后,钧座是否仍拟留其在华供职,抑或乘机更换,另选他员,请即确示,以便相机进行。史梯威对我之态度,久在愚虑之中,若早日得知,美方接济或不致为此延宕。一般客卿待遇过厚,往往失其戒惧之心。此辈宽不知恩,于此可见外事局太不得力,不能为钧座应付,似须改组。拙见伏乞谅察,并请赐复。○鱼。卅一. 七. 六

352. 宋子文致蒋介石报告美方派员赴印度调查电(1942年7月16日)

另缮发 7/16

介兄:关于租借案中印军输事宜,数月前派美人 Shaugnessy 赴印度调查,彼对于军部苟且点缀态度极为不满,屡电实情,供我向军部交涉资料。兹已饬其来渝,呈报一切。此君对我方甚忠实且详知史梯威、白来顿②等及英美人士在印度内容情形及关系,已饬其如垂询实告一切,如蒙约见③

353. 宋子文致蒋介石报告美卫生署拟派专家前往滇缅路电(1942年7月17日)

呈委员长电　七. 十七

委座钧鉴:窃查滇越铁路建筑时,员工因疟疾死者五万余人。今滇缅路经过

---

① 该电文已收入《中华民国重要史料初编》第三编战时外交(三),第610~611页。
② 白来顿,即勃兰特。
③ 以下脱稿。

区域,疟疾更盛。预计工员廿五万人。是以向美国卫生署请求,由其完全负责办理疟疾及防疫,拟派专家十五人,前往保卫,为期二年,所需及医生之薪津约美金拾万元及各项药料,概由贷借法案内供给。惟需用医生看护等,中国人员甚多,要求我方划出适合美金拾五万元之国币,随时应由我政府一次拨给,交其支配。愚见该署既允负责,成效可期,条件亦不苛细。是否可行,仍乞裁示祗遵。

354. 宋子文致蒋介石请告居里收复浙赣区计划电（1942 年 7 月 19 日）

加码　呈委员长电　卅一．七．十九日

委座钧鉴:总统迭接英美各方报告,日敌近对中国,未用重兵,所有冲突不过较大之游击战,故中国无危险,不必太注意,且中国已抗战五年,再支持一二年,尚无不可。文为打破此种论调,屡次陈说:珍珠港之变后,沪、港、缅甸相继沦陷,中外交通阻断,武器行将用罄。敌伪复于沦陷各地,排斥我法币,极力封锁我行政区,因此物价愈高,通货膨胀益甚。最近敌据浙赣铁路,鄱阳湖一带米区悉被占领,沿海物资,尤其食盐,来源被截;长沙本只受岳州敌人威胁,今加以东面之敌,有夹击之虞且危害我洞庭湖粮食区;广州越南则不时增兵,有三路攻滇之势。凡此危虑,并托克罗白同时解释。因恐当局始终迷信,或托词中国必能持久□口号,故须以事实详切说明。此为消极方面应支持中国之理由。但仍恐美方不能动听,必须加以积极说明其本身利害关系。查苏联军队恐将崩溃,届时美方舆论必不满其政府,而议会行将选举,为美国政府着想,只有不断大举轰炸日本,以获得一般人民信任之心理。我浙赣机场虽一时被占,美方如能执行钧座三项要求,我军不难收复,并示以较详实行克复浙赣路及各飞机场计划,以冀引起美当局切实援我之决心。钧座如以为然,请与居里谈话时,亦告以收复浙赣区原阵地之计划。如何之处,敬乞核示。○皓。卅一．七．十九

355. 宋子文致蒋介石报告昨太平洋会议情形电（1942 年 7 月 22 日）

新加码　呈委员长电　卅一．七．廿三日

委座钧鉴:昨太平洋会议:(一)文照皓电所陈,说明中国军事经济种种困难情形,并特备地图指示敌封锁我交通状况,力言非中印空运达到目的,则行将告罄之弹药无法接济,何以抗战。各代表颇为动容。(二)总统告,上月赴木

漫斯克①运输舰卅五艘中,沉没三十,而苏大使衔史丹林命,仍欲美方运械至该港口接济,余不得已答复史公,若非利用木漫斯克港,苏联即不能支持,则余当继续冒此极大危险,但其责任请史负之。总统又谓,苏大使对战事极悲观,余不知其用意为何云。退席后,文访苏大使,据云:南北铁路线既被敌冲断,事实上苏联战线已截而为两,此后虽必继续拼死力战,但已失去战斗效力。至第二战场,恐成画饼,日敌无攻印度必要,不久将进攻西比利亚云。(三)军部友人密告,苏军将崩溃,美国将有最重要之决定。此后方针,不出以下三项:(甲)不顾一切倾全力由法国攻德;(乙)全力攻日;(丙)以一部力量支持印度及中国,以一部力量计十师,攻取法属北菲【非】,夹击罗末尔②军队,完全占领地中海北岸,恢复地中海海运。文告以甲项由法登陆,援苏已太迟,且在外线背海作战,遭遇坚强之敌军,甚为危险,万一失败,则大势去矣;丙项办法,分散力量,恐将两者俱失;在此情势之下,只有依照乙项,及蒋委员长前提办法,合中英美苏力量速攻日本,一年之间,必能解决;再以欧洲大陆外世界之全力攻德,彼德虽强,溃败只时间问题耳。此为我联盟国万全之策。等语。当否,乞示。○养。文。卅一.七.廿二

356. 宋子文致蒋介石报告美方解释史迪威职权电(1942年7月23日)③

加码　呈委员长电　卅一.七.廿三

委座钧鉴:史梯威事,军部转达总统意见云,史为中国区参谋长,当然听命于蒋委员长,同时为美国驻渝租借法案代表,及国际军事会议美国代表,当然听命于美方。蒋公如以为不便,可将史职权划分由两人担任,即:(一)参谋长职务,(二)美国代表职务。但总统因史梯威对中国及蒋公一向友好,且熟悉中国情形,甚盼蒋公能继续任用之。文以其语气仍不免袒护,乃往亲谒总统,解释内中情形及史函之不当。总统云:史职权中,代表美国出席在渝国际军事会议一项,既无此类会议,事实上形同虚设。关于租借法案,此后一切由君代表蒋公,霍布金代表余,在华府共同解决。此两种职权划分清楚,史事实上即专属参谋长地位矣。如蒋公仍以史为未妥,余当更换之,但美国干练适当之军官甚少,另觅妥员,确有相当困难。文允将此意转陈后,请总统俟参谋总长及霍布金日内返美,即饬其与文切商钧座三项要求,切实答复钧座,且克罗白在此,正可著其供【贡】献意

---

① 木漫斯克(Murmansk),现译摩尔曼斯克,北冰洋沿岸最大的港口城市,亦是苏联西北著名的不冻港。

② 罗末尔,即德国陆军元帅隆美尔(Erwin Rommel)。

③ 该电文已收入《中华民国重要史料初编》第三编战时外交(三),第611～612页。

见,以备参考。总统允于照办。所陈各节,钧意如何,敬候复示。○梗。文。卅一·七·廿三

357. 宋子文致蒋介石请迅饬滇缅路速运积存器材函稿(1942 年 7 月 29 日)

呈委座函稿 七·廿九

委座钧鉴:窃查兵工署积存仰光器材甚多,闻滇缅路由腊戍至昆明,每月平均仅运四百余吨。该项器材,多属制造枪弹之原料,为前方所急需,现在敌占越南,该路益受威胁,用特恳请迅饬该路局速予内运,至少亦须以百分之五十运量,专事输送兵工原料。敬求核夺饬遵。肃叩钧安。文。

358. 宋子文致蒋介石提议向居里直告对史迪威之不满事实电(1942 年 7 月 30 日)

加码 呈委员长电 卅一·七·卅

委座钧鉴:军部麦次长①密告文,参谋本部现正讨论钧座要求供给空军五百架战斗机计划,颇有端倪,出其意料之外,并嘱暂勿宣泄。另据军部友人密告,此次钧座向总统表示对史梯威不满意,反使参谋本部不能不注意中国要求,促现加紧援华之事实云。钧座乘居里在渝,凡不满史梯威之种种事实,最好向其直言无隐,因史氏将与居里同赴印度,难免以一面之词告之也。○陷。文。卅一·七·卅

359. 宋子文致蒋介石报告英方对印度问题方案电(1942 年 7 月)

致委座电

○电计达。英大使已赴伦敦,其对印度方案,形式上采取大理院推法官佛兰佛向其谈话备忘录。佛为总统亲信,方案之理论即总统屡次向文所表示。佛之谈话因总统阅甘地致钧座函,及渝英使向钧座表示,不便向邱直说,授意请佛出面无疑,摘要如下:
一、如甘地有举动,而英国不得不予以扣留,美国人士原来不同情于英国之印度政策将复燃,因克利浦斯②赴印努力而美舆论对英渐有好转之观念当逆转。

---

① 即麦克洛依(John J. McCloy),时任美国陆军部次长。
② 克利浦斯,即英国爵士克里普斯(Sir Stafford Cripps),曾赴印度试图说服国大党与英印当局合作。

二、为英国计,莫若使美国参入印度问题,万一印度态度无理倔强,则美国人士可料【了】解应付之困难。

三、各联盟国由英美或加中国在内领袖,取原则:

(甲)印度问题即联盟国问题;

(乙)印度应有自由;

(丙)但世界和平需要印度之统一。

四、如此,则英国可表示美国对菲律宾之政策可由英今日行之于印度,足使世界明了英帝国制度善于应变,非为欧战时之奥帝国陈旧不合潮流。

五、是以敢建议邱相代表联盟国尤其英美中发表:(甲)目的在兼要印度之自由及统一;(乙)决定印度自治之期,此期应确定不改而最近之日期;(丙)自治之方案及日期由联盟国担保,联盟国有此责任方能对事有咨询及批评明文;(丁)自治日以前,印度须自动定宪法,限定中央及各省或各区之权,其宪法适合印情形,不必仿效美国或任何国制度,但关于国防及外交当然属中央范围;(丑)如预定自治之日各党派不能完成宪法,则各省各区无条件得以自治;(己)印度既不能统一对外之关系,须有同盟国负担之,尤其负责诸国之责任,指英美中。如以上各点可蒙采纳,则英美间之感情从此可增加不少。云云。

以上各点,英大使及佛兰佛友谊上交阅,兹转钧座采考,请勿发表或对印度人提及。文。

360. 宋子文致蒋介石并转周至柔关于美国供华飞机情形电(1942年8月10日)

新加码　呈委员长电　卅一.八.十日

委座钧鉴并请转示周主任至柔:

(一)军部友人密告,美空军在华作战成绩甚佳,故军部对增加飞机队赴华颇感兴趣。中国空军用P四三作战,必须著有同样战绩,庶将来增请飞机,可有办法。军部信P四三机已有八十二架装配完竣,其中六十七架,已由我方接收。

(二)但据我方人员报告,到华P四三机,仅廿九架,其中十二架,业经损坏,在印之P四三,因不适于我飞机司之用,均已交还美方,且其发动机亦经拆卸,供C五三机之用。

(三)军部得有报告,谓P六六型机六十五架,已到达印度。我方报告,仅收九架,且均在卡拉其①。两方报告,相差甚远,请注意。

---

① 即卡拉奇(Karachi),城市名,位于印度河三角洲西部,现为巴基斯坦最大城市和经济中心。

（四）美在华空军及供给中国空军原来之秘密计划为：

　　甲、P 四零型一五零架,每月补充卅二架;

　　乙、轻轰炸机卅二架;

　　丙、重轰炸机四十八架,分四队,每队十二架之中,以九架前线作战,三架补充;

　　丁、供给中国空军前线驱逐机一百架,准备机五十架,包括 P 四三及 P 六六,另轻轰炸机 A 二九卅三架。

（五）友人好意密告,A 二九机,较 P 四三更难驾驶,且式样陈旧,与新出之 B 二五,效力相差极大。该型飞机,在飞华途中已毁四架,死十二人,故条陈该机到华之后,最好拨给陈纳德,由美国驾驶原机至华之美机师飞行作战,俾资熟手。盖我方驾驶,倘有疏虞,恐美方借口,于增请飞机反不利也。美友此项主张,是否可行,务祈裁夺,惟切勿告美军事团。再我如能托故放弃 A 二九,要求以 B 二五机替代,效能必更大。○蒸。

361. 宋子文致蒋介石并转周至柔密告 A29 轰炸机等性能电(1942 年 8 月 11 日)

致委座电　8/11

（一）委座钧鉴并请转示周主任至柔：军部友人密告,即将抵华之 A 二九轻轰炸机式样陈旧,且较 P43 更难驾驶,在飞华途中已毁四架,死十二人,故秘密条陈该机到华之后,最好托故词拨给陈纳德,由美国驾驶原机至华之美司机飞行作战,并要求 B25 以替代。盖我方驾驶倘有疏虞,恐美方借口,于增请飞机反不利也。查 A29 为首次拨我空军之轰炸机,我方等待已两年,不知能否再等候。但友人条陈出于至诚,请从长考虑。文。

（二）美拨我之 P66、P43,闻国内多不能用,请将原因详告,以便与美方接洽。文。

362. 宋子文致蒋介石报告罗斯福关于印度问题谈话电(1942 年 8 月 13 日)①

加码　呈委员长电　卅一. 八. 十三日

委座钧鉴：总统英文复电计达。昨太平洋会议,总统云：印度问题,余与蒋委员

---

① 该电文已收入《中华民国重要史料初编》第三编战时外交(三),第 484 页。

长电讯频繁,互悉最后之目的相同,即一致希望印度得以自治。余素注意把握时间,美国各州之逐渐联合统一,菲律滨四十年之培养,俱为先例。英国为同盟好友,印度之事,中、美若被邀请出面斡旋,自当尽其友谊上之责任,否则似有未便,故余意此时以缄默为是。等语。意含中、美最好不向英国公然有所表示。总统因英人告以印事不日可了,故持观望,似尚未到动转时期。文意两三星期英人如不能制止甘地运动,美舆论将转变,届时当审择良机,遵照钧座意旨,再向总统恳切陈词,较有效果。仍乞裁示。文。

363. 宋子文致蒋介石请速示知日敌集结消息电(1942年8月18日)

致委座电 最密

英大批军械飞机由主力艘队护送至 MALTA①,中途被德空军不断轰炸,海军损失奇重,折回。东地中海控制权已操诸德国。同时(二)埃及德军已开到援军二师。罗末尔将继续进攻。此间对埃及战事极悲观,认苏彝士不久将被夺。(三)日敌似已中止其攻西比利亚计划,然亦不见其有攻印度模样。近来美空军在中国活跃,日敌窥破中国为最后反攻日本根据地,或将集大力再向我压迫。钧座如有此类消息,迄速示知,以备催其增援我空军。文。

364. 宋子文致蒋介石代拟致居里备忘录稿电(1942年8月20日)②

致委座电

委座钧鉴:侵、寒各电奉悉。至缅甸失陷后,自本年五月起,文处鉴于运输困难,即集中一点,要求空运月五千吨,战斗机五百架,及紧急运输军械每月三千五百吨,此外并无奢求。军部亦无特别隔阂。居里所谓容易引起误会,似可不必为虑。美参谋总长向文告以美军部与英、苏、澳、荷及南美诸国,无一日不有争执,向文叫苦。足见各为其国主,人情之常。当时不免争执,事后无不谅解。今美方既提议以后申请物品,先在中国由我军政部与美国代表团商定,再通知美军部及文处执行,根据事只求成之原则,自不妨与其试办。钧座与居里连日洽商,经过情形必多,为求意见一致起见,谨根据侵、寒电代拟备忘录交与居里,即乞速示。其内容如下:

---

① MALTA,即马耳他,地中海中部岛国,是时为英国殖民地。
② 该电文已收入《中华民国重要史料初编》第三编战时外交(一),第506～507页。

兹为告知中国军部及中国国防物资供应公司①连日与君在渝谈话结论，特编备忘录为左，请查照。

（一）在中印空运困难情形之下，决定目前最急需要每月中印空五千吨军需及前线五百架空军之支持。

（二）每月三千五百吨紧急运输军械应照常施行，不得停止。

（三）美租借案物资抵印后，由美方代办库储，并由美方将库储纪录抄知我方。该项物品不得蒋委员长同意，不得拨借任何方面。为中国在印度之军队需要，该项物品由蒋委员长或其驻印代表通知提用。

（四）美方代办该项物资，中印空运应遵照运统局之优先顺序及比率进行。

（五）以上各点为运输困难时期临时方案，俟运输畅通再修改之。

如钧座认为备忘录适宜，请修正。可否由文代致居里，乞裁核夺示遵。

365. 宋子文致蒋介石请示有关泰国问题电（1942 年 8 月 29 日）

蒋委员长

□电敬悉。经与驻美泰国公使洽谈，据称：泰国在美资金约有一千万元，现款有三百万元，美政府特许其提动，以供自由泰运动之用。泰幼皇及母后现仍在瑞士，被轴心包围，即欲脱离亦无法。至逊位皇后在英，泰人民并不拥戴，故不易产生合法的流亡政府，以资号召。此时自由泰运动，以驻美使馆为中心。现有泰国学生四十人，在美受军事训练，内中五人为官，准备派到中国及缅甸等处，担任秘密工作。此事业由美军事情报当局与史梯威将军有所接洽。云云。泰使又谓，在英资金约计五千万镑，仍受封锁。泰人在英原被视为敌伪，但最近英军队已许泰人入伍。月前泰使由美派遣代表赴英，亦获得英方赞助。彼现拟派自由泰代表驻华，以期与我国当局合作，并推进现在云南边境及阿萨密等地之泰难民反日活动，要【邀】请我国政府同意。如何，敬乞核示。○

366. 宋子文致蒋介石密告美军部关于中印空运消息电（1942 年 8 月）

委座钧鉴：中印空运，军部消息如下：

（一）军部拟在最短期间，完成中印空航共百架运输机之计划。其中七五架归军

---

① 即 CDS（China Defense Supplies, Inc.），1941 年由宋子文在美国注册成立，负责接洽援华租借物资。

部运输队,二五架归中航公司。

（二）史梯威拟与中航订运输合同,运价根据成本计算。惟此项合同须得钧座同意,俾中航公司运输优先可由钧座定。史梯威并称,在原则上,已得钧座之同意。

（三）美运输队飞航员报告,中印路线,每机运量超过一吨,即感困难,最多每次飞航,每机载重为二吨。我告以最近文处辛克莱君试航汀江昆明线,于来回汽油外,曾载货三吨半。

367. 宋子文致蒋介石报告居里复函电(1942 年 9 月 7 日)①

D838　新加码　呈委员长电　卅一.九.七

委座钧鉴:哿电拟致居里备忘录,经遵照梗电修改译转,据居里九月四日复函称:

"备忘录所述各节,大致与蒋委员长在渝对鄙人表示之意见相符,但有一二点亟欲预先声明,因有误会之可能也。（甲）鄙人赴渝,政府并未授权决定任何问题,蒋委员长亦必明了此种情形;（乙）关于第三节甲项,鄙人曾向蒋委员长解释新办法,即本年五月一日以后运出之租借案物品,在所有权实际转让中国政府以前,得由军货分配委员会支配之"等语。查该函末节,盖指五月一日后运出之租借案物品虽已抵印,所有权仍属美政府,美方有权拨让他方,不必得我政府同意,物品抵华,所有权始属中国。至于五月一日前运出物品,则所有权属中国,除中国同意外,不得拨让他方。敬乞裁示。○阳。文。卅一.九.七

368. 宋子文致蒋介石报告对于印度问题美舆论转变电(1942 年 9 月 16 日)

最新加码　呈委员长电　卅一.九.十六

委座钧鉴:关于印度问题,美舆论之转变,果如八月元电鄙意所料。美初受克利浦斯愚弄,迨甘地等被捕,及种种压迫事实发生后,一般人士,虽谓甘地确难应付,然英人以在香港、马来亚、缅甸失败之政策,重演于印度,自当归咎英方。邱相及印度事务大臣艾曼雷氏日前演说,反予美方恶劣感想,以为邱相等只知用高压手段,尤以演词中明示英国已加派大军赴印,露出长久把持印度之目的。原来同情英方,如纽约时报,最近社论已变更论调,特嘱中央通讯社电呈备考。○谏西。文。

---

① 该电文已收入《中华民国重要史料初编》第三编战时外交(一),第507～508 页。

369. 宋子文致蒋介石请准予回国一行电(1942 年 9 月 18 日)①

居里回美,叠次与其开诚商讨钧座提出三项要求。彼向文及各人袒白表示: 在渝不能撤【彻】底解决钧座与史梯威间之误会。及返美后,军部除对空运稍有进步外,恢复缅甸及五百架战斗机之计划不能切实接受,总统亦不能时时□促,原因皆在注重对德。在此根本观念不能转变前,难有显著之进展云。文深觉自缅甸失陷,此间接济日形困难及竭蹶,为打破此种难关及明了情形,极有向钧座面陈并请示以后方针之必要。② 可否准予回国一行,乞电示遵。

370. 宋子文致蒋介石谈对苏过境运货案电(1942 年 9 月 24 日)

呈委员长电　卅一.九.廿四

委座钧鉴: 养电敬悉。

(一) 接邵大使③皓电略称: 向苏提过境运货新案,暂照我国每年依约应交苏联农矿品吨数二万四千吨,扣去我向苏商购油料五千吨,暂定过境运货为一万九千吨。苏政府认本案有肯定解决之可能云。以文观察,限制吨数或系根据苏方空车来华取运农矿品之吨位计算,若我能另外自备车辆,由苏边境接运内地,或可不受此限制。

(二) 驻美英大使馆及英购委会,向文处商洽伊朗首段运输即须筹备,拟:

　　甲、由彼方电伦敦特饬 UKCC④ 驻印代表与沈士华⑤接洽,即乞特饬沈代表知照,并查明由克拉奇⑥至 MESHED⑦ 铁路及公路运量各若干,UKCC 有无充分车辆及设备。

　　乙、苏境内由 MESHED 到 ASHKHABARD⑧ 公路八十哩一段运输,归英方或苏方办理,由驻苏英大使交涉。

　　丙、如中国境内运输车辆,由我自备,则 SARGIOPOL⑨ 到中苏边境公路一段运输,归何方担任,请饬邵大使商洽。

---

① 　该电文已收入《中华民国重要史料初编》第三编战时外交(一),第 723 页。
② 　宋子文本人在此处原写"拟回国向钧座请示"一语,原稿未删除。
③ 　即时任中国驻苏联大使的邵力子。
④ 　即 United Kingdom Commercial Commission,英国购料委员会。
⑤ 　沈士华,浙江吴兴人,时任国民政府外交部驻印度专员。
⑥ 　即前注之卡拉其。
⑦ 　即麦什德,亦译作马什哈德,伊朗东北部城市。
⑧ 　即苏联城市阿什哈巴德。
⑨ 　SARGIOPOL,苏联地名。

（三）中苏运输问题复杂，应否饬由交通部办理，以专责成。

统乞裁夺。〇迴。文。卅一.九.廿四

371. 宋子文致蒋介石请饬江杓购办礼物分赠居里等电（1942 年 10 月 23 日）

呈委员长电　十.廿三日

委座钧鉴：圣诞节近，美方与我有关人士，如居里君及将官一员、上中校廿三员、少校十员、尉官七员，素日热忱相助，备极辛勤，拟以钧座名义，分赠礼物，以示慰勉。可否请饬江杓购办带美，尚祈裁定。

372. 宋子文致蒋介石报告抵加与史迪威谈话情形电（1943 年 2 月）

委座钧鉴：文抵加后，即将钧嘱各节转达史迪威。彼极为懊丧，并谓当时谈话有失体统，甚以为慊，但信钧座必谅其忠实及一番热忱。又谓，钧座如不切实声明，英方恐借此拖延，至一万吨运输必为力争，云云。在加开会时，彼本提出中国务须有每月万吨之接济，魏佛尔声明种种困难，而其参谋长莫力斯将军谓，铁道及水运无论如何能追上空运力量。文遂向亚诺将军郑重声明，英国方面既有负责表示，此后万吨空运之责任当视阁下之努力。亚诺谓，尚须英国方面增加三个飞机场，及中国方面增加机场。文答，中国方面我委员长已有负责表示，英方是否能同样努力。魏谓自当尽力。等语。顷史梯威来告，九号下午英美将领开会，英方允另辟三个机场，美方亦决定积极增加飞机，等语。是钧座七日上午向亚诺之谈话已完全收效，致九日上午军事会议情形甚佳。当由何总长①将会议记录译呈。文抵 Ramgarh② 即病，热度甚高，几成肺炎，幸服新发明之 Sulpha③ 药，顷已脱险。文。

373. 蒋介石致宋子文附与史迪威谈话记录函（1943 年 4 月 20 日）

委员长来函

子文吾兄勋鉴：兹将与史迪威④将军谈话稿附录一份，请察核。自敌寇上月占领

---

① 即时任国民政府军政部部长的何应钦。
② Ramgarh，印度地名，位于印度比哈尔邦，当时中国驻印军正在该地接受美式训练。
③ 即 Sulphonamide，磺胺类药物。
④ 史迪威（Joseph W. Stilwell），美国陆军中将，后出任中国战区最高统帅蒋介石的参谋长。

长江以南之华容、石首以后，其海军舰艇可由岳州直达宜昌。今夏水涨季节实为最危险之时。此时应急之空军，必须有三大队驱逐机，掩护陆军扫除华容、石首一带之敌，且须在六月以前派到也。余录于谈话记录中，故不赘述。顺颂近祉。中正手启。四月廿日

委座接见史迪威参谋长谈话记录

时间：四月十九日下午五时

地点：曾家岩官邸

史问：反攻缅甸之总司令人选，钧座有何意见否？若英国指派奥钦勒克(Auchinleck)(前任英国北非军总司令)担任总司令之职，钧座是否赞成？又，将来中国之远征军由印入缅后，究竟听何人之命令以为行动之准绳？

委座答：对反攻缅甸总司令职位一事，无任何意见，可由英美会商决定。驻印中国远征军仍由汝用参谋长名义指挥。至于反攻时整个华军之作战，余决亲往指挥，希向罗总统及马歇尔参谋长说明。反攻缅甸时，除安诺得①将军在渝所报告计划中之美国海军及空军外，希望美国派遣陆军三个师至印度，协同英军攻占仰光。

史答：派遣陆军困难之处，即在于船舶缺乏，当遵命报告罗总统及马参谋长。

委座答：希向罗总统及马参谋长说明现今中国严重之形势。中国之士气及民气，均极低落，其情状实为六年来所未有。敌人在华容、石首一带渡江后，由武汉至宜昌之长江水路业已打通，夏季江水上涨时，敌人即可以炮舰艇只溯江而上，威胁重庆外围之江防工事。此点实至可忧虑。现我方要求美国在今年六月前务必派遣三个驱逐大队来华助战，如此则我军可将在长江以南华容一带之敌军逐至长江之北，解除此严重威胁。再则民气士气，因之即可提高。不然敌人利用汪伪组织强化伪军，动摇我军民抗战意志，夏季敌方若沿长江发动一大攻势，则中国恐难再支持。又，现今中国朝野上下，均希望美国更多之援助，美国飞机产量如此之高，但对吾人仅仅三个大队之要求，尚迟迟不予实现，实使余个人对于中国军民亦无以解答此一疑问。此点务希郑重向罗总统及马参谋总长说明。希与贵国军方，就上次安诺德在渝所会商之反攻缅甸作战方案，再定更具体之实施计划，并于雨季结束以前，完成一切准备事项。

史答：遵命。

委座答：在美晤及蒋夫人②及宋部长时，请特告今日谈话之内容。又，蒋夫人若可能与汝一同返华则更佳。请向总统及马参谋总长致候。

---

① 安诺得(Henry H. Arnold)，亦译为安诺德、阿诺德，时任美国空军(隶属于陆军)司令。
② 即蒋介石夫人宋美龄。

374. 宋子文致蒋介石报告今后十二个月内加拿大可拨械弹货单电(1943年4月24日)

D1127　加码　呈委员长电　卅二.四.廿四

委座钧鉴:加拿大为欧战起后兵工业新兴国家,文与其总理①及国防工业部长等交谊素笃,屡告以军事工业战后必将停顿,改为普通工业,届时可与我积极合作,助我建设新中国,彼此互相有利。该国人民对于钧座及我国抗战亦极钦佩,鉴于英美支配一切,暗中颇为不平。总理等日前特约文赴加,会商结果,谈定拨赠大宗军械。今后十二个月内,可拨下列各项器械。此项提案俟下月国会通过后,即可定案。此不过形式而已,惟在此期间,仍请暂守秘密。

子,七九轻机枪三万挺;

丑,强力式手枪十八万枝,附子弹五千四百万粒;

寅,三英时七高射炮二百四十门,附榴弹四十八万发;

卯,一公尺基测远镜两千具;

辰,六倍望远镜五万具;

巳,六磅战车防御炮三百六十门,附破甲弹廿四万发;

午,九米厘手提机关枪六万挺,附子弹五千万粒;

未,廿五磅轻榴弹炮七百廿门,附榴弹百一十五万两千发,烟幕弹十四万四千发;

申,机枪履带车或名小战车一千二百辆;

酉,四公分高射炮六百门,附榴弹一百六十二万发,破甲弹十八万发。

上列各项枪炮之备件、车辆、通信器材等,均照英国制式配齐。

文复以美方海运困难,请其拨我万吨最新式货轮三艘,亦允照拨。关于该轮所需人员等事项,另电奉陈。窃以加拿大以千数万人民之小国,为此热忱援助,崇尚正义,殊堪钦佩。俟最近形式上定案后,拟请钧座电总理等表示谢意,伏启垂察。

○敬。文。卅二.四.廿四

375. 宋子文致蒋介石报告陈纳德与亚诺会议结果电(1943年4月30日)②

加码　呈委员长电　卅二.四.卅日

委座钧鉴:昨陈纳德与亚诺及其他高级人员会议,结果至为圆满,陈纳德一切要

---

① 即加拿大总理麦肯齐·金(Mackezie King)。

② 该电文已收入《中华民国重要史料初编》第三编战时外交(三),第223页。

求,亚诺完全应允,并谓总统急欲在中国区以空军打击敌人云。但空军方面虽赞成此项计划,马歇尔尚未同意,且计划能否实现,问题仍在中印空运。文是以致总统备忘录一件,大意译呈如下:

(照译附件)蒋委员长经缜密考虑,认为所有战时资源,暂须全部致力于空中攻击之准备。故五、六、七三个月空运吨位,宜全部候运汽油及飞机器材之用,使有效的空中攻击早日得成事实。七月以后空运,除少量空军补充材料外,再运陆军所需器材。以美国生产力,此项准备空中攻击必须之飞机及器材数量并不甚大,是以吾人切望早日拨交起运,俾得完成一切准备事项。蒋委员长并嘱余声明,敌人如用陆军进攻我航空根据地,阻挠我空中攻击计划,中国陆军力量足资应付。蒋委员长前请总统令陈纳德将军返美,面陈空中攻击计划内容,陈将军刻已抵此,必能详细上达也。等语。再,备忘录送达时,史迪威尚未交阅钧座手示及谈话记录,故关于敌寇渡江后之严重情势各节,日内另向总统面陈,乞鉴察。○卅。文。卅二.四.卅

376. 宋子文致蒋介石报告美参谋本部会议情形电(1943年5月1日)①

D1140　加码　呈委员长电　卅二.五.一日

委座钧鉴:(一)昨美参谋本部会议三小时,史梯威、陈纳德到会陈述意见。陈纳德主张,中美空军用五百架飞机大举空中攻击,足可消灭大部敌在华空军力量,并予敌船运以极大打击,敌交通线被破坏,则缅甸及中国本部之陆地战事较易为力。(二)史梯威称,在充实陆军力量以前,大举空中攻击不能实现。彼觉华军现有军械给养训练,均不足坚守、支持、保护前线各机场。史对兰木加②受训华军,称扬备至,深信此项军队由缅苦战返华,用以保护机场,将可再作大举空中攻击。如空攻计划实施过早,敌恼羞成怒,袭取机场,则收复不易,而大举由华空袭日本本部之机会,亦将丧失。(三)马歇尔将军先告陈纳德,彼对此问题与史梯威意见一致。参谋本部会议中,马在陈发言以前,即已离席。(四)文向总统及霍金斯③力主即刻完成空中攻击之准备,以免坐失事机。霍告陈纳德云,文日前致总统备忘录,予总统以难题,盖总统须驳斥军部主脑主张也。(五)三妹星期一来华府,文④拟协同向总统陈说,如空中攻击不能早日实现,则敌乘夏季水涨

---

①　该电文已收入《中华民国重要史料初编》第三编战时外交(三),第224页。
②　兰木加,即Ramgarh,印度地名。
③　霍金斯,即时任美国总统罗斯福政治顾问的霍普金斯。
④　该处原稿为○。

进攻重庆,事势之险,莫过于此。此后中国区战场之支持,全视美方能否采纳钧座意见。谨陈。文。

377. 宋子文致蒋介石密告出席英美参谋团会议情形电(1943年5月17日)①

D1185　加码　呈委员长电　卅二.五.十七日

委座钧鉴:今日英美参谋团会议,总统之参谋长李海②主席,除总统及邱相外,各要员均出席,请文报告钧座意见。

文谓:自敌占领缅甸,中国完全陷于包围,因此不能获得军火补充及物资接济,国内经济衰落,通货恶性膨胀。敌复改变以前侵略方法,利用傀儡,煽惑人心,一面以全力进犯晋、豫、鄂、湘,意图威胁重庆。凡此事实,当荷洞悉。但中国处兹危境,并无意外要求,只请同盟国实践诺言,履行总统、邱相北菲【非】之决议③而已。此可代表蒋委员长禀告诸君者。查北菲【非】关于中国事项之决议有二,请分别言之。

(一) 决定增强空军,攻击在华之敌及日本本土。因空运不足供应增加空军,此项决定,迄未实行。目前美驻华空军只能保卫中印空运线,中国陆军从未得美空军之掩护。在此敌人企图进攻各要点及陪都之际,最迫切需要者,为美空军力能助我陆军作战及破坏敌交通。然以现状而论,殊不可能。且须知数个月内同盟国所能实际有效援助者,亦只有空军而已。是以蒋委员长请总统以最近三个月之空运,完全供应空军,以达到增强陈纳德空军之目的。关于空军作战计划,陈将军已有详细说明矣。

(二) 决定反攻缅甸。

总统、邱相曾自北菲【非】电告蒋委员长,以海、陆、空军完全克复缅甸,打通滇缅路线。复派狄耳④元帅、亚诺空军司令亲赴重庆,面述一切,并在加埠会议⑤出席者,英、美各高级将领,何部长及本人,决定各国所负任务。至此,文乃朗读二月九日加埠会议英武官之记录,并指出:

甲、魏佛尔开会辞曾有根据北菲【非】及重庆决定之语;

乙、何部长报告中国参加作战之兵力;

---

① 该电文已收入《中华民国重要史料初编》第三编战时外交(三),第230页。

② 李海(William Leahy),美国海军上将,原驻法国维希政府大使,1942年7月起即出任美国陆海军总司令即罗斯福总统的参谋长。

③ 即1943年1月罗斯福、丘吉尔在北非摩洛哥的卡萨布兰卡(Casablanca)举行会议达成的决议。

④ 即迪尔(Sir John Greer Dill),英国陆军元帅。

⑤ 即中英美军政高级幕僚人员于1943年2月9日在印度加尔各答举行的会议。

丙、魏佛尔决定由印度派遣十个师；

丁、何部长提出须有强大之海军参加，经英海军提督保证；

戊、何部长提须获得制空权，经亚诺保证。

又指出，魏佛尔结论，各方既皆同意，只须各方以最大之努力，准备反攻之语。

文续谓：请诸君注意，攻缅并非一普通计划，实为三国共同决议案。中国方面部队已集中备战，并将各机场扩充整顿。本人谨再重复声明，蒋委员长今日并无新的要求，只请英美同盟国实行共同议决案，告知攻缅之海空军配备情形。英美政府要人已向世界履次宣布本年攻缅，故请诸君恕我直言，万一有放弃攻缅之决定，中国军民必以为英美背信违约。英美表示无决心以武力强迫日敌投降，不但中国人心绝望而瓦解，同盟军若无中国根据地，亦将无法消灭日寇。

再者北菲【非】会议以前，史迪威将军曾提议仅攻缅北，委员长未加许可。盖因敌人据有铁路、伊落瓦底河及公路之交通路线，我如不占领缅南，断其后路，必归失败，徒作无为【谓】之牺牲。蒋委员长彼时之决心如此，今日对此之决心益坚。等语。

查上星期五英美军事会议，史迪威公开批评钧座，谓诸事犹豫，于战略无一定见解，文趁此次会议机会，补充声言蒋委员长并非初次与外国军事专家合作，前在张古峰①、诺门汉②击败日敌之加伦③将军，曾追随数年之久，创造德国之防军之塞克特④及曾充卢登道夫⑤作战科长之佛采耳⑥及最近在史太林格勒⑦击破德军之崔可夫⑧，均曾充任顾问，无一不恪遵蒋委员长意旨。若谓我辈遵从蒋委员长或陷于错误，则错误不止我辈，上述各世界名将亦共同犯此过失，且蒋委员长负中国区安全之责任，凡所筹画，必以全局为主体，如我辈对彼怀疑，反对其主张，则我辈应有担负中国区安全之能力。文此言不仅对史，且使美陆、空军当局

---

①　张古峰，位于中国东北图们江下游。1938 年 7、8 月间，日本与苏联曾在这一地区发生大规模武装冲突。

②　诺门汉，即诺门坎，位于中国边境。1939 年 5 月，日本与苏联在此地区发生大规模武装冲突。

③　加伦(Vasily K. Bleucher Gallen)，苏联将领，曾于大革命时期在国民革命军中担任军事顾问。

④　塞克特(Hans Von Seecket)，曾任德国国防军总参谋长、总司令，1934 年 5 月至 1935 年 3 月任德国驻华军事顾问团总顾问。

⑤　卢登道夫(Erich Ludendorff)，曾任德国国防部部长。

⑥　佛采耳(George Wetzell)，即魏采尔，曾任德国陆军军务局局长，1930 年 5 月至 1934 年 3 月任德国驻华军事顾问团总顾问。

⑦　即斯大林格勒(Stalingrad)。

⑧　崔可夫(Vasily Ivanovich Chuikov)，苏联将军，曾担任国民政府军事顾问。

对于中国不能以一隅之见任意支配也。谨闻。○篠亥。

378. 宋子文致蒋介石报告太平洋会议与丘吉尔争辩西藏问题电（1943 年 5 月 21 日）①

D1195　加码　呈委员长电　卅二.五.廿（关于西藏事在第二页）　复　R1180

委座钧鉴：本日太平洋会议，总统报告：太平洋一般局势及亚都 ATTU② 战况均佳。关于中国方面，现正采取步骤，增进空军战斗及运输力量，空运数量将大为增加，致陈纳德空军力量亦可增加三倍，邱相亦愿派遣驱逐机三队赴华。文谓，此项消息，本人至为欢迎，犹忆珠港事件发生前，英相已曾拟派空军赴华矣。邱相谓，近闻中国有集中队伍准备进攻西藏之说，致该独立国家大为恐慌，希望中国政府能保证不致有不幸事件发生。文答，并未闻有此项消息，且西藏并非首相所谓独立国家，中英间历次所订条约，皆承认西藏为中国主权所有，当早在洞鉴之中。邱谓：西藏为不毛之地，英国对之并无野心，只希望吾人此时集中力量对付公敌，万勿分耗力量而已。吾人现正设法增近对华空运，足致超过历来滇缅公路所载数量。顷知缅甸为蛮瘴之区，在此种艰苦情形下作战，白人不如日人，现在印度边境英印军队颇众，但因交通困难，不易运用，亚拉铅 ARAKAN③ 之役，可为前车之鉴。文谓：收复缅甸虽然困难，但为一劳永逸之举，亦属当前最急之务。目前增强对华空运之步骤，固至重要，但滇缅路恢复后，运输可进展至每月十万吨。现中国所急盼望于英美者，即执行攻缅之决议，中国政府与军事最高领袖，均视此为肯定之诺言。北非【非】会议所决定之方针，中国一般人士及全世界人民亦已知其大概，倘不予实行，中国军民人心摇动，前途至为危险。邱谓，此项计划，英国方面实非肯定之承诺，自可随局势之缘进而有所变更。文谓，总统与首相在北菲时曾将所决定之方针电达蒋委员长，又经英美高级将领亲赴重庆会商，文与何部长又曾参加加埠魏佛尔将军主持之军事会议，决定各项详细计划，中国政府当然视此项决议为肯定之承诺。邱相仍坚持只有计划并无决议，且谓，英美军事当局如有所允诺，实属越权。文谓，加埠会议决定各方应即采取之步骤，中国在过去数月中，已尽力准备。邱谓，前数日始看见加埠会议报告。文谓，此种重要计划系二月九日决定，何以迟至前数日首相始看见，殊属

---

① 该电文已收入《中华民国重要史料初编》第三编战时外交（三），第 233～235 页。
② 即阿图岛，位于美国阿拉斯加州西南部、阿留申群岛西端。
③ 即阿拉干，缅甸古城，距孟加拉湾八十公里。

不解。邱无以为答。文续谓：至于在缅作战之困难，新岁亚战须亦有同样情况，皆赖将士之决心与技能，借以克服诸般困难。瘴气虚疾，日本士兵亦受同一影响，分别不在种族之黄白，而在决心之有无。北菲【非】联军之胜利，实赖指挥之得人。且据经验可得，澳美陆军在蛮瘴之区作战，实不亚于敌人。中国以收复缅甸为解除危机之唯一途径，极盼英美克践诺言，否则前途殊不堪设想。邱谓，彼意并非限于空运及空军力量，将来当极力设法致印度与中国军队得以连合，或须经缅甸北部。总统谓，文可不必过虑，军事上攻缅政策，自当固定，但战略或须变更，将来取道仰光或其他地点，均未可知。文谓：中国现最盼望收复缅甸，前所拟定援华计划，应即执行。本人以国家存亡所系，不略择言，总统与首相为联合国中重要领袖，当然能谅解其关键所在。邱谓：彼虽无确实消息，但深信苏联如能支持度过本年夏间，将必愿意参加抗日。目前能援助中国之处，自当尽力。但纵使缅甸收复，滇缅路亦非如一九四五年前可得恢复，每月亦仅能运二万吨云。总统问，中国军队撤退时是否将滇缅路破坏。文答：只破坏一部份，日敌早已修复。据美国方面计划，该路若经改良，每月可有十万吨之运量，故非空运所能代替。等语。邱相于会后又切望文暂缓将本日会议情形报告政府，希望日后再与文会商。云云。谨闻。○马亥。文。卅二.五.廿

379. 宋子文致蒋介石报告与罗斯福谈丘吉尔昨日所言情形电(1943 年 5 月 21 日)

加码　呈委员长电　卅一.五.廿一日

极密。委座钧鉴：马亥电计达钧览。今午谒总统，彼谓，邱首相昨日所言殊不得体，但其目标与文所主张无大出入，故彼当时特为调解。文谓：邱所言实在可归纳为三点：（一）并无诺言。（二）加尔加答会议时，倘有承诺，实并未得其许可。（三）二月九日加埠会议报告，彼于五月下旬始得看见。邱昨于会后，又劝文暂缓报告蒋委员长，但文不得不即作报告。文于前日甫将总统所示攻缅计划电达蒋委员长，刚隔一日，又有此关于邱氏主张之报告，蒋委员长对之作何感想，自可想见。须知蒋员长为实行加尔加答所定计划，业已抽调部队赴滇，虽因此减弱其他战区兵力，亦在所不顾，此系完全信赖英国之诚意。今英又欲食言，是不仅为攻缅计划问题，且根本牵动联合国间之互相信任，关系尤为重大。此次英方诺言犹可推翻，则下星期如有所决定，是否可保证其必能维持。此中真相倘为中国人民所知，其影响诚不堪设想。总统谓：可报告蒋委员长，攻缅计划定必进行，参

谋部对此问题现正积极策划,下星期一即可完成报告。现可秘密相告者,魏佛尔形式上虽返原任,但指挥作战则将以一四十二岁富有魄力之师长升充。总统又问:报载日军距渝只一百二十七英里,是否属实。文答:扬子江以南局势确甚危急,前已报告矣。邱相昨放弃攻缅计划,而欲以未来之苏俄参战为替代品,未免近于幻想。苏俄情形,我方至为熟悉。苏在与德战前,本以大量军械助我,但现非俟败德后,必不加入对日作战。总统谓:德国败后,俄当愿加入,但届时吾人所需者不为苏俄之军队,而为空军根据地。文谓:更有欲进言者,史迪威将军在华时曾拟具一有限度的进攻北缅计划,委员长曾告以不予赞同,并于其回美时,嘱将不能赞同之理由转达总统。其理由在缅甸之地势与后方给养及补充之重要。盖六年来我方与日作战之秘诀,在迫使机械优越之敌人,运用恶劣之交通线,使其机械设备失其效用。试观缅甸地图,可知北缅形势适得其反。日人可利用伊落瓦底河及仰光铁路,而我方只有现正在建造中之里多(LEDO)①及英坊尔(IMPHAL)②两条公路。纵使我方在北缅立即成功,日人仍得藉马来亚与泰国之交通便利,继续派军增援。故委员长对史迪威一再说明不可再蹈前次失利之覆辙。总统问,然则北缅作战是否不能成功。文答,非以在缅南作战,遮断敌人后路不可。总统谓:是则有海军动作之必要。英国在印度洋只有旧军舰,又无飞机母舰,故全靠美国海军。且闻仰光附近有二十三处飞机场之多,海军将必受重大牺牲。文答,仰光一带飞机场均可自中国及加尔加答轰炸,因此目前我方在缅已占空中优势,日机无法截击我方空运,即其明证。总统谓,余曾语参谋团人员,何不在加尔加答建造一极大空军根据地,足使仰光炸为粉碎。文谓,同时使陈纳德队炸毁日军之交通线。总统谓,陈纳德需要战斗机及运输机都不成问题,余当力为设法。文谓,邱相拟派英国空军三队赴华,我方固甚感谢,但此举未免有碍空军指挥之统一,何不指定英空军保护阿萨密省③各飞机场,以替代现驻之美空军,而使美空军赴华。总统谓甚是,并谓拟给我载重车一千五百辆,用于伊朗公路,使每月运输可达四千吨,倘汽油缺乏,美方可供给木炭机。文再次申述,史迪威之攻北缅计划,徒耗军力,蒋委员长绝不能接受。总统谓,攻复仰光,确有困难,但可先向西南岸进攻,以从后面袭击仰光。又谓:英方前拟调纽丝兰④军队赴北非作战,余告以久战之兵应使憩息,因而劝止。目前在北非之美军队,余亦拟着休憩,故余将来如派军赴缅,必为新锐部队。请告蒋委员长攻缅计

---

① 地名,位于印度东北部,史迪威公路的印方起点。
② 地名,亦作因帕尔,位于印度东北部,印缅边境。
③ 即印度东北部的阿萨姆邦(Assam)。
④ 即新西兰(New Zealand)。

划,余有决心进行,下星期一英美参谋团当提出方案。云云。箇亥。文。卅一.
五.廿一

380. 蒋介石致宋子文告以丘吉尔干涉中国内政必坚决反对电(1943年5月 22日)

委员长来电

邱吉尔称西藏为独立国家,将我领土与主权,完全抹煞,侮辱实甚。不料英国竟有如此言动,殊为联合国共同之羞辱。应向罗总统问其对于邱言作何感想及如何处置。西藏为中国领土,藏事为中国内政,今邱相如此出言,无异干涉中国内政,是即首先破坏大西洋宪章。中国对此不能视为普通常事,必坚决反对,并难忽视。又,本月初英使①见吴次长②,面称西藏闻中国军队已进至昌都附近,其为恐慌,在此美国正对中国加强空运之时,不宜对藏用兵。其词气一如邱所言。当时吴即拒绝其请,声明此为我国内政,不能接受此等劝告,并由王雪艇③派杭立武④以私人关系警告英使,勿再提此事,故至今彼未敢再提也。此电请转三妹阅。中○。祃戌。

381. 宋子文致蒋介石报告与麦克洛依谈话情形电(1943年5月23日)

D1202　急　加码　呈委员长电　卅二.五.廿三日　复R1190

委座钧鉴:祃、祃戌、梗、养各电敬悉。

(一)顷往晤陆次⑤及史迪威,面述钧电所示情况,允即由昆明调驱逐机两队、轻轰炸机一队,赴渝助战,并增调驻印空军赴华。彼等意见,有空军掩护及由第九、第五战区夹击,敌无法得逞。

(二)关于西藏事,在此危急之时,务恳避免冲突。文观察英方将来对于西藏交涉,必能让步。英国已失数百年之积蓄,故希望战后中国建设获得一部贸易也。且即使开辟公路,如无英方合作,亦恐无益于事。罗总统曾口头告文,希望千万勿因此酿成意外。请即示复,以便转达。文俟此间各事就绪,

---

① 即时任英国驻华大使的卡尔(Sir Archibald Clark-Kerr)。
② 即吴国桢,字峙之,湖北建始人,时任国民政府外交部政务次长。
③ 即王世杰,字雪艇,时任军事委员会参事室主任、国民参政会秘书长。
④ 杭立武,安徽滁县人,时为中英文教基金董事会总干事,中英文化协会秘书长。
⑤ 即时任美国陆军部次长的麦克洛依(John J. MacCloy)。

即拟赴英与各当局接洽,随时秉承指示。勉力为之,自信或有相当成效。乞行钧意。

(三)顷陆次又告文,英美参谋团对于反攻全缅计划,态度较前似有进步。并陈。〇梗。文。

382. 蒋介石致宋子文指示应向罗斯福严重表示电(1943年5月23日)

R1182　委员长渝来电　加码　卅二.五.廿三　复　D1202

养(廿二)电悉。我政府只有对藏开辟公路以利运输,而决无集中十一个师进攻西藏之事。此说完全为英国所捏造,其用意欲我发表并无攻藏行动之宣言。务声明与对英保证,此决不能为也。余照前电之意,应向罗总统严重表示,英国在事实上已首先破坏大西洋宪章矣。此首先二字,应特注重。中正手启。梗(廿三)。

383. 宋子文致蒋介石报告此次英方较前似有诚意电(1943年5月24日)

致委座电

文昨与总统邱相会议,本日复与英美参谋团洽商。此次英国方面较前似有诚意,英美对日敌作战有全盘大举计划,非仅关于缅甸局部而已。因恐泄漏,不便电陈,拟派朱世民①武官下星期飞渝面陈详情。可否,乞示。文对此计划未表示意见,仅谓须先报告钧座后再复。文。敬(廿四)。

384. 蒋介石致宋子文告以关于西藏问题不能轻忽电(1943年5月25日)

R1190　委员长渝来电　加码　卅二.五.廿五　复 D1208

梗(廿三)电悉。关于西藏问题,不能轻忽,应照前电对罗总统严重表示,使其注意。如罗总统有勿因此发生意外之语,则我更应申明立场主权为要,否则其他军事要求与我之主张,更被轻视,以后一切交涉,皆必从此失败矣。切盼遵令执行,勿误。盼复。中正手启。有。

---

① 即朱世明,时任中国驻美国大使馆武官。

385. 宋子文致蒋介石报告当重复声明我国立场与主权电(1943 年 5 月 25 日)

D1208　极密　加码　呈委员长电　卅二.五.廿五日

委座钧鉴:有电敬悉。邱吉尔当日提及西藏,文立即郑重声明,西藏为中国主权所有,哈力法克斯①亦表示承认,次日总统亦云邱所言殊不得体。兹拟下次见总统时,遵令重复声明我国立场与主权,对任何人绝不能发表并无攻藏之言论。惟务乞饬令军队,千万不可发生冲突。英美反对我者,已谓中国一旦成为强国,必为侵略者。西藏为我国土,即使用兵,固绝非侵略可比,但不明真象者,必当误解。且将谓中国生死关头、一发千钧之际,不一致对敌,反分散兵力于和平之边境。在法律上,英国绝无干涉我内政之权,万一中藏间稍有冲突,事实上英国势必借题发挥,至少可能阻碍中印国际交通,破坏攻缅计划。钧座烛照无遗,毋待晓渎。伏乞垂察。○有西。文。卅二.五.廿五

386. 宋子文致蒋介石报告美现已决定进行攻缅计划电(1943 年 5 月 25 日)②

极密　加码　呈委员长电　卅二.五.廿五

本日罗总统面告,攻缅计划现已决定进行,并授文关于此项决定之通知书。原文另达,并闻另由美军事代表团呈。文谓,蒋委员长亟欲知作战之详细计划,首先愿知美国部队是否可派三师参加。总统谓,现只决定派工兵,其余则尚未决定。文问,将派作战部队否。总统谓,美方固愿,但英方称在印度精兵有六十万之众,故似无派兵渡洋之必要。依彼个人意见,美国部队一师,可等于英印部队三师。文谓,实可等于五师。总统谓:美方可派遣部队,但须视局势发展情形而定。惟美国海军陆战队,自文参加登陆作战,仰光附近可登岸者有五六处。英美联合参谋部现正在研究,期于四五日内完成工作。余曾说过,美海军定当助英作战。文谓,对此项详细计划,愿知其详,以资呈报蒋委员长。总统谓:恕不能尽量预告,军事上详细步骤,往往只可告知直接负责执行之人员,蒋委员长必能谅解此点。譬如经何处登岸,此时未曾决定,自不便转告,在登陆二三十日前可预告并拟在日军后方袭击之。至在何处开始亦不便说明。军事上原则,以知者愈少为妙。

---

① 即时任英国驻美大使的哈利法克斯。
② 该电文已收入《中华民国重要史料初编》第三编战时外交(三),第 242~244 页。

邱相现已决定派魏佛尔统率印度内地之印度部队,其地位实等于督察长官。同时,邱相已急电亚力山大及蒙哥利①两将军于北菲【非】作战最著功绩之师长中推选一人,并选兵站勤务能员一人,即以此二人充任攻缅指挥。故关于调派美国部队,须俟英方指挥人选决定,视其意见如何方能定夺。至关于史迪威,马歇尔已对余表示,如以大量中印空运供应空军,彼对于派史迪威回任有疑问。余以无可无不可答之。文谓,其善,但陈纳德宜早日返华。总统谓,拟先派陈纳德与史迪威赴英,俾与英方详细讨论关于伯勒马柏特勒河(Brahmaputra)及阿萨密交通等问题。总统末谓,两日来,彼与邱相商讨攻缅计划,直至早晨三时卒使邱折服,承诺一致进行。总统又问,日军威胁重庆情形如何。文谓,势甚危急,在过去数月中,我方曾屡向美方陈说应防止日军犯渝,惜美高级军官未能高瞻远瞩,至此时须仓促济急。总统谓,愿我方确知彼现正极力援助中国云。谨闻。文。

387. 宋子文致蒋介石报告与罗斯福谈西藏等问题电(1943年5月)

委座钧鉴:本早谒总统,先转钧座艳酉电,继遵照艳、戌电,向其提出各点。总统逐条答复为:(甲)英已决定派有力海军,控制缅甸海。彼已决定截断敌交通线,至先占仰光,或先占仰光附近城市,此乃战术问题,要在占领缅南。邱现在北菲【非】,本应早告余英国攻缅新司令,近日恐因帮于调停法国、北菲【非】两派争执,故尚未有电来,但日内必有消息。英方一定司令人选,彼与史梯威当可作一个完善计划。(乙)此次海军,英为主体,美为附助。现英美已亟力损害义主力舰队,觉颇有把握,此事能有相当成功,可操【超】过原定之控制缅甸海军力量。(丙)固当注意时时刻刻设法推动英方实践其诺言。(丁)所谓同时行动,如以同刻进攻,恐难办到,但至多亦不过两三星期之先后。余虽非军人,但以余判断,英度及中国方面先在缅土发动,俾敌人不能调动队伍,在二三星期后,以登陆之步【部】队,作背海之动作。末关于美国队伍参加,总统谓,目前只派工程队伍,但当考虑派一二师海军陆战队参战。总统续问宜昌战况。文答,此次充分证明美军部判断敌无攻重庆企图之错误,并证明总统注重派遣美国空军助战之大成功,但须继续增强补充在中国之空军,将第十大队之战斗机悉调中国。总统颇以为然,并即饬副参谋总长执行。最后文述钧座对西藏事各电意旨,请总统注意,并告以中国方面不能接受英方对西藏任何提议。总统谓:邱行前,余问其何以提西藏问题,

---

① 即蒙哥马利(Bernard Law Montgomery),英国将领,曾率英国第八集团军在北非与盟军协同作战,取得阿拉曼战役的胜利。

邱答英方并无占领西藏之企图。余又追问西藏乃中国帝制时代之一部份,现乃民国之一部份,与英国无涉。邱答中国政府在西藏无实权。余谓中国政府有无实权,与英国何涉。邱无以为答云。文谓:邱相□云中国集中十一师攻藏,实属荒谬。中国只有开辟公路,是以总统屡向文提议修筑中印间公路,以利运输。总统谓,此类事余亟盼早日与蒋委员长、史丹林、邱相四人会面,但邱不忘其英国独霸世界之传统观念,最好余与蒋委员长两人在四人会面前,早二三日畅谈云。

388. 宋子文致蒋介石报告与艾登等谈话情形电(1943年5月)

(一)艾登已赴加拿大转英,文与谈过四次。

(二)(甲)艾谓,攻缅计划,本年决执行,当调大量海空军参加,此次目的仅在恢复缅甸,打通中国陆运,至恢复泰、越、马来亚,俟第一步目的达到再谈。(乙)英决无姑息日本之意,愿以对付德之手段加于日本,战事了结后,处置日本方法,当适从中国意。(丙)英苏同盟,照苏联建议,包括欧洲,并未提及远东问题。(丁)战后国际组织当以四大国为主体,负责领导,不能如前次国联各小国之放纵,是以四大国应及早有共同一致政策。(戊)对战局甚乐观,但战后解决极难。美苏之间,美国太理想,苏联太实际。(己)文提及西藏问题,探询印度何以藐视中国主权,对他国中国毫无土地野心,但本土主权丝毫不能放松。彼因不知内容,愿文赴英时与文研究。嗣后彼告外次 Welles①,谓文曾提出此问题,彼已电伦敦问讯。据彼所推想,如有侵犯中国主权,必下属举动而已。

(三)艾登来美后,文连日与总统、霍尔、韦尔思、霍布金数次见面,探询英美间讨论内容。

(四)②艾注重讨论欧洲、亚洲问题。霍尔谓,英美对华,均极尊重中国权利,台湾、流球、东三省、大连,自当归还中国。至东三省问题,总统及韦尔思谓,中苏应直接谈判苏联过去铁路等特权。文谓,苏已将中东③售于日本,故已不成问题。外蒙古问题,总统亦谓中苏应直接谈判。文指出,全世界作应有战后全世界解决之方案,两国间之国疆问题,是以成为各国关切之问题。霍布金对此极同意。朝鲜问题,英美认为须独力【立】,但一时须同盟国 trusteeship④。香港问题,总统谓,可得英国之同意,但英方宣布之日期,当绝对守秘密,一方面中国自动宣布自

---

①　即时任美国副国务卿的韦尔思。
②　此处原稿为"甲"。
③　即位于中国东北的中东铁路。
④　指由同盟国行使托管权。

由港,因【应】在英国宣布后一两星期并事前绝对不使外间泄漏,以维持自动之本旨。

(五)印度问题。总统告前在 Cripps① 未起印度之前,曾带信邱吉尔,劝英国即宣布印度自治,不必谈去脱离英帝国制之权,以免印度宗教之争。艾登竟谓,总统信邱,未曾告渠。

(六)总统与艾登谈属地问题以同盟国 Trusteeship,艾登似颇能融【容】纳,英方且表示马来亚、星加坡可由同盟国 trusteeship。但据霍尔告文,邱吉尔既表示不愿放弃属地,此意义恐难对英国实行,但可施之于法属及前国联共管之旧德国属地而已。

(七)美方各人对邱吉尔演说轻视中国,甚为反对。文告总统,邱相主张设一欧洲国际集团、亚洲国际集团,实等于恢复强权政策,中国不能赞同。总统谓,曾告艾登,美国决不参加欧洲集团。

总统告艾登,美国只能参加世界集团,美国不能参加欧洲集团,即本人赞成,美国上议院决通不过。艾登对此坚决态度,甚为诧异,云云。查英国原来欲英美支配世界,继欲英美苏独霸世界。美方谓,欲白种人支配世界,决酿起色种大战。

(九)韦尔思谓,英、苏关于战后诸大问题不能公开讨论,恐美国战后仍回至孤立态度,一如第一次大战后之政策,故美国朝野应充分表示战后必负责参加世界集团。

(十)美苏间问题,艾登意欲英国居间商洽。惟美国表示直接磋商,不久霍布金或再赴莫世干,与史丹林直接谈判。

(十一)艾登来美,一切尚称顺利,英美间局部谅解可进一步。惟关于世界集团及集团安全等问题,无具体结论。

(十二)霍布金密告文,总统与渠意,中美间此时无须再非正式交换意见,尽可与美正式谈远东诸切实问题及中国关于世界集团意见。中美能谅解后,文宜赴英正式谈判。惟此类谈判,虽属正式,但仍保守秘密,同时希望中国与苏联开始交换意见。

389. 宋子文致蒋介石报告在英美参谋团会议发表主张电(1943 年 5 月)

(一)英美参谋团会议,各重要人除罗、邱外皆参入。李海主席邀文报告钧座意见。文谓:中国局部被围五年,敌占领缅甸,完全包围,因此军货接济无着,经济衰落,通货恶性澎涨【膨胀】。敌改变以前方准【针】,利用傀类【儡】买服人心,并

---

① 即英国爵士克里普斯。

不断用武力压迫政府区域，最近如攻晋豫鄂湘。此种危险情形，诸君在洞鉴之中。惟今日中国并无新要求，中国只欲同盟履行 Casablanca 总统、首相之决定①。

（二）Casablanca 决定：（甲）增强空军力量，攻击在华之敌及日本本部敌；（乙）克复缅甸。因空运之不足供应，增加空军此项决议至今未能实现，故美国在华空军，只能保卫中印空运路线，中国陆军从未得美国空军之掩护。关于空中作战计划，陈纳德已有详细说明矣。敌人企图进攻陪都、长沙及其他要点，最重要为美空军□力能□我共同作战。须知此数个月内，陆运中断，海运□□，同盟国只能空军予有效之援助，中国□处孤危之境，同盟国□□有效之□□，惟有空军而已，是以蒋委员长请总统在最近三个月内，完全运输空军需要，俾增强陈纳德将军之空军。

（三）查上星期五美参谋团会议，闻史梯威公开反对钧座计划，谓钧座对诸事皆犹豫不决，对于战略无一定之见解，故文补充几句：诸君须知此次同盟国作战，蒋委员长与当局并非初次与外国军事专家合作，在张古峰、NOMAHAN 破日敌之加伦将军，数年追随蒋委员长，创造德国防军之塞克特，及卢登道夫作战科科长佛采耳，及最近在史丹林克落②击破德军之 CHUKOV，皆当钧座顾问，无一不遵钧座意旨。是以如我辈顺钧座而误事，与我共同误识【事】者有世界之名将不少。且钧座负中国区安全之责任，如我辈不从钧座意旨，则我辈自应有能力负中国区之安全。

（四）决定反攻缅甸。总统、邱相 Casablanca 曾有电告，以海陆空军完全收复缅甸，打通滇缅路，复派狄而（Dill）③元帅、亚诺尔④航空司令，亲赴重庆，面陈一切，并在加埠会商，参加者有何部长、英美各高级军官及本人，决定各国所负任务。至此，文遂朗读将二月九日加埠英国武官之纪录，并指出：（甲）魏佛尔开会词有根据北非决定及重庆决定之语。（乙）何部长报告中国参加之兵力。（丙）魏佛尔决定印方派近十师队伍。（丁）何部长提出须有强大之海军力量参加，并经英海军提督之保证。（戊）何部长提出空军控制权，魏佛尔经亚诺尔之保证。及最后魏佛尔谓，各方既皆同意，现只须各方最大之努力准备反攻等语。文续谓：请诸君注意，攻缅并非一普通计划，确为三国共同之决议案，中国方面部队

---

① 1943 年 1 月美国总统罗斯福、英国首相丘吉尔在北非摩洛哥的卡萨布兰卡（Casablanca）举行会议，决定于当年 11 月反攻缅甸。
② 即斯大林格勒。
③ 狄而（Dill），即英国陆军元帅迪尔。
④ 亚诺尔，即前注之安诺得、安诺德。

已准备备战,并将机场完全扩充。今日蒋委员长并无新的要求,只须英美切实履行决议,以解除中国危机而已。且查本年攻缅计划,已为公开秘密,英美各政府要人曾向世界屡次公布,今我方待英美告我海空军布置情形,兹请诸君允□。万一攻缅计划放弃,中国全国军民必以为英美失约负友,美已表示无决心以武力强迫日敌投降。不但中国人心瓦解,失却中国根据地,同盟军实无法向敌作战。再者,北非会议以前,史梯威将军曾提议攻缅北,当时蒋委员长未允。盖因敌有铁路及 Irrawaddy 公路之交通,我如占领缅南,断其后路,必遭失败。蒋委员长今日之决心,更为坚定。

390. 宋子文致蒋介石关于如能收复宜昌影响重大电(1943 年 5 月)

致委座电

实行攻缅尚有数月,在此期间,美国空军或攻广州一带及沿海敌人船艘,或在扬子江活动。查国内经济及政治种种困难,如能收复宜昌,影响甚大。陈纳德深信,即可以空军力量阻扰敌人长江运输,同时以轰炸机协助陆军克复宜昌。如钧座以为然,请召陈纳德、陈辞秀①在渝开会。乞裁断。文。

391. 宋子文致蒋介石说明史迪威函件下星期方能回复电(1943 年 5 月)

致委座电

巧电敬悉。(一)克罗白昨始抵此,本早晤谈,甚融洽。其意见与我方颇同,已与其联络一致进行。史梯威函件因参谋总长下星件【期】始由伦敦回国,且此事与克罗白向其军部报告有关,故下星期方能电复。

(二)邱相抵美,原来为开辟第二战场洽商事,迨抵美,Tobruk② 被陷,遂注重托论如何援近东。至英苏同盟,美国之策不愿与任何国发生单独同盟关系,更不愿与苏联有此关系。英苏在托论同盟时,美已有明白表示,故邱相此次限于解识【释】英苏间不能不有同盟之苦衷。至中美同盟,鄙意时期尚未成熟,类如英法之同盟。及最后英国提议英法合并,世界战争须至最危急阶级民主国方有此决心。谨陈。

---

① 即陈诚,字辞修,浙江青田人,时任军事委员会第六战区司令长官、湖北省政府主席。
② 即托布鲁克,利比亚东北部港口城市,北非战略要地。

392. 宋子文致蒋介石报告美军人有不利于我之感想须设法补救电(1943 年 5 月)

本日太平洋会议,总统告,埃及事出于仓卒,不及待告即抽调第十大队一部份赴援,因此蒋委员长颇为着急,但埃及事即中国事,近东一失,中国运输道断绝无余。继谓,又曾电史丹琳,请临时交回四十五架抵波斯驱逐机,史即答允,可知:(一)苏俄对全部关系较前关心;(二)苏德战事不如外间所传之紧张。文不愿当众表示异议,故谓,关于此事,文接长电,容开会后报告。

继总统谓,中国抗战已五年,目前虽有困难,但全盘大局颇容乐观,中国只须支持,即可获最后胜利。文谓:中国领袖及上下皆有决心无疑,但五年之长病,发现种种困难,请略陈。自缅甸失陷,中国军械来源断绝;自沪、港、星加坡、菲岛、荷属沦陷后,我金融已受莫大打击,伦【沦】陷区币纸之战争,已告失败,通货澎涨【膨胀】已在危境;自敌占领浙赣铁路,盐粮均感恐惶,危机四伏,敌虽不加兵于陪都,是以最大之压迫。

总统继谓,日对西比利八月间进攻之模样,蛛丝马迹,如此事发生,则可解中国之危不少。云云。

查美国人民虽极同情于中国,而新自中国来之美人,尤其军人,十之八九有不利于我之感想。此系事实,务须设法补救。其论调:(甲)日木近来对华如浙赣等攻击,以小【少】数部队进攻,并未大举,而中国无力抵抗。(乙)中国自十二月八日以后,倚赖美国出力制日本,不愿自己牺牲。(三)中国军队无组织作战,力量极微,即予以军械,亦无大作用。(四)中国军政内部分烈【裂】。以黄秉衡归时,托其带函美政府各机关,派员至内地调查,我不应取完全开放主义。苏联对外国人士,即美国军官团,始终不准其赴内地或前线,用意不谓不深。

393. 宋子文致蒋介石密告美愿意担任中国军饷名义电(1943 年 5 月)

连日与各面洽商,感相【想】如下:

(一)推测其心理,罗、邱及财长极愿取盟国担任中国军饷名义,不用借款性质,可向世界表示其对友国之热忱。我可扩大其范围为担任此后中国一切军费,每月担任若干千万元。一切人数表【标】准不必提及。

(二)为整理已发行之法币,另提出向英美一次借若干万万元。

(三)第一项之心理甚热烈,我不可完全不顾,且为镇定军民心理,源源有固定友邦军费,较之龙【笼】统借款,觉更实在,可争取其信仰,且每月军费加之另订一次借款,其总数可达钧座之期望。

394. 宋子文致蒋介石报告赴纽约见宋美龄情形电(1943年5月)

致委座电

虞、佳各电敬悉。文昨赴纽约见三妹,交阅关于四人会面及盼望美方派有力海军控制各电。文并提议催促总统派正式陆军参加战事。三妹与文同意关于四人会面事不必太客气。至派正式陆军参战,三妹意,前渠向总统谈时,要求派美军参加【战】缅北,故此时最好亦请其派兵参战缅北。惟文意此次决定缅北缅南同时进行,最多亦不过二三星期之差,故最好不指明参加【战】缅北。如指定缅北,则参谋本部或将谓缅北运输困难,有中英军队作战,美军为运输关系〈参〉加不上。如何之处,仍请钧裁。

395. 宋子文致蒋介石报告陆海空军会议讨论钧座两项要求电(1943年5月)

昨午陆海空军会议,邀文及史梯威、陈纳德参加讨论钧座关于陆空军两项要求。文根据钧座叠电所示各节陈明及四月十九日与史梯威谈话记录详细说明:(甲)六、七、八三个月中印空运,专运空军需要。九月起四千八百吨,以资六月增添驱逐机三大队及此后扩充维持五百架计划。(乙)攻缅计划印度方面力量不足,最近缅南 ARAKAN 阿拉铅①英印军为少数敌军击溃可为一证。是以根据 CASABLANCA 决议派英美海陆军占领仰光,断绝敌人后援,请速派美军三师赴印完成此项任务。中国六年抗战,疲劳已极,今敌人打通岳州宜昌路线,威胁陪都,国内陆军无空军掩护,无法活动。国际陆地交通年内不能恢复,殊属万分危险等语。史对美派三个师并不表示意见,但谓中国陆军六年来无军械物资补充,万一空军活动,敌全力来攻,届时滇、桂、湘飞机场恐难坚持。文谓敌人深知中国区战场重要,如其有力量占领各飞机场,不论空军活动与否,亦必倾全力来攻。且关于此事,蒋委员长已郑重向总统说明,如有空军掩护,中国军队力能保卫各飞机场。史谓中国军队如有力量,何以委员长对敌人占领华容、石首,引以为虑? 文答:第一点,无论保卫滇、桂、湘飞机场及恢复华容、石首,均须有空军掩护;第二点,华容、石首之敌,有长江之交通线,与滇、桂、湘之间交通及地势困难情形不同。史梯威谓:中国陆军勇敢苦战,损失极大,顷集中滇、桂、黔一带之卅二师炮

① 即缅甸古城阿拉干。

兵,几等于无轻武器,兵额亦欠缺甚多,一连华容不满五十支步枪。彼现正设学校训练并有陈将军诚整理。目前情形实不堪一战。如按月印度有军械物资补充,深信九、十月间可成劲旅,如六、七、八三个月专为空军运输,则反攻缅甸殊无把握。文谓:今日谈话本为自己人事,陈纳德空军为援我,史梯威奋斗亦为援我,各有理由,钧座同等感激,同等维持。但以中国区总司令地位权衡轻重,为保卫重庆,为支援中国各地区战场,为振奋中国军民心起见,目前最需要为增加空军力量,三个月过后仍可分运陆军、空军物品,是以对史将军计划并无多大阻碍。且余以为史将军未免对中国陆军太悲观。今日之所谓不堪一战之队伍,即文在渝时其日夜催促本年三月一日反攻缅甸之队伍,云云。言毕,参谋总长向文道谢,文遂退席。顷三妹告昨晚与总统谈话,经过长时期催促,总统允:(甲)空运百分之五十为空军物品,百分之五十为陆军需要;(乙)返【反】攻缅甸缩改为占领缅北,至孟得来线为限,至派遣美国军队,俟魏活尔①将军来华府再商;(三)以中国在美训练之飞机司,利用现在 KARACHI 之飞机成两个总队。查目前空运月只四五千吨,如以半数供陈纳德,只能维持现有之飞机,决不能达到钧座所要求之六月增添三大队驱逐机,九月前扩充至前线五百架机。且第三项所谓 KARACHI 飞机,数目甚少且为旧式驱逐机,成立两个总队只空名。至原在 Casablanca、重庆、Calcutta 攻缅计划缩为攻缅北计划,钧座已再三声明,如非有海陆空军占领仰光,绝断敌人后援,缅甸事决不能取胜。邱相下星期将来华府。在其未到前,急切请示久【究】竟应接受总统昨日所谈,抑仍坚持钧座前议。文。

396. 宋子文致蒋介石密告台维斯谈中国近况函(1943 年 6 月 8 日)

6/8　外交部邮包寄复

委座钧鉴:据确息,国务部派在史梯威部下任政治顾问之约翰台维斯(John Davies)②对友人谈中国近况,称:

(一)共党军队努力抗敌,而中央以四十万大军监视共党。日同盟社报告,近月日军与共军接触次数,较与中央军接触次数多至二倍以上。花旗银行行员赫尔(Hall)及英国牛津大学倍利奥书院教务长(Master of Balliot)林赛(Lindsey)之子,均身历共区,对共军抗日成绩,颇致赞美。

(二)共党确信蒋委员长为联合中国唯一领袖,但蒋委员长仍反对共党。共党曾

---

① 即时任驻印英军司令的魏佛尔(Archibald P. Wavell)。
② 约翰·台维斯(John Davies),时任美国驻华大使馆二等秘书。

向中央主张厉行民主。

（三）蒋委员长地位颇有困难，彼在政治方面，注重事实，既不喜共党，亦不喜国民党，但其政治势力，仍以国民党为根基，并使党内各派之势力不失均衡。

（四）蒋委员长要求强大空军，用以维持其本人将来国内势力。美军部早经决定之步骤，为先供给中国以陆军军械。史梯威主张，即秉承军部意旨。陈纳德在中国政治方面极为活动，对军部计划予以阻碍。宋部长在国内时赞助史梯威，现则与史意见相左。中国军队能力薄弱，如实行空中攻击，日军不难袭取云南、广西之机场。

（五）美军部曾令史梯威，应利用一切机会统率中国军队。

（六）史梯威与罗总统会谈，结果甚觉不满。彼认罗总统对远东问题意见空洞，而对史所提出主要问题之取决，均作漠然之表示。

（七）史对罗总统深加批评，认为总统对彼与陈纳德，应决定孰用孰舍，但彼同时感觉总统素日对各派人物一体优容，对此亦必不采取断然之处置。

（八）史与华方关系，不如陈圆满。盖史每使华人进行华方所不愿担任之工作，而陈则每对华方让步也。

（九）中国通货膨胀，日形恶化。美国务部曾讨论此项情势是否有引起革命或内战之危机，结论认为膨胀必致增加人民痛苦，但无碍大局。

（十）日本出三师兵力，可以随时攻取云南。云南主席①一受攻击，即可倒戈。中国第六十军并无作战能力，现与日方勾结，专营走私，竟由安南运私酒售于驻华美空军之类。

（十一）美驻华军官每对华人发生恶感，主因由于路斯②系刊物"生命"Life、"时代"Time、"幸运"Fortune 杂志等，代华过度宣传，及到华目睹一切，感觉失望。

（十二）蒋委员长企图发展空军之目的，不外继续维持战后政权，消灭共党及各地方及政府份子。彼时美方所拥护者，不啻一中国"佛郎哥"（Franco）（西班牙独裁者），必致引起俄方反感，演成混乱局势。云云。

以上各节，颇堪注意，因史梯威、台维斯向美政府之正式报告，内容恐相类似也。谨此函陈，伏希鉴察。敬颂崇安。

397. 宋子文致蒋介石报告与罗斯福谈中英香港交涉情形电（1943 年 6 月）

昨谒总统。据告：艾登来美，拟与讨论欧洲善后问题。邱相不能脱离十九世纪

---

① 即龙云,时任云南省政府主席。
② 即前注之鲁斯。

思想,对艾登可坦白交换重建新世界意见。中英关系,彼拟提出交回香港问题,
英方初必不允,前曾将意见告蒋夫人,一面英自动将香港交回中国,一面中国自
动将香港九龙一部或全部划为自由港区,在该区内不征一切捐税。英国经营香
港百年,中国宣布自由港,可保全英侨民一部分权利,此乃中国为建设世界之供
【页】献。等语,并询文意见为何。文答:(一)卡尔大使在渝曾表示,英愿放弃香
港。顾大使①在英亦获得英方同样感想。(二)此次洽商废除不平等条约,英方
则表示愿在战后再商交还九龙问题。(三)香港已无军事重要性,至经济地位,
中国如严格以香港视为外国属地,香港必行破产。因未奉训示以前,文不愿对香
港制为自由区有所表示。此点伏乞钧裁赐复。总统又谓,钧座托亚诺将军带来
要求之事,已决定完全照办。运输机已增加至每月一万吨运量,战斗机队,军部
已允十二月前,在中国扩充至五百架。总统亟欲轰炸日本及其航线船只。文谓,
最好利用昆明湖,派海军、鱼雷、飞机轰沉敌人船只。彼颇以为然,将与海军部研
究。文续谓,中国重视攻缅计划,惟英方出击队伍以印度军队为主力,英印间之
隔阂如此,用以与日本军队作战,恐难出力。为占领缅甸及此后美国在亚洲及太
平洋发言地位关系,亟应遣派一个军团,至印度加入攻缅战事。总统谓,此点亦
彼所愿,大约一二师不成问题。文与军部继续讨论。最后总统谓:蒋夫人此次
莅美,予美国人以深切之好感,惟旅行目的,已完全达到,最好不再公开演说,至
阻碍其病体复原。彼与总统夫人意见,蒋夫人不必赴西方,即加拿大之行,亦无
多大作用。文谓,三妹此行,本专为治疾,蒙总统及夫人、朝野盛情特别款待,我
辈非常感谢不荷。

398. 宋子文致蒋介石报告十八日与罗斯福谈话情形电(1943 年 6 月)

(一)文于十八日谒总统,总统告完全了解钧座在军事经济上种种困难,故亟欲
增强驻华空军力量,因有下列之决定:

　　(甲)七月一日起,中印空运每月定为七千吨。首先应以四千七百吨供应陈
纳德之空军,其次以二千吨供应陆军,再其次以三百吨供给空军。

　　(乙)九月一日起,每月空运一万吨,并再逐以增加。

(二)文向总统问,五、六月份之空运可否完全供应空军。总统谓,此事请与副参
谋总长协商,恐不免小部份供应陆军。

(三)文旋与副参谋总长协商,双方决定如左:五、六月份,每月供应陆军五百吨,

---

①　即时任中国驻英国大使的顾维钧。

其余悉数供应空军;自七月一日起,供应空军吨位,每月有绝对之优先权四千七百吨,其余之数可归陆军;追陆军在十月底前,一共收到一万吨。

(四)总统命 Wheeler① 将军修理印度方面若干机场,其余机场,由邱相命令赶修。

399. 宋子文致蒋介石报告加拿大延缓拨给军火原因电(1943 年 7 月 1 日)

加码　呈委员长电　卅二.七.一日

委座钧鉴:四月敬、五月勘电陈加拿大拨给各项军火,顷始接该国国防工业部长正式通知,其延缓原因,关系美国军部托词,加拿大制造军械,有若干种附件及原料,向恃美国供给,且中印运输归美方负责,故美方亦应参与其事。其实有不识大体之军官,欲使所有供给中国之军械,须得史迪威查核,俾其权限愈重,地位愈高,在华便于支配。文获此密讯,即向加总理及霍布金揭破内幕,并谓,此类操纵,殊悖美国爱护盟邦之本旨。军部自知理屈,卒未发生波澜。事已告一段落,具见应付艰难。前请钧座电谢加总理及国防工业部长,兹将英文稿另电呈核,候示遵办。将来是项军火运抵印度,拟于文赴英时,与其当局切商,由我兵工署派员接收储藏,请示钧座起运及分配,不经史迪威之手,以免操纵。如何,并乞示遵。

400. 宋子文致蒋介石分析罗斯福与斯大林会晤可能性电(1943 年 7 月 26 日)

D03　加码　呈委员长电　卅二.七.廿六日

委座钧鉴:敬电敬悉。六月廿一日密函曾提及总统有与史丹林晤面之意。最近战局演变,且因苏联推动在莫斯科组织自由德国政府,与英美意见相左,罗更有晤史之必要,其约会地点,将在西比利亚。似拟罗或于回美时,欲在亚拉斯加②与钧座晤面。文离美之前,霍浦金③曾再询钧意,已遵马电特告矣。○宥。文。七.廿六日发

---

① 即韦洛(Raymond A. Wheeler),时任美国空军补给司令,史迪威之参谋长。
② 即阿拉斯加(Alaska),地区名,位于美国西北部。
③ 即霍普金斯(Harry L. Hopkins)。

401. 宋子文致蒋介石报告丘吉尔对苏深怀疑虑电(1943 年 7 月 27 日)

加码　呈委员长电　卅二.七.廿七

委座钧鉴：昨邱吉尔宴波兰外相时，表示对苏联态度深怀疑虑，且谓苏联无外交道德，与史丹林有何协定，每不践诺。又暗示万一苏方先进柏林，真不堪设想。云云。

402. 宋子文致蒋介石密告钱端升致丘吉尔及英阁员函内容电(1943 年 7 月 29 日)

D07C　呈委员长电　廿二.七.廿九.

委座钧鉴：少川言，克利浦斯告彼，钱端升①分函邱相与重要阁员及本人，谈中国政局：一、国民党专制；二、党外优秀份子，无法参加政府；三、经济状况危急，弊端百出，政府要人亦通同舞弊。克利浦斯谓，此类破坏英方对中国观感之事甚多，余虽百口称辩，不如中国人此类函件影响之深也，云云。乞赐注意。○艳。文。卅二.七.廿九日发

403. 宋子文致蒋介石报告丘吉尔言攻击日敌具有决心电(1943 年 7 月 29 日)

D08C　加码　呈委员长电　卅二.七.廿九日

委座钧鉴：本日邱相告文最近对义战事进展，又言攻击日敌，具有决心，除海空军外，正在筹画调遣大部陆军参战，俟下次与罗总统晤面时商决。文进问攻缅准备。邱答，当于雨季后进行。文以所言含浑【混】，告其钧座特欲明了英方攻缅详细计划。邱云，余欲彻底击溃日本，但攻击敌人，必须出其不意，攻其无备，不可限于人人所能预料之目标。此次北菲【非】战事胜利，亦即恃此策略。下星期二余将召集重要将领开太平洋会议，请阁下参加，当可得知内容。文云，依本人经验，重要决策，往往在正式会议之外举行会议，有时不过为通告已决定事项之大概而已。邱云，阁下之言诚然，兹请于下星期一先与海陆空军各最高当局协商，次日再参加太平洋会议，等语。再者，狄而元帅适在伦敦，顷来访晤。文询及攻缅计划，据云，雨季后攻缅，当无问题，

---

① 　钱端升，上海人，时任西南联大教授，国民参政会参政员。

但目标及所用力量，全视一二星期内新总司令派定后，彼之主张如何，及义大利之变化而定，义事两星期内当可分晓，如能速了，则用于彼方之登陆舰队及有力之海空军，可移调印度矣。云云。并陈钧察。○艳戌。文。卅二.七.廿九日发。

404. 宋子文致蒋介石请详示远征军最近情形电（1943年7月30日）

致委座电

文与陆、海、空军各参谋总长约下星期二检讨双方攻击缅甸准备情形，请钧座速将我出征军①最近整备情形、兵力番号、现在位置、训练程度、编制人数，及将来补给补充办法，以及目前粮弹交通、通信、卫生、器材储备状况，详示数字。我方应知英方情形并祈急电示复。○陷午。文。卅二.七.卅日午发。

405. 宋子文致蒋介石告以我方军事宣传幼稚恳请切实调整电（1943年7月）

致委座电

○电奉悉。二日合众社渝电，军部发言人谈称：鄂西五月四日至六月卅日战事激烈。日军死伤五万五千八百七十名，其中被俘者四十八名。战利品甚多，计获步枪六百四十六枝、机关枪卅挺、迫击炮十尊、战马三百余匹。又击落敌机三架、击沉日军内河航船十艘。云云。文意稍具常识之人，必觉我方如仅获此少数战利品，敌人决无五万余人之死伤。以各国战事常例判断，敌方死伤不能超过五千人。无怪美军部及史梯威不信鄂西战事之激烈，更不信敌人此次有胁迫陪都之企图，而证明文以前向军部及各人所述鄂西战况，为不实不尽。窃查我方军事宣传之幼稚，已非一日，往往以儿戏视之。且其报告损害政府之威信甚于敌人之宣传，其效用等于第五纵队参加工作。文代表钧座驻外三年之间，工作受其影响殊深。是以恳请钧座切实调整，以精干人员主持军事宣传。缺乏常识者，仅授以宣传大纲数条绝不能纠正此种错误。务乞赐予特别注意为祷。

---

① 即中国入缅远征军。

406. 宋子文致蒋介石报告与英陆海空三参谋长会谈情形电(1943 年 8 月 3 日)①

加码 呈委员长电 卅二.八.三日

密呈委座钧鉴:今午文偕顾大使②、蔡文治③与英陆海空军三参谋总长开会,陆军参谋长主席。

(一) 文首先告以我方已按照加尔各答所商攻缅办法进行,军队及给养补充等等均循序准备无误,钧座丞欲得知英方准备情形。另欲声明者,英方一部份人士以为滇缅路已彻底破坏,修复后运量亦只每月万吨左右。此类意见与事实不符,须知滇缅路不易破坏,为前线军运,中国段已增加工作,敌占领段亦然。沙尔温江④桥虽已破坏,但不难修筑临时军桥。我第二预备师早在该江西岸。以前滇缅路虽因缺乏车辆、汽油等,运量不大,但美国后勤部已有切实计划,每月可运十万吨。其方法为:甲、改良滇缅路工程;乙、利用滇缅铁路路基为第二条公路;丙、利用汽油输运管,供给沿途卡车;丁、编大部车辆运输队。此每月十万吨之计划,虽需数个月内逐渐实现,然第一步即使只运五万吨,对于反攻在华日敌,及空军轰炸日本,截断日本与南洋交通,或掩护英、美海军在中国沿海作战,已有极大效用。且得缅甸后,空运可不必绕越山岭。主席谓,英方所得报告,运量及该路情形与此不同,请义书面详告。又谓:七月卅一日加尔各答以西铁路均被河水冲毁,由加埠至阿萨姆铁路未受影响。目前英、美工程师组织委员会研究,并调查解法,或可利用海运至加埠补救若干,但已影响反攻之准备无疑,加以机场若干处亦被冲毁,至影响准备之程度如何,俟数日后详告。

(二) 文问海军准备如何。海参长答,义事变化,英国不久当可不必在地中海留大部海军,届时即可调至印度洋作战,不过调遣及稍加修理,均需时日。惟陆空军如准备完成,海军必不延缓。文复问义海军有无被德夺占之虑。彼答无此危险,但义军何日归降,不能预料。

(三) 文问空军进行如何。空参长答,飞机场虽被冲毁若干处,飞机已较前加多,惟需增加重轰炸机,亦与对义用兵相关,义事早决,当可抽调(据艾登密告,英、美无进攻巴尔干企图)。联军在缅制空权已渐加强。据报,本年一月在缅日机有二

---

① 该电文已收入《中华民国重要史料初编》第三编战时外交(三),第 254~256 页。
② 即时任中国驻英国大使的顾维钧。
③ 蔡文治,字定武,湖北黄冈人,时任中国驻美军事代表团代理团长。
④ 沙尔温江(Salween River),亚洲南部大河,中国境内称怒江,流入缅甸后始称沙尔温江。

百七十架,现只一百三四十架。又,二月至四月,联军空军出击次数,比敌多六倍,五月至七月,比敌多廿五倍。

(四)文问,首相见告英、美正讨论另以其他方法攻击日本,愿知其详。主席答,远东作战有下列各办法:甲)攻缅;乙)切断泰南 KRA 克拉半岛;丙)收复苏门答腊;丁)攻占南洋群岛,夺复石油、橡皮等原料区。但两国洽商尚无头绪。邱相欲用北菲【非】作战出其不意之战术,强敌作战,一举而击溃之。文问之,如采乙、丙、丁办法,是否甲项亦同时进行。彼答,战术虽时时重新考虑,但在未商定改变以前,仍依原来计划进行。文续问,攻击日本,英方是否准备调大部陆军前赴远东。彼答,依甲项办法,大部可自印度调派及接济,如依乙、丙、丁项,则须自英国调遣,给养亦须由英国输送。至军队调动之多寡,须视船舶吨位而定,目前海运已大见进步矣。

(五)文问,依照加尔各答议定办法,由印度应出军数,是否已达准备位置。主席答,未,因该区患疟,调回后方训练区,俾保持康健。(未完)

(六)文问,联军在准备期内,以空军尽量轰击缅甸敌根据地与交通线,削弱敌力,最近情形如何。主席答,进行正顺,现注重敌占码头与船只,计自二月至七月,炸毁大小敌船七七三只。主席又告,最近华府会议,将来攻缅统帅问题,因有英、美军参加,当仿南太平洋办法,另设统帅,不归印度总司令统帅。人选现与美商,亟希早决。

(七)主席问,由泰南至缅敌造铁路情形如何。文答,据我方消息,业已通车,设备尚不完全耳。

(八)文问,联军在北非及西雪利①登陆所用登陆驳船,收效宏,损失少,将来可大量照此以攻缅否。主席答,西雪利之役,损失之少,出乎意外,但蚀耗亦重,能调若干未可定。

(九)主席问敌在华活动及中亚西藏两运线,文均酌量答复。

(十)综核会谈情形,英方攻缅,据云虽依序准备,而因水患影响运输,且义战牵连,海、空军调动全视地中海事何时可了,故恐本年雨季一完,未必即可进攻。与美商各种制胜日本之其他计划,尚未决定究采何种办法,但表面上,主席谓攻缅为恢复与华交通,故无变更之意云。谨闻。文。卅二.八.四日午后六时发完。

---

① 即西西里岛(Sicily),位于亚平宁半岛西南,1943 年 7 月盟军在该岛登陆。

407. 宋子文致蒋介石请饬令驻昆明部队抽调空运赴印电(1943年8月10日)

D22C **加码** **呈委员长电** **卅二.八.十日**

委座钧鉴：顷接马歇尔参长急电称：中国驻印缅第卅八师、第廿二师各团尚缺步兵五千人,第卅师仅九百人到印。现作战期近,务请转陈钧座,急速调运补足为要。等语。查我方屡对英美宣称,中国惟富于人力,而我方早允于春季各师补足缺额。今情形如此,不免贻人口实,且罗、邱及两国重要将领,即将在坎拿大①举行会议,此事千万不能再缓。务恳饬令即刻驻昆明部队抽调空运赴印,如数补齐。如由〈内〉地调运,需时更多矣。乞核示后转达。再,此间各事粗毕,文定十一日离伦敦,次日由苏格兰飞返华府,并陈。〇蒸。文。卅二.八.十日发

408. 宋子文致蒋介石报告在伦敦与朝野晤谈情形函稿(1943年8月17日)

呈委员长函稿 **卅二.八.十七**

委座钧鉴：文留伦敦三星期,与彼方朝野名流及各国使节、流亡政府领袖等晤谈之余,见闻所及,或有呈供钧座参考之处,谨择数端,录陈于次。

一、此行自以探询英方对于远东战事之真实态度为主要目的。文与邱相谈话内容,前于艳戌电详陈,已可知其大概。虽自英皇以次,艾登、邱吉尔、陆海空军各部长及各党领袖,无不表示对日作战坚持到底,但所谓攻缅战略,另谋捷径,即便实行,为期尚远。一般以为欧战乃生死关头,德败则轴心瓦解,远东战事非目前之急务,即亚洲英帝国权益,只可暂时不顾。此类观念,与美国不同。美国人民一致要求扩展对日战争,视为国家必需之政策,不仅为同情援助中国,且舆论影响甚巨。英国战时内阁实权庞大,一切政策之决定,全在政府。人民虽亦同情我国抗战,但政党意见、人民舆论,影响甚微。故太平洋作战之最后决定,仍在美方。美国若供给陆海空军力量,英国亦必合力作战。盖能左右英政府者,惟罗总统一人而已。

二、墨索里尼意外失败②,无疑为意大利崩溃之开始,大举轰炸德境,秋季更将加甚,以及苏联抗战之坚强,轴心〈国〉潜艇之失效,联盟国军需生产之激增,凡此种种,俱使英当局确信德国不久必不能支持。空军总司令言,德国有效防空方法若

---

① 即加拿大。
② 1943年7月意大利发生政变,墨索里尼被捕,法西斯政权倒台。

无进步,联军陆海军若速合进攻顺利,则仅以空军之力量,即足使德国于本年底投降。此言虽过于乐观,然一般人俱以为至迟不过来年春夏季间事耳。

三、英国战时社会生活完全改观,人民自五十五岁以下,均须服役工场或补助战事之业。劳工部长严厉执行此项政策,无分贵贱,待遇一律。生活必需品,一切企业、交通、金融,无不受政府严格有效之统制。社会秩序井然,优于美国,颇足取法。一般政党领袖、企业家、银行家、教会,公认最前进之社会保护政策为战后所必需,但在战争时期,自以政府主持设计及统制管理为适当。不若美国人民,反有私管企业之趋向也。

四、英国外交方针,胥以能否制止德国再起为转移。英苏廿年不侵犯条约之签订,英本以为唯一解毒之方,其实苏联不过为求得物资上之援助,及至开辟第二战场未能实现,渐感失望。目前苏联实力强大,已有单独行动之势。且参加对日作战,须在德败以后,乃有可能。但亦不过坐享其成,一九三九年对波兰之故智。艾登因此希望法国复兴,加入同盟,抵制苏联,复拟划分其他欧陆为英苏两势力范围,再由列强保证世界安全。邱吉尔怀疑苏联,力图取得美国共同负责之外援。在战时,美国应不惜牺牲人力物力及海军,一切按照两国资源比例分担损失。战后恢复远东失地,甚至扩充英属政策于欧洲大陆,香港至少须为英海军根据地。海陆空军均将保持战时全部力量,以便配置于欧陆及远东。英外部意见,日本战败后仍当维持其皇室,以秩父代昭和。

五、英国对于印度及英属各地,负债达四十万万美元,加以战时每年举债十万万零两千万元,对美所负债额,更属惊人。英政府负责者,正考虑设法销除。战后复兴,势将倚赖国外市场,并愿恢复日本市场。罗总统曾明告艾登,希望中国因美国之协助,于五十年内成一强国,此言或足以增加英方误会。邱相深知英美对华之最后决定在华府,只有以其毅力试为操纵而已。

六、文曾与欧洲各流亡政府首领,及前西班牙共和党各领袖晤谈,彼等一致畏惧德国之再起及苏联势力之影响,虽明知若无苏联之抗战,联盟国早已战败。欧洲沦陷区内秘密活动,颇有社会主义之趋向,政治组织虽不显明,或有联合为一欧洲集团之可能。

七、最难解决之问题,即为苏联与波兰之争端。苏联希望或者成立一独立之波兰,与苏联缔结军事同盟及共同一致之外交政策,或者以分割土地及无产宣传,使沦为弱小国家。苏联显然争取一九四一年与芬兰所定之边界,割取挪威北端,以达大西洋,并获得波罗的海诸小国、罗马尼亚、沙罗尼加埠之管理权。英国最初受美国影响,反对战时关于土地疆界之谈判,但目前英美或将变更此政策。

八、德国国防军内部分为三派,旧军官派已渐失势,其余两派势均力敌。附属戈林①及沙特者主张与西欧各国成立谅解,共同对付苏联;另一派则主张苏德同盟为德国称雄世界唯一办法,即使赤化,亦所不恤。苏联现拟成立自由德国委员会。此举足以操纵现局,英美颇抱不安。后因史丹林再三拒绝与罗总统会商,于是奎贝克②会议后,艾登乃不得不赴莫斯科一行。

综核上陈各节,欧洲战事,虽有进展,政治内幕,则愈趋复杂。对日作战,英美未趋一致,最后决定,仍须总统努力。

409. 宋子文致蒋介石报告今日抵达魁北克电(1943年8月22日)

加码　呈委员长电　卅二.八.廿二日

委座钧鉴:文今日午后四时抵奎贝克,加总理亲莅机场欢迎,其他要人尚未晤面。闻会议对苏联空气甚恶劣,一般不赞成即辟第二战线。苏政府除撤换驻美大使李维诺夫③外,现又召回来奎贝克之塔斯社访员,表示对英美冷淡。顷晤某重要美国将领,据密告:此次英美攻缅,具有决心。本日电驻印总司令积极准备运输线,并即由美起运油管,一并装置加尔各答经 Fort Herz④ 至云南之线,每月可运飞机汽油一万八千吨。一备滇缅路至昆明之线,月可运油三万六千吨,一备前方军队用,月可运九千吨云。文。

410. 宋子文致蒋介石报告与罗斯福丘吉尔谈话情形电(1943年8月23日)

加码　呈委员长电　卅二.八.廿三日

委座钧鉴:总统、邱相顷约午餐,只霍布金作陪。入席前总统先见文,密告战事计划进行顺利,但关于战后政治问题,邱仍固执不悟。入席后,邱首谓,此次用尽心力筹划对付日敌,结论请总统讲明。总统云:

(一)即日由美起运油管,装置加尔各答,经阿萨密及 Fort Herz 至昆明之线,三个月可抵加,到后五个月完工。无论如何,明年夏季每月可运飞机汽油一万五千吨,足供需要。

(二)加阔列多 LEDO⑤ 道路,俾缅北与昆明通车。

---

① 戈林(Hermann Wilhelm Goering),纳粹德国帝国元帅,空军总司令。
② 即加拿大魁北克。
③ 李维诺夫(Litvinov),时为苏联副外交人民委员,驻美国大使。
④ 应为 Fort Hertz,即赫兹堡,缅甸北部小城。
⑤ 即前注之里多(Ledo)。

(三)派遣受过森林作战训练之美军渗入英军,在缅北作战,打通至中国陆路,详细计划请文及早与英美参谋团接洽。

(四)中印空运现达七千吨,下月可达万吨,明春可达二万吨,驻华空军之增加,当以中方空运能力为标准。

(五)驻印军出征后,如中国愿意,可续派部队至兰木加训练。

邱告,英出征军总司令已内定某皇族。文在伦敦时,邱曾介绍晤谈。此君年富力强,颇有资望。邱云,现当未到宣布时期,请文暂勿电陈姓名,以免电报传递泄漏。文询究竟缅南进攻之议,何时执行,两人仍以须视驻地中海舰队何时可抽调为词,但用海军掩护登陆当进行无疑。文告以俟明晨与参谋团接洽后,转陈钧座核夺。再,钧座致罗电,已遵照面转。

411. 宋子文致蒋介石报告蒙巴顿不久到印后即赴渝电(1943年8月25日)

加码　呈委员长电　卅二.八.廿五日

委座钧鉴:文今晨抵美。奎贝克会议时,邱相密告,英远东军总司令已内定皇族 Lord Louis Mountbatten 蒙培登①,曾充著名航空母舰 Illustrious 舰长,海军中将,即将升上将,现任海陆军联合登陆部队参谋长,深得邱信任。文在伦敦时,邱曾介绍晤面。彼亦出席此次会议。数度倾谈,知为能将,年富力强,对钧座极致敬仰。美方认为资望允孚,不久到印后,即赴渝晋谒,请暂勿与任何人提及。将来远东战事,此人关系最大。以前我国对于盟军,每因联络不得其人,吃亏甚大。此次似应遴派干员,随时周旋应付。驻澳联络员王之②,深谙南太平洋区战况。今后与□区联合作战,亦熟悉该区者。文意拟请将该员调驻印度英远东军联络处。尚乞钧裁。○有。

412. 宋子文致蒋介石报告与英美方面谈战后内河沿海航线问题电(1943年8月)

最密　致委座电

文在伦敦时,怡和太古③代表来访,征求中国关于内河及沿海航线最后计划及与

---

①　即蒙巴顿,时任英国海陆军联合登陆部队参谋长,后出任东南亚战区盟军总司令。

②　王之,字淡如,湖南长沙人,时任军事委员会委员长侍从参谋,正辗转于西太平洋南北,担任中国与盟军之间的情报联络工作。

③　即英国怡和洋行(Jardine Matheson)和太古洋行(Swire),航运是其重要业务之一。

兹两公司合作方案。文以此问题关系我国复兴建设计划至巨,仅虚与委蛇。今美国战时海运局表示愿协助我国:(一)训练航行及管理人员;(二)商讨供给战后我方需要船只,或向美国租借或购造,目的在希望其太平洋航线与我国内航取得联络。战后远东航线必为英美竞争之点,我国暂时似不必有所明显表示。惟为运用机会起见,请饬曾养甫①速派□□来美,助文随时策划,呈候钧座核定。但关于英美内容等情,请勿告任何人,告之□其对外言论太随便。敬乞钧裁。文。

413. 宋子文致蒋介石报告美方对战后世界性组织设想电(1943 年 9 月 3 日)②

加码　呈委员长电　卅二.九.三日

委座钧鉴:霍尔告文,总统所云世界性组织③,数日内将以书面交文,希望不久成立。以四强之间先订协约为根据,大致:(一)四强为最高委员会,负有以武力维持世界安全之责;(二)十一国为理事会理事(COUNCIL MEMBERS);(三)所有联合国均为大会会员(ASSEMBLY MEMBERS)。此组织系临时性质,战后再成立永久机关云。文。

414. 宋子文致蒋介石报告与魏道明刘锴等会商情形电(1943 年 9 月 9 日)

加码　呈委员长电　卅二.九.九日

委座钧鉴:本日召集魏大使道明④、刘公使锴⑤、夏晋麟⑥、卢祺新等,至医院会商,谨遵虞电指示,积极准备,并与各重要新闻随时联络。各员金谓最近此间各报登载山东共军与保安队冲突消息,美方一般人士多重视,因此可能发生之影响,深以为虑,此点实堪注意。各员走后,文反复筹思最好办法。大会宣言,侧重实行宪法时期及战后政治经济之方针各点,此间加以积极宣传,必能得国际舆论上之最大同情。若连带共党问题,一般不明真象者"左倾人士",必曲解本党大政

① 曾养甫,广东平远人,时任国民政府交通部部长、军事工程委员会主任委员。
② 该电文已收入《中华民国重要史料初编》第三编战时外交(三),第 798 页。
③ 即 1945 年成立的联合国(United Nations)。
④ 魏道明,字伯聪,江西德化(今九江)人,1942 年 9 月 11 日起任中国驻美国大使。
⑤ 刘锴,字亦锴,广东香山(今中山)人,时任中国驻美大使馆公使衔参事。
⑥ 夏晋麟,字天长,浙江鄞县人,时为国民党中央宣传部国际宣传处纽约办事处负责人。

方针,不过为解决共党之手段。故宣言不如不提处置共党问题,俟一两个月后,根据此项大政方针,促使共党就范,一面更广事宣传,必有良好效果。谨贡【供】参考,仍乞钧裁。〇青。卅二.九.十

415. 宋子文致蒋介石提议与英美军事关系调整方案电(1943年9月)

委座钧鉴:联军对日攻势渐趋积极,我方与英美军事关系,亟应调整。文拟下星期一先与总统作原则上之检讨,迨下月偕陆次①来渝时,再切实商承钧座决定。调整方案可分二类:(甲)属于最高级之组织者如下:华府之联合参谋团及军械支配委员均应有中国代表参加。而供给中国之军械应由中国直接申请,毋须史梯威或其他驻中国之美国军官过问。(乙)属于中国战区组织者如下:史梯威即行撤调,但只撤换史一人不足以根本改善中国战区内之中美军事关系。不久将来中国为联军与日敌之大战场,届时英美有极大部份之陆海空军参战。如该项军队仍由英美将领统帅,一如今日美方在中国、缅甸、印度之空军,直接受史梯威之指挥,则中国战区统帅徒有其名,危险殊甚。鄙见改善之途径,在仿效麦克阿瑟②、艾森豪③、蒙培登所指挥之战区组织,改组中国战区。钧座为最高统帅,以美国将领充任副统帅,以中国将领为参谋长,以美国将领充副参谋长,统帅部各处长以中美军官分任之,副处长亦然。

416. 宋子文致蒋介石报告与罗斯福讨论中国战区等问题电(1943年9月)④

急

委座钧鉴:顷与总统讨论各问题甚久,详细容面陈。兹□简单结论如下:

(一)中国战区并无变更,仍包括越泰,邱相虽欲划归蒙培顿区⑤,美必坚持。

(二)中国大军入缅,毫无不欢迎意。此点文以为必然。

(三)遵撤史梯威。

(四)总统意在华府另组织太平洋军事参谋团,中国参入。此事迨文回国再商。

(五)遵照文〇电改组中国战区。

---

① 即时任美国陆军部次长的麦克洛依(John J. McCloy)。
② 麦克阿瑟(Douglas MacArthur),美国将领,时任西南太平洋战区盟军总司令。
③ 艾森豪,即艾森豪威尔(Dwight David Eisenhower),美国将领,时任北非与地中海盟军总司令。
④ 该电文已收入《中华民国重要史料初编》第三编战时外交(三),第267页。
⑤ 即以英国将领蒙巴顿为总司令的盟军东南亚战区。

大纲如上,明日续谈。至文回渝事,因与英美约定,且蒙培顿此行①关系甚重大,故难于变更。再,文亟须报告国际情形,并与钧座洽商将来与罗邱晤面时诸问题,故决于星期五动身飞 New Delhi②,偕蒙培顿同来。文。

417. 宋子文致蒋介石报告关于地中海委员会情形电(1943 年 9 月)

呈委员长电

委座钧鉴:○电敬悉。塔斯通讯社消息,大致属实,美方亦予确认。其所称军事政治委员会,即指所谓地中海委员会。邱首相于本月廿一日在英众院演说,曾声明系苏俄主张设立。赫尔于廿二日与记者谈话,解释该委员会之作用,曾谓该委员会并无决定政策之权,仅为一承转机关,随时就地搜集有价值与有重要性之情报,以报告与建议于各该政府,是于俄、英、美及中国等国,实有便利之处,云云。记者有问中国是否参加,赫尔谓尚未与总统谈及,但地中海区之进展情形,无论与中国有无切身关系,亦自当尽量通知中国政府,云云。又,美外部面告,该委员会所注视者为义大利军事局势所产生之政治进展,美代表人选尚未决定。苏俄以地中海区进展与将来巴尔干军事动作极有影响,故特别注重。文告以我国素重视此次战争之世界性,地中海区之政治进展,我国自亦关心,宜有代表参加,亦足以表示四强之团结。美外部愿以我方意见提出考虑。又,前○○电所陈对义休战条件,据美外部告:当时爱森豪将军③提前于九月三日与义代表秘密签字,仅限于军事条款,其内容已电由美大使转呈。其余关于政治及经济部份,原拟继续谈判,但现时义政府实际上无统治能力,义皇与其首相逃避南部,故除军事休战外,其他条件或暂无签字之必要,但将来拟设立一管理委员会,隶属于联军总司令,以处理民事事务。届时有关政府可派员与该委员会联络,管理各该国权益。云云。○

418. 宋子文致蒋介石报告关于国民党五届十一中全会美国舆论情形电 (1943 年 9 月)

全会④对共党案之原文暨全会宣言尚未详载各报,惟委座对战后实行宪政与解

---

① 根据 1943 年 8 月英美最高当局在加拿大魁北克会议确定的反攻缅甸方案,蒙巴顿将赴印度考察缅北战事的准备工作并赴重庆向蒋介石说明魁北克会议的决定。
② 即印度首都新德里。
③ 即艾森豪威尔(Dwight David Eisenhower)。
④ 即 1943 年 9 月在重庆召开的国民党五届十一中全会。

决共党问题之训辞,已见各报,并深引起美国各方之好感与希望。关于战后经济建设暨中外合资比率不加限制之议案,美方亦颇有好评。兹再详述如次:(一)委座久为政府重心,世所共知,今兹升任主席①,总管政军两政,实属至当之选,有非斯人不可之意。在宪政未实施以前,权威当更高于昔。(二)中国一党主政,颇引起美方誉【舆】论之疑惧,以为将趋于专制,背反【叛】民主,或将无期延搁宪政。此次确定期限召集国民大会颁布宪法,并指定实施日期,可谓排除此种疑虑,使战后有与民主中国提携合作之希望。(三)美方对共党处置问题颇多注意,此次宣布容忍,以政治方法解决,已博得各方一致之赞称。纽约论坛报有希望容忍态度实施于战地,使破坏和平之责由共党负之一语。

---

①   国民党五届十一中全会通过《修正国民政府组织法案》,废弃四届一中全会关于国民政府主席不负实际行政责任的规定,同时正式选举蒋介石为国民政府主席。原国民政府主席林森于 1943 年 8 月 1 日去世后,蒋介石曾代理国民政府主席。

Select Telegrams between Chiang Kai-shek and T. V. Soong, 1940 – 1943

Translated by Hsiao-ting Lin and Jiang Shaoqing

Editor's Notes

1. All telegrams collected in this volume are selected from the Boxes 59 – 61 of T. V. Soong Archives at the Hoover Institution, Stanford University. With the permission of the Hoover Institution and Madame Laurette Soong Feng, this is one of the volume of the Hoover Institution and Fudan University Modern China Research Series: Leadership and Archival Documents.

2. Most of the telegrams in this volume are correspondences between T. V. Soong and Chiang Kai-shek during 1940 and 1943. A small portion of the correspondences are letters that T. V. Soong wrote to Chiang Kai-shek and hand-delivered by Soong's personal envoy. All are transcriptions of the original handwritten documents.

3. The titles of the telegrams, including names of the sender, receiver or third party are added by the editor for the reader's convenience.

4. All texts in the original documents are accurately transcribed in this edition. The punctuation has been duly edited to correspond with the original.

5. Notes of names of people, places, nations, organizations, as well as terms for positions, titles, major events, etc. are marked at the bottom of the page where these terms first appear. In addition, an index of names and special terms is appended at the end of the volume.

6. All personal names are spelled in the pinyin romanization system, with exception for the most popularly used spellings of names such as Chiang Kai-shek, T. V. Soong, H. H. K'ung, etc.

7. The original text is in Chinese. The English version is a translation of the original Chinese texts.

8. This book is co-edited by Wu Jingping and Tai-chun Kuo. Notes are made by Wu Jingping and Cao Jiahan. English translation is done by Hsiao-ting Lin and Jiang Shaoqing. Chinese and English introductions are contributed by Wu Jingping, and Ramon H. Myers, respectively. The Chinese and English indexes are done by Cao Jiahan, Wang Li, Shi Tao and Mr. Li Hui. Chinese proof reading is done by Wu Jingping, Cao Jiahan, Wang Li, Shi Tao, Wan Liming and Mr. Tian Xingrong; English proof reading is conducted by Tai-chun Kuo, Hsiao-ting Lin and Jiang Shaoqing.

TABLE OF CONTENTS

Casting New Light on Modern Chinese History: An Introduction

Ramon H. Myers

Senior Fellow Emeritus

Hoover Institution, Stanford University

The private papers of T. V. Soong have long constituted an important part of the Hoover Institution archival collections in modern China. In April 2004, T. V. Soong's family granted permission to the Hoover Archives to open nineteen file boxes that had been previously closed to the public, and then provided an addition of three thousand documents hand-carried by Michael Feng, T. V. Soong's grandson. Among these new materials are more than five hundred telegrams between T. V. Soong and Chiang Kai-shek. These telegrams provide a clear picture of Soong's political and diplomatic careers in World War II, when he was, firstly, Chiang Kai-shek's personal envoy to US President Franklin D. Roosevelt, and then Chinese Foreign Minister. The significance of these telegrams, carefully selected, translated and published in this volume, show how and why the Sino-American relationship was revitalized during wartime, and how T. V. Soong had contributed to that relationship.

After Pearl Harbor in December 1941, the United States joined with a non-Western country, China, to defeat an Asian power: the empire of Japan. At first, Washington's leaders welcomed this alliance and provided China with loans, economic and military materials, and personnel assistance to help China become stronger and more effective against the Japanese imperial army. But China's image as a great power began to fade in Washington, particularly after the Cairo Summit in November 1943. Disillusioned with Nationalist China's limited ability to engage Japanese troops, the US Government now criticized Chiang Kai-shek, his administration, and his armed forces for ineptitude and corruption. In fact, historians have concluded that it was the corrupt and inept Chinese leadership that brought about the Nationalist Government's eventual defeat in 1949. Some have also tried to explain "who lost China?" Many accused Chiang Kai-shek and his in-laws, namely T. V. Soong and H. H. K'ung, as responsible for communist unification of the Chinese mainland.

However, the new T. V. Soong telegrams have much to tell us about the US-China relationship during World War II. They reveal close, friendly relations between Washington officials and the representatives of Chongqing (China's wartime capital in Sichuan Province) during 1940 – 1943. They also describe in detail the financial and military aid to China arranged by T. V. Soong. Close Sino-American relations even helped elevate Nationalist China's international status to one of the "Big Four".

How did Chongqing leaders in these few years convince the US and its allies to place their trust in Nationalist China? Why was this period of trust and friendship so short-lived? Did Chinese leaders like T. V. Soong make a difference? If so, then how? The selected telegram correspondence between Chiang Kai-shek and T. V. Soong in this volume offers new insights into these intriguing questions.

Born into a wealthy family of Shanghai Christians in December 1894, the son of Charles Soong and brother to the eminent Soong sisters, T. V. Soong obtained a B. A. in economics from Harvard in 1915. In 1917 he returned to China and became a secretary in the famous Han-Yeh-Ping Iron and Coal Company. In 1923, he joined Sun Yat-sen's revolutionary campaign to unify China, thus beginning his political career. After serving as Sun's private secretary, he held high positions in Sun's Canton government, including Central Bank Manager and Finance Minister. After Chiang Kai-shek completed his Northern Expedition in 1928, Soong joined the Nationalist Government, serving as Minister of Finance (1928 – 1933), Governor of the

Central Bank of China (1928 - 1934), and Acting President of the Executive Yuan (1930 - 1933). During the early years of Nationalist rule, T. V. Soong simplified the tax system, increased tax revenue, and established China's first bond and stock markets in Shanghai. In 1931 he helped establish the National Economic Council (which in 1934 became the China Development Finance Corporation) to supply credit for China's industrialization and attract foreign capital to China.

In the summer of 1940, three years after the Japanese invasion of China, T. V. Soong went to Washington as Chiang Kai-shek's personal representative to the Unied States. Chiang wanted him to work with the US and win President Franklin D. Roosevelt's support for China's war with Japan. Until late 1943, Soong negotiated substantial loans from the United States to support the Chinese war effort. In December 1941, immediately after the attack on Pearl Harbor, Chiang Kai-shek appointed Soong Minister of Foreign Affairs to remain in Washington and to manage China's alliance with the United States and Great Britain.

After his arrival in Washington, T. V. Soong spared no effort to build the US-China alliance. With his political skills and Chiang's trust, Soong brought all his talents into full play. As demonstrated in his telegram correspondence with Generalissimo Chiang Kai-shek in Chongqing, he gave speeches to Americans and wrote articles for newspapers; he made friends and built alliances. Soong's hard work and management skills soon paid off. Within six months, the network for China's lobby to obtain more US aid was in place. Soong had developed many strong and mutual friendships in the White House, the Treasury, the War Department, and at the *New York Times*. Now Soong's important friends were Stanley K. Hornbeck, William Youngman, Thomas Corcoran, William Pawley, Claire L. Chennault, and Joseph Alsop. On December 4, 1940, Soong reported his progress to Chiang Kai-shek, "I was helpless for the first six months here in Washington, but in the past two months I began to get the knack."

On October 22, 1940, Soong represented China in signing an agreement with the United States, receiving a credit of $25 million for the Nationalist government. Soong was not content with this success, but considered it a good beginning. In a series of confidential telegrams to Chiang Kai-shek, Soong expressed confidence that, in addition to the $25 million loan, he could secure more financial support for China and minimize China's wartime financial difficulties.

After Japan joined the Axis powers in late 1940, more American officials now believed that the Japanese military was determined to destroy Chiang Kai-shek and his Nationalist government. War with Japan was inevitable. Soong, taking advantage of the changing situation, urged Frank Knox, then US Secretary of Navy, to submit a proposal to aide China. The Secretary of State, Cordell Hull, also pressed Roosevelt to respond to china's requests. When President Roosevelt instructed Morgenthau to negotiate the details with Soong, Soong proposed that Washngton combine all loans into a total loan of $100 million. President Roosevelt accepted. Excited by the good news, Soong did not forget to remind officials in Chongqing that "more efforts should be done in order to secure trust and sincere friendship from the United States."

How well did Soong perform in Washington? Historians hitherto have known little about his opinions regarding Sino-American relations, or how he persuaded his American partners to support China. But from the new T. V. Soong telegrams we learn that Soong played a crucial role in obtaining aid when China desperately needed it.

T. V. Soong strengthened US-China cooperation in other ways as seen in the example of the Flying Tigers. By late November 1940, Soong sensed that high officials in Washington would recognize China's new importance now that war with Japan was inevitable. He submitted to Henry Morgenthau a proposal drafted with Claire Chennault advocating a plan for strategic bombing. They argued that if Chennault and Nationalist China "were given a 500 – bomber force that was piloted, supplied and maintained by the United States," the Nationalist Government "could virtually annihilate the Japanese forces within China and neutralize Japan's naval striking ability." According to Soong, this "Special Air Unit" could "operate independently in attacking Japan proper," and would "surely undermine Japanese public morale."

Although Soong's ingenious suggestion persuaded some US officials like Henry Morgenthau, his proposal soon met strong opposition from the War Department. High officials in the Chiefs of Staff and the Department, such as George Marshall and Henry Stimson, vehemently opposed any diversion of limited bombers and crews to China that would deprive the British of more airpower. Their thinking was understandable, as the concept of "Europe first" was deep-rooted in the minds of most high military authorities in Washington. But Soong refused to give up. He soon drafted another project to avoid antagonizing the War Department and still help China. Soong proposed a new scheme-to create a non-government, volunteer air force to fly and fight for China. These officers would resign their official tasks and sign contracts as civilian agents. US Government leaders quickly accepted this plan.

By early 1941, Soong and Chennault, assisted by the White House, worked out a plan to establish the American Volunteer Group (AVG) in Washington. With the consent of President Roosevelt, the AVG began to recruit pilots and sign contracts with them acting as agent of the Central Aircraft Manufacturing Corporation, a Chinese government entity. As an initiator and creator of the AVG, Soong named these energetic fighters the "Flying Tigers." In a letter to Chennault, Soong said that China's air force, with the assistant of AVG crews, would be greatly enhanced "just like a tiger (which) gets two wings." In the eyes of the Flying Tigers, Soong was AVG's "old friend and protector."

Telegrams in this volume also demonstrate T. V. Soong's strategy that created strong relations between China and the US government. As American military and financial aid to China was drastically expanding, the Universal Trading Corporation (UTC), the Chinese aid mission in Washington, had to be reorganized. Soong seized this opportunity to create a new agency in Washington aiming at "establishing helping hands around President Roosevelt to ensure the aid policy will practically meet China's needs." China Defense Supplies Inc. (CDS) was established in early 1941 as a joint Sino-American enterprise to manage military aid and Lend-Lease between the US and China, while the UTC only handled commercial procurements. The CDS soon replaced the UTC and became an active and influential arm of the Nationalist Government in the US.

T. V. Soong and the CDS grasped every opportunity to support China's war against Japan. In July 1941, at Soong's request, the US Government agreed to set up an American Military Mission in Chongqing. Stationing a US military mission in China's wartime capital was supposed to help boost Chinese public morale. By August 1941, around $600 million worth of military equipment had been assigned for the Nationalist Government, although supplies would not be shipped until 1942.

Soong worked hard to elevate China's strategic importance in the Allied command structure. In August 1943, he attended the Quebec Summit. Soong understood very well the political difficulties and military significance of this new allied command structure. During the summit, Soong argued with Churchill and Stilwell. He stressed the importance of the China theatre and China's urgent need to open the Burma Road. He also defended Chiang's strategy for the Burma campaign. After the summit, Soong took the initiative to discuss with President Roosevelt China's future role in the alliance. Then, in a new proposal submitted to the White House on September 15, 1943, Soong argued that Lord Mountbatten's new appointment as Supreme Commander of the Southeast Asia theatre made it unnecessary for General Stilwell to be the proposed commander of allied troops in Southeast Asia, particularly in Burma. Soong said that "Stilwell should be replaced by a Chinese general who should have authority over the Air Transport Command in the China-Burma-India theatre, as well as over all other military units of whatever nationality operating in China." Soong also insisted that China should be included on the Combined Chiefs of Staff and Munitions Control Board, and have equal status with its American and British allies. He wanted the US government's assurance that there would not be any change in Chiang Kai-shek's position as Supreme Commander in China theatre. As his telegram correspondence unearthed, Soong's ultimate goal was to have China, Burma, and Thailand under Chiang's control, and that the Nationalist Government control all

Lend-Lease materials.

President Roosevelt agreed to Soong's proposal, but Chiang Kai-shek had a different opinion about restructuring the Allied command system. Instead of joining the Combined Chiefs of Staff and Munitions Control Board, Chiang wanted to create a new Joint Chiefs of Staff for the Asia-Pacific region with China taking the lead. After receiving Soong's proposal, Chiang urged Soong to adopt his advice. Soong, however, did not believe Chiang's opinion was sound, and he insisted that his original plan was best for China's future relations with the Allies. Chiang eventually agreed.

In spite of T. V. Soong's active lobbying in Washington, evolving military and allied relations between Chongqing and Washington were poisoned by the Stilwell issue, damaging wartime US-China relations. Many publications have described the troubled Chiang-Stilwell disputes. The new T. V. Soong telegrams in this volume not only document many details of this issue, but also reveal a Chinese perspective not mentioned by Barbara Tuchman (*Stilwell and the American Experience in China, 1911– 45*) and others.

The Chiang-Stilwell problem first surfaced in January 1942, when the Allies agreed on a unified command structure in the Asia mainland theater of operations. British General Sir Archibald Wavell was to serve as Supreme Allied Commander, but Chiang Kai-shek would serve as commander of all land and air forces "which are now or may in the future be operating in the China theatre." Adding further confusion, the United States would send a representative to China to act as Chiang's chief of staff and serve as liaison between Chinese, British, American, and other allied troops. That representative would also speak for the United States on any international war council in China, and he would control and maintain the Burma Road — the crucial supply route into China.

Relations between Stilwell and Chiang further worsened after the Allied defeat in Burma. Between June 1942 and October 1943, Chiang and Soong had twice considered replacing Stilwell. Stilwell berated Chiang for his failure to "appoint a real commander, give him real authority, and hold him responsible for results" and complained of poor Chinese military leadership. Demanding that Chiang reform his military forces, Stilwell referred to one Nationalist general as "a second-rate man" and warned Chiang that if he continued to entrust large forces to such a general, "the effort will be wasted" and "will give China a black eye in America and Britain."

Disagreements between Chiang and Stilwell reached a climax in late spring of 1943 over the use of American airpower and the appropriate strategy for recovering Burma. The new Soong telegrams document that as Chiang became even more furious about his perception of Stilwell's arrogance and ignorance, Soong again lobbied hard in Washington to replace Stilwell. In a confidential dispatch to Chiang on September 29, 1943, about his meeting with Roosevelt, Soong reported that he had reached several important agreements with the US government, including the removal of Stilwell "at any cost." When Soong accompanied Lord Mountbatten, the Allies' new Supreme Commander in the Southeast Asian theater, to Chongqing in October 1943, he confirmed to Chiang the "good news" and urged him to telegram President Roosevelt at once.

But Chiang Kai-shek changed his mind. Recognizing Stilwell's solid connections with the US War Department and his new position as Lord Mountbatten's deputy, together with the overall situation in the China-Burma-India theatre, Chiang decided to keep Stilwell as long as he maintained the current level of Lend-Lease aid. Soong felt embarrassed and betrayed. In mid-October, there was a fierce quarrel between Chiang and Soong. Chiang was furious and reportedly threw a rice bowl on the floor. Soong also became angry, and he slammed the door when leaving Chiang's residence.

For the next three months, T. V. Soong was left cooling his heels in his residence in Chongqing. He was no longer allowed to participate in official events or to return to Washington; and he was not invited to join the Cairo Conference with the Generalissimo and Madame Chiang although he had worked hard in Washington for Chiang's participation in Cairo. Chiang's refusal to replace Stilwell did not improve Sino-American relations; and his reluctance to do so worsened the situation. Then, in September 1944, Chiang formally requested that President Roosevelt recall Stilwell.

In spite of any disputes or disagreements, Washington's relationship with the Nationalist Government during 1940 - 1943 was basically friendly and based upon trust. As the new T. V. Soong telegrams show, T. V. Soong played a crucial role in securing American military and financial aid for China at a critical time in the war effort; and these telegrams show that Sino-American relations were revitalized in 1940 - 42. But tensions in the relationship increased in 1943 - 1944 as the military balance between Nationalist China and Japan shifted further in favor of Japanese abilities to attack Chinese military forces and put them on the defensive. T. V. Soong's diplomatic contributions had improved Sino-American relations, but future historians will continue to seek information in order to identify when and why the alliance began to suffer. Did Sino-American relations improve for a period of time because of T. V. Soong's leadership and creative management? These new documents suggest that this seems to be the case.

Soong believed that American technology and organizational innovations could help save China and enable it to reform itself. Soong himself demonstrated networking and strategy skills with the mass media and public relations skills and an appreciation of the potential of air power he had learned from the West. While Sino-American relations declined precipitously after Soong left Washington at the end of 1943, we cannot answer the question of whether the relationship would have progressed more positively if Soong had somehow stayed more involved in Washington during the immediate postwar period. However it is clear that Soong's efforts during the war brought valuable help to the Chinese war effort against Japan, tying down Japanese troops, and buying time for the Allies to prevail in Europe without Japanese troops being thrown into the fray against the Soviet Union or against British forces in India.

This large body of telegram correspondence, in addition, provides unusual access to further understanding and reevaluating wartime US-China political, military, and financial relations. Unlike many official papers which contain political rhetoric and obscure diplomatic terms, Soong's personal correspondence vividly reveal how top-ranking officials in both Washington and Chongqing truly perceived their war agenda, as well as how their mutual relationship were shaped and conceptualized, thus enabling us to closely examine the differences in political culture, cognitions and beliefs of two nations.

Select Telegrams between Chiang Kai-shek and T. V. Soong, 1940 – 1943

1. Telegram from Chiang on Soong's meeting with Roosevelt (June 26, 1940)

A101

I hope you arrived in US safely today.

Since France surrendered to Germany, international situation has changed dramatically. This is however not unexpected. As long as British and French navies can continue joint combat, war in Europe will not end Soon. But during this period Japanese will surely launch unbridled attack in Far East and do whatever they want. Particularly recent cutoff of transportation in French Vietnam was a heavy blow to morale of our army and general public. If US continues to step aside and does not take immediate action to intervene, there will be negative effects on our war against aggression. I am eager to see US government find ways to aid us. When you meet President Roosevelt, please stress first point above, i. e. , France surrendering to Germany has brought tremendous effects to Far East. Cutoff of transportation in French Vietnam is particularly damaging to our war efforts. Please ask for President's detailed advice on settlement of Sino-Japanese conflicts and his opinion on this "war or peace" situation.

Also please raise following issues when you have chance (in meeting with President Roosevelt):

A. Whether US fleet now in Pacific Ocean could stay on rather than be transferred to Atlantic Ocean.

B. If Japanese army invades French Vietnam, their next step must be to invade Dutch Indonesia. To protect American interests and position in this region, US should stand up now to preserve justice regarding French Vietnam and transportation issue. This is actually only chance for US to curb Japanese "Southward Advance" policy.

C. Is there any improvement in recent US-Russian relations? Is it possible for US and Russia to cooperate in dealing with Japan?

D. Japanese planes are bombing Chongqing violently everyday. If US could warn Japan to stop bombing, or US would implement oil embargo against Japan, it could be effective (to stop Japanese).

Kai-shek

2. Telegram from Chiang on military procurement and on loans (July 7, 1940)

A102

I received all your previous telegrams and am relieved.

A. As to military procurement, please negotiate based on largest amount in the list that Yu Dawei[1] has submitted to you, i. e., US $30 million.

B. If purchase of fighter planes is possible, please make an order of 150 planes. Please ask Wang Chengfu[2] who is now stationed in US to decide on specific models. I have ordered him to come meet you.

C. Amount of requested loans is at your discretion according to current conditions. I hope you will not leave for Europe until after finishing your important assignments in US

All goes well here. My son Weiguo will visit you soon. Please give him your instructions on my behalf.

Kai-shek

---

[1] Head of Ordnance, Ministry of Military Affairs, Nationalist Government.

[2] Then serving as a counselor of the National Aviation Commission.

3. Telegram from Chiang on Yu Dawei petition regarding to military procurement (July 10, 1940)

A103

Yu Dawei reported the following:

At T. V.'s request made in person, I prepared purchase list of 20 million US dollars worth for negotiating with US side. He also said since there's no guarantee in purchasing weapons, it's better to negotiate purchase of materials. I therefore submitted to him two purchase lists, one for weapons and one for materials, each of US $10 million. Weapons list composed of 10,000 light machine guns and 300 million cartridges. If weapon purchase value can be increased to US $20 million, I suggest adding rifles, anti-tank guns, field artillery guns and mountain artillery guns. The quantity cannot be decided until we get the price quote from US side. I have told Soong in person.

Could you please discuss above issues with US government?

Kai-shek

4. Telegram from Chiang on procurement of fighters and bombers (July 10, 1940)

A104

Please proceed according to my instructions in telegram of 6th. (We hope that) US government can transfer to China all airplanes previously sold to France. If US could provide us now with 300 fighter planes of latest model and 50 to 100 long-range bombers, China could win war against Japanese aggression sooner. Should you meet President Roosevelt, please inform him of my above words. Please also tell him the reason why Chinese troops could not gain final victory is that Chinese air force is less than even one percent of Japanese in quantity. I eagerly hope he can help us with those planes.

Kai-shek

5. Telegram from Chiang on US governmental loan negotiation (July 12, 1940)

A105

[replied on July 12]

You need not discuss loan issue with Ambassador Hu Shi. It will be more convenient if you handle this on your own. I plan to recall Ambassador Hu now. Is there any problem?

If you meet President Roosevelt, please tell him the following: if US government could aid China with even one tenth the quantity of airplanes and other materials sent as aid to France, China could not only win the war, but also reconstruct our country (after war) with American aid. This magnanimous help from US would be unprecedented in China's history and we would never forget it. No one is expected to be able to bring this about except President Roosevelt. Please tell President the above when you have a chance.

I heard US ambassador to France William Bullitt returned to US. China wishes to invite him to serve as senior consultant. I wonder whether this is workable. Please consider it.

Kai-shek

6. Telegram from Chiang on interruption of Burma transportation (July 16, 1940)

A109

[Replied on July 17, 1940]

I received your telegram on the 12ᵗʰ.

A. If Burma Road transportation stopped, all British and US aid except financial loan would be ineffective.

B. Half of Russian loan is pending. One reason is difficulty of land transportation.

C. There is little hope American goods can be transported via Russia.

D. UK's decision on stopping Burma Road transportation shattered any hope in Chinese public of prospective British and American assistance.

E. If US determined to talk with Russia on assuming joint responsibility for Far East, it is still possible to turn things around.

F. Executive Yuan just set up a new Ministry of Economic Warfare and appointed you as minister. I will be acting until you come back, or you may choose to take over another ministry. But this new ministry is important and we need to set it up as soon as possible. Gu Yichun[1] and Zeng Yangfu[2] are candidates for vice minister subject to further discussion when you get back.

Kai-shek

7. Telegram from Chiang on UK-Japan negotiation over Burma transportation (July 17, 1940)

A110

I received your telegrams dated 13th and 14th.

A. Since Soviets concluded Nomonhan Agreement[3] with Japan last month, no (Russian) supplies arrived despite the orally promised immediate delivery. It could be because Soviet Union intends to reconcile with Japan for the moment because of uneasy situation in Near East. Therefore there is little hope of purchasing Russian ordnances with US loans. As for already ordered supplies, they haven't arrived yet and any excuse may be made to procrastinate with new orders. My observation is that, even though we negotiate with Soviet Union, there won't be any definite answer because Russia does not want to irritate Japan. If we seriously want to strengthen our resistance to Japanese invasion, it's impracticable

[1] Then serving as a member of the Guangdong Provincial Government and head of the provincial Finance Chamber.

[2] Then serving as board member of the Sino-British Boxer Indemnity Fund and supervisor of the Office of the Yunnan-Burma Road Construction.

[3] In the summer of 1939, Japan and the Soviet Union had a short but bitter conflict over a disputed section of the Manchurian-Mongolian border. A ceasefire was reached in June 1940.

to rely on remote aid to remedy immediate calamities. The only solution is direct aid from US which may also engage Soviet Union and (consequently) reach consensus with Soviet Union on effective solution of Far East issue. As to your previous suggestion on transportation of American supplies to China via Vladivostok, I will surely discuss it with Russian side. But US should mediate in this; otherwise our talk may not have results.

B. Though transportation route in Northwestern China is not currently blocked by Japanese, it is in fact as good as blocked. Burma Road is now the only alternative. This is highly important for US to understand, and please ask US to do its best to prevent UK from compromising with Japan on Burma Road issue.

C. Chinese statement on UK's (Burma Road) attitude was published last night. You must have read it already.

Kai-shek

8. Telegram from Chiang on Japanese invasion into Vietnam and on US financial aids (August 11, 1940)

A113

I received all your telegrams. At this stage, most serious difficulty in our war against aggression is (weak) economy, with (lack of) weapons second. Price of rice is now more than seven times last year's. Inflation should not reignite. If financial situation cannot be improved, civilian public will suffer from shortages of foods and clothes, thus communists will take advantage for sabotage. As result, war against Japanese aggression will not last long. If US does want to aid China, please tell US authorities frankly the following:

A. It may be effective if immediate actions are taken to stop Japanese enemy from invading French Vietnam. Otherwise Japanese will take Yunnan shortly via French Vietnam. Should Yunnan be occupied by Japanese, US and UK would be unable to aid China even though they hold Singapore.

B. China's internal and external situation cannot sustain long if US doesn't extend financial aid immediately.

Hope US authorities give me a hand by taking action on above two things in near future.

Kai-shek

9. Telegram from Chiang on Southwestern Transportation Administration's Manila office setup (August 14, 1940)

A114

Southwestern Transportation Administration proposed to set up a branch office in Manila. Philippines authorities telegraphed US for instructions. US Secretary of State Cordell Hull has not replied yet. Besides ordering Foreign Ministry to make formal negotiations, I like you to discuss with US authorities for (obtaining) approval.

Kai-shek

10. Telegram from Chiang on reorganization of the Executive Yuan (August 15, 1940)

A115

Swedish government does not oppose transferring to us airplanes ordered from US, as long as US government agrees. There won't be any other obstacles. Regarding import port, if Burma is not available, airplanes can be assembled in Singapore and India then fly to China directly, if UK and US are sincerely willing to help us.

In my previous telegram I asked you to lobby US government for loans. You may proceed according to your assessment of the conditions, and you do not need to transliterate my original telegram.

Executive Yuan is to be reorganized. I look forward to seeing you back soon.

Kai-shek

11. Telegram from Chiang on reorganization of the Executive Yuan (August 23, 1940)

A116

I received your telegrams dated 15th and 20th. General plan for strengthening administrative organs is same as you suggested. Final decision is to be made after your return.

It would be good if you dropped by Russia on your way back. We simply need to show good will on our side.

Kai-shek

12. Telegram from Chiang on transportation of medicines (September 2, 1940)

A117

I received your telegram dated August 28th. It would be convenient to ask Red Cross be responsible to ship those medicines to Kunming from Rangoon. Transportation from Kunming to Chongqing will be carried over by trucks provided by Southwestern Transportation Administration, while we'd ask Red Cross to provide gasoline either. Upon shipping of these medicines from US, please inform Mr. Wang Ru-tang[1] of Red Cross at 111 Austin Road, Hong Kong. Please be noted of above.

Kai-shek

13. Telegram from Chiang on Tungsten Loan (September 11, 1940)

A118

I have ordered Ministry of Economic Affairs to follow my instruction on tungsten issue.

---

[1] Former Chinese ambassador to the United States. Then chairman of the China Red Cross.

Kai-shek

14. Telegram from Chiang on Soong as delegate plenipotentiary for loan negotiations (September 26, 1940)

A119

I received your telegram dated 23rd. The 50 million dollars is indeed not enough to meet our emergent needs. It is, however, impolite to decline, and this amount is of some help anyway. We should accept it. My only hope is these 50 million dollars will be disbursed as lump sum. If not, at least public statement should (be made to) indicate total amount is 50 million dollars. It would be better not to mention the sentence ". . . half of which is subject to further discussion over coming period. " By doing so, it would be beneficial to (public) impression outside China as well as to morale in our country. According to brother Yong (Dr. H. H. K'ung[1]), as long as we deliver tungsten as collateral on time and in full, we will keep good credibility and can obtain this loan. You are fully authorized to handle this matter.

Kai-shek

15. Telegram from Chiang on formation of the Axis and on US aids to China (September 28, 1940)

A120

[replied on Sept. 28th and on Oct. 2nd]

It's confirmed that Germany, Italy and Japan have formed the Axis. Hence US will very likely provide us with more aid. Please pay special attention to this scenario. I hope US will extend additional financial loan to us in near future. If US government does want to cooperate with us (in military aid), the only weapons we need are airplanes. Whereas main assistance we need is economic and financial, for reinforcing civilian and military morale to sustain our war against Japanese

[1]Then Vice Premier and Finance Minister of the Nationalist Government.

aggression. We don't have any other requests than this.

Please pay special attention to Russia's attitude while you are in US. The essence of (the idea of) current Axis actually originated from anti-communist agreement. No matter whether its specific provisions evidently relate to Russia or what Russia's recent attitude is, Russia is destined to be Axis's ultimate prey. I sincerely hope and will be glad to see that UK, US and Russia can make an allied front with China to check aggression. The key is now in US hand. Therefore we need to put this plan forward skillfully rather than forcefully. Pushing too hard will raise suspicion. Please engage wisely and don't miss favorable opportunities.

Kai-shek by hand

16. Telegram from Chiang on tungsten output and transportation (October 1, 1940)

A121

Decode and forward to Mr. T. V. Soong

According to Minister (of Economic Affairs) Weng (Wenhao)'s report, tungsten ore needed to service new US loan is about seven thousand tons a year. Current output of tungsten ore is enough to cover this amount. The only concern is transportation. Discussions are under way to expedite shipment. Above is for your reference.

Kai-shek

17. Telegram from Chiang on loan agreements execution and on airplane procurement (October 1, 1940)

A122

I received your telegrams dated 26th and 27th. I asked Ambassador Hu to handle signing of loan agreement according to your suggestions. How you handle remaining issues is at your discretion.

As to purchase of airplanes, I'll forward you plan within days. If enemy occupies Singapore, supplying aviation gasoline will become difficult too. Large cargo planes should be prepared to transport gasoline from the Philippines to Chongqing or Guilin. If 500 new type fighter planes and 150 heavy-duty bombers are not shipped to China by next February, we will be unable to continue our resistance to Japanese invasion. Please deliver this message to US government now.

Kai-shek

18. Telegram from Chiang on analysis of Japanese army activities (October 2, 1940)

A123

According to confidential and reliable information, purpose of Japan's recent invasion of Vietnam was to incorporate Thai army in order to attack Singapore. This strategy was proposed by Germans. Germany has decided to launch final offensives against UK and US before US election. At that time, in West, Germany will help Spain to take Gibraltar; in Middle East, Italy will attack Suez Canal; in East, Japan and Thailand will jointly attack Singapore and Hong Kong, thus exposing UK to attack on all fronts and finally forcing UK to surrender. I personally believe this strategy will be duly executed. If Japan can't make war against UK and US now, its power won't match UK and US after next year, and would have to allow itself to be trampled by UK and US. Therefore, I predict that Japan will attack UK and US before (this) year-end or before US election. It is regrettable that UK and US are indecisive and hesitant in taking actions, and have lost the advantage of timing and opportunity to Axis countries. If UK and US do not actively and promptly defend Singapore, if Singapore is in danger, the whole Pacific area will be lost. Please frankly convey my above opinions to UK and US authorities.

Kai-shek

19. Telegram from Chiang on procurement of airplanes, fuel and ammunition (October 4, 1940)

A124

[replied on Oct. 8 th]

The airplanes, gasoline, ammunition and equipment to be purchased are as follows:

A. Quantity of airplanes:
   a. 300 fighters, of which 150 are for combat against bombers and 150 against enemy fighters
   b. 200 bombers, of which 100 with single-engine shall engines have diving ability (part of these will be transferred to reinforce reconnaissance squadrons) and 100 with double engines

   There should be extra 30% of the total on monthly basis as back-up, i. e., (a) 90 fighters per month, equally divided into above-mentioned two types; (b) 60 bombers per month, equally divided into above-mentioned two types.

B. The planes should better be models currently used by US Air Force. Because production (of those planes) takes a long time, we suggest US War Department pick out currently in-service planes that fit our needs and ship them to China immediately after changing their engines to new ones.

C. The planes should mainly use air-cooled engines, because China's air-force mechanics are more experienced in maintaining air-cooled engines, such as model CYCLO E, F, and G engines produced by Wright and the WASP, TWIRWOSP engines produced by Pratt & Whitney. Our mechanics are less familiar with liquid-cooled engines such as Alyson model. Besides, liquid-cooled engines need special cooling liquid such as Glycol, which is difficult to resupply and match. Therefore we hope only small quantity of liquid-cooled engine planes be supplied at this stage for training purpose.

D. Planes can be equipped with (guns of) 12.7 mm, 7.62 mm or 6.3 mm (caliber). The cameras and sight equipment should be most advanced models. Other spare parts, such as bomber's cockpit i. e., nose of plane, landing gear and tail wheel of fighters and bombers, wingtip and propeller, etc, should be at least equal to 100% of quantity ordered.

E. For above-mentioned quantity of airplanes and for training use, we need gasoline ranging from 25 to 30 million gallons per year, plus compatible lubricating oil.

F. For above-mentioned quantity of airplanes, we will need 30, 000 tons of bombs, 100 million 7. 6 mm cartridges, 10 million 12. 7 mm cartridges and 2 million 23 mm shell cartridges per year.

G. Airplane delivery: Above-mentioned airplanes as well as gasoline, ammunition and equipment should be shipped to China as soon as possible for fear that transportation will be cut off in the future.

Regarding training:

a) Venue (for training) should be where supplying materials is convenient, either in US or in the Philippines, subject to US government approval. But the Philippines are more preferable because of their proximity to us and low cost entailed. If training venues are in both locations, ask US to train as many overseas Chinese as possible.

Moreover, when number of senior-class cadets in military academy is insufficient or equipment supply is difficult, just train cadets of mid-level class (as supplement). In this case, training equipment now used by senior class of military academy can be reallocated to sergeant training school.

b) Size of training class is temporarily set at 1, 000. Other than training Chinese pilots, please train a western bomber operator, and better hire some mechanical staff. Specific percentage of divisions should be decided when types and quantity of planes purchased is confirmed.

c) Duration of training is temporarily set at three years.

d) This training plan will be delegated to Colonel John Jouett for careful implementation.

To obtain backup airplanes sooner and to reduce effects of US's war participation, and for international support, please negotiate with US government to immediately transfer to us airplanes that are now in service (in USAF). This is critical to our future. You must negotiate earnestly with US and ask for a decision as soon as possible.

Kai-shek by hand

20. Telegram from Chiang on failure of Russian airplane delivery and demands for American airplanes (October 7, 1940)

A125

[replied on Oct. 8th]

I received your two telegrams dated 4th.

A. Airplanes promised by Russia have not yet been delivered. Even if they arrived, their performance would be inadequate in combating current models used by enemy, and would cost us the lives of air force servicemen in vain. These planes are far behind (than enemy planes) in speed and other features. Recently enemy bombers ran wild over city of Chengdu, thus rocking morale of our civilians and troops. Our war cannot last long unless US provides us with latest-model planes.

B. We have three large-scale air bases in Zhejiang Province, namely Quzhou, Lishui, and Yushan, which are closest to naval ports in Japan. If US can keep supplying 200 new-model heavy-duty bombers a month, plus fighters we requested earlier, it won't be difficult for us to destroy major fleets of Japanese navy in coming months. Please remind US that this is not exaggeration.

C. If US is sincere in cooperating with us in both land and air forces, I will send out a senior officer to US for further discussion.

D. Main issue of Sino-Russian relationship is that Russia wants us to be distant with UK and US and to cooperate solely with Russia. Otherwise Russia will by no means give us aid. I am still working on our policy for cooperating with Russia.

Kai-shek by hand

21. Telegram from Chiang on the urgency of American airplane procurement (October 7, 1940)

A126

[replied on Oct. 8 th]

You must have received my two previous telegrams. Enemy fighter planes taking off from Yichang can now reach Chengdu and Chongqing covering their bombers' unbridled attacks. While it takes only 6 minutes to climb to altitude of 6, 000 meters for Japanese fighters, Russian-made counterparts would take 15 minutes, lagging far behind and letting enemy planes run wild. It is completely different from air battles (happened) in Chongqing when you were here. We don't expect Russia will deliver us its newest model planes if they send us any. If we don't receive fighters of the newest models from the US to curb the enemy, the army and general public's morale cannot hold up any longer. Therefore, obtaining new model US planes is our most important task. I have to bring up this issue with you again.

Kai-shek by hand

22. Telegram from Chiang on verification of Associated Press news report (October 9, 1940)

Reference is taken to your telegram dated September 27th. I transferred your telegram to brother Yong (H. H. K'ung) for investigations. He replied that Associated Press's news from Chongqing on the 26th was released by United Press. There were no words of "official spokesperson" in original news. Original telegraph reads that if Burma Road continued to be closed, there would be no outlet for China to export tungsten ore. Therefore, to facilitate trade between China and all other peaceful countries, it is necessary to open Burma Road. Government's censors passed this news report because its intention was to facilitate re-opening of the Burma Road. After careful reading of original news report, there was no malicious intention. Please be informed of this issue.

Kai-shek

23. Telegram from Chiang to welcome American Air force Volunteers (October 12, 1940)

A129

US Air Force volunteers' coming to assist China's war is highly welcome. If US is willing to cooperate with us, she should designate General Chennault to contact our high-ranking officials in US. If US government is determined, she should proceed as quickly as possible. Otherwise I am afraid transportation will become a problem.

There won't be any problem for us to cooperate with US Marine Corps stationed in Shanghai. My only suggestion is that US Marines in Shanghai and our counterparts should be made acquainted beforehand, though purpose of this acquaintance should not be disclosed.

Kai-shek

24. Telegram from Chiang on dispatch of Mao Bangchu to US (October 15, 1940)

US government has recalled consultant General Chennault to US to serve in US Army Aviation Department. I plan to send General (Mao) Bangchu to US along with him. You can consult him on air force cooperation plan. Please find out US government's resolution on this plan so that Bangchu can decide whether to go.

Kai-shek

25. Telegram from Chiang to Soong and Hu Shi on Chiang's interview with US ambassador on Oct 18, 1940 (October 20, 1940)

A132

To be copied to Ambassador Hu:

I met American Ambassador Nelson T. Johnson on the 18th and told him that since Burma Road blockaded, not only American goods can not be transported to China, but aid from Russia is cut off too. In last two months, Chinese Communist Party (CCP) has been particularly active, which has already cast shadows over China's future. This is only one of China's crises. Although CCP has not taken explicit actions against central government since Burma Road blocked, it has created some negative propaganda. I'd just like US government to know this fact. If Burma Road was not re-opened and US government did not extend loan to China, this would have severe effects on our political and economic conditions. This is another of China's crises. I firmly believe that Chinese army will not be defeated by Japanese. My only concern now is Communists' sabotage (efforts) and the dwindling public resolution in war against Japanese invasion.

Situation improved since last week, owing partly to re-opening of Burma Road and partly to improvement in Soviet Russia's attitude toward us. To keep up momentum of this good Russian attitude and to strengthen general public's will to continue war, we need active and substantial aid from US. UK's recent reopening of Burma Road was largely encouraged by President Roosevelt. This is indeed most critical turning point of China's war against Japanese aggression, from failure to victory and from danger to safety. Chinese government and people are deeply grateful to Tresident Roosevelt for his good will. Mr. T. V. Soong is now in negotiation with US government on details of US aid to China. In general, whatever the international situation turns out to be, China will keep cooperating with US and UK.

But most critical issue for US aid is timing, because this aid will be helpful only before Burma Road is under enemy's heavy bombing and (possible) blockade. In addition, if enemy attacks and takes Singapore, sea route will be cut off too. At that time it will be impossible for US to aid China even if she wants to. Therefore, timing is most critical now. I am anxious to receive large quantity of fully equipped American airplanes in next two to three months so as to encourage our military and civilians to keep fighting. We will need 500 to 1,000 planes a year and must have 500 shipped to China in next two to three months to meet our urgent needs and before transportation is cut off.

We have several ready-to-use air bases in Zhejiang province, from where our bombers can take off to attack Taiwan and all major naval bases in Japan. If we have as many planes as we just discussed, we can destroy Japanese naval forces. This is indeed US's best and only way to avoid war with Japan. Even when war between the US and Japan finally breaks out, as long as China has air force equipped with new models to support our army's operations, US may not need to send naval forces to Far East, because joint force of Chinese army and part of US air force will be adequate to eliminate Japanese navy and (thus) lay solid foundation for long-term stability in Far East.

Besides above-mentioned airplanes, it will be better if US air force volunteers can come to China's aid. Or Chinese pilots could operate new-model planes after proper training.

US ambassador responded that he would be glad to see this plan realized and was willing to offer assistance. He would report our conversation to Washington.

I said that in Sino-US-UK alliance, China will surely follow US leadership. Recent three US loans to China totaling 75 million dollars have already produced positive results. I hope future loans can be consolidated into one lump sum in large amount so as to encourage Chinese people's morale.

In short, we don't worry now about Japanese enemy's aggression, but do worry about possible collapse of domestic economy and social stability. Only US air force and economic aid can help us stabilize shaky economy and public morale. If we can obtain this aid, Communists won't have a chance to play their tricks. Therefore, if China loses this war, Japanese will establish hegemony over eastern Asia, and Communists will rise and become a threat. Its influence on future of Far East will be worrying.

US ambassador agreed to relay these points to US government, too.

Kai-shek

26. Additional Telegram from Chiang on interview with US ambassador on Oct 18, 1940 (October 20, 1940)

A133

You must have received my previous telegram. I now add following points to my (report of) interview with American Ambassador:

A. I have detailed plan on delivering large quantity of airplanes to China before transportation routes are cut off. Mr. Soong is negotiating with your government for assistance. We hope to (be able to) use these planes within three months. Therefore time does not permit ordering them from manufacturers. US government has to allocate (to us) those that are already made or now in service in US Air Force and ship them to China. This would encourage our troops and general public to continue resistance.

B. At beginning of war, I promised the nation publicly that war would last for three years. Now it is already more than three years but we still haven't defeated enemy. In July and August this year, we still had small quantity of fighter planes to intercept enemy planes, and morale was not rocky as today. Now our air force is exhausted and unable to (have enough planes to) take off to fight. That's why enemy planes are now bombing brutally all over the country and running wild. Our people, especially businessmen, are seriously disquieted. Words are spreading that if US does not provide assistance to us, then what is the meaning of our continuing sacrifice? If international transportation route is cut off before US planes arrive, general public's morale will go further south.

The above two points are most important. I am afraid that the US ambassador would not report them in detail. Please emphasize on these two points with US authorities.

Kai-shek

27. Telegram from Chiang on Stalin's stand on the Axis (October 23, 1940)

A135

I received yesterday reply telegram directly from Stalin dated 17th. The meaning of this telegram is subtle. But as to the Axis, he clearly stated that China and Russia have common interests. And he implied at last that both China and Russia have no room to reconcile with Japan. He stressed mostly that he believes China has strong army and will finally overcome all difficulties and win independence and freedom. Please note this telegram and keep it strictly confidential. Don't release it to anyone without particularly important reason.

Please also be informed that Mao Bangchu and his entourage will probably leave Hong Kong for US on 26th.

Kai-shek

28. Telegram from Chiang to Soong on Yu Dawei's petition regarding to procurement (October 26, 1940)

A129

Yu Dawei reported that he dispatched Jiang Biao[1] to head a team of technical personnel to US to assist ordnance procurement. Until Jiang and his team arrive, Office of Ordnance Corps will assist Mr. Chen Guangfu[2] in buying ordnance materials. And engineers Han Chaozong and Wang Naikuan will receive Mr. Soong's instructions.

I approved his report. Please note.

Kai-shek

---

[1] Then serving as representative of the Commission of Arsenals, Ministry of Military Affairs to the United States.

[2] Director of board of the Central Bank of China.

29. Telegram from Chiang on expectation of airplane delivery within 1940 (October 27, 1940)

A136

We strongly hope US will re-allocate to us all planes originally planned to sell to Sweden. In addition, we hope 200 more planes will be transferred to us from those sold to France or French Vietnam. Among those the new model fighter planes are urgently needed. Please convey my message to US authorities. In short, we expect to have 300 US planes arrive in China within this year to strengthen military and civilians' will for war.

Kai-shek

30. Telegram from Chiang on situation of transportation via Vietnam (October 29, 1940)

A138

Tse-liang's telegram from Hong Kong dated October 26th reported following:

There were reports that on the 24th, French ship Xi Jiang, which was rented by Far Eastern Trading Corporation in Haiphong and loaded with 8,500 tons of cargo, was searched by Japanese Navy and Army personnel. They found gas masks, identified them as military equipment, and demanded unloading of the whole cargo. Vietnamese authorities took a surrendering attitude. Customs Office is now making final efforts but chance of success is slight, etc.

According to our investigation, cargo on that ship had been sold in June by several entities to American Far Eastern Trading Corporation, which is registered in Delaware, USA. In fact, this company is a US business organization, and transaction with payment procedure was legally completed. Therefore cargo is now American property and has no relation to China. Besides, gas masks are for sanitary usage. They, as other common goods, are civilian rather than military. We will notify American Ambassador of truth of this incident and ask him to intervene to release this ship. Please decide whether we should notify Ambassador Hu Shi and ask him to handle this, etc.

Please ask US government to intervene actively for cargo release.

Kai-shek

31. Telegram from Chiang on procurement of anti-air guns and airplanes (November 14, 1940)

A139

(replied on November 15, 1940)

In order to address our urgent needs, can you manage to order and ship along with airplanes various anti-air guns that are in the list mailed to you earlier? I look forward to your reply.

Kai-shek

[draft reply added on the same page:

I will proceed as instructed simultaneously (with airplane purchase). (Mao) Banchu[1] will arrive today. — T. V.]

32. Telegram from Chiang on Bank of China to receive US loan proceeds (November 22, 1940)

A141

Please send directly to brother Yong (H. H. K'ung) your telegram dated 19th suggesting Bank of China to receive 25-million-dollar loan on behalf of central bank. I think this has been done according to formal procedure. As to Gu Mengyu[2], I will follow your suggestions as long as he himself agrees.

Kai-shek

33. Telegram from Chiang on Russian weapon delivery (November 25, 1940)

A142

---

1 Head of Chamber of Military Ordinance, National Aviation Commission.
2 Head of KMT Central Propaganda Department.

Russian ambassador told me in person yesterday that his government has all weapons promised in our earlier agreement ready for shipment. It's evidence that Russian-German relationship and Russian-Japanese relationship have not improved after Molotov's visit to Germany. Possibly those relationships are even deteriorating. Please, at your discretion, inform American and British governments of this news. Supplies from Russia, however, can't be counted on until they arrive in China.

Kai-shek

[draft reply on the original page] :

[A. I appreciate your informing me of Russian ambassador's message on imminent weapon delivery. Please also inform me of specific date of delivery when available. But since this has not yet been accomplished, please don't release this news for the time being. I am afraid that once American and British governments know we have supports (from Russia) ,they will not give us full-scale aid. B. The government . . . [1]]

34. Telegram from Chiang on announcement of Sino-US Loan Agreement (November 29, 1940)

A143

I received your two telegrams dated 27th. Regarding to US consent on 20-million-dollar loan, please do not announce the news after signing until our proposal is also approved and then announce both together. Otherwise, our people's morale will be negatively affected.

While Japan recognizes (Wang Jingwei) puppet regime, if US does not announce large-amount loan as economic aid to us, our government's position and public confidence will be shaken and war against aggression cannot last long.

If US government is not willing to cooperate in any form, ask whether they will possibly agree to follow my proposal C? Please question them in detail.

---

[1] The original text interrupts here.

As to economic development in western China, we need to compose comprehensive plan as soon as possible. If US is willing to help us on that, we will start discussion now, for fear that Japan would make claim (on the resources) when peace one day restored. Please study this issue carefully. It would be better if US economic delegates could be dispatched to China to discuss it.

Kai-shek

35. Telegram from Chiang on cooperation of power supply development with US (November 30, 1940)

A144

I believe you received my telegram of yesterday. Japanese have often said that materials and mineral resources in western China are so rich that such resources will not exhaust even if all East Asian countries exploit them at full speed for next three hundred years. This revealed their greed. Foundation of our (economic) infrastructure and defense industry in the future will be laid in western China, including provinces of Sichuan, Xikang, Yunnan, Guangxi, Guizhou, Guangdong, Hunan and Jiangxi. If peace is restored between China and Japan, Japan will definitely be eager to compete for exploitation of resources in western China. So we should act in advance. Our postwar economic construction will completely relied on US. Otherwise Japan will take advantage of us. If we can lay a foundation now for Sino-US cooperation on western China and sign agreement or if, as I suggested, US pays 300 million dollars as deposit, Japan will then be forced to take their hands off. But we need to have an overall plan and design now. Please urge US government to dispatch economic, transportation and military advisers to China to push forward this matter. Please convey my opinion to US government for immediate action.

Kai-shek

36. Telegram from Chiang on Japan-Wang (Jingwei) Pact and message to Roosevelt (November 30, 1940)

Japan and Wang Jingwei puppet regime just signed official agreement, which marked Japan's de facto recognition (of Wang regime). If US and UK do not express their serious concern and announce large-scale aid to China, public morale and economic situation in China will experience unpredictable changes. If US does not want to issue a joint statement with UK, then is it possible for the two countries to reach a mutual agreement on a principle and then issue parallel statements? It will be even more helpful if US announces a large-scale loan to us. Please convey my opinion to President Roosevelt.

Kai-shek by hand

37. Telegram from Chiang on transferring of C. C. Chang and on his successor (November 30, 1940)

I received your telegram dated 27th. The transferring of Mr. C. C. Chang[1] to Gansu province has already been publicly announced. Please find someone to replace him and ask Chang to take office as early as possible so as to (put his) focus on frontier affairs.

Kai-shek

38. Telegram from Chiang on Soong's trip to UK (December 3, 1940)

A146

As US loan agreement has been announced and memo on supply of airplanes has been delivered to US and UK governments, please push them to grant approval as soon as possible. I hope negotiations on airplanes can finish at the

---

[1] Member of the Gansu provincial government and head of the construction chamber of the provincial government.

time you return to US from UK. Please go to UK first to close loan negotiation and then return to US immediately.

Kai-shek

39. Gratitude Telegram from Chiang on completion of US loan negotiation (December 3, 1940)

A147

Please copy to Ambassador Hu.

Attaining this loan can be fully attributed to the hard work of you both. I'm wholeheartedly grateful.

Wish you good health.

Kai-shek

40. Telegram from Chiang via Hu Shi on transportation via Vietnam (December 4, 1940)

A145

To Ambassador Hu Shi and forward to brother T. V. Soong,

Southwestern Transportation Administration forwarded the following report from Haiphong:

1. Japanese enemy has loaded off Far Eastern Trading Corporation's cargo, which originally was loaded in ship Xi Jiang, and moved away with trucks. The cargo is (now) said to be shipped out by another ship. We should ask US government to protest against French government or to detain French assets in US.

2. Saigon authorities received orders from French Governor in Vietnam to transfer to Japanese embassy all transit cargos of Chinese governmental and private ownership. Since all Chinese government's properties and rights in Vietnam have been entrusted to US consulate, US consul Mr. Little secretly advised us to have Ambassador Hu discuss this matter with

Washington to recourse and detain Banque Indosuez's ten million US dollar worth assets (in US as revenge). The French authorities in Viet Nam has not only seized our properties, but also infringed US interests. So US should adopt swift counteractions.

Please consider carefully above suggestions and take necessary actions.

Kai-shek

41. Telegram from Chiang on the amount of UK governmental loan (December 6, 1940)

A148

I received your telegrams dated 4th and 5th and learned that British Under-Secretary of Treasury Sir Frederick Phillips has come to US. I agree that you don't need to go to UK. Your telegram on 5th coincides with my opinion. British loan should be no less than equivalent value of 100 million US dollars. Please convey this message to British government. US loan to China already totaled 150 million. If UK shall commit to give us loan, it should be at least 100 million. The form and method of payment is however negotiable in order not to disturb UK's ongoing warfare.

Kai-shek by hand

42. Telegram from Chiang on Japanese fuel transportation via Shanghai (December 9, 1940)

According to intelligence report, to salvage oil shortage, Japan sent out envoy named Saito to US and made agreement with American oil merchants to ship oil to Japan secretly by using Shanghai as transit station. This is for your notice.

Kai-shek

43. Telegram from Chiang on approval of heavy-duty truck purchase (December 9, 1940)

A149

I received your telegram dated 3rd, and hereby approve your suggestion to transport mineral resources by ourselves and to allocate proceeds from US loan to purchase heavy-duty trucks. I have informed this decision to Vice Premier H. H. K'ung and Minister of Economics Weng Wenhao.

Kai-shek

44. Telegram from Chiang on UK government's decision on loan amount (December 9, 1940)

A150

We know for sure that British government has decided internally to lend China 10 million pounds, of which 5 million is credit loan and rest 5 is cash loan.

I just summoned British ambassador and told him the loan should not be officially announced if total is only 10 million pounds. The announcement should be released to press only if loan totals 20 million pounds which will benefit our war of resistance and keep our people from being disappointed by British government. I discussed the matter with him for two hours but he still felt it would be difficult. Finally I told him to convey my opinion frankly to his government. Even if difficult, total loan announced should be 20 million pounds. Of that, 10 million is cash loan; 10 million is credit loan which is not in urgent need and its terms could be subject to further discussion. If British government really finds it difficult to pay that amount in full, Chinese government will not insist (on paying). But total amount of loan announced should be 20 million pounds. He agreed reluctantly to report my stance to his government and promised me a reply by about Thursday. Thus we infer that (British government will announce) loan news on Wednesday or Thursday.

Please inform immediately British friend in US if total loan is 10 million pounds, do not release news right now. Note that information of this confidential figure is not from British ambassador. So don't make clear statement on this while talking to your friend in US. You may simply tell him that you read it in newspaper.

Kai-shek by hand

45. Telegram from Chiang on request to increase UK governmental loan (December 10, 1940)

A151

According to Reuters news, British government officially announced it will provide us with a loan of 10 million pounds. Please follow my prior telegram and do your best to negotiate with British side for a 20 million pound loan. If they insist that this amount is set, we can argue this 10 million is currency loan with another credit loan pending negotiation. I sent telegram to brother Fuchu (Guo Taiqi)[1]. Please discuss (this proposal) with British side immediately pursuant to this telegram. I look forward to your reply.

Kai-shek

46. Telegram from Chiang on free pound suggestion (December 11, 1940)

A152

I received your telegram dated 7th. Regarding "free pound" suggestion, I asked British ambassador to China Sir A. Clark-Kerr to report it to British government.

Kai-shek

47. Telegram from Chiang via Hu Shi on improvement of Russian aids (December 11, 1940)

A153

To Ambassador Hu and to be forwarded to brother T. V.

---

1 Chinese ambassador to UK.

I received Ambassador Hu's telegram dated 5th via Foreign Ministry. Please deliver a confidential oral reply to US State Department making the following points. Soviet Union's material aid to us is on barter basis according to (Sino-Russia) credit agreement. In view of recent failure of Japan's peace-seeking efforts and our resolute fighting against Japanese aggression, Soviet Union sent envoys several times to me saying that they are willing to execute the agreement and deliver immediately ordnance promised to us, including field cannons, machine guns and others. But number of airplanes (to be delivered) is insignificant and we have not been informed of any specific quantity or delivery date. Moreover, Russian envoys asked me about progress in obtaining American ordnance aid to China and expressed that they hoped US would provide enough such aid to China. So now Russia's attitude on aiding China is getting more active, and more closely related to American attitude. Please ask (State Department) to keep the above confidential.

Kai-shek

48. Telegram from Chiang on Chiang's telegrams to Roosevelt and others (December 12, 1940)

A154

Please translate the following four telegrams and deliver them respectively.

1. Telegram to His Excellency President Roosevelt:

Given Japanese recognition of (Wang Jingwei) puppet regime and signing of treaty with it, our country is at critical moment. Your Excellency President at this moment announced loan to China of currency reserve and credit loans in significant amounts that will tremendously strengthen our military forces to fight against aggressors, uplift confidence and stability of general public, and reinforce our social and economic basis. Your Excellency's lofty spirit of justice in helping the weak and checking the powerful has actually stricken heaviest blow to aggressors and paved bright way toward eternal peace in the Pacific region. I have been struck with wholehearted admiration while witnessing all these happenings, and firmly believe that settlement of chaotic Far Eastern situation and realization of eternal peace will be fully accomplished only with inspiration of your wise policy and your great spiritual power. To me, and all my military and civilian compatriots, this has been an unchanging belief for past five years. And we believe it now more than ever. The struggle for peace and revitalization in Far East requires our joint efforts. I look forward to receiving your continual advice and guidance.

Another confidential letter will be handed to Your Excellency by Mr. T. V. Soong in person. I would appreciate it if Your Excellency could meet him at your earliest convenience.

With my highest respect and sincere wishes for your health.

2. Telegram to Secretary of State Mr. Hull:

I am extremely grateful to His Excellency President and Your Excellency for practical policy you adopted to aid China and checkmate aggressors. Loan agreement signed in Washington D. C. is most recent proof of American goodwill to China at our most critical moment. This makes me further believe that His Excellency President and Your Excellency not only understand accurately China's needs but have also resolved to take leadership in aiding China. My appreciation of United States government augments every time you take a new strategic action in confronting Far Eastern situation. So does my confidence and resolution in winning final victory of our war against Japanese aggression. Please allow me to take this opportunity to express my utmost gratitude.

3. Telegram to Morgenthau:

I am extremely grateful for Your Excellency's repeated manifestations of support of China's fight for freedom and independence. All United States' generous financial assistance to China can be attributed to Your Excellency's initiation and mediation. The recently approved loan showed anew United States' willingness to provide enough aid to countries in Pacific region that are undertaking all-out war against aggression. Please allow me to avail myself of this opportunity to express my utmost gratitude.

4. Telegram to Mr. Jesse Jones[1]:

United States government's repeated loans to China have greatly benefited our war against Japanese aggression. I can foresee that the loan this time will be of more benefit than ever. Your government's policy of aiding countries suffering aggression is being implemented under Your Excellency's instructions and supervision. Please allow me to take this opportunity to express my utmost gratitude for Your Excellency's important achievements.

Kai-shek

49. Telegram from Chiang on Chiang's letter to Roosevelt (December 13, 1940)

A155

To be translated and presented to H. E. President Roosevelt:

My telegram of gratitude dated December 12th must have reached Your Excellency's attention.

After US government lent us large amount loans, British government followed suit with another loan to us. Now we have no serious difficulty in terms of economic resources to continue our war against Japanese aggression. We however expect to have Your Excellency's vigorous support in providing us with air force weapons as well as other ordnance supplies. Please allow me to explain in detail my plan and requests to Your Excellency.

I think the wars in Western Europe and in China are inseparable. As to time manner (of war settlement), it's easier to curb Japanese aggression first and thus end Sino-Japanese war, and stabilize Far East situation earlier. As result (of peace in Far East), it will also be easier to end war in Western Europe and achieve overall world peace. This is the key to current global situation, which I believe Your Excellency must have observed clearly. To achieve this goal, we must act now before Japanese army launches and expands its southbound aggression, i. e. , deal a decisive blow to its air forces or pin it down by

---

[1] Head of the US Federal Loan Agency.

consuming its combating resources consistently. According to intelligence we obtained, by next April, Japanese army will not be able to launch southbound offensive campaign nor withdraw a substantial number of troops from China and use them to invade Southeast Asia. Therefore, at current stage, to attack or hold up Japan's air force, prevent its expansion of southbound invasion, or even preempt any attempt of southbound invasion at all, is necessary and imminent in the context of overall Far Eastern as well as global situation.

And this plan is not infeasible. I firmly believe that, with this strategy, we can obtain significant benefits by investing only a small amount of resources. The essence of this strategy is to deal enemy surprise blow within shortest time range.

Japanese air force is estimated to have about 2,500 to 3,000 airplanes with combat ability. Their ammunition load and speed is inferior to newest model American planes. According to our previous combat experience, if we have 500 new American planes, we can pin down 1,500 enemy planes, i. e. , more than half of enemy planes will be stopped from going south. If this number of Chinese air force high-quality planes can be maintained continually, we can keep on fighting enemy air force and erode their fighting capability consistently. With that, Japanese army and navy without air force cover can hardly expand their aggression in the south. Even if they do have a plan, and have prepared to go south, they will be forced to abort it. Therefore, this is most fundamental solution to eliminate the danger of Japan's further aggression in Pacific region.

My urgent request to Your Excellency on supplying and strengthening our air force is not only to obtain 100 to 200 planes and protect our communication routes and major cities. I firmly believe we should take offensive, rather than defensive, strategy to shatter enemy's military ambition. We must have enough air force to launch active and overall counteroffensive, which is only effective strategy. If we get only 100 to 200 planes each time, we will not be able to launch counteroffensives. Besides, those newly arrived planes may be consumed up in enemy's constant raids. It is very likely that, before we could (gather enough strength to) launch counteroffensives, enemy have already defeated us through constant engagements. All external support and aid to us would be in vain in this case and Your Excellency's precious goodwill and help would be fruitless.

Purpose of my next stage counter-offensive plan is not only to use our air forces to cover our army's land combat and to defeat enemy air force in China, but also to project our forces to Japan to bomb their air bases, airplane plants, important military facilities and industrial centers. Only this strategy can turn war around and end it completely. To accomplish this purpose, we must obtain within a certain time range at least 500 newest model planes from United States in one batch, equipped with most sophisticated long-range air weapons that Japan doesn't yet have.

To summarize above arguments, and in consideration of current supply level in United States, I submit to you two minimum requests:

1. We hope at least 5% to 10% of airplanes made for American and British air forces can be transferred to us. These planes should be delivered as a priority so that we could receive more than 500 planes in next three to four months. My plan can not be realized unless Your Excellency grant special approval. I hope Your Excellency will grant approval and authorize immediate execution to ensure completion of our minimum air force expansion plan and thus begin effective counteroffensives.

2. Please send us certain number of US-made Air Fortress bombers to enable us to develop long-range bombing capability and make heavier and more effective strikes in Japanese territory. (By doing so,) we could let known (to Japanese people) the weakness of Japanese warlords and impel them to remorse.

During last year's Nomonhan Incident between Japan and Russia, Russians with less than 500 new model planes destroyed over 600 Japanese planes during half month. Japanese have bowed to Russians since then, not daring to challenge any longer. This is a graphic example of Japan's failure in air combat as well as a precedent of its real lesson to come.

I weighed this plan for a long time, and didn't want to translate it into empty words. Now only in view of making due contributions to Far Eastern situation do I dare disclose this plan frankly to Your Excellency. As to technical details such as personnel, equipment, supplies, delivery dates and methods and so on, I entrusted T. V. Soong to discuss these in person. Please assign your officials-in-charge to negotiate with him.

I sincerely hope United States' goodwill and precious aid will be used in a timely manner and bring China maximum results in order to defeat Japan and to eliminate sources of peril in Far East in the interest of global peace. Your Excellency's valuable support of approving of this plan early will be extremely appreciated and honored.

Chiang Kai-shek

50. Telegram from Chiang on withdrawal of air force cooperation proposal and on recall of Hu Shi (December 13, 1940)

A157

US is still reluctant to establish any form of military cooperation with UK. Therefore proposal for air force cooperation among China, UK and US will be abandoned. Now our only hope is that US could do what I requested in my letter to President Roosevelt, and this may be easier to bring about.

Ambassador Hu's performance is not satisfactory. So I'd recall him before formal plan is submitted. However, according to information I received, if I recall or transfer him now, he may stay in US and not come back as instructed. I will not make final decision before careful and thorough study of this issue.

Kai-shek by hand

51. Telegram from Chiang on Chiang's telegram to Knox (December 13, 1940)

A158

To be translated and presented to His Excellency Secretary of Navy Knox:

I read with gratitude Your Excellency's letter dated November 15th brought to me by Lieutenant Commander John McCloy. I interviewed with Lieutenant Commander, informed him of and asked him to report to you current progress of China's war against Japanese aggression and our needs of military aid.

Since outbreak of war, we received from your country substantial sympathy as well as financial and many other forms of aids, which enhanced our confidence that justice must win final victory. Increasing aid to China is attributed not only to His Excellency President's wise policy, but more to your foresightedness and ardency. All particularly moved by this, I and all Chinese people will drive ourselves to fight harder against enemy and deal heavier blow to that peace-threatening aggressor country and eliminate eternally the source of peril in the Pacific region.

To achieve this goal, we urgently need supplies of military equipment, especially airplanes, from your country that will enable us to launch effective counterattack to aggressor country before it invades Southeast Asia outrageously.

I have submitted my such views to His Excellency President via Mr. T. V. Soong. I firmly believe, with your superior military insight, Your Excellency will kindly tender valuable assistance to our early realization of the above strategy.

With my utmost gratitude.

Chiang Kai-shek

52. Telegram from Chiang on settlement of Sino-UK loan argument (December 14, 1940)

A156

I received your telegram dated 11th. Since British loan already announced officially in parliament, it is now meaningless to argue more, which would only hurt Sino-British relationship. Please extend (to UK government) our gratitude on my behalf.

You should agree to visit U. K. when you finish your negotiation in US Before that, you could entrust Guo Taiqi and Guo Bingwen[1] to start negotiation (with UK government). If you could finish your work on US loan early, please visit U. K. as soon as possible to reward their good will to us.

Kai-shek

53. Telegram from Chiang on amendment to telegram to Roosevelt (December 15, 1941)

A155

Please insert in my telegram to President Roosevelt dated 13th the sentence of "The essence of this strategy is to deal enemy surprise blow within shortest time range" directly after the sentence "... *we can harvest significant benefits at the cost of much smaller amount of resources.*" If the said telegram has not yet been forwarded to President, please make sure to add this sentence.

Have brothers Tse-liang and Tse-an arrived in US? I like to know. Weiguo arrived in Chongqing safely.

Kai-shek

54. Telegram from Chiang on treatment of banks affiliated to Wang Jingwei administration (December 17, 1940)

A160

As for how best to deal with puppet regime's banks in Shanghai, we hold same principles here as you suggested. So don't worry.

We have not heard rumors here that loans we received were in form of public bonds.

---

[1] Member of the Chinese Trade Commission in London and financial attaché in Chinese embassy in London.

What I said in my telegram to President Roosevelt that "... *to deal enemy surprise attack ...* " refers to "blitz" attacks. Please explain this to President if you could meet him.

Kai-shek by hand

55. Telegram from Chiang on transferring of Willington Koo (December 18, 1940)

A161

I received your two telegrams dated 16th. Only two to three persons here know content of Stalin's telegram to me. It might have been leaked by embassy in Moscow, and thus is known by UK and France.

Selection for ambassador to US aroused guesswork overseas. It's not strange. My opinion is that Gu Shaochuan (Wellington Koo)[1] is currently the most appropriate candidate. Please consider timing (of transferring) and let me know your opinion.

Kai-shek

56. Telegram from Chiang on airplane procurement (December 23, 1940)

A162

Flying Fortress cannot be put into actions without sufficient cover from fighters; otherwise they would be easily shot down by enemy planes even before operation. Therefore adequate amount of fighter planes are necessary. Besides, runway for Air Fortress will not be ready until end of March at earliest. It is impossible to finish preparation work within one month.

Kai-shek by hand

---

[1] Then Nationalist China's ambassador to France.

57. Telegram from Chiang for Christmas greeting (December 24, 1940)

Wish you a merry Christmas and pray for your good health.

Kai-shek

58. Telegram from Chiang on Soong Tse-liang's position (December 24, 1940)

A163

How is brother Tse-liang? How long will it take before he recovers? I worry very much. Since brother Liang (T. L. Soong) left, operation of Southwestern Transportation Administration has deteriorated. The nature of work is complex and nobody takes charge. The current transportation tonnage is less than one-third of planned capacity. Such scenario is dangerous for military and transportation outlook. Currently, brother Liang is taking nominal and real responsibility, but it will become burdensome for him in future. My opinion is that, if brother Liang cannot come back soon, it is better for him to resign his duties and mandate that all his subordinates do their jobs as usual. I will assign another trusted and able person as acting officer or successor. Thus somebody will take charge, and brother Liang can have good treatment without worrying about office work. To avoid interruption of office operations, all current staff should be given strict orders to stay on position, keep to their duties and not be allowed to resign. This arrangement takes into consideration both personal and public interests and brother Liang's heavy burden of work load will thus be alleviated.

I wonder what brother Liang would think about this suggestion. Waiting for your reply.

Kai-shek by hand

59. Telegram from Chiang on loan agreement terms and signatory capacity (December 25, 1940)

I received both your letters dated 11th and 20th. Sino-American Metal Loan Agreement has been transferred to brother Yong (H. H. K'ung) and the National Resource Committee for record. I asked brother Yong to check records on Loan Terms Ratification Outlines together with assignment of authorized signing representatives, and mail them to you.

Kai-shek

60. Telegram from Chiang on procurement of guns and ammunition (December 26, 1940)

A164

Please place following orders with US suppliers as quickly as possible:

1. Ten thousand 7.9 mm light machine guns
2. Three hundred million 7.9 mm cartridges
3. One hundred and twenty 75 mm field guns, each with three thousand shells
4. One hundred and twenty 0.5-inch anti-air machine guns, each with five thousand cartridges

The light machine guns and cartridges are necessary for our weapon and ammunition reserves. Please take immediate action and telegram me results.

Kai-shek

61. Telegram from Chiang on Rogers' visit to Chongqing (December 29, 1940)

A165

Brother Yong (H. H. K'ung) did not try to prevent Mr. Cyril Rogers[1] from

---

1 British representative to the Sino-British Stabilization Board.

going to US. Instead, he invited Mr. Rogers for talks in person, and asked him to bring comments here in Chongqing to your attention when he comes to US.

Kai-shek

62. Telegram from Chiang on signatory capacity of loan agreement (January 5, 1941)

To be decoded and presented to Mr. T. V. Soong

I received your telegram dated 3rd and asked Ambassador Hu Shi by telegram to notify US government that you and other two are authorized to sign (the loan agreement).

Kai-shek

63. Telegram from Chiang on directorship of the Stabilization Fund (January 5, 1941)

A166

I received your telegrams dated 31st (December 1940), 2nd (January 1941) and 3rd (January 1941). You must have received reply from brother Yong (H. H. K'ung). Please follow his instructions after careful review.

As to your participation at Stabilization Fund Board, both brother Yong and I agree. Please proceed.

Kai-shek by hand

64. Telegram from Chiang on Mao Bangchu's press interview (January 5, 1941)

A167

New York Tribune carried interview with Mao Bang-chu at the end of last month. I wonder whether this is true. Please ask him why he met with reporters. It absolutely should not happen again.

Kai-shek

65. Telegram from Chiang on Southwestern Transportation Administration (January 5, 1941)

A168

I received your telegram dated 31st (December 1940). How is brother Tse-liang after operation? I worry much about him.

It has been decided not to reorganize Southwestern Transportation Administration, and current Vice Director Chen Ticheng[1] is appointed acting director to take full responsibility. To improve efficiency, Yu Qiaofeng[2] (a.k.a. Yu Feipeng), chief of staff of Transportation Administration Bureau, has been dispatched to direct and supervise Burma Road (transportation). Brother Tse-liang needs only to instruct all his subordinates to obey absolutely Qiaofeng's orders.

Kai-shek by hand

66. Telegram from Chiang on airplane procurement and Universal Trading Corporation (January 7, 1941)

A169

I received your telegram dated 5th. Airplane purchase affairs shall not be entrusted to Universal Trading Corporation[3]. Please take this as your foremost task and go all out to fulfill it.

Kai-shek by hand

---

1 Acting director of the Southwestern Transportation Administration.

2 Then serving as Minister of Logistics, Military Affairs Commission.

3 The Universal Trading Company was set up to purchase supplies in the United States using US credit given to China from 1938 to 1940. T. V. Soong had previously operated as an agent of the company.

67. Telegram from Chiang on truck purchase (January 8, 1941)

A170

Please allocate funds from US loan to buy 1, 000 three-ton-load trucks for National Aviation Committee's transportation use.

Kai-shek

68. Telegram from Chiang on dispatch of air force personnel (January 9, 1941)

A172

[replied on Jan 13 th]

I received your telegram dated 6th. Do you need me to send air force personnel besides Shen Dexie (Shen Te-shek)[1] , or just ordnance technicians? Please reply in detail.

Kai-shek

[Soong's draft reply in original text:

I received your telegram dated 9 th. Shen Te-shek by himself is good enough. Please also send me ordnance technicians familiar with American or European ordnance affiars]

69. Telegram from Chiang on funding of Stabilization Fund (January 10, 1941)

A171

I received your two telegrams dated 23rd (December 1940), and forwarded them to brother Yong (H. H. K'ung). He replied as follows:

A. As to news that Ministry of Finance allegedly stated that it will not abandon *Fabi* Nationalist currency in Shanghai, in fact, the ministry never made statement about abandoning *Fabi* in any city during past several

---

1 Supervisor of training programs, National Aviation Committee.

years. In view of such rumors month ago, a statement released in English language reiterated that government's policy on *Fabi* currency has not changed, and after receiving US loans, our currency reserves are stronger than ever. Thus public should not believe in rumors and fall into trap.

B. There is no change in foreign exchange policy. To avoid any possible unexpected troubles, preferably that this loan should be disbursed in lump sum.

The above is for your information.

Kai-shek

70. Telegram from Chiang on military procurement and Universal Trading Corporation (January 10, 1941)

A173

I received your telegram dated 8th. You may entrust Universal Trading Co. to go through (trading) procedures as you suggested.

Kai-shek

71. Telegram from Chiang on Southwestern Transportation Administration affairs (January 15, 1941)

Please ask brother Tse-liang to have good rest and not to resign. He only needs to order Southwestern Transportation Administration staffs to reorganize strictly following my instructions and to obey Minister of Logistics Yu Feipeng's supervision.

Kai-shek by hand

72. Telegram from Chiang on approval of reply to British memorandum (January 18, 1941)

I received your telegram dated 9th, and sent out ten photo pictures via airmail.

Regarding to reply to British memo, I hold same opinion as yours.

Kai-shek

73. Telegram from Chiang on the New 4th Army Incident (January 18, 1941)

A174

I received your telegram dated 15th. The (communist) New 4th Army disobeyed orders and planned to betray government. This troop has been completely disarmed and I have ordered its name and designation cancelled. All communist troops south of Yangtze River were eliminated, so we don't need to worry about this threat at our backs any longer. Without military power, Communist party can only expand propaganda to confuse international audience. They are doing this in hope that a civil war would not be in interest of central government, thus they would not be punished. As matter of fact, central government, while waging war against Japanese aggression, is in position to control domestic affairs without any misgivings. Foreigners may not know the story and are prone to be misled by Communist propaganda. Please explain in detail to our friends and ask for their credence.

Kai-shek

74. Telegram from Chiang on code book for Soong (January 21, 1941)

To be decoded and forwarded to T. V. Soong c o Ambassador Hu:

Director Soong Tse-liang brought you a code book. Have you received it? Please check and reply.

Office of Classified Affairs

[Soong's draft reply shown in original text:

Chongqing Military Committee, Office of Classified Affairs

Telegram received. Be informed Director Soong has given me the code book. Soong]

75. Telegram from Chiang on recruitment of American transportation specialists (January 23, 1941)

A175

Could you give priority to hiring American personnel who have rich experience in transportation administration and ask them to come to China as early as possible? What's your opinion?

Kai-shek

76. Telegram from Chiang on misbehavior of Rogers (January 23, 1941)

A176

Please note that Rogers is not honest in his words or behavior. Control of financial and foreign exchange affairs should be in our own hands. We cannot trust foreigners (on this issue).

Kai-shek

77. Telegram from Chiang on Currie's visit to China (January 25, 1941)

A178

International News Agency reported in Washington D. C. on 24th that:

President Roosevelt announced appointment of Mr. Lauchlin Currie as special envoy to undertake a field investigation of China's economic situation. State Department announced simultaneously that US was concerned about dispute between Nationalist Party and Communist Party in China. As economist, Currie will leave for Chongqing soon with letter from President Roosevelt to Generalissimo Chiang. It is said that Currie was directed by US government to investigate into Nationalist Party's accusations of Communists' disobedience and other betrayal schemes, as well as Communists' counteraccusation about Nationalist Party's suppression of peasants. US government's concern about China's internal friction has led to delay in approving proposed 50 million dollar loan.

How reliable is this report? You'd better ask US government to issue a denial statement and to expedite disbursement of the loan.

Kai-shek by hand

78. Telegram from Chiang on recruitment of American Volunteers (January 27, 1941)

A180

Regarding American volunteers (recruitment), please proceed according to conditions and principles set out in your telegram. But pay special attention to detailed definition of their rights and obligations and requirement that they absolutely obey command's orders.

Kai-shek by hand

79. Telegram from Chiang on announcement of the New 4th Army Incident (January 29, 1941)

A181

I received your telegram dated 27th. Truth of New 4th Army incident was disclosed in my public speech today. It is indeed well known domestically that Communist army is very weak, less than 2% of total army soldiers in China. China has now 119 armies, out of which New 4th Army and 8th Route Army are just two. Please relay the truth about this to US authorities.

Kai-shek

80. Telegram from Chiang on Japanese offensive along the southern Peking-Hankow Railroad (January 29, 1941)

A182

I received your telegram dated 27th. Enemy is launching offensives along southern section of Peking-Hankow Railway. They will be defeated soon as before. Please do not worry.

Kai-shek

81. Telegram from Chiang on China's joining of the Allies (January 30, 1941)

A183

I received your telegram dated 29th. While it is better if we could officially join British-American Alliance (and become a member), it is fine if we establish indirect relationship with Alliance, which could secure full-scale aid to China's economy.

Russian attitude is same as before in both military and political terms. There is no sign of change. Weapons are being shipped here as usual.

Communist Party announced formally today their intention to obey orders and no longer engage in conflict.

Have American newspapers reported my interview with United Press reporter? What are their comments?

Kai-shek by hand

82. Telegram from Chiang on the diplomatic influence of the New 4th Army Incident (February 3, 1941)

I have received all your telegrams dated January 31st. Now we don't need to explain too much in our public communications with US. Truth should be well known soon. After New 4th Army incident, new shipment of Russian weapons arrived in Gansu Province last week, including 150 new model airplanes and 100 field canons and so on. This shows that N4A incident has not affected our political and diplomatic positions. But please keep this information from US senior officials if possible.

Germany's counterpropaganda is absurd, and merely intended to sow dissension. Fortunately Russians still continue their assistance to us. I hope US government will watch out for this kind of propaganda made by Third International, whose purpose is to damage Sino-US friendship and to make

Chinese people rely more on them.

Kai-shek by hand

83. Telegram from Chiang on Currie's arrival in Chongqing (February 6, 1941)

A185

(Mao) Bangchu is already back. Currie arrived in Hong Kong yesterday and is arriving in Chongqing tomorrow. Brother Yong and (Gu) Mengyu will receive him as director and vice director (of the welcome board).

Preferably you should come back at end of March. But if the negotiation not finished then, you may postpone your trip.

Can Air Fortresses (B-17 bombers) be delivered to us as agreed? Airport (for Air Fortress bomber) here will be ready by about end of March.

Kai-shek by hand

84. Telegram from Chiang on the political influence of the New 4th Army Incident (February 8, 1941)

A186

Central government's disarming of New 4th Army was merely a military disciplinary action, absolutely without any political or partisan consideration. That explains why we central government, knowing well New 4th Army is closely related to Communist Party (CCP), adopted a lenient attitude towards CCP (after this betrayal incident), and has never suppressed communists or censored their publications.

At present, China has over 220 armies, totaling more than 4 million (formal) troops participating in the Anti-Aggression War. Among those formal troops, only several tens of thousands, or less than 1 – 2 percent in quantity, are under communist influence. Even if CCP continues to pursue the wrong course, there will be few chances to bring about a full-scale civil war, and consequently jeopardize our war against Japanese invasion. Central government consistently believes that the world's anti-aggression forces shall always unite together. China, UK, US and Russia should work particularly closely with each other and take uniform actions. CCP, on the contrary, opposes (China's) close cooperation with UK and US in the name of anti-imperialism, while in essence hinder the implementation of our (Nationalist Party's) foreign and war policies. Please have British and US governments know of CCP's real and malicious intention.

Kai-shek

85. Telegram from Chiang on possibility of China's civil war (February 13, 1941)

A187

It was decided as early as last December that Russian chief adviser would return and new chief adviser take his place, before New 4th Army Incident. CCP's propaganda is only designed to confuse domestic and international audiences. It is impossible for division and civil war to occur. Central government doesn't want to see a civil war. Please don't worry.

Kai-shek by hand

86. Telegram from Chiang on negotiation of new US governmental loan (February 21, 1941)

A190

Earl H. Leaf, our representative of International Communications Agency in New York, reported that US Congressmen Andrew L. Somers and Mr. Thomas K. F. Moloney suggested our Consul-General in New York Yu Junji in person to start formal negotiation for a new loan of 150 million dollars. This loan will be used to revitalize some idle or deserted American factories to produce ordnances for China. They suggested this loan could be repaid either with dollar currency or with goods when China is able to do so. It's quite similar to that of Lend-Lease Act currently under debate in US Congress, though with zero interest and indefinite date on repayment. Factories should be jointly invested by China and US, while managed by China. This congressman is sympathetic with China, and asserted that he is confident in presenting this bill and getting it passed in Congress. Please contact him and proceed according to your judgment.

Kai-shek

87. Telegram from Chiang on Currie's leaving of Chongqing (February 25, 1941)

A191

Mr. Currie is leaving Chongqing on 28th and will bring you all the documents.

It is true that CCP set up a military committee. But their purpose is to threaten and blackmail (central government). Generally, CCP's actions are aiming to produce (political) tension domestically and overseas. They don't actually have the ability to take formidable actions. Rumors that CCP has raised conditions (to central government) and (central government has) detained Zhou Enlai were utterly groundless. While spreading such rumors, CCP in fact has never dared to raise a single condition to government in an official manner. We can see from this that (CCP) is simply making propaganda.

Kai-shek by hand

88. Telegram from Chiang on the Yunnan-Burma Railroad negotiation (February 27, 1941)

A192

I received your telegram dated 26th, and hereby authorize you to take charge of negotiations with British and US governments on Yunnan-Burma Railroad (construction). I have also informed Vice Premier (H. H.) K'ung and Minister of Communications Chang (Kia-ngau) to follow this instruction and dispatch Du Zhengyuan[1] to US immediately.

Kai-shek

89. Telegram from Chiang on Executive Yuan's resolution on the Yunnan-Burma Railroad issue (March 2, 1941)

A194

I received your telegram dated February 27th. As to Burma Road issue, Executive Yuan discussed and approved the same suggestions put forward by the British ambassador, as well as British suggestions on Yunnan-Burma demarcation.

Kai-shek

90. Telegram from Chiang on transferring of Alfred Sao-ke Sze (March 3, 1941)

A195

I received your telegram dated February 25th. I agree with your suggestion of dispatching Shi Zhi-zhi (Shi Zhaoji; Alfred Sao-ke Sze)[2] to US to assist (you). Please proceed to send him invitation on my behalf.

Kai-shek

91. Telegram from Chiang on dispatch of senior US air force officers (March 5, 1941)

A194

1. Before leaving China, Currie advised us to send senior American air force officers to undertake field observation in China. Please contact Currie upon his arrival.

---

[1] A well-known engineer who was then responsible for constructing Yunnan-Burma and Xikang-India Roads.

[2] Former Chinese ambassador to the United States, then serving as senior advisor to the Chinese embassy in Washington, D. C.

2. When will American air force volunteers arrive in China and start work? Please reply. Also please order a jumbo passenger plane and a cargo plane for me. Passenger plane should have seating capacity for 20 people. I hope this plane can fly to Chongqing from US directly.

Kai-shek

92. Telegram from Chiang on execution of Stabilization Fund Agreement (March 13, 1941)

A196

Mr. Currie must have come back to Washington. After approval of Lend-Lease Act, I hope other aid projects for China can be approved as soon as possible. Quick signing of Stabilization Fund is particularly important for preemptying malicious Communist propaganda. As to air force volunteers, Air Fortresses as well as quantity and transportation of air force plan agreed on earlier, I hope concrete plans can be decided as soon as possible. Weapons list composed by Minister of Military Affairs Yu Dawei and installment schedule also need to be completed.

Kai-shek by hand

93. Telegram from Chiang on American Volunteers (March 13, 1941)

Nationalist Aviation Commission forwarded Shen Te-shek's telegram reporting that:

Claire Chennault's recruiting of volunteer group is at standstill. My opinion is that Commission should gather enough personnel before receiving new planes.

While Russian planes are arriving, commission does not have enough fighter pilots to operate American planes. Please do your best to encourage American volunteers to come to China.

Kai-shek

94. Telegram from Chiang on Bank of China's management positions (March 21, 1941)

A198

I received your telegram dated 15th. I have asked Minister (H. H.) K'ung to handle your recommendation that Mr. Wu (Dingchang) and Wang (Yansong) appointed as Bank of China's director and supervisor on behalf of government ownership (in the bank).

Kai-shek

95. Telegram from Chiang on development of vegetable oil vehicles (March 22, 1941)

A199

Reference is made to your telegram dated 13th of last month on dispatching specialists to participate in designing and manufacturing vegetable-oil-driven vehicles. This has been checked out and there are no suitable specialists in China. But Universal Company established by Trade Committee at 630 Fifth Avenue, New York, which manages US loan-related purchasing affairs, does have mechanical and engineering personnel. I have asked Vice Premier K'ung to instruct (the company) to send suitable personnel to participate in this project.

Kai-shek

96. Telegram from Chiang on Chiang's letter regarding to freezing of bank deposits (March 24, 1941)

A200

I received your telegram dated 21st. On February 27th, I asked Currie to take with him a letter regarding to freezing of bank deposits, which is outlined below:

1. United States has taken certain actions regarding deposits and securities

belonging to citizens of some European countries now undergoing foreign aggression. If applied in Far East, this action would benefit China significantly. I hope Your Excellency will take this into consideration.

2. Dramatic changes in Far Eastern situation and various rumors caused feelings of uncertainty and consequently speculation in financial markets, which resulted in more currency out-flows (from China). This makes it increasingly difficult for China to maintain face value of *Fabi* (the national currency).

3. As currency is unstable, it largely flows into your country as refuge. If Your Excellency's government would freeze China's private deposits and put them under supervision and custody of Chinese government, or use them as collateral for China's borrowings and thus enhance China's financial strength, it would benefit not only our wartime economy but also general financial situation (of our nation).

4. Moreover, most of China's US dollar-dominated foreign exchange from export and remittance of overseas Chinese, which always falls in pockets of foreign exchange speculators in Shanghai, will thus be under Chinese government control and used to purchase urgently needed goods from United States.

5. A similar action by British government would be very helpful too. I already drafted a memo and will also encourage British side. UK is actually tightening restrictions on foreign exchange. I therefore dare to predict that UK would be happy to fill up this last loophole in Shanghai.

6. I am clearly aware that your government's export license system treats without discrimination both aggressor countries and countries suffering aggression. Therefore, to freeze Japanese deposits in the US would entail review of this policy. But Japanese aggressors sell resources they stole in China to US in exchange for their badly needed US dollars. If US government could apply export license system to Japanese deposits, Japan would be forced to export only its own manufactured goods in exchange for US dollars. Thus Japan's robbing China of wealth could be effectively stopped.

7. If you kindly accept this suggestion, please keep it utterly confidential when enforcing it. Otherwise Chinese depositors in US will transfer their money into American citizens' accounts.

The above is for your reference and look forward to your valuable assistance on this matter.

Kai-shek

97. Telegram from Chiang on Jiang Biao's trip to US (March 27, 1941)

A201

I received your telegram dated 20th. Yu Dawei reported that Jiang Biao and his companions leave for America in April.

Kai-shek

98. Telegram from Chiang on procurement of military and transportation equipment (March 30, 1941)

A202

I received your telegram dated 27th.

1. Categories of ordnance and transportation equipment are numerous and complicated. A detailed list is being mailed to you. For now, please refer to totals of each category in original list for negotiation. This is of utmost urgency.

2. As to weapons, it seems unnecessary to divide them into "urgent" and "no rush" categories. You may aggregate subtotals of original A and B items and submit total (result) to US side. But be sure to note clearly that most urgent needs are 15,000 light machine guns with 500 million bullets; 480 mountain cannons with 2,000 shells for each; 1,000 anti-air machine guns with 5,000 bullets for each; and 360 0.37-inch anti-tank guns with 1,500 shells for each. We also hope US will transfer remaining items on the list to us from (US army's) inventory as soon as possible.

3. As to medium-sized tanks and light tanks, please (request for) quantity of

vehicles along with all matching weapons and equipment to meet needs for two to three armored divisions according to current US army establishment. They however can be delivered after October.

4. Please purchase transportation trucks according to list brought by Currie.

Kai-shek

99. Telegram from Chiang on Xikang-India Road plan (April 9, 1941)

A203

I received your telegram dated March 26th. The original Xikang-India Road construction plan was composed and submitted by Director Du (Zhengyuan). I ordered Transportation Ministry to do terrain survey and other preparation work first and complete it in 12 to 18 months. Du has been put in charge (of this project). I also asked brother Yong (H. H. K'ung) to raise funds to ensure all work finish on time. As to questions raised in your telegram, Transportation Ministry will answer you by airmail. Besides, this planned railroad, though it will pass over mountains, is not especially difficult to build.

British Conservative Party leaders used to think that, to protect India, it was necessary to keep India's northeastern plateau and mountains neutralized. They were unwilling to connect that area with Tibet for fear that our influence would get into. Even now, they are still hesitant about building international transportation route close to Tibet.

This road is however critical to our frontier area as well as to southwestern international transportation, not to mention importance of promoting political and economic development in western China with this opportunity.

Now we can encourage British government officials to make up their mind by taking advantage of this opportunity, and promote it while relying on American economic power. This is only way to be successful. Please keep that in mind as guidance in mediating this matter. As to technical issues, please consult Du Zhengyuan.

Kai-shek

100. Telegram from Chiang on procurement list from the Ministry of Military Affairs (April 10, 1941)

A204

I received your telegram dated 2nd. Military Affairs Ministry reported that procurement list in 1941 included four types of THIONOL, which are not cloth, but pigment materials to dye "straw yellow" and "grey" colors.

I have ordered K. S. Lim[1] to prepare and mail you a list of medical equipment and tools.

Kai-shek

101. Telegram from Chiang on recruitment of air force instructors and volunteers (April 12, 1941)

A207

I received your telegram dated 10th. Are they two separate things to hire instructors for Kunming Air Force Academy and to recruit American air force volunteers? Have you recruited the volunteers? I look forward to your reply.

Kai-shek by hand

102. Telegram from Chiang to enquire on US government's China policy (April 14, 1941)

A205

According to Japanese news, in Russia-Japan Neutralization and Friendship Pact there is a clause regarding to their mutual recognition of territorial integrity of Outer Mongolia and Manchuria. This must be true. We can expect

---

1 Director of personnel training program in the Ministry of Military Affairs.

that Russian diplomatic policy toward us will be more problematic. Please inquire immediately US authority's policy toward China. If they are sincere in supporting China, they will announce quickly a complete and effective plan and guarantee its implementation, in order to erase suspicions (on US policy) among our Chinese people.

In addition, it's quite disappointing that we were not even informed beforehand of recent meeting US, UK and Netherlands held in the Philippines. Please convey my views to US government.

Kai-shek by hand

103. Telegram from Chiang on execution of Stabilization Fund Agreement (April 14, 1941)

A206

I received your telegram dated 11th, and asked Vice Premier (H. H.) K'ung to authorize you and Li Gan to sign Sino-British Stabilization Fund Loan agreement.

Kai-shek

104. Telegram from Chiang on Russia-Japan Pact (April 17, 1941)

A208

I just received telegram from brother Shao Lizi[1] reporting following:

I met with Molotov at 5: 30 this afternoon, and asked, pursuant to your instructions, whether the second clause (of Russian-Japanese Pact) involves Sino-Japanese war situation. Molotov replied that Russian-Japanese Pact is to secure peace for Soviet Union and does not affect China. Nor did Soviet Union even mention relationship with China during bilateral negotiations. He also said that Soviet Union would continue to support China and there would be

---

1 Nationalist China's ambassador to Soviet Russia.

no policy change. I did not ask about Russian aid to China as instructed, but in response to his friendly attitude, I extended our gratitude for Russian aid. I then told him that there was difficulty in discussions with Ministry of Foreign Trade on transporting goods, and asked for his assistance in mediating with foreign trade minister. Molotov first claimed that this was purely an issue of transportation and that reason (of delay) was on China's side. But he later added it would not be difficult to satisfy Chinese ambassador's demand. With this conversation, I think Russian aid to us will continue.

The above is for your information.

Kai-shek

105. Telegram from Chiang on conditions for Stabilization Fund Agreement (April 17, 1941)

A209

I received your two telegrams dated 15th. To date Russia has been delivering weapons to China as usual. There have been no changes. Russian ambassador received telegram from his government, indicating no signs of policy change.

I just asked American ambassador to report to his government that if Stabilization Fund is not disbursed in lump-sum, Chinese people may have misgivings about American goodwill. It seems that US Treasury Department does not trust our government. If loan is paid by installment, Chinese government's domestic and international dignity will be compromised. Therefore, I ask you not to sign loan agreement, and hope US government will fully understand our difficult situation.

Regarding military weapon (aids under) Lend-Lease Act, I share your opinion that an agreement on total amount of all lease goods should be reached and signed first, and actual delivery schedule can be discussed later. This will satisfy our Chinese people's anxious expectation of American aid and (thus) uplift public morale and confidence to continue anti-Japanese war.

As CCP absolutely obeys orders from Third International, its assertion of its belief in Three People's Principle is utterly false. After recent disclosure of Russian-Japanese Pact, Chinese youth and intellectuals were disillusioned by Soviet Union and Chinese Communists. CCP's propaganda in past now proved completely futile. There is no doubt that CCP itself will break up from inside. CCP's military strength in anti-aggression war is negligible and is not an obstacle to our war.

Kai-shek by hand

106. Telegram from Chiang on directorship of Stabilization Fund (April 22, 1941)

A212

I received your telegram dated 19th. You should not refuse position on Board of the Stabilization Fund. Please kindly take this position to avoid any misunderstanding.

Kai-shek by hand

107. Telegram from Chiang on Chiang's telegram to Roosevelt via Currie (April 24, 1941)

A213

I just telegraphed Currie to forward this telegram to President Roosevelt. Outline is as follows:

Since announcement of Russian-Japanese Pact, our civilians and soldiers are angry and sad. It is widely expected that there will be serious negative developments in Far East. I believe military failure in Greece and Yugoslavia also lowered our public morale and affected result of recent battles in Fujian and Zhejing coastal areas. This time in those battles, Japanese army used crack troops that they have rarely used in past. At this critical moment, Chinese government is eager to see American government take decisive action in aiding China. As Lend-Lease Act of your country including plan to aid has been approved, I hope anxiously that Your Excellency will announce total sum of aid according to detailed weapons list we submitted. The earlier announcement, the better.

Kai-shek

108. Telegram from Chiang on directorship of Stabilization Fund (April 25, 1941)

A214

I received your telegram dated 22nd. Again, please do not decline the appointment.

Kai-shek by hand

[A draft reply was added on the page:

I received your telegram dated 25th. Indeed please do not appoint me (to this position).

April 25th, T. V. Soong]

109. Telegram from Chiang on financial personnel in Shanghai (April 25, 1941)

A215

I received your telegram dated 22nd. Our special agents will never impose any financial personnel in Shanghai.

Kai-shek

110. Telegram from Chiang on appointment of Bei Songsun as Stabilization Fund Director (April 27, 1941)

A216

I received your telegram dated 25th. Since you brother indeed cannot take this position in addition to your current responsibilities, I asked Vice Premier

K'ung to appoint Bei Songsun (Bei Zuyi)[1] to fill this position.

Kai-shek

111. Telegram from Chiang on airplane procurement (April 27, 1941)

A217

[replied on April 29th]

Does the term "high-angle cannon" in your telegram refer to mountain cannon? Please also negotiate and decide quickly on models and quantity of the airplanes. I look forward to your reply.

Kai-shek by hand

[On the original page, a "yes" was added by the word "mountain cannon".]

112. Telegram from Chiang on weapon orders (April 27, 1941)

A218

I received your telegram dated 24th.

1. The 7.9mm machine guns and matching bullets are most urgently needed now. Even if US side cannot deliver now, we hope they expedite production and delivery. Director Yu mailed to US all engineering drawings needed to manufacture 7.9mm gun and bullets.
2. We would like 15,000 0.3-inch machine guns promised by US side delivered immediately. Each gun should come with 20,000 bullets.
3. Of all cannons, the mountain cannons are needed most urgently. We were informed in your telegram that they would not be delivered until next June. It will be too late then. Please request US side to allocate from their inventory and deliver to us now.
4. As to other cannons and tanks, please ask US side to deliver immediately, and telegram me specific amount and delivery date.

---

[1] Member of Board of Overseers, Central Bank of China.

5. The 480 "high-angle cannons" of your telegram must refer to 480 75mm mountain cannons. Moreover, the reported 140 mobilized field cannons were not on original purchase list. Is this a new item added by US side or a mistake in your telegram? Please check and reply.

Kai-shek

113. Gratitude Telegram from Chiang to Hu Shi and Soong for execution of Stabilization Fund Agreement (April 28, 1941)

Ambassador Hu Shi:

I received your telegram dated 25th. And also please forward this telegram to brother T. V.

Congratulations on signing of Stabilization Fund Loan, which is largely attributed to your diligent work. Please also extend my gratitude to Treasury Secretary Morgenthau.

Kai-shek

114. Telegram to Chiang on Soong's joining of Anti-War Alliance (May 6, 1941)

S328

I received your telegram dated 4th. My participation in Anti-War Alliance was in response to Madame Sun (Yat-sen)'s invitation to her fund-raising. Now that there is unfavorable report , I telegraphed its office in Hong Kong to check it out and execute your instructions.

T. V.

115. Telegram to Chiang and K'ung on responsibility of Lend-Lease negotiation (May 6, 1941)

As to military aid affairs under Lend-Lease Act, (Financial) Minister K'ung said in a telegram dated 2nd that he hoped me "could work together on it." I wonder whether this was to instruct me to share responsibility with Ambassador Hu? Please reply so that we can be clear about our respective responsibilities.

T. V.

116. Telegram from Chiang on Vice Premiership of Executive Yuan (May 6, 1941)

A219

Vice premier of Executive Yuan is a position that I always wanted to offer you but failed to do so, for reason that bureaucratic structure should not change too frequently, which might cause public criticism. This change, moreover, would have to go through legislative procedures and could not be done as conventional proposal or by executive order. I therefore feel hesitant to do it now. It will be easier to do when other parts of bureaucratic system undergo reform.

At present, the only possibility is chairman of the Economic Conference, which I currently occupy. I plan to recommend you to take my place, or to restore National Economic Committee and recommend you as chairman. Neither of these two positions requires legislative procedure and would thus be easier to carry out. What's your opinion? I look forward to your reply.

Kai-shek by hand

117. Telegram to Chiang and K'ung on appointment of Fox as Stabilization Fund US director (May 7, 1941)

S329

The State Department informed me that US Treasury Secretary Morgenthau recommended that A. Manual Fox, currently member of Tariff Commission, be appointed as American director on board of Stabilization Fund and

William H. Taylor, now staff member of Currency Section of Treasury Department, as assistant director. Fox asked for an annual salary of 25,000 dollars plus a daily allowance of 10 dollars. Taylor asked for 10,000 dollars as annual salary plus 8 dollars as daily allowance. Their flight tickets should also be covered.

If you agree to these terms, please telegram me and I will forward to them. At same time, our government will announce appointment of Fox as director of fund. Appointment of assistant director does not need to be announced.

T. V.

118. Telegram to Chiang on quantity of cotton uniforms (May 7, 1941)

The quantity of cotton cloth noted in Mr. Currie's list is 2 million bolts, equaling to about 80 million yards. Please check and inform me of how this figure was calculated, i. e. based on how many soldiers and how many sets of uniforms per soldier, in case US side inquires.

T. V.

119. Telegram to Chiang on US military forces maneuvering (May 8, 1941)

S330

My friend informed me confidentially that US government ordered transfer of most of Pacific fleet to Atlantic Ocean. It is generally expected in inside circles that military conflict will break out between United States and Germany in coming weeks. In the Pacific area, a large amount of US army, air force and a part of navy have been built up in Bengal to confront possible southbound invasion by Japanese enemy.

The above is for your confidential information.

T. V.

120. Telegram to Chiang on Mme. Sun Yat-sen's political activities (May 9, 1941)

S331

According to telegram I received from Hong Kong, organization sponsored by Madame Sun Yat-sen and called "China Defense League," is solely for raising funds for refugees and has never engaged in anti-government propaganda. As to "Anti-War Alliance" mentioned in Your Excellency's telegram dated 4th, I didn't take part in it. Is it possibly so-called International Counter-Aggression Conference, in which Zheng Yanfen[1] is general secretary? Since outbreak of anti-Japanese war, miscellaneous organizations have emerged and are indeed difficult to tell apart.

T. V.

121. Telegram to Chiang on transportation of Red Cross goods (May 14, 1941)

S338

American Red Cross complained that many relief goods have piled up in Rangoon and can not be transported to China. I wrote letter to Davis, President of Red Cross, stating that Burma Road is being upgraded and transportation capacity will increase two to three times in the future. I just received reply from Davis saying that, considering probable upgrading of transportation capacity, American Red Cross has decided to supplement 900,000 dollars worth more aid such as medicine to originally approved (quantity of) relief goods. They will be shipped as soon as purchased. I expressed gratitude (to American Red Cross) on Your Excellency's behalf. Please instruct transportation authorities to pay particular attention to granting priority to transporting Red Cross goods.

T. V.

---

1 Executive officer of the China Defense League who was associated with Madame Sun Yat-sen. He later became secretary-general of Guangdong provincial government.

122. Telegram to Chiang on Fox's trip to China (May 15, 1941)

You must have received my telegram dated 7th. I am looking forward to your reply given that Fox and his companion are about to leave for China.

T. V.

123. Telegram to Chiang on transportation of Lend-Lease goods (May 15, 1941)

First consignment of US Lend-Lease military equipment has been loaded for shipment. It is expected to arrive at Rangoon on July 6th. I am sending equipment list for your inspection. This shipment includes 240 military vehicles, which are heavy-duty and good for any rough roads. In addition, US authorities have agreed to bear unloading cost when first several shipments of military equipment arrive at Rangoon. Unloading costs for later shipments are subject to future negotiation.

T. V.

124. Telegram to Chiang on needs for submachine guns (May 15, 1941)

S339

Negotiations on light machine guns have progressed slowly. At present, however, 10,000 Thomason 0.45-inch hand-carried machine guns, each with 2,000 bullets, are readily available. Are they needed? Please kindly check and reply with your instruction.

T. V.

125. Telegram to Chiang on Arthur Young's return to Chongqing (May 16, 1941)

Finance Ministry consultant Arthur Young accompanied me to US last year. He is now about to go back to Chongqing. Would you please inform Minister

(H. H.) K'ung that Finance Ministry will grant him permission to travel only if I need him to convey messages in Chongqing and Rangoon on issues of Burma Road and air transportation?

T. V.

126. Telegram to Chiang on Soong's meeting with Halifax (May 17, 1941)

S332

1. Lord Halifax[1] just informed me that UK government won't blockade Yuannan-Burma Road. In his judgment, Japanese government is aware of British position, and unlikely to request UK to do so. Should Matsuoka Yousuke[2] or Shigemitsu Mamoru[3] make such request, UK Foreign Ministry will notify Lord Halifax.

2. I briefed Halifax that US, under Lend-Lease Act, in addition to weapons, would supply trucks, gasoline, technicians needed for construction of Yunnan-Burma Road and materials for Yunnan-Burma Railroad, for total of US $15 million. It would be great contribution to China's anti-Japanese war if UK could assist China in transportation from Burmese territory to inland China. I advised UK government to designate a representative in Burma to assist us in following pursuits:

   (a) Expeditiously completing railroad construction from Lashio to border of Yunnan;

   (b) Measuring and constructing Xikang-India Route; and

   (c) Increasing transportation capacity of Yuanan-Burma Route.

Lord Halifax agreed to convey above suggestions to UK government by telegram, and hoped Your Excellency would give same suggestions to Sir A. Clark-Kerr (British ambassador to China) directly.

3. Regarding US Air Force volunteers mentioned in last telegram, Mr. Currie proposed to discuss this first with President Roosevelt before contacting

---

1 British ambassador to the United States.
2 Japanese foreign minister.
3 Japanese ambassador to the UK.

British. Thus I didn't mention this to Lord Halifax during our conversation. US Department of State will of course not inform British prior to President's authorization.

T. V.

127. Telegram to Chiang on procurement of vehicle parts (May 19, 1941)

In response to your instruction in telegram dated 11th to buy spare parts for "Universal" brand trucks, I have added this item to Lend-Lease purchase list.

T. V.

128. Telegram to Chiang on list of first Lend-Lease goods delivery (May 20, 1941)

S333

First shipment of Lend-Lease goods is expected to arrive on July 6th. Total load is 7,000 tons, including 250 field freight trucks, 2,000 tons of aluminum for military use, 1,000 tons of copper, along with airplane gasoline and lubricating oil and so on. A detailed list will be mailed separately.

T. V.

129. Telegram to Chiang on Guo Taiqi's return trip to China (May 21, 1941)

S334

My humble opinion is that, on his trip back to China, Fuchu (Guo Taiqi) should take route via Rangoon. Fuchu maintains a good relationship with Burmese Governor and can take this opportunity to discuss Yunnan-Burma Railway and Xikang-India Road issues. It would be too remarkable if he made a special visit to Burma after going back to China, which might not prefer British side. I look forward to your decision.

T. V.

130. Telegram to Chiang on approval of military procurement (May 22, 1941)

S335

Because of negotiations with US side, ordnances we obtained under Lend-Lease Act will be shipped to China soon in several batches. Part of second batch and planes are expected to be approved by President within days.

From now on, there must be many liaison affairs in Chongqing and Rangoon with various government entities. Matters relating to transportation and takeover will be numerous and complicated too. I need special representatives to deal with those matters in Chongqing and Rangoon to speed up the process. I'd ask Qian Changzhao[1] to assist in Chongqing and former Bank of China Rangoon branch manager Chen Changtong to assist concurrently in Rangoon. I will still report to you directly on important issues.

T. V.

131. Telegram to Chiang on second Lend-Lease goods delivery (May 24, 1941)

S336

Second lot of Lend-Lease military equipment approved this morning includes:

A. 600 fully equipped mountain cannons, with 1.2 million shells;
B. 144 75mm mobilized field cannons, with 144 thousand shells;
C. 360 tanks, with affiliated weapons and equipment;
D. 1,000 field light jeeps.

Above four items are worth 49 million US dollars. Delivery time will be reported to you once decided.

T. V.

---

1 Acting secretary-general of the National Defense Planning Committee, Nationalist government.

132. Telegram to Chiang on resignation of Soong Tse-liang (May 27, 1941)

S340

Brother Tse-liang has undergone three operations and not yet fully recovered. He just told me in person that Southwestern Transportation Administration's affairs are many and complicated. Feeling deeply uneasy that he is now unable to execute the duties of his position, he asked repeatedly and sincerely to resign. What he said is true. I humbly ask your approval of his resignation. He will serve country again as soon as he recovers. I am looking forward to your decision.

T. V.

133. Telegram to Chiang on appointment of Huo Yamin (May 27, 1941)

S341

I received your telegram dated 27th, and will follow your instruction that Qian Changzhao is not suited to take another position. I hereby propose appointing Huo Yamin, currently deputy general auditor of Bank of China, as my representative in Chongqing, responsible for liaising with various departments. I look forward to your approval.

T. V.

134. Telegram to Chiang to propose cancellation of Yunnan-Burma Railroad Bond (May 27, 1941)

S342

According to US news agency from Chongqing, Chinese government plans to issue public bonds of 10 million US dollars for Yunnan-Burma Railway, and is dispatching overseas Chinese Kwong Ping Shun[1] to US to sell bonds. An official of State Department was surprised and expressed displeasure because

---

[1] A rich overseas Chinese who was then head of the anti-Japanese association in San Francisco.

they were not informed beforehand. Moreover, judging from overseas Chinese communities, it might be unlikely we could raise funds in that amount.

If the news is true, is it possible to withdraw this decision or adopt an alternative? This is at Your Excellency's discretion.

Ambassador Guo Taiqi is also familiar with this issue. Please refer to him for more information.

T. V.

135. Telegram to Chiang on withdrawal from Anti-War Alliance (May 28, 1941)

S343

With reference to your earlier telegram dated 4th. I just received from Dong Xianguang (Hollingtong Tung)[1] communist propaganda publications distributed by "Anti-War Alliance," which used my name in attempts to mislead public opinion. I therefore followed your instructions and made public statement by telegram that I intended to resign from that organization. Just for your acknowledgement.

T. V.

136. Telegram to Chiang on pricing of tungsten (May 28, 1941)

S344

Under Tungsten and Metal Loan Agreements, price of granulated tungsten was calculated according to published price in American mineral magazine, i.e., 16 or 17 dollars per unit, equaling about 1,050 per ton. Given Japan's purchase of granulated tungsten from Bolivia at high price, American Metal Reserves Company ordered Bolivia's whole output of granulated tungsten in next three years at comparable high price, i.e., 21 dollars per unit, equaling

---

1 Then serving as deputy director of Nationalist Party's Central Propoganda Department.

about 1,360 dollars per ton. The company will be compensated for its loss by US Treasury. Although price of granulated tungsten rocketed during last European war, (price of) major materials in US are currently under control and price rise is prohibited. Now granulated tungsten unit price of 21 dollars is much higher than current market price, and this will likely benefit us in the long run. I thus ordered my staff to negotiate with Metal Reserves Company, asking an equal price for our granulated tungsten to that for tungsten from Bolivia in next three years. American side has accepted (this idea) in principle. Since this relates to collaterals of loan arrangement, I hereby ask you to instruct National Resources Committee to give its comments.

T. V.

137. Telegram to Chiang on military procurement petitions (June 2, 1941)

S346

Reply to Generalissimo's telegram dated May 31st, 1941

Your telegram dated May 31st 1941 acknowledged. I already requested the US War Department in writing to deliver us all weapons' manuals, instructions, checklists of establishment and equipment, and all related technical documents. They are, however, highly classified and take very complicated procedures to obtain. As of today, we have received only a portion of them. I instructed the ordnance group of the China Defense Supplies, Co. to send home as many documents as they have received. The above is for your information.

T. V.

138. Telegram to Chiang on procurement and transportation of trucks (June 2, 1941)

S347

Your telegram dated May 28th acknowledged. Prior to the request made by

General Director Huang Zhengqiu[1], 250 GMC 4-ton field trucks were already shipped. These trucks are very useful for transporting weaponry, and supposed to arrive in Rangoon in about two months. Moreover, we placed an order with the US for 35 air force engineering trucks. I respectfully reply as above and beg for your instructions.

T. V.

139. Telegram to Chiang on Currie's enquiry on airplane purchase (June 3, 1941)

S348

I noted your telegram of June 2nd. Mr. Lauchlin Currie came and said that it would be better if he submitted this telegram himself to urge approval for the supply of airplanes to meet our urgent needs. Afterwards, we can follow normal procedures. The account of (Ambassador Clarence E.) Gauss delivered similar message, revealing to us what's going on behind the scenes. It also reminds us to take into serious review of our personnel in Washington D. C. (Li) Shizeng[2] understands this matter very well. I beg Your Excellency to inquery him about this matter.

T. V.

140. Telegram to Chiang on Soong's meeting with Lattimore (June 3, 1941)

S348

Mr. Currie and I just met with Owen Lattimore[3], who is Chinese-speaking and quite familiar with Northern China and the Far East issues. He does not know the President personally, but is a man of integrity and learning,

---

1 Then serving as director general for air defense, National Aviation Commission.

2 Also known as Li Yuying. He was then traveling between Europe, Hong Kong and Chongqing in China's diplomatic activities.

3 A well-known sinologist who was then recommended by the US government to serve as Chiang Kai-shek's political advisor.

and willing to be Your Excellency's personal advisor. I have negotiated with him the following terms: 1. A six-month trial period. Should he be dismissed upon expiration of the contract, he will be paid 10,000 US dollars in addition to travel allowance. 2. If he could serve more than a year, 15,000 US dollars per year would be paid to him in addition to travel allowance. Mr. Currie suggested that if Your Excellency approves this appointment, I can inform him. Because this is personal advisor, there is no need to go through the US embassy. Whether it is appropriate, I beg Your Excellency's decision.

T. V.

141. Telegram to Chiang on Soong's meeting with former Burma Governor (June 3, 1941)

S349 (Replied by Chang kia-ngau on June 10th)

I met with former governor of Burma yesterday. According to him, Burma welcomes air transport between Yunnan and Burma, and hopes it will take place as soon as possible. They hope to build an airport in Myitkyina. As soon as our Yunnanyi airport (in Kunming) is constructed, we can acquire a stable, fast and direct air route. Since US has good relations with China National Aviation Corporation (CNAC), my humble opinion is that the Burma-Yunnan air transport should be managed by that corporation, so that the transfer of airplanes can be dealt with more conveniently. Moreover, as soon as the four-year contract of CNAC is due, we can reclaim it and manage by ourselves. If Your Excellency approves, please instruct the Ministry of Transportation to negotiate with that corporation.

T. V.

142. Telegram to Chiang on Arnstein's trip to Chongqing (June 3, 1941)

S350

I received your telegrams dated June 1st and 2nd, and asked Daniel

Arnstein[1] bringing his technical staff to fly to Chongqing on June 24th. Upon their arrival, please grant them an opportunity to meet you. Thomas Baker is an expert in railway statistics, but inexperienced in road transportation. Residing in our country for long, he is deeply aware of worldly wisdom. However, as he was recommended by Mr. Currie, if we place him under Arnstein, Mr. Currie would not be pleased. Rather, it is better to appoint Baker as Superintendent, and Arnstein as Deputy-superintendent. Arnstein is a road transportation specialist. If Your Excellency tells Baker to authorize Arnstein with real power, then Arnstein would work to his best, and the two would get along. I await Your Excellency's instruction. Moreover, the person previously addressed by Mr. Currie is exactly Arnstein. He was originally introduced by Hopkins to me and Mr. Currie. His resume is attached in the written report for your information.

T. V.

143. Telegram to Chiang on US-Japan relationship (June 4, 1941)

Nomura, Japanese ambassador to the US, had negotiated with the US Secretary of State about some arrangement similar to the Soviet-Japanese Pact. Last week, he proposed the negotiation again. Yet, the US Secretary of State refused politely on the ground that Japan repeatedly broke its promises, such as Open-Door Policy, thus had lost all credibility. The US can no longer trust Japan. In addition, Mr. Joseph Clark Grew, the US ambassador to Japan, reported that the Japanese navy is reluctant to enter into a war with the US, and the Japanese elite is also discontented with the government policies. This news has been secretly forwarded to *New York Times* by the State Department and supposed to be released next week. The purpose is to show that there is no fundamental change in Japan-US relations. Take the speech of the President on last 27th as an example; there is not a single word blasting Japan. That is evidence that the US does not want to worsen its relations with

---

[1] Then serving as head of the US transportation and communication mission to China.

Japan. I respectfully report the above for your reference.

T. V.

144. Telegram to Chiang on US-Germany and US-Italy relationship (June 4, 1941)

S352

As US relations with Germany and Italy have became intense lately, the Pacific Fleet has been gradually transferred to the Atlantic Ocean. This has proved my previous report true, and given marked rise to the notion that it is not good to fight in two oceans simultaneously. The group advocating appeasement of Japan gains ground again. The renowned American lawyer William J. Donovan[1], a colonel during World War I, and an expert in strategy, is also a close friend of the President and Secretary of Navy. He has some influence in military and political affairs. This spring, he was secretly commissioned to conduct an investigation in Europe and Africa. He is deeply familiar with world affairs, and knows the significance of China's war of resistance to the international community. I would like to invite him to visit our country on behalf of Your Excellency. His report of the field investigation would challenge the views of those American navy and army officers who look down on our war of resistance. If Your Excellency agrees, he can thus start off after getting the President's approval. He is quite well off, and will travel on his own. I beg Your Excellency's instructions.

T. V.

145. Telegram to Chiang on Johnson's report on Nationalist-Communist relationship (June 5, 1941)

Mr. Nelson T. Johnson has returned to the US. He has deep insight into the problems between the Nationalists and Communists, and also is familiar with

---

[1] Donovan later became director of the Office for Strategic Service.

tricks played by the Communist Party. In addition, he said while staying in Hong Kong he acquired information that the enemy is training parachute troops quite hard. If those troops land in the Burma-Yunnan road, for example, in the surrounding areas of Yunnanyi, occupy the airports and obstruct traffic, then it will cause great damage that will not be easily repaired in short time. We should pay attention to this information. Furthermore, the most dangerous place in military view is plainly Yunnan. We will need to adopt some preventive measures in this regard. I respectfully report this.

T. V.

146. Telegram to Chiang on Louis Alley's trip to US (June 5, 1941)

S353

People in the US who are interested in (Sino-US) cooperation are all hoping that Louis Alley[1] will be able to come to the US to help in raising large-scale funds for assistance. I beg Your Excellency to agree and offer your instructions.

T. V.

147. Telegram to Chiang on transportation of P-40 fighters (June 6, 1941)

S354

The 36 P-40 airplanes have arrived in Rangoon. Since the second and third shipment (of Lend-Lease supplies) are also under way, Director Zhou Zhirou has sent our personnel to prepare for the takeover. These kinds of airplanes are known for fairly high speed and great performance. Our crew has yet to become familiar with them. Any oversight will give the US an excuse, and affect cooperation between the air forces of our two countries. Moreover, the

---

[1] An active New Zealander who was then in China launching an industrial cooperation movement for the Nationalist government.

munitions of the airplanes are to be delivered together with the second and third batches and therefore we will not be able to make use of them in such short time. My humble opinion is that the one hundred new airplanes should be allotted to American Volunteer Group (AVG), and AVG should train our pilots. After our pilots become skillful and experienced, we can begin to take over. I beg your instructions on whether this proposal is appropriate.

T. V.

148. Telegram to Chiang on proposals regarding to military procurement (June 6, 1941)

S355

The Universal Trade Company received an order by telegraph from the Finance Ministry dated May 9th to purchase 45,000 pistols and a batch of military equipment, totaling 2,680,000 US dollars, to be disbursed by Central Bank of China. I find this order of military ammunition can be included in the Lend-Lease program and should not be paid for in cash. If the order doesn't work in the Lend-Lease framework, this company will not be able to handle it either. During the war of resistance against Japan, all materials and supplies we need from the US are military-related. My humble opinion is that the order should be (1) included in the Lend-Lease program first, or (2) paid for by Export-Import Bank loans, or (3) as a last resort, paid for in cash. The above sequence would conserve our financial resources and suit the principle of Lend-Lease Act. Yet implementation of the above three methods must depend on the varieties of materials and supplies, as well as on the situation. Moreover, the domestic situation of the US is quite intense now, and strict controls have been adopted. Even the purchase and export of civilian necessities is under control. To get priority from the US in processing our purchase and shipment requests, we should establish a centralized controlling mechanism. I would just like to telegraph you my humble views. That is, from now, all the materials and supplies we request from the US should be listed by the home authorities concerned first, and then forwarded to me. I will review and decide which of the above methods of payment should be applied, then report to

Your Excellency for your instructions.

T. V.

149. Telegram to Chiang on Currie's report on Lattimore (June 11, 1941)

S356

Your telegram dated June 7th acknowledged. I have followed your instruction and asked Mr. Currie in person. According to him, John McCloy[1] also received Your Excellency's telegram and made the same inquiry. Currie also said that Owen Lattimore had no close friendship with the President. Yet because of his wisdom learning and reputation, Lattimore is respected, and Currie would like to recommend him. I just report this to Your Excellency.

T. V.

150. Telegram to Chiang on Lattimore's trip to China (June 12, 1941)

S357

Your telegram dated June 11th acknowledged. Mr. Lattimore is scheduled to fly to China on July 1st.

T. V.

151. Telegram to Chiang on situation of airplane procurement (June 13, 1941)

S358

Though some progress has been made in implementing the Lend-Lease Act, to date there are no definite results regarding our urgently needed airplanes. I am very worried. Shen Te-shek and I made a 1,000-plane plan earlier, the first item of which was 500 planes, including 350 fighters and 150 bombers. I tried my best and elaborated our reasons to the US side repeatedly. There is some hope for fighters but little for the bombers. Currie told me that he also

---

[1] Then serving as councilor and navy attaché in the US Embassy to China.

was exhausted and couldn't go further. Though the difficulty may stem from great demand due to urgent needs in US and UK, the arguments we presented also may not have impressed them. I pondered the matter and concluded that we can only tell them about the critical situation and military crisis we are facing, such as our recent military failure in Shanxi, which was not because our soldiers weren't brave or loyal enough, but mainly because we lacked airplanes. Only by listing the facts and telling them frankly what's at stake, can we successfully persuade President Roosevelt to allocate some planes to us from American and British arsenals. Considering the immensity of the stakes, I dare not make decision alone. Feeling great anxiety, I hereby report to you my humble views and wait for your instructions so I can follow through and avoid any possible mistakes.

T. V.

152. Telegram to Chiang on announcement of Lattimore's employment (June 16, 1941)

S359

Since Your Excellency invited Owen Lattimore to be your political advisor, Sino-American cooperation has been getting steadily closer. As to whether we should extensively publicize this news in the US, I beg Your Excellency to offer your instructions.

T. V.

153. Telegram to Chiang on chaos of Burma transportation (June 17, 1941)

S360

According to the report from the US military attaché, the transportation in Rangoon is extremely chaotic. This is what I have heard.

T. V.

154. Telegram to Chiang and He Yingqin on communication equipment procurement (June 18, 1941)

The communication equipment ordered by the Ministry of Military Affairs is for two-year use. We had submitted 60% of the original order to the US War Department. However, the specifications of the War Department are too strict. Moreover, over 20 items are not available in the US Army. The value of all items we requested estimated at around $30 million. Thus it's difficult to work out. Since the Lend-Lease program will continue to support our order, to save time, we have selected about 30 items which are available in the US Army. These items comprise roughly one third of the original order plan and valued at around $4 million. The unavailable 20 items should be made with a special purchase order. The most urgent (of these 20 items) is valued at about $1 million. I beg Your Excellency's instructions on whether these items could be paid for by the loans.

T. V.

155. Telegram to Chiang on communication with Roosevelt regarding to airplane procurement (June 18, 1941)

Your telegram dated 15th acknowledged. I have used Your Excellency's telegram to try to urge the President to provide us with airplanes. Please allow me to report to you the follow-ups later.

T. V.

156. Telegram to Chiang on leaving of American Volunteers for China (June 19, 1941)

S361

Your telegram dated June 18th acknowledged. The 31 members of the AVG have set off for China, and the other 90 members will leave the United States on 30th of this month. The rest will depart according to vacancies on the ship.

And General Chennault will fly to China on July 8th. The above is my respectful response to Your Excellency.

T. V.

157. Telegram to Chiang on Burma transportation and Sino-US relationship (June 20, 1941)

S362

I received your telegram dated 19th. In my previous telegram I mentioned that the American military attaché reported on the chaos of the Yunnan-Burma road transportation. After a thorough inquiry, I found this was not John McCloy. McCloy has recently forwarded a telegram to Currie via the American ambassador and reported that the cargo transport in May was 19,500 tons, two-thirds of which was directly shipped to Kunming, and the rest was unloaded at stations along the road. The volume greatly exceeded previous records. Meanwhile, Mr. Currie has received a report from the War Department stating that the transportation volume was only 4,000 tons last month and the situation in Rangoon was in disorder. Currie thus asked me about the disparities in the above information. I found the truth is this: though this matter was not reported by McCloy, it is better to let the secretary of the navy Frank Knox know Your Excellency's attitude toward his honesty. Besides, transportation on the Yunnan-Burma road is the only means that the US could help us with and that depends on the road's transport capacity. A close friend in the US government told me secretly that if the transportation is smooth and unimpeded, it should not be a problem for the $500 million worth of munitions as requested by Your Excellency. According to their confidential plan, they are prepared to supply us with $1 billion worth of military equipment. He conveyed the message to me because of our personal friendship, and wanted to keep it off of the record. Yet it is absolutely reliable. I respectfully send this confidential telegram.

T. V.

158. Telegram to Chiang on announcement of Lattimore's employment (June 23, 1941)

S363

The President agreed to publicize the appointment of Owen Lattimore as advisor, and stated that Lattimore was introduced by the President to Your Excellency, to show the close cooperation between our two countries. The original text of the announcement was revised by the President himself. I telegraphed Huo Yamin a request to translate the text and submit it to Your Excellency. If Your Excellency agrees, please publish the original announcement in Chongqing and inform me. The US will announce the news simultaneously here.

T. V.

159. Telegram to Chiang on augment of Lend-Lease Act goods (June 23, 1941)

S364

The US government requested the Congress to increase the quantity of munitions prescribed under Lend-Lease Act, and asked China and Britain of their needs. When we first handled such a case, we had little time and there were some omissions. Yet now that we have this good opportunity, please instruct relevant authorities to make a comprehensive plan and draft a list, then send to me so I can respond as soon as possible. I look forward to it.

T. V.

160. Telegram to Chiang on possible Japanese southward invasion (June 23, 1941)

S366

After the breakout of Soviet-German war, President Roosevelt was anxious to know whether there was a secret agreement between Adolf Hitler and Yosuke

Matsuoka. Assuming any, Japanese may take this opportunity to head south. I'd predict Japanese might make full-out attack on us, and invade Siberia as soon as Soviets seem to lose war. Is this correct?

People here are also eager to know any message Soviet Union sent to us after German declaration of war. Please kindly inform. Your Excellency's reply will be passed on to President Roosevelt directly without a third party. In addition, it seems to me that US government, because of public opinion, finds it difficult to assist Soviet Union as persistently as Britain did. How would Your Excellency comment?

T. V.

161. Telegram to Chiang on quantity of approved airplane purchase (June 25, 1941)

S367

The President has approved the plan of supplying us with 269 pursuit planes, along with earlier approved 100 P-40 airplanes, meeting the original target of 350 planes. As for the bombers, we are still pushing for their supply, and have made some progress already. According to your telegram dated June 12th, air force personnel are supposed to be dispatched to the US for training. After discussions with others, I feel the number of personnel is too small, and plan to ask the US to approve our sending 500 personnel. This request is under discussion. I respectfully report this.

T. V.

162. Telegram to Chiang on Long Yun's request to purchase trucks (June 25, 1941)

I received a telegram from Miu Yuntai[1], which says that Governor Long Zhizou[2]

---

[1] Also known as Miu Jiaming. Then serving as an advisor to the National Resources Commission and director of the Economic Commission of the Yunnan provincial government.

[2] Also known as Long Yun. Then governor of Yunnan Province.

asked to purchase 100 trucks and 500 motorcycles for military transport and police use, and said he will pay for them himself and so on. Since I have not received your instructions, I haven't replied to him yet. I beg your decision on whether I should proceed.

T. V.

163. Telegram to Chiang on procurement of anti-tank guns in Canada (July 1, 1941)

S370

Your telegram dated June 29th has been noted. Because of slow delivery by the US government, I propose purchasing 3. 7-inch Anti-air guns and munitions from Canada, which would still be conducted within the Lend-Lease framework. I cautiously send Your Excellency this proposal.

T. V.

164. Telegram to Chiang on telegram to Roosevelt regarding to airplane procurement (July 1, 1941)

S371

The US government has agreed in principle to give us the airplanes we requested. But delivery is worryingly slow. Today, following your instructions in telegram dated June 15th, I drafted a telegram on your behalf and handed it over to Currie, who will pass it on to the President. The content of the telegram is outlined below:

A. According to your telegram dated 15th, I told him that the enemy planes are increasingly reckless in violent bombing. Our army soldiers could not even come out to fight back. Our lack of planes is the real reason for the failure of the recent Zhongtiaoshan battle[1].

---

[1] In May 1941 the Japanese attacked the Zhongtiaoshan area in the south of Shanxi Province. The Nationalist troops were defeated, and the whole area was occupied by the Japanese.

B. It is likely that, before the result of the Soviet-German war becomes foreseeable, the Japanese may full out attack us with their army and air force now stationed in northeast China. If the Soviet Union is defeated, the Japanese will surely advance and take Siberia. If they succeed, the Japanese will become stronger and try their best to end the war. China would face a much more dangerous military situation at that time.

C. The incessant bombing by enemy planes, the outbreak of Soviet-German war and the increasing strength of the enemy army against us are the reasons for our dwindling public morale. This is now the most serious concern during Your Excellency's four-year leadership of our war. The only way to encourage morale is to strengthen our air forces.

D. We have requested 500 planes. It is a negligible quantity. Major General Clark completely agreed to this plan after his field observations in China.

E. As to fighter planes, only 100 have been delivered in the past twelve months. Though the other 250 have been promised us, the delivery is too slow. We learned that the UK now has enough fighter planes to meet their needs. We hope the delivery can be sped up.

F. The problem of bombers is still unsolved. How can we organize an air force without bombers? The bombers not only can attack enemy airports, i.e., to preempt their bombing operations, but can attack enemy cities as well.

G. The Generalissimo believes that 150 bombers will not be decisive in the Atlantic battlefield, but they will make a huge difference for us. They will greatly encourage the morale of our people and army who have experienced four years' hard fighting against enemy. And this would turn the war around.

I also noted that the above-mentioned points, especially our concern over low public morale will be kept confidential from all US officials except the President.

I hereby report to you the above.

T. V.

165. Telegram to Chiang on procurement of communication equipment (July 1, 1941)

I gather that my telegram of June 18th has reached Your Excellency's attention. Concerning communication equipment of the Ministry of Military Affairs, except the 30 items that can be executed within the Lend-Lease framework, the other 20 items worth US $1 million must be purchased separately. I beg Your Excellency to give your instructions on whether the amount can be allocated from the Lend-Lease program.

T. V.

166. Telegram to Chiang on negotiation with UK regarding to airplane allotment (July 2, 1941)

S372

The US negotiated with the UK about transferring part of the airplanes to us since we urgently need bombers. To date the UK has not agreed. Now the Russian troops' defeat is imminent, and the international situation will change abruptly. If the UK takes a long view (on the global situation), she shall cooperate with the US in every aspect and do her best to assist us with planes. The recent bombing of the British embassy in Chongqing should have shocked them. I beg Your Excellency to state to the British ambassador the stakes and request him to telegraph Churchill about having thorough negotiations with President Roosevelt. Now when we have few ways out, this is one anyway. I beg for your decision.

T. V.

167. Telegram to Chiang on analysis of war situation in Russia (July 2, 1941)

S373

According to sources from London, the Soviet troops might not be able to sustain within four to five days.

T. V.

168. Telegram to Chiang and K'ung on extension of Stabilization Fund Agreement (July 2, 1941)

S374

The agreement on Sino-American Stabilization Fund was originally planned to expire this June. Now the US Stabilization Fund Act has been extended, and therefore, the Sino-American agreement on this Stabilization Fund can be extended to next June. In consulting with the US Department of Treasury, I was told that a signing is needed. Please telegraph our embassy to inform the US that the original signatories will sign on behalf of our government and Central Bank of China. With my best wishes.

T. V.

169. Telegram to Chiang on involvement of diplomatic personnel (July 6, 1941)

S375

Previously, I asked Li Shizeng to submit a letter to Your Excellency for your inspection. During the one-year extension of my stay in the US, I followed Your Excellency's instructions and diligently performed assigned tasks, and was lucky to be able to avoid the roundabout course. Yet, there have been some difficulties and twists in conducting various business affairs, external relations in particular. Since I sometimes have to negotiate directly with the highest US military authorities without following normal procedure, the criticism has been raised against me that I've stepped out of line. As a result, business affairs were obstructed. The fact that Mr. Gauss stated that from then on all telegrams concerning his government should follow official procedure is evidence. I pondered this issue, and begged Your Excellency in my telegram of April 29th to offer me the title of vice premier. I have concerned myself just with state affairs and made bold to express my views, thus ignored legislative procedures. I am deeply grateful that Your Excellency has forgiven me for my reckless proposal. Since it is difficult to give me the title of vice premier, only by appointing an able and efficient ambassador to the US who is thoroughly cooperative, can everything be done smoothly. Now Shi Zhizhi[1] stationed in the US is the most suitable person for this job. At present since world politics are changing rapidly, Sino-American relations are extremely important. If I am only in charge of Lend-Lease affairs, I won't have much to do with foreign affairs. If I need to look after special international affairs, I won't succeed without the concerted efforts of a diplomatic envoy. I have been in this job for years, and received Your Excellency's trust. Your Excellency would not regard my proposal as an attempt to seek private interest. I beg your decision on whether the above idea is feasible.

T. V.

170. Telegram to Chiang on Soong Tse-liang's resignation (July 7, 1941)

I read your telegram to brother T. A.[2] dated June 21st and learned that you approved my stay in the US for medical treatment. I am deeply grateful. The Southwest (Transportation Administration) affairs are extremely important. Please approve my resignation, so that somebody else will take charge to avoid disruption. As regards to the transportation between Kunming and Wanting, I followed Your Excellency's instructions and urged all staff to hand over authority to and assist Mr. Baker[3], and keep on working contentedly. While staying in Washington D. C., I will seek medical advice to cure my illness as soon as possible and help brother T. V. deal with the matters concerning procurement of materials for transportation. I respectfully write you of the above and beg for your consideration.

---

1 Alfred Sao-ke Sze, who was recommended by T. V. Soong to replace Hu Shi as China's new ambassador to the United States.

2 T. A. Soong, the youngest brother of T. V. Soong.

3 An American expert on transportation who was then in China.

T. V. [on behalf of T. L.]

171. Follow-up telegram to Chiang on Soong Tse-liang's resignation (July 7, 1941)

S376

According to confidential information from a friend in the State Department, the department received a report from Ambassador Gauss which states that Yu Qiaofeng [aka Yu Feipeng] of the Southwest Transportation Administration was afraid of offending the Soong family and dared not restructure the organization thoroughly. I do not believe a word of this information. Yet before the resignation of my junior brother Liang is approved, all sorts of speculations are inevitable. Brother Liang is even firmer about his resignation now after learning the news. I beg Your Excellency to grant your permission in consideration of both public interest and personal friendship.

T. V.

172. Telegram to Chiang on construction of Xikang-India Road (July 9, 1941)

S377

According to observations from various sources, the Japanese army will attack Thailand and French Vietnam in the near future. If the Burma Road becomes the target of intense enemy intense bombing, severe damage will be inevitable. The task of building the Xikang-India Road is now urgent. That's why I sent you several telegrams repeating this proposal. I asked Halifax his opinion of the plan and got his consent. I suggest that our government start discussions with the British ambassador immediately on cooperation in construction. The first step should be topographic survey. All the materials and instruments needed could be supplied by the US through the Lend-Lease program. Could Your Excellency please order the related ministries including foreign affairs, finance and transportation to prepare properly and work concertedly to finish the construction as soon as possible. With my best wishes.

P. S. The airports along the Sadiya-Xichang air route will also be constructed quickly. Please extend your approval on that.

T. V.

173. Follow-up telegram to Chiang on Long Yun's request to purchase trucks (July 10, 1941)

Previously I submitted a telegram to Your Excellency concerning Yunnan Governor Long Zhizhou's request to purchase vehicles. I have not received your response yet. I beg Your Excellency to give me your instruction on how to deal with this.

T. V.

174. Telegram to Chiang on communication with US Army regarding to ammunition development (July 11, 1941)

S379

There have been reports that the Commission of Arsenals has gained some results in its study of explosive bullets. The US army urgently needs this study for reference. I propose that Your Excellency order the Commission to hand the related drawings over to the US military attaché in China, who would make a gift of them to the US War Department as a sign of friendship. I beg for Your Excellency's instruction on this matter.

T. V.

175. Telegram to Chiang on Roosevelt's opinion on Sino-UK-Russia Military Pact proposal (July 12, 1941)

S378

I received your telegrams dated July 3rd, 5th and 11th, and hereby submit my humble response as follows:

1. In response to our telegram requests, President Roosevelt made following reply after consulting with high-ranking US military and political officials:

    a. President Roosevelt thought it beneficial for China to enter into Sino-Russian Military Agreement. He made same comment regarding Mutual Military Agreement among China, UK and Soviet Union. US, however, cannot participate, nor render a guarantee.

    b. President Roosevelt hopes to be informed confidentially and promptly should there be any military consultation between China and Russia.

2.

    a. I met and discussed with Lord Halifax on British-Russian relationship, and was told that UK would surely assist Russia in fighting Germany. Nonetheless, a military coalition is impossible because of differing political ideologies in the two countries. I inquired of some friends close to President Roosevelt and was told, however, that Prime Minister Churchill holds a different opinion on this issue.

    b. Japanese would take actions targeting Vietnam, as Lord Halifax learned from London.

    c. According to information received by US Secretary of Navy, Japanese will attack Russia on August 1.

    d. Morgenthau just informed me secretly that no Japanese ships have been sailing toward US in past two weeks. Also, manager of Japanese shipping company in US secretly sent his family and appliances back home, and he appears to have gone back too. Observing above information, I predict Japanese will surely take action against US, probably going southward. The first step will be to occupy all of Vietnam and expand airports in Thailand, preparing for invading Singapore, Dutch Indonesia and so on.

3. I am deeply moved by Your Excellency's considerate telegram on the 11th. Your graceful approval of Zhi-zhi's [Alfred Sao-ke Sze] appointment as ambassador to US showed your wise planning. Given intense international

situation, our country cannot succeed without contributions on diplomatic frontier. When I have discussed urgent issues with President Roosevelt, only after many twists and turns have I received concrete responses. This demonstrates our difficult situation. If this situation continues, not only I will be unable to fulfill my responsibility, but also Shizhi (aka Ambassador Hu Shi) might be in awkward situation. I plead Your Excellency and announce your decision swiftly. Should you regard it improper for time being, I would stick with my job relating to Lend-Lease Act during this period. Your Excellency will kindly understand my situation and make proper decision.

I present this letter with respect and look forward to your orders.

T. V.

176. Telegram to Chiang on Japan's withdrawal of bank deposits in the US (July 14, 1941)

S380

(Henry) Morgenthau just informed me secretly that Japan has continually transferred back its bank deposits in the US.

T. V.

177. Telegram to Chiang on latest approval of fighter purchase (July 15, 1941)

S381

Your telegram dated July 14th has been noted. The pursuit planes approved this time include A) 125 REPUBLIC P43; B) 92 VULTEE P48C and 52 P48D. The total numbers of the two items are 269. I have conveyed Your Excellency's gratitude to the US government.

T. V.

178. Telegram to Chiang on transferring of commercial staff from Berlin (July 16, 1941)

Your telegram dated June 27th acknowledged.

(1) The forthcoming visit of the commercial attaché staff stationed at our embassy in Berlin to US is more than welcome. I will follow your instruction to keep them stay.

(2) The Japanese Cabinet has resigned. Please instruct me with the details.

(3) According to Russian Ambassador to China Alexabder Paniushkin, Leningrad and Kiev are indeed in danger, but Moscow is able to stand.

T. V.

179. Telegram to Chiang on Japan's intention to invade Siberia (July 17, 1941)

S382

According to sources from Tokyo and the observations of the US Secretary of Navy (knox) and Mr. Morgenthau, the target of the Japanese enemy seems to be Siberia. And your telegram dated 16th also noted. I will follow your instructions and take good care of the said matter.

T. V.

180. Telegram to Chiang on airport construction in Sadiya (July 21, 1941)

S383

I heard that the construction of airfield in Sadiya may face opposition from India's small tribe states. I found that Mr. DaCooper, former British Minister of Information, is currently the Cabinet's representative in the Far East. It seems feasible to ask brother Fuchu (Guo Taiqi) to approach him and have him mediate inbetween.

T. V.

181. Telegram to Chiang on approval procedure of Lend-Lease affairs (July 22, 1941)

S384

I received your two telegrams dated 21st. The means of communication is extremely important. Yet, since I undertook the military procurement affairs under Lend-Lease Act, as it concerns military affairs, I have been directed by the Military Affairs Commission, and conducted all business under Your Excellency's instructions. Now the new four rules seem change the whole system. The Ministry of Finance will take over all matters related to procurement, shipment, and allocation of the loans. I strongly feel that during this critical moment of war, there will be too many barriers in both internal and external relations (if the new rules are adopted). After long weighing, I would suggest to keep the existing rule, i. e., to submit all cases to Your Excellency for instructions to the proper authorities to deal with them, or to concentrate them under the Military Affairs Commission for designing alternative means of communication. I beg for your instructions on how to deal with this.

T. V.

182. Telegram to Chiang on French concession to Japanese occupation of Vietnam (July 23, 1941)

S385

According to intelligence US State Department received from ambassador in France William Leahy, the French Minister of Navy Admiral Francois Darlan came to tell him that the Japanese urged full occupation over Vietnam by force on the 24th. The French Government had no way out but agreed. It seemed that US and UK are about to launch their economic sanctions on Japan.

T. V.

183. Telegram from Chiang on proposal of US-Russia negotiation (July 23, 1941)

I received a telegram from Ambassador Shao[1] dated July 19th. He reported that from his observation during the past month, the Soviets do not want the alleged Soviet-US joint actions. Talking about this with the Soviets may make things worse. However, if the US offers something practical and concrete, the situation will be quite different. The US ambassador to Russia will return to his position soon. Ambassador Shao very much hoped that the US ambassador would be authorized to initiate sincere and frank negotiations with the Soviets. He asked if Mr. T. V. could help. Would you please make this suggestion to the US government?

Kai-shek

184. Telegram to Chiang on Roosevelt's approval of bomber purchase (July 23, 1941)

S386

President Roosevelt approved 66 bombers, including 33 Lockheed Hudsons and 33 DB-7s. These are the result of negotiations with UK to transfer their allotment to us. I hereby report above to Your Excellency.

T. V.

185. Telegram to Chiang on US reporter's visit to Russia via Xinjiang (July 23, 1941)

S388

A newspaper in Chicago run by US Secretary of Navy Frank Knox intends to send a reporter (Archibald T.) Steele to Soviet Russia as a battlefield correspondent. The Secretary asked me on his behalf to beg Your Excellency

---

[1] Shao Lizi, then Chinese ambassador to Soviet Russia.

to render your kind assistance so that Mr. Steele will be able to fly from Chongqing to Moscow via Xinjiang. The Secretary of Navy is always enthusiastic about helping us. Could we grant him gracious permission? I beg Your Excellency to give me your instruction.

T. V.

186. Telegram to Chiang on French volunteer pilots (July 23, 1941)

S389

A French pilot coming from Vietnam expressed his willingness to recruit local residents to join in the war against Japan. I beg Your Excellency's instructions (to approve), and ask him to fly to Chongqing to contact our Aviation Committee.

T. V.

187. Telegram draft to Chiang on gun procurement in Canada and US (July 24, 1941)

S390

Your telegram on the 18th acknowledged. Following your instructions, I ordered 360 3.7-inch Anti-air guns from Canada and the US respectively. The delivery date for the new 7.5-inch Mountain guns has not been confirmed. I plan to watch for an opportunity to increase the purchase number after the delivery begins. There shouldn't be problem in principle.

T. V. (drafted by Jiang Biao)

188. Telegram to Chiang on military procurement in Canada (July 24, 1941)

S391

Herewith I submitted for Your Excellency's review the detailed order for munitions we gave Canada. After discussions, our application of ordering five kinds of Canadian munitions has been sent to the US War Department today.

The order includes:

(1) 15,000 Bren Light Machine Guns, to be delivered from August to next September;

(2) 3,000 0.55 rifles, to be delivered during next January and June;

(3) 360 37-mm anti-tank guns, to be delivered from August, and completed by 12 months installment;

(4) 180 4 mm Bofors anti-air guns, to be delivered from October and completed by next June;

(5) 48 3.7-inch anti-air guns, to be delivered from next January to September.

All guns are equipped with ammunition.

T. V. [Drafted by Jiang Biao]

189. Telegram to Chiang on US freezing of Japanese possessions (July 24, 1941)

S392

The US decided to (1) freeze about $150 million USD worth Japanese assets in the US, (2) stop buying Japanese gold and silver. The above two decisions were announced today. In addition, the US intends to (3) detain Japanese ships in the US (4) embargo gasoline and engine oil to Japan. This is what I heard.

T. V.

190. Telegram to Chiang on secret meeting between Yan Xishan's representative and Japanese (July 31, 1941)

S393

An important figure here told me that, according to reliable sources from Shanghai:

1. The representative of Yan Xishan[1] held a meeting with Tanaka, enemy's

---

[1] Former Shanxi warlord who was then serving as Nationalist commander of the 2nd Military Zone. It was reported that Yan was also then secretly negotiating with the Japanese.

representative, in Taiyuan on June 30th. It was agreed to increase the Shanxi troops to 300,000, with munitions and supplies to be provided by the Nanking puppet regime on behalf of the Japanese enemy.

2. The representative of Yan requested that (a) 30 million in paper currency be issued, backed up by the Japanese enemy with reserves, (b) Yan's properties be reclaimed, and (c) thirteen (occupied) counties of north Shanxi be returned to (Yan's) Shanxi administration. Mr. Tanaka agreed to negotiate the first two requests. The third one is not negotiable because the Japanese enemy and the Inner Mongolian puppet regime already had an agreement on it.

3. After the agreement between Yan and the Japanese would be signed in Taiyuan on about August 1st, the two sides would cease fire. Yan would declare his anti-communist stance, participation in the so-called East Asia New Order, and disengagement from central government. The singing representative of the Japanese enemy is the commander of the First Army or their chief of staff, and the representatives of Yan are Zhuo Jingchu and Wang Xiguo (Cho Kyo Su and O Sei Koku in Japanese spelling). Moreover, Yan's arsenals in Shaanxi and his family dependants in Sichuan are moving back to Taiyuan now. He also carried out conscription in Shandong and Shanxi provinces. To deceive the government, he purposely spread the news that the meeting with Japan had failed, and so on.

I secretly report the matter to you.

T. V.

191. Telegram to Chiang to request for explanation on procurement purposes (August 5, 1941)

S394

I found that our government organizations didn't specify the uses for materials and supplies they requested to purchase under the Lend-Lease Act. Since the US examined these requests carefully, only after many setbacks was each order approved. I beg Your Excellency to direct those organizations to bear this in mind in order to avoid back-and-forth inquiries and delays.

T. V.

192. Telegram to Chiang on dispatch of senior-level communication personnel (August 6, 1941)

It is difficult to find an appropriate person at the moment to handle telecommunication equipment in my office. Now Wen Yuqing is in interim charge. But he is sick and asks for leave quite often. I am afraid of causing delays and thus beg Your Excellency to send to the US a telecommunications specialist who is proficient in English and familiar with situation here. I beg with anxious expectation.

T. V.

193. Telegram to Chiang on possibility of export from Sichuan and Yunnan (August 6, 1941)

S396

The US authorities banned the import of Japanese silk, but demand is great. Is it possible for our provinces of Sichuan and Yunnan to export some? Is there any way to smuggle some from the Japanese-occupied coastal provinces? I beg your further instructions.

T. V.

194. Telegram to Chiang on air-survey of southern Xikang-India Road (August 7, 1941)

S395

I received your telegram dated 2nd. As regards to the Xikang-India roadway, originally it was designed to go westbound from Xichang to upper Yangtze River (Jinsha River), and then divide in two directions: (1) northern line to India via Atunze, Yanjing and Zayul, about 1,500 kilometers, and (2) southern line to India from Upper Burma via Gongshan and Jiangxinpo in

Yunnan Province, roughly 1, 200 kilometers. This is the alternate route via northern Burma that the American embassy proposed hoped in its memo be surveyed simultaneously. The southern line is shorter and does not pass through the area of Xikang and Tibet, where the boundary is blurred and could cause contention. As for foreign relations, there will be no other problems if Britain and Burma agree to assist. I beg Your Excellency to instruct concerned agencies to survey the southern line at the same time. It will be more efficient if they use aerial survey. Moreover, for the sake of the Sino-India transport, the aerial survey is indispensable. If the Ministry of Communications does not have the equipment for aerial survey, it can negotiate with the CNAC for assistance. Mr. Duff Cooper, the representative of the British cabinet in Singapore, will arrive in the US soon. I will discuss this with him and ask for his assistance. I respectfully reply to you the above.

T. V.

195. Telegram to Chiang on transportation priority of Red Cross goods (August 7, 1941)

S397

After I explained to the American Red Cross that the transport capacity of the Yunnan-Burma road has been enhanced, the Red Cross agreed to provide medical products over and above the original relief supplies. I reported this to you in my May 14th telegram. However in June, only 22.5 tons (of Red Cross goods) have been shipped: 780 tons are stored in Rangoon, while another 780 tons are on the way to Rangoon. Red Cross has decided to stop supplying until the stored materials (in Rangoon) have all been shipped out on the ground that the slow transport and hot weather in Burma would cause those medicines to deteriorate easily. Though transportation on the Yunnan-Burma Road is improved now, shipping of all supplies inland should be done in order of importance and urgency, and under a comprehensive plan. Or we can set up an organization to take exclusive charge of this matter. The Red Cross supplies in particular should have priority in shipping to avoid delays and prevent giving our ally an excuse. I beg your decision.

T. V.

196. Telegram to Chiang on approval of DC-3 air freighter delivery (August 7, 1941)

S398

The US authorities agreed to dispatch ten DC-3 planes (to us) from their cargo fleet in 1-2 months. Please instruct the Ministry of Communications to discuss with CNAC how to allocate them.

T. V.

197. Telegram to Chiang on delivery of uniform cotton (August 8, 1941)

The 10 million yards of cotton fabric for uniforms ordered under Lend-Lease Act will be delivered in the following months: August, about 400 thousand yards; September, one million; October, two million; November, 3. 4 million and December, 3. 1 million. I beg you to inform the Ministry of Military Affairs. The detailed list will be sent out separately.

T. V.

198. Telegram to Chiang to request for Chiang's interview with Arnstein (August 8, 1941)

S399

(1) Daniel Arnstein has finished his inspection of the Yunnan-Burma Road, and is returning to Chongqing on 11th. Please meet him at your convenience and listen to his report as Your Excellency's reference for future reform. (2) Chen Zhiping[1] and Chen Changtong[2], stationed in Rangoon, have proposed setting up a

[1] Then serving as head of the Sino-Burma transportation administration and representative of the Executive Yuan to Burma.

[2] Then serving as governor of a branch of the Bank of China in Rangoon, where he was also representative of China Defense Supply Inc. , Burma and India.

committee to identify order of importance and urgency for supplies to be shipped inland. Their opinions are valuable. I beg your instructions on whether the proposed committee should be headed by Yu Qiaofeng[1]. (3) Since the Lend-Lease Act does not cover the transport expenses of the materials requested by Chen Zhiping and others for shipping inland, and I am only responsible for delivering those materials to Rangoon, please instruct the Ministry of Finance to appropriate funds for that shipping. I wrote this respectfully.

T. V.

199. Telegram to Chiang to request for investigation on paralyzed Burma Road transportation (August 12, 1941)

S400

According to American reports at this moment, several hundred trucks and other Lend-Lease Act materials have arrived in Rangoon. Yet because no one takes care of transport expenses and customs duties, the shipment has been halted. Though Your Excellency has stationed Deputy Foreign Minister Zeng Rongfu and Chen Zhiping to Rangoon, they have not been able to do anything owing to lack of funds and other reasons. The American Military Mission (AMMISCA) is coming to China. It is feared that they will take this situation as an excuse to delay future supplies. I am very worried, and beg Your Excellency to find out the truth about this and formulate a solution. I beg with great expectation.

T. V.

200. Telegram to Chiang on dispatch of naval intelligence officer to US (August 12, 1941)

S401

The President's intelligence unit expressed their hope that we will select and

---

[1] Director of Southwest Transportation Company.

send a navy officer to station in Washington D. C. because the situation in Pacific area is getting tenser. The candidates should speak English and be familiar with Japanese matters. I beg your decision and look forward to your reply.

T. V.

201. Telegram to Chiang on Soong's meeting with British delegate to Singapore (August 14, 1941)

S402

I just met Duff Cooper, the representative of the British cabinet in Singapore. (1) I welcomed on behalf of Your Excellency his visit to Chongqing; (2) I stated to him the need of holding a meeting of China, the UK, the US and Netherlands in Singapore to discuss the fight against the enemy; (3) Regarding levying duties for our Lend-Lease materials via Burma, Mr. Cooper promised to telegraph the US to request duty exemption. Cooper plans to fly to Singapore next week. I wrote this with respects.

T. V.

202. Telegram to Chiang on US government's dissatisfaction on Burma Road transportation (August 21, 1941)

S404

Daniel Arnstein telegraphed that he wants to go back. Mr. Currie asked me to request Your Excellency's opinion on whether Arnstein's report on the Yunnan-Burma road is substantial and grounded. Recently, the US government received all sorts of news reporting complaints about transport conditions on the Yunnan-Burma Road. Our request for Lend-Lease supplies amounted to US $900 million. If transport on the road is not quickly improved, the US will take this as an excuse and delay the supplies. In fact, there is no way to execute shipment (of more aid supplies). Considering this prospect, I am deeply worried about how we can accomplish the task under such circumstances. Your Excellency is cristally clear (about the situation) and will be able to find out the real problems. Whether they stem from the mismatch of authority and responsibility, from the inability of the chief officer to implement fundamental reform, or from other reasons, I beg Your Excellency to investigate the matter. I wrote this with great expectation.

T. V.

203. Telegram to Chiang on US Military mission's visit to Chongqing (August 22, 1941)

S406

I received your telegram dated August 15th. The dispatching of US Military Mission is in slow progress due to the State Department's cautiousness. I therefore wrote an enquiry letter to President directly, and have just received his reply. The President said he is very willing to consent. Secretary of War has already chosen Major General John Magruder[1] as Chief who is now recruiting staff and going to Chongqing very soon. The President hoped the Mission would do their best to provide effective assistance during China's war against the Japanese.

General Magruder and some of his staff will leave for Chongqing in two to three weeks. The specific date will be reported separately. The rest of his staff will follow later in several teams. Please have their residence in Chongqing prepared and decide whether on the south bank or the north bank of the River.

T. V.

---

1 Later to be Head of the American Military Mission to China.

204. Telegram to Chiang on meeting between representatives of Yan Xishan and Japanese (August 22, 1941)

S407

Hope you have read my telegram dated July 31st. The US was informed on August 7th that the representative of Yan Xishan and representative of the Shanxi Province governor (the puppet regime) met and agreed that the troops under Zhao's command will be dispatched to Xiaoyi [in central Shanxi] so as to make contact with the enemy troops. In the meeting of Xiaoyi on August 6th, the enemy side participants were the chief of staff of the Japanese First Army and the head of Taiyuan Secret Service. The results of the meeting have been reported to the Nanjing puppet regime and so on. I found that according to the telegram by United Press from Chongqing on 15th, the Chinese army has recovered Xiaoyi which had been occupied by the Japanese troops for three and half years. I do not know whether the event correlates with the above news. I wrote this respectfully.

T. V.

205. Telegram to Chiang on airplane procurement under Lend-Lease Act (August 22, 1941)

S408

I received your telegram dated August 21st. According to the Lend-Lease Act, we planned to request 1,000 airplanes. Soon afterward, we altered to request 500 planes instead on the ground that it would be easier to proceed. Besides the 100 P-40 airplanes we have already purchased, the planes we request now include 125 P-43 fighter planes, 144 P-48 planes, 33 Hudson bombers, 33 DB-7 planes, 138 B-25C planes and 70 basic training aircrafts. This number of airplanes seems to be enough to meet our original expectation of 350 fighter planes and 150 bombers. The US has accepted our requests. However, because of production constraints, and because demand exceeds supply, it is difficult to anticipate the actual quantity of planes to be delivered. Now we are trying every means to urge their delivery as soon as possible. I respectfully wrote this (for your reference).

T. V.

206. Telegram to Chiang on organization of US Military Mission (August 26, 1941)

S409

The US government announced the dispatch of the American Military Mission to China (AMMISCA), and they will depart around mid-September. The organizational structure of the Mission is as follows: a Chief of the Mission, one office and five divisions: (1) The Office of Chief-of-Staff directs four Sections: Finance, Administration, Medical and Commissioner; (2) Division for Personnel Administration; (3) Division for Intelligence Communication; (4) Division for Organizational Training; (5) Division for Logistics; (6) Division for Operation and Planning.

Under Divisions Two to Five, there are 11 Sub-divisions: Air Force and Infantry, Engineer Corps, Communications, Transportation and Maintenance, Delivery Corps, Chemical Corps, Wild Artillery, Antiaircraft Artillery, Armored Troops, and Miscellaneous. Under Division for Logistics, there are four groups: Transportation, Yunnan-Burma Road, Distribution, and Railway.

The Mission headquarters is in Chongqing, with branch offices in Guiyang, Kunming and Lashio. Moreover, there are five liaison officers stationed in Shanghai, Manila, Singapore, Hong Kong, and Rangoon. The Washington Office is headed by a Director, and directs seven Sub-divisions: Air Force, Munitions, Communication, Engineering Corps, Transportation and Miscellaneous. The Washington Office would handle China's Lend-Lease affairs that relevant to the War Department. The Mission will have a 40-delegate team, which is currently being organized. It is better we organize corresponding liaison and reception offices in advance. Besides the organizational structure chart which will be reported to Your Excellency separately, I will follow up (new information) and report as soon as I acquire more details.

T. V.

207. Telegram to Chiang on background information of Lattimore (August 26, 1941)

S410

Your two telegrams dated August 21st acknowledged. I will probe into US intentions and report to you later. Your Excellency could consult with advisor Mr. Lattimore who has deep insight into Mongolian and Xinjiang issues. In my opinion this matter concerns not only technical but also political and diplomatic aspects. It would be better to formulate an overall plan among China, Russia and the US. As the Germans might soon occupy the oil fields in the European part of Soviet Russia, exploitation of new oil fields could solve the problem for both China and Russia, and the Russians would benefit from it greatly. Yet the Russians used to regard Xinjiang as their exclusive domain of influence, and have been reportedly assisting Governor Sheng Shicai in administration (of Xinjiang). Now that US offered only limited ordinance assistance to the Russia, thus may not be able to hold strong and effective stance over the Russians. Therefore, political solution is the key to this matter. Once the political issue is solved, all difficulties will be overcome. I beg Your Excellency's advice on whether my views are feasible.

T. V.

208. Telegram to Chiang on Lend-Lease Act negotiations and allotment of aids (August 27, 1941)

US Congress passed Lend-Lease Act this spring to assist those democratic countries under invasion. Since then the Act has experienced several changes. Herewith I submit to Your Excellency a summary of all the changes and the allocation of (Lend-Lease) funds.

A. Our portion according to the Lend-Lease Act passed by the US Congress on March 27th this spring is as follows: (in US dollars)

1. Weapons	47,876,181
2. Aircrafts	50,000,000
3. Armored and military vehicles	67,282,585
4. Shipping expenses	5,000,000
5. Military Miscellanea	9,841,234
6. Defense industry	(not allocated yet)
7. Agricultural and industrial commodities	50,000,000

(including 15 mm dollars worth of railway materials)

Total:　　　　　　　　　　　　　　　230,000,000

B. Under the President's authorization, the military equipment, munitions and other goods purchased by US government before March of 1941 could be transferred to democratic countries. Among them USD 25, 503, 500 was allocated to us.

C. The President will request the Congress appropriate the second round of funds under the Lend-Lease Act. The US government informed us on July 9th that we need to submit for examination, within two days, a detailed list of the military equipment we need from now to the end of next year. Since this matter was urgent, after talking with the staff of the Directorate of Ordnance, the Aviation Commission, and other government departments stationed here, I took the liberty of having a detailed list made of needed equipment. The total budget amounts to roughly US $1,500,000,000. The breakdown list is as follows (in US dollars):

1. Weapons	296,865,000
2. Aircrafts	676,450,000
3. Military vehicles	167,200,000
4. Transportation	50,000,000
5. Military Miscellanea	83,800,000
6. Defense industry equipment	25,100,000
7. Agricultural and industrial commodities	191,700,000
8. Other management and inspection costs	8,400

On August 15th the US government examined the above budget, and will allocate 600,000,000 USD out of the total budget before the end of this year. The US government will soon send this bill to Congress for approval. The breakdown of this allocation is as follows:

1. Weapons   179,128,500
2. Aircraft   201,000,000
3. Military vehicles   76,020,000
4. Transportation   35,000,000
5. Military Miscellanea (mostly communication equipment)
                                                                          27,836,000
6. Defense industry equipment   6,000,000
7. Agricultural and industrial commodities   75,000,000

I stated to the US government that the above items may be subject to minor changes according to actual needs. The US government has agreed.

The above A, B, and C are assistance the US government extended to us for five months under the Lend-Lease Act. The total amount of the approved budget is US $855,103,100, excluding the funds we expect to receive in next fiscal year. Generally speaking, the US feels that she has done her best in providing supplies to China. It is also true that production is slow and demand exceeds supply. It is reported that the total assistance Latin American countries to receive is less than this amount.

T. V.

209. Telegram to Chiang on Roosevelt-Churchill summit (August 28, 1941)

I gathered several pieces of news from the Atlantic Conference between Roosevelt and Churchill as follows:

(1) As the Russians retreat in defeat, they may repeat the practice of the last European war and make peace with Germany unilaterally. Though the UK and US are willing to offer assistance, their production of ammunition is unable to meet Russia's need. For example, the Russians requested 6,000 airplanes; yet the UK and the US could only offer 205 planes, including 140 pursuit planes allotted by the UK, 60 allotted by the US, and only 5 bombers. They were worried about Russia's

disappointment, and therefore held this conference between the UK and the US in Moscow to show their firm determination to offer assistance and to procrastinate.

(2) Roosevelt insisted that the UK should adopt hard line stance on Thai issue. Yet he does not want to say explicitly that the US would be involved in the event of a war between the UK and Japan because of this. That was why Churchill in his speech on the South Pacific issue last week took precedence over the US and tried to involve the US in the storm. The US was very angry at Churchill's maneuver. US Secretary of State Cordell Hull stated to the press, "I always admire the eloquence of Prime Minister Churchill's speech, yet I do not wish to make any comment on this one," and so on.

(3) The UK expressed concern over the production of munition in the US. The US and the UK decided to collaborate effectively in munition production in hope that the output of airplanes, tanks and firearms would exceed the German's in the latter half of next year. As regards the US entry into war, Roosevelt stated that timing is not yet an opportune. However, he promised he would propose to the Congress that American fleets should be sent to protect British transport. Moreover, I repeatedly expressed our complaints to the US that the Atlantic Conference had not mentioned China at all, and China had not been able to participate in the Moscow Conference. That might be the reason why the US State Department, which originally opposed the dispatch of AMMISCA, requested the President to announce the dispatch officially. They are very likely afraid that we will turn to Soviet Union, thus made a preventative friendly gesture. Russia knows clearly that if Japan continues advancing to the south, the US will inevitably join the war, but if Japan attacks Siberia, then the US will not necessarily take part. As Japan's attack of Siberia is imminent, the Russians try their best to involve the US in this whirlpool, just as Churchill did in his speech.

(4) I repeatedly expressed our complaints to the Americans that they had not mentioned China in the Atlantic Conference, and they had not let China participate in the Moscow Conference. That was why the State

Department, which originally had opposed the dispatch of AMMISCA, now changed its attitude and supported the dispatch to show they had not forgotten China.

T. V.

210. Telegram to Chiang on US-UK-Russia meeting in Moscow (August 29, 1941)

I received your telegram dated August 4th. The news I gathered from the Atlantic Conference between Roosevelt and Churchill is as follows: The Russians retreated in defeat with heavy losses. Worrying that the Russians would repeat the practice of the last European war and make peace with Germany unilaterally, the UK and the US expressed their good will by offering assistance. However, their ammunition production is unable to meet Russia's demand. For example, the Russians requested 6,000 airplanes, yet the UK and the US could only offer 205 planes, including 140 pursuit planes allotted by the UK, and 60 allotted by the US plus only 5 bombers. Afraid that the Russians would be disappointed, they held the Moscow Conference to show their determination to provide assistance. That is why this conference was not as significant as outsiders thought. As to US, it wanted to procrastinate about Japan for some time, and therefore, it did not wish China to participate. Ambassador Hu had proposed to the State Department earlier that China did not have to take part.

Roosevelt insisted that the British adopt a hard line stance toward the Thai issue, yet he did not wish to say explicitly that once the war between the UK and Japan breaks out, the US would be involved in. Two weeks ago, when Churchill made a speech concerning Thailand, Dutch Indonesia and Singapore in the Pacific Ocean, he pushed the US to the forefront with the U. K playing the role of a helper. His attempt to embroil the US in the war irritated the US Mr. Cordell Hull stated to the press, "I admired the eloquence of Prime Minister Churchill's speech deeply, however, I do not wish to make comments upon this speech," and so on.

At the Moscow Conference the Russian Deputy-Minister of Foreign Affairs openly said to Ambassador Shao Lizi that the purpose of the Russia-US-UK conference was to discuss (issues regarding) the ammunition for war against fighting Germany, and so China had no need to participate. Now the Russian advisor expressed to Your Excellency that he'd welcome Chinese participation. It is unknown whether this was a shift of responsibility onto others, or was for some other reason. The Russians know very well that if Japan continues advancing to the south, the US is very likely to join the war, but if Japan attacks Siberia, then the US does not necessarily have to take part. At the moment Japan's attack on Siberia is imminent, which is why Russia wants to involve the US in the war, as Churchill did in his speech.

My colleagues and I repeatedly expressed our complaints about not mentioning China in the Atlantic Conference, and not letting China take part in the Moscow Conference. That was probably why US State Department officials who originally opposed the dispatch of AMMISCA shiftcd their attitude and requested the President to announce the dispatch officially. This was to show they had not forgotten China. I wrote this with respect.

T. V.

211. Telegram to Chiang on shipment of trucks (August 29, 1941)

S412

I received your telegram dated August 27th. 1,500 10-wheel military trucks will be shipped out before September 18th. 733 of the total of 2,500 4x2 trucks for Yunnan-Burma Road, Gansu oil fields and Yunnan-Burma Railway have already been shipped out. 1,131 more trucks will be delivered before September 8th. The rest 636 trucks will be shipped in early October. I beg Your Excellency to acknowledge this and forward the (attached) detailed shipping documents to Minister He (Yingqin) and Mr. Yu Feipeng.

T. V.

212. Telegram to Chiang on letter from Fumimaro Konoe to Roosevelt (September 3, 1941)

S414

The letter from (the Japanese Prime Minister Fumimaro) Konoe to President Roosevelt is as follows: (1) During the European war, Japan promises not to expand their military forces beyond its current control territories; (2) the number of Japanese troops stationed in Vietnam will be decreased to 10,000, and they will not undertake any constructions in Vietnamese military harbors; (3) Japan will maintain status quo in China proper and three northeastern provinces, and hope the US persuades China to accept a long-term cease-fire; (4) Japan hopes to restore economic relations with the US, lift the blockade, conclude trade treaty, and persuade the UK and Netherlands to restore diplomatic relations with Japan. The US government keeps the above information absolutely secret. I hope Your Excellency will not mention me as the source of this news if Your Excellency needs to make use of it.

Moreover, the US government knows well that Konoe's statement is nothing but a means of procrastination. If Germany wins, then Japan would be able to succeed eventually. Even if Germany is defeated, Japan would still have the chance to maneuver with democratic countries. During this critical, uncertain moment, Japan would enhance its military and economic strength, just as a beast use spare time to digest swallowed food. The US government clearly knows Japan's tricks. Nevertheless, US government does not wish to disclose them publicly in fear that Japan's military authorities would rally and attack the Konoe cabinet. Yet the US is confident that the Konoe cabinet will by no means be able to sustain itself during these two months. By then, the time of launching the Pacific war will come to maturity. The US does not wish to see the Konoe cabinet fall from power at this moment, and therefore it does not want this news leaked. I report this with respects.

T. V.

213. Telegram to Chiang on Soong's meeting with Magruder (September 4, 1941)

General John Magruder of American Military Mission to China (AMMISCA) will fly to Chongqing with a team of his staff in middle of this month. Here I humbly present my views and the course of our conversation in following for your inspection:

1. I instructed Qi Jun[1] to translate organizational structure and ranking of officials of previous German Military Mission to China, as well as their good comments about us, and forward them to AMMISCA for reference.

2. I told General Jiang Biao, commissioner of Arsenal Division, to inform AMMISCA of fire arms previously supplied by German Military Mission for their observation.

3. Mr. and Mrs. Henry Luce paid a visit to our troops stationed at Tongguan last spring, and were very much impressed. General Magruder used to be military attaché to China during 1925 – 26. Now, our troops are very different from in that period. The great progress our troops have made is widely recognized. We should invite AMMISCA upon arrival to visit our finest troops, so that they will get a good impression and will not look down on us.

4. I told General Magruder frankly that quantity and quality of our troops are beyond question. Yet what we lack are airplanes and ammunitions. I hope he will report this to US government to help increase weapons supply and expedite delivery. This will be one of AMMISCA's most important tasks. Whether the mission of AMMISCA is successful depends on their fulfillment of above tasks. Delivery of US weapons is too slow. There are two alleged reasons: (a) production of ammunition and warplanes is low, (b) transport in China is not smooth. Although these reasons are not merely excuses, yet we should try to argue that we have tried our best to improve transportation on Burma Road and, if necessary, present facts to

---

1 Then serving as a secretary in the Chinese Military Affairs Commission.

them as proof.

5. General Magruder is military man, yet he is also highly skilled in politics. Therefore, we cannot treat him simply a military mind.

Your Excellency's fame and prestige are widely spread and acknowledged both inside and outside China. There is no doubt that AMMISCA will follow your instructions. I pray Your Excellency be healthy.

T. V.

214. Telegram to Chiang on shipment of materials for the Yunnan-Burma Railroad construction (September 4, 1941)

S413

The materials for the Burma Railway (construction) were shipped out on August 29th. The shipment contains twenty five thousand items in total, including six hundred tons of dynamite and other accessories, one hundred tons of surveying equipment, tools for building the roadbed, and medicine. The inventory list has been sent to the Ministry of Transportation. I hereby inform you on this and request that you instruct the Ministry.

T. V.

215. Telegram to Chiang on employment of American technical advisors (September 4, 1941)

S415

Because of technical problems, the National Aviation Commission cannot send technicians to the US now. I propose hiring one or two American technical advisors to assist us with urgent needs. However, their salaries will be high. Therefore I beg your instructions on this matter.

T. V.

216. Telegram to Chiang to request for Chiang's interview with Arthur Young (September 4, 1941)

Arthur Young, the advisor to the Ministry of Finance, is very familiar with the situation on the Burma Road. Please grant him an audience when you have time, and instruct him to show you the translation of his report on the inspection of the Burma Road, which can serve as the basis of your decision.

T. V.

217. Telegram to Chiang on visit of US Military Mission (September 5, 1941)

The American Military Mission to China (AMMISCA) consists of 28 officers, and 14 attaches. They are leaving in succession. The core members will gather in Hong Kong around October 7th and 8th, and then fly to Chongqing. The attaches will travel by ship to Rangoon. It would be better if we prepare offices and guesthouses in Chongqing and Hong Kong as soon as possible. The requirements are as follows: (1) Three lodgings and offices to accommodate 25 mission members and 14 attaches in Chongqing. I'd advise that accommodations in Jialing village of Chengdu-Chongqing Railway be allotted to them. In addition, we need to find lodging in the neighborhood for 25 people and lodging in the north bank for more than ten people, with parking spaces for ten more cars. (2) The bedding such as pillows, sheets, woolen blankets and other daily necessities should be prepared as soon as possible. (3) Personnel should be assigned along with Chen Kangqi, secretary of the Bank of China in Hong Kong, and Chen Changtong, governor of Bank of China in Rangoon, to discuss with the Mission the reception and aforementioned preparations.

T. V.

218. Telegram to Chiang on UK tax exempt on Lend-Lease goods transported via Burma (September 8, 1941)

S417

The British embassy secretly informed me that the British government agreed that no duty will be levied on our Lend-Lease materials passing through the Burmese territories. Instead, the British government will compensate the Burmese government 10 rupees for every ton of such goods. This news will be published tomorrow. The British representative in Singapore Mr. Cooper contributed most to this matter while he was in US. Please send him a telegram to express our gratefulness and invite him to visit Chongqing.

T. V.

219. Telegram to Chiang on shipment of military equipment (September 9, 1941)

Your telegram dated September 7th acknowledged. (1) The US is expediting production of bullets for own use. Thus US cannot yield them to other countries within this year. In South America only Ecuador has 79 mm bullets. But the amount is small and thus I have given up. Our arsenals have reduced the production of bullets because of shortages of raw materials. Now large amounts of materials are continually shipped to Rangoon. Please instruct the responsible authorities to transport them to China as soon as possible for ammunition production. (2) One thousand Canadian light machine guns will be shipped out within the month. (3) Twenty mountain guns and fifty 75 mm howitzers will also be shipped out within the month. I am trying to obtain rifles.

T. V.

220. Telegram to Chiang on construction progress of the Burma Railroad (September 9, 1941)

Your telegram dated September 3rd acknowledged. Whether the Burmese authorities will do their best to connect the railroad is the key to finishing the Burma Railway construction on schedule. I have told the American advisors to pay attention to this matter. They will help us by urging the Burmese authorities to speed up the construction work. I beg you to instruct Director-General Zeng[1] to do as told.

T. V.

221. Telegram to Chiang on issues regarding to Myitkyina airport construction (September 9, 1941)

S419

The British authorities agreed to provide the funds for building Myitkyina airport to connect air transportation among theaters in western Yunnan. But the British authorities hope we will provide the funds for constructing the airfield buildings according to the model required by the China National Aviation Corporation. Please instruct Deputy Foreign Minister Zeng Rongfu to follow your orders in managing this matter.

T. V.

222. Telegram to Chiang on employment of US military advisors (September 9, 1941)

Your telegram dated September 7th acknowledged. The President-appointed American Military Mission's duties, besides consultation, include management of the (China related) Lead-Lease affairs. Members' salaries are paid by the US Army. We had better observe their service for a certain period before concluding a contract. I beg Your Excellency's decision.

T. V.

---

[1] Zeng Yangfu, then serving as Nationalist supervisor-general of the Burma-Yunnan Road.

223. Telegram to Chiang on arrival of US Military Mission (September 11, 1941)

Your telegram dated September 10th acknowledged. The departure dates of the American Military Mission slightly changed because of the availability of flight seats. The first group of three members will depart on September 14th. The second group of five, including General John Magruder and Commissioner Jiang Biao is scheduled to depart on September 21st. They will all fly from San Francisco. The rest of the mission members will follow later. Jiang Biao will inform you of the dates of their arrival at Chongqing at due time.

T. V.

224. Telegram to Chiang on tasks of US Military Mission (September 12, 1941)

S421

Your telegram dated September 11th acknowledged. The President stated to the Congress the duties of the American Military Mission as follows: (1) overseeing the uses of Lend-Lease supplies (in China), the same duty as that of the US Military Mission in Britain; (2) consulting with Chinese officials. The title "military mission" itself explains this. The Mission is naturally subject to Your Excellency's command. Commissioner Jiang Biao will report the details to Your Excellency in person. General Claire Chennault has not been officially appointed, and his status is different from this Mission's.

T. V.

225. Telegram to Chiang on transferring of military equipment allotment from UK (September 12, 1941)

S422

The British embassy in the US has agreed to allocate one thousand light machine guns, a hundred tons of incendiary bombs, and the sixty-six bombers that the President promised us. Could I beg your Excellency to express our gratitude to Ambassador Sir Archibald Clark-Kerr for all this assistance? I beg that Your Excellency consider this and make a decision.

T. V.

226. Telegram to Chiang on possibility of building a fuel pipeline between Lashio and Kunming (September 17, 1941)

S423

According to a proposal of Asiatic Petroleum Co., a light-duty pipeline (can be built) along the road between Lashio and Kunming as a replacement of the gasoline transportation by trucks could save four thousand tons of gasoline monthly in Burma Road. The company could first do a survey at our expenses. It said that Germany also uses this method to facilitate its military advance. I beg for your instructions on whether this is workable.

T. V.

227. Telegram to Chiang on miscellaneous affairs (September 18, 1941)

Commissioner Jiang Biao went to Chongqing with AMMISCA. As to those matters that could not be described in detail by telegram or post, I told him to discuss them with Your Excellency personally. On top of that, I list the following points:

1. The production of American munitions is still unable to meet the need. From past few months' experience, I can only anticipate that the American production of ammunition will still be less than demand. Once production increases, we should alter our demand in response.

2. The supply materials that the Americans offered to us have mainly been provided out of comradeship. From now on, we should try our best to let them realize that the Chinese war is vital to the international community, the Sino-US relation in particular. Since the US and China have common interests, the supply from the US to China is to help us accomplish the task

[of fighting against the common enemy], not just to express friendship. Otherwise, we will be in the position of a hanger-on forever, and there will not be equal cooperation between us.

3. For the above reasons, my humble opinion is that Your Excellency (supervise to) compose an independent and comprehensive counter-offensive plan to eliminate all invading enemies, which would explain clearly the priority and steps of attacking targets over time. (To execute this plan,) we need to organize a keen and able troop of 300-400 thousand strong, equip them with new weapons including tanks, heavy artillery, antiaircraft artillery as well as airplanes to cover from the air. This plan should be very detailed and practical.

4. After drafting a thorough counterattack plan, please consult General Magruder. Once he agrees to the plan, I will submit it to the US and ask for supplies, so that we can achieve distinguished results. By that time, please dispatch senior staff to Washington D. C. to help me negotiate with highest ranking officers of American military forces. I express my limited view here, and beg for your decision.

5. I received the telegram of brother Fuchu (Guo Taiqi) today. (According to him,) the British Ambassador Clark-Kerr proposed to set up a Sino-UK-US Joint Committee in the US capitol, and a branch in Chongqing. Your Excellency has also already endorsed the proposal. I have been supporting this idea for a long time, and we can expect that the cooperation of the three countries will be closer with the establishment of said committee under way. Previously, I had entrusted Li Shizeng with submitting a petition that mentioned the US would take action soon. For this reason, the cooperation among China, Britain and the US in the Pacific region is even more urgent. I will consult with British Ambassador to the US Lord Halifax as soon as he returns to America, and report to Your Excellency. I pray for your good health.

T. V.

228. Telegram to Chiang on the employment of US technical advisors (September 18, 1941)

S424

(1) In your telegram dated September 13th, Your Excellency inquired about the employment of the American Technician Mission. Since last European war, the US sold most overproduced equipment as scrap. Once this war is over, we can make use of most of the discarded equipment. Since we have good relations with the President, it is likely we can obtain a special discount or means for buying these. Though the US pays extraordinary attention to the current war, they will not easily agree with the proposal for employing a technician mission. They will either reckon the state of the Yunnan-Burma Road transport does not allow shipping such heavy equipment, or say that it is the very time to train needed military specialists, or our fallen areas have not been recovered and the whole national defense project is not yet in place. I deliberate on the possible solutions and think that it is not yet a good time to bring up the proposal. As the US Military Mission to China has many technicians, I beg Your Excellency to start discussions with them. Meanwhile, I will submit the proposal to the US National Defense Committee. Once the timing is opportune, I will bring it up with the US. I beg for Your Excellency's decision. (2) I negotiated with the US according to the instructions prescribed in the previous telegram. They promised to send specialists to investigate the quantity of the Xinjiang oil fields' output. However, what really matters are political issues. I beg Your Excellency to notify me by telegram whether we can reach a compromise with the Soviet as well as the locations of the oil fields. (3) I received your telegram dated September 16th. The US has agreed to employ our Staff Officer Liu Tianpu. Though he does not have good command of English, we can help him improve this shortcoming.

T. V.

229. Telegram to Chiang on Soong's meeting with Stimson (September 25, 1941)

S425

The war situation in Russia is getting critical. I was informed that someone here proposed to set priorities for the shipment of military supplies to Russia as much as possible. Today I visited US Secretary of War Henry Stimson and told him urgently that, though the war in Russia is important, China has been warring with the Japanese for over four years and our military supplies are exhausted. I hope the military supplies that were assigned to China will not be reassigned to Russia. Stimson agreed to do his best on this issue. He then asked me to report to Your Excellency confidentially that the US is increasing military forces in the Philippines aggressively and is dispatching most heavy-duty bombers there to distract the Japanese navy from invading to the south. He regarded this as indirect assistance to China. I expressed my gratitude for his good will and reminded him that, since the enemy is now attacking Central China violently, the direct shipment of sufficient US military supplies to China should not be delayed. I hereby report the above.

T. V.

230. Telegram to Chiang on plea to expedite anti-air guns delivery (September 26, 1941)

S426

I heard that, because of the critical war situation in the Soviet Union, the half-inch antiaircraft machine guns that the US authorities are expected to provide us will be diverted to the Soviet Union. I request that Your Excellency pretends not to know this but telegraphs Lauchlin Currie directly, stating that the battles in central China are critical and our troops urgently need antiaircraft guns and requesting him to urge the Department of War to allocate one thousand such machine guns to us. The telegram could be forwarded by James Mchugh. Whether or not this should be done is Your

Excellency's decision.

T. V.

231. Telegram to Chiang on shipment of communication equipment (September 30, 1941)

I have your earlier telegram dated 24th which contains the points that Supervisor-General Zeng Yangfu has stated. I have carefully read it and am urging the US authorities to ship out the urgently needed machinery for laying the roadbed [of the Burma Road] and other telecommunication equipment. I will contact Supervisor-General Zeng about dealing with this matter. I hereby report the above.

T. V.

232. Telegram to Chiang on organization and staffing of the Burma Road transportation (September 30, 1941)

I received your telegram dated 26th. (1) Mr. Currie reckoned that as the transactions concerning Yunnan-Burma road transport are taken charged by numerous governmental authorities. Even if Mr. Wilson demobilizes from military service and engages in [helping the transactions], he can not do much about [improving the transport]. Now the road transport is improved, and the merger of these authorities concerned is underway. Mr. Currie does not object Wilson's employment anymore. Yet, Wilson is under AMMISCA's command now. I beg Your Excellency to consult with General Magruder directly about his demobilization procedures and his employment as Deputy-Chief (of the Southwestern Transportation Administration); (2) We plan to employ 32 personnel as motor repair technicians for the Yunnan-Burma road, and 6 persons as motor dispatch specialists. Their travel allowances and salaries will be paid by the US. Now, the selection of the personnel is underway. The selected personnel will start to depart in groups on October 10th; (3) another group of motor assemblers led by Mr. Lartin is sent by General Motors

Corporation to help assembling vehicles. They are now rushing to China. I respectfully wrote this. Please inform Chief Inspector of Military Supplies Department Yu Qiaofeng of this matter.

T. V.

233. Telegram to Chiang on issues regarding to news censorship (October 1, 1941)

S427

According to United Press telegram report from Chongqing dated September 30th, some Mr. Pan's conversation in Chongqing touched on some matters such as arrival of American pilots to China and American naval convoy. US government is very discontented about disclosure of such information. I wish Your Excellency to instruct press censorship officers to pay extra attention in order not to divulge any military secrets.

T. V.

234. Telegram to Chiang on US enquiry on China's three-year raw material demands (October 1, 1941)

S428

Munitions control Board chaired by US Vice President Henry Wallace devised three-year plan for 120 major types of raw materials needed in national defense and for aiding China, Britain and Russia. Edward Stettinius, chief of Military Lend-Lease Office, just wrote to inquire about amounts of various types of raw materials we need in coming three years, and asked us to provide an estimate for consideration. My opinion is, first, the amounts of many goods and materials China needs have yet to be calculated in detail. Amount of raw materials needed is even more difficult to estimate. Second, with respect to goods we leased and purchased from US, most are manufactured products; it is difficult to determine major components of raw materials in each product. Third, supplies were purchased from US batch-by-batch or piece-by-piece, and ordered according to needs, except for military Lend-Lease goods which were ordered altogether according to plan. Thus it is really difficult to set forth overall plan. This US government survey, however, constitutes blueprint of her future production plans. If our requests not placed on time, raw materials we need may not be included in its national production plan. Even if we have cash in hand, there may be nothing to purchase. Now I'm going to negotiate with the Board proposing that we submit list of our Lend-Lease military equipment we now request for procurement. Next, Board would help us estimate amount of raw materials needed. But this is only temporary expedient that does not cover all our needs. I therefore earnestly request Your Excellency to instruct responsible institutions to (1) estimate, if possible, amount of major raw materials of products for military, civilian and export use during three-year period. These raw materials can be temporarily restricted to iron and steel, chromium, nickel, aluminum, alumina, cobalt, vanadium, copper, brass and molybdenum, and indicated as (a) self-produced (b) supplied by Britain, Soviet Union and the Netherlands (c) supplied by US. Estimates can be inaccurate, but should not be excessive or too broad. (2) urgently compile and send complete list of goods we request from US under military Lend-Lease Act for 1943. (3) indicate by telegraph China's three-year total output of tin, tungsten, and tung oil, together with estimates of exports of these goods to US. By the way, list of major raw materials attached to airmail letter dated September 17th is actually same as described in this telegraph. Here I attach again for your review.

T. V.

235. Telegram to Chiang on dispatch of Sun Zheng (October 4, 1941)

Your telegram dated October 2nd acknowledged. Ministry of Transportation is proposing to send Mr. Sun Zheng to come here, who is a suitable candidate. Please inform the ministry of this decision.

T. V.

236. Telegram to Chiang on resignation of Chen Changtong (October 6, 1941)

S430

I learned of your telegram dated 3rd, and just received Chen Changtong's telegraph stating that he was extremely uneasy as appointed manager of Southwestern Transportation Administration. He asserted he's been serving in banks, and has no experience in transportation field. He asked to decline this position in order not to hinder military transport. What he stated is really true. Given that Lend-Lease supplies are already on the way, and number of American specialists dispatched to China increased, it is indeed extremely complicated to handle all the work related to receipt of goods, investigation and communications. It is advisable to appoint another officer experienced in transportation to take over these tasks. Besides, Chen Zhiping, unfamiliar with foreign affairs, has displeased US and Burma. But he worked hard in protecting security along transportation lines. Is it possible to order him to assume responsibility of security only? Look forward to Your Excellency's instructions.

T. V.

237. Telegram to Chiang on candidate of Polish ambassador to China (October 6, 1941)

S431

Ambassador of former Polish government to Japan, Mr. Romer, has been deported by Japanese authorities because he submitted to authority of his new anti-Axis (Polish) government (in exile). Allegedly this person stayed in Japan for eight years and was familiar with inside information of the Japanese army military and government. If China agrees, Polish government (in exile) would like to appoint him ambassador to China. Perhaps he could be taken advantage of. I look forward to Your Excellency's decision. [Note added: Poland was opposing Soviet Union back then, and Japan spared no effort to cooperate. Hence, he gathered considerable military news.]

T. V.

238. Telegram to Chiang on telegram from US Lend-Lease Chief Officer (October 7, 1941)

I expect you received and read my telegram dated October 2nd. For your reference, I hereby translated and submit to you letter (dated September 24th) from Edward Stettinius, chief of Military Lend-Lease Office:

For the sake of foresight and future planning, US decided to make total calculation of raw materials needed for production of military and civil supplies to be provided to China, Britain and the Soviet Union, in line with domestic production, for current year, 1942 and 1943. We are asked to submit as soon as possible estimates of major raw materials needed for next three years in tabular form for (Lend-Lease) office's review. This matter is, in my view, of utmost importance. If future needs of our country are not estimated in advance, US may use this as excuse to stall and hold us. Please instruct all responsible organizations to work jointly and draw up plans in proper and prudent manner. Our foreign procurement has always lacked overall planning. Each entity, for instance, Universal Trading Company (UTC), Hua Chang Company or other private companies, acts in their own way without standards and coordination. As a result, overall demand and production for national defense could not be met, and intangible loss can well be imagined. Taking this opportunity will not only benefit us in coordination of overall situation, but also facilitate US future supply. This US plan is not restricted to Lend-Lease Act, but covers raw materials for other civilian goods as well. Our needs under Lend-Lease Act for current and following year added up to plan of $150, 000, 000, and this estimation should be submitted to US before October 10th for preliminary assessment. Commissioner Jiang Biao in his letter to Your Excellency put forth counterattack plan of organizing 300,000 to 400,000 crack troops, equipped with different kinds of weapons. This plan requires circumspect and careful consideration, as well as consultation with US military advisor, General Magruder, and would take quite a long time. It is advisable to attribute it to request contained in 1943 Lend-Lease authorization. What could be handled from abroad is only (estimate of) Lend-Lease items. It is not easy to gather comprehensive and accurate information. Besides, we should rely on survey and statistics conducted by our responsible governmental organizations. In my view, Resources Committee is very experienced in research work on domestic and foreign resources. Is it possible to order this committee to call responsible organs together for planning and preparation? Among organs which should be called together for meetings are: (1) Ordnance Administration, about raw materials needed for each ordnance factory, as well as raw materials for finished goods to be supplied by US ; (2) Aviation Committee, about its needs in airplanes, spare parts and maintenance centers; (3) Trade Committee, about output of our raw materials and export and import of raw materials; (4) Health Department and Military Medical Department, about different kinds of medicine and sanitary equipment; (5) Ministry of Transportation, about communications equipment and transportation vehicles; (6) Ministry of Economics, about industrial and mining equipment. Apart from above-mentioned organizations, meetings of all other relevant organizations should be called. Please take note of Mr. Stettinius's letter and go into details to come up with survey and estimation as soon as possible. Make sure to complete report and send it by air-mail to US before November 15th. Stettinius will submit it to US government after his review and editing. Since this matter is vitally important to our national defense, I pray for Your Excellency's full support.

T. V.

239. Telegram to Chiang on US government analysis of war in Russia (October 9, 1941)

S432

According to various sources, Soviet army has some signs of total collapse. US government is quite pessimistic about prospect of Soviet on continuing war of resistance.

T. V.

240. Telegram to Chiang on Jiang Biao's return to US (October 14, 1941)

Commissioner Jiang Biao is in charge of munitions affairs here. His task is extremely onerous and complicated. He was previously assigned to accompany General Magruder to go to Chongqing. After this job is done, please instruct him to return here as early as possible.

T. V.

241. Telegram to Chiang on allotment of fuel under Lend-Lease Act (October 17, 1941)

As regards to thirteen million gallons of truck gasoline allocation under Lend-Lease Act, US government has already ordered oil companies to supply. Gasoline will soon be barreled in Singapore and is scheduled to arrive at Rangoon by end of this month, then be handed over to Chen Changtong. For the sake of overall coordination and allocation, I suggest Military Commission be advised to allocate gasoline among the following orgnizations: (1) Military Affairs Ministry; (2) Aviation Committee; (3) Yunnan-Burma Road Bureau; (4) former Southwest Transport Administration; (5) Yunnan-Burma Railway Bureau. All aforementioned orgnizations are applicants included in Lend-Lease program; (6) Liquid Fuel Committee, who had originally entrusted Universal Trading Company to purchase gasoline but was put off since Lend-Lease gasoline was shipping out. So please allocate some (to Liquid Fuel Committee) too. In response to Minister He Jingzhi's[1] request of fuel purchase in his telegram dated October 1st, I have asked Universal Trading Company to place order for extra one million gallons. Above is for your information. Also please inform Minister He Jingzhi and Chief Inspector Yu Qiaofeng.

T. V.

---

[1] He Yingqin, minister of Military Affairs.

242. Telegram to Chiang on issues regarding to fuel pipeline (October 17, 1941)

S433

Your telegraph dated 9th acknowledged. Concerning oil pipes, Daniel Arnstein is good at road transportation but unfamiliar with engineering or technical issues in other fields. Moreover, even if Yunnan-Burma Railway is completed in two years as scheduled, freight capacity would not be able to meet demands of our anti-Japanese war. By laying oil pipes, 16,000 tons of oil can be carried monthly, and fuel problem can be completely solved. After careful study and discussion, for the sake of circumspection, I decided to fly pipeline expert Mr. Hull to Rangoon on October 21st to survey on possible line routes and make appraisals. Airfare and other expenses will cost only several thousand dollars. If he concludes this (pipeline) project practicable in his final report, I will suggest he submit the report directly to Your Excellency for your final decision. I have also informed Director Yu Qiaofeng and report to you for your information.

T. V.

243. Telegram to Chiang on war situation in Russia (October 20, 1941)

S434

Soviet Union is moving its capital toward the southeast, and there are indications that it may move further to Iran in future, not in the direction to Siberia. Please note this development.

T. V.

244. Telegram to Chiang on progress of military procurement negotiation (October 23, 1941)

S435

1. A top secret meeting of US War Department was held yesterday to discuss report presented by US representative to Ammunition Board who just

came back from Moscow. Report highlighted heavily Red Army's achievements, asserting that Germany lost one-third of its troops invading Russia. Though factories in western part of Russia are occupied by German troops, factories in eastern part can still provide military supplies for one hundred divisions. Report particularly praised Russian air force, which is superior to British air force in manner of skill and courage. US observations on Red Army always go to extremes and fail to reveal truth. Meeting ended with conclusion that key to war is in Russia. US government should strengthen supplies aids to Russia. UK comes second (in aiding list). (Quantity of) Aids for China is subject to leftovers after other aid programs, and will most likely be symbolic. I was very concerned after learning this news. No matter whether US observation is accurate or not, I decided to make following proposal to US government: China's resistance and counterattacks are the only means to stop Japanese army from invading Russia. This is an important component of the overall world situation. US should be more active in assisting us to fulfill this mission. Before Japanese army starts to act, Your Excellency (China) would urgently need following weapons:

a. Airplanes. Original requested number is 350 fighters, of which 100 already delivered and 83 more are supposed to be delivered within this year. I would ask instant delivery of 177 more, all should be drawn from existing fleets of American and British Air Force. Original request for bombers is 150, 66 have been promised, of which 24 are supposed to be delivered in this year. I'd ask for instant delivery of 160 more.

b. 0.5 inch anti-air machine guns. 285 guns have been approved to deliver within this year. I'd ask for instant delivery of additional 750.

c. 37 mm anti-tank guns. 60 are supposed to be delivered within this year. I'd ask for instant delivery of additional 300.

d. 75 mm field guns. Original request was 600, of which 178 are already approved to be delivered within this year. I'd ask for instant delivery of additional 300.

e. 13-ton light tanks. Original request is 120. I'd ask for full delivery.

f. 90 mm anti-air guns. 96 already approved. I'd ask for instant delivery of at least 24.

g. I'd ask for immediate delivery of 800 tons of gunpowder.

I'd ask for immediate response and then report results to Your Excellency.

2. All above items are urgently needed. Based on current US output, these requests should not be extravagant. I ask Your Excellency to put forward serious request to General Magruder concurrently with mine.

3. General Magruder telegraphed US War Department, suggesting postponement of non-urgent goods shipment because of limited transportation capability of Burma Road. Please pay attention to this issue so that our military supplies shipment is not delayed by this excuse.

Above is my report and am waiting for your reply.

T. V.

245. Telegram to Chiang on transportation of US military aids to Russia (October 24, 1941)

The American Aviation Commission announced that the munitions aids to Russia would not be shipped via Vladivostok, but across the Atlantic Ocean and landed at Arkhangelsk in the White Sea instead. This move concerns only shipping line, and has no political meaning. The President was very displeased with the publicity (of this change), fearing it would raise public misgivings that the US intended to appease Japan.

T. V.

246. Telegram to Chiang on Jiang Biao's trip to US (October 25, 1941)

The US army and navy officers related to China aids affairs have always been cordially helping us. In addition to entertaining them occasionally, since Christmas approaches, I suggest Your Excellency instruct Jiang Biao to bring some gifts to the US for these officers in recognition of their assistance. I look forward to Your Excellency's instruction.

T. V.

247. Telegram to Chiang on confidential telegram from Magruder to Stimson (October 27, 1941)

S436

I just had access to the top-secret telegraph from General Magruder to Secretary of Army. The contents are as follows:

1. The Chinese army launched a counterattack targeting Yichang to support Changsha campaign, and retreated after the mission was accomplished. This was not against the military strategy.
2. The Chinese army is incapable of launching a large-scale counteroffensive unless reinforced with artillery forces.
3. At present, China's most urgent needs include (a) raw materials for ordinance factories (b) cartridge (c) light machine guns and infantry artilleries. Without these, the current situation can not be maintained. Howitzers and anti-tank guns are also needed. Air force affairs will be reported in another telegraph.
4. The War Department shall handle affairs related to quality of and procedures for military aids to China merely based on my telegrams. Requests from Mr. Currie and Chinese offices in Washington D. C. are excessive and can be ignored.
5. I suggest including China in all US government's announcements regarding British and Russian (cooperation) affairs. It will cost US nothing, but would boost morale among Chinese people.
6. Comprehensive plans to be reported after meeting with Generalissimo, etc.

My comment is, although the content of this telegraph is not unreasonable, the weapons (mentioned) falls far short of our expectations. Items listed in my telegrams of 23rd including tanks, anti-air machine guns, anti-air artillery guns, 10.5 mm and 15 mm howitzers and fieldpieces, etc, are not mentioned at all. Besides, the (proposal in) paragraph 4 went beyond his duty, by which he would have sole discretion (on military aids) and left no room for Your Excellency. Besides, there are many political parties and groups in the US. Not only is General Magruder divided in opinion with Mr. Currie, but he cannot cooperate well with War Department's Lend-Lease Office. It may be all right if General Magruder takes on everything and assists us full-heartedly. But he has definitely not the capacity to achieve that. I ask Your Excellency to tell Magruder and Ambassador Gauss the following: (1) as regards to the matters about requests and supply (of Lend-Lease weapons), they should follow the existing rules. The Military Mission is simply an advisory body to offer necessary assistance, and cannot represent our government in coming up with requests. The US mission in Britain does not have such authority either. All British demands are discussed directly between the British representatives to Washington and the US government. (2) The US shipment of military equipment is too slow. A complaint should be lodged on this matter. This telegraph is an off-the-record report, please keep it classified. Whether it is appropriate, I look forward to your instructions.

T. V.

248. Telegram to Chiang on Ministry of Finance advisor's stay in US (October 28, 1941)

Mr. D. F. Myers, advisor to the Ministry of Finance, was previously dispatched by Your Excellency to the US to assist US government in the planning and construction of maintenance centers at different locations (in China). He just received a telegraph order from Minister H. H. K'ung to return to China. Is it possible for him to stay for two more months and hand over his work? I look forward to Your Excellency's decision.

T. V.

249. Telegram to Chiang on Indian government's attitude towards China-India Road (October 30, 1941)

S437

A source in the British government told me privately that the Indian government was rather estranged from us over the issue of Sino-Indian transportation route for following reasons: (1) The Indian government intended to make aerial survey on the route for us at their own expenses, but we refused to accept. (2) Our Executive Yuan secretly sent a Customs Officer named Naberator to the Indian military zone to survey the route but had not notified Indian government. (3) Our response to the alleged US policy toward Tibet remains indefinite. I report this information as it says, just for your information.

T. V.

250. Telegram to Chiang on air force training program in US (October 30, 1941)

S438

Reference is taken to the training of air force cadets in the US. Considering the unpredictable changes of American ship-lines schedule, it is difficult to know in advance the vessel names and exact leaving dates. Therefore, I suggest that Your Excellency order to dispatch one batch of cadets every five weeks for Hong Kong and wait there for the ship (to US) to avoid any delay. It would be even better if 200 to 250 cadets could be dispatched to the US at one time and wait here for training. I look forward to Your Excellency's instruction.

T. V.

251. Telegram to Chiang on Soong's meeting with Roosevelt (October 31, 1941)

S439

I received telegram from sister Mey-ling (Mme. Chiang Kai-shek) and learned Your Excellency met General Magruder, and there are signs of Japan planning an invasion of Yunnan Province. I made special appointment with President Roosevelt this morning to convey Your Excellency's opinions and talked privately with him for 45 minutes.

President said: according to US Army, Japan can not invade Yunnan without four additional divisions. Since battlefields (in Yunnan) are extremely mountainous and transportation conditions poor, even if Japan takes Yunnan-Burma Road, it won't keep the road for long. I replied: Although unfavorable topography is barrier to military actions, well-organized, motorized troop with air cover can overcome such barriers. Latest example is German army's swift seizure of Yugoslavia. There is no lack of German technical experts in Japanese army. We should not underestimate it.

President said: China has been fighting bravely for over four years. Even if Yunnan-Burma route is taken, China should be able to resist for another year. I replied: To continue anti-Japanese war to end is the Generalissimo's unswerving determination. However, without continual supply of weapons from abroad, it's uncertain whether general public's confidence can maintain high. In case Yunnan-Burma route is taken and Chinese army can no longer hold out, Japanese enemy can spare at least one million soldiers from its forces in China to attack Soviet Union or head southwards.

President said: Firstly, regarding this matter, US plans to warn Japan, but has not come to the stage of issuing ultimatum. After discussion with Hull this afternoon, President would warn Japan that attack on Yunnan-Burma route infringes US interests. Secondly, it is improper for UK to dispatch airplanes from Singapore base to fight jointly with us. British-Japanese war could otherwise break out, and Japanese could cut off sea-lane between Australia and Suez Canal. President suggested British repaint their airplanes with Chinese Air Force insignia and fight jointly as volunteers. I said it would take much time. President said he would make proposal and expect to get response from British within 2 - 3 days. I said: President's goodwill is highly appreciated. Nevertheless, enemy's invasion of Yunnan is imminent while overdue delivery of weapons promised by US might not meet current needs. It would be desirable if US could spare some supplies used in US army to reinforce China in short term.

I handed the President a list of weapons described in my telegram dated September 23rd. After discussing with me item by item, President added a note before passing it over to Harry Hopkins. I said: if weapons are delivered to China in time, it will be not only a benefit to China, but also indirect support to Soviet Union, and a heavy blow on Germany's nose. If Soviet army retreats to east of Urals, (Russia will be left) with population of only 51 million, it will be hard to keep fighting Germany. In comparison, with population of 450 million, China is the largest reserve (of manpower) among all democratic countries. President paid much attention to this point and said it is possible that Russians will retreat to east of Ural this winter. President followed with detailed questions on transportation between China and Russia, and on whether China could send troops over western border to reinforce Russia if Siberia were cut off.

I replied: there is Xinjiang route, by which many Russian arms are transported to aid China. President said: the Generalissimo should be confident in all circumstances. Alliance of Germany and Japan has population of no more than 150 million. In comparison, all anti-aggression countries in world, including China with the strength of her vast population and territory, are many times more formidable than enemy.

President at last implied that even if Yunnan-Burma route were taken, Japan wouldn't win, because the war would thus be expanded. This statement might mean something.

Our conversation concerned other topics. I have chosen only most important (matters) to report to Your Excellency. Then President dispatched an adjutant to accompany me to meet Hopkins and discuss arms supply. Hopkins contacted Department of War at once and promised to give concrete reply in a few days.

T. V.

252. Telegram to Chiang to request for investigation on fuel sale in Burma (November 3, 1941)

S440

US War Department just received a report stating that our National Liquid Fuel Administration commissioned Texaco office in Rangoon on September

22nd to ship ten thousand odd barrels of light diesel and four thousand odd barrels of heavy diesel to India for sale. The Department was surprised and questioned us that, if the Chinese government has fuel stored in Rangoon for sale, why does it still urge the US authorities to provide the same fuel? This matter concerns our credibility under the Lend-Lease program and our future requests for raw materials. Please do order an investigation into the reason for the sale and grant me a reply. Then I can explain it to the US authorities. Also please order all government departments that similar incident should not happen again.

T. V.

253. Telegram to Chiang on manager candidate of Southwestern Transportation Administration (November 3, 1941)

S441

Your earlier telegram dated October 28th acknowledged. It's true that Chen Changtong is inexperienced in transportation. He is afraid of committing mistakes. Lend-Lease affairs in Rangoon are complicated and many. Hence, I specially transferred and have him be stationed there to deal with everything. Now he is gradually becoming familiar with the environment and people there. At the moment it is difficult to find another commissioner to take over the task. The manager of Southwest (Transportation Administration) is easier to find. I beg that you appoint other candidates to take over the task.

T. V.

254. Telegram to Chiang on Soong's talk with Roosevelt regarding to US-Japan negotiation (November 3, 1941)

S442

I believe Your Excellency has read my previous telegram dated October 31st. I talked with the President about the US-Japan negotiations the other day. President said, "Japan wishfully thought to exchange empty words about restoring economic relations. Yet my genuine thought is that other issues should not be touched on unless the Sino-Japanese problems are settled first. Japan asked me to meet Konoe somewhere in the sea. I didn't agree. In the end, Japan discovered that I intended to procrastinate. Soon the Konoe cabinet fell. Nevertheless, this negotiation was not insignificant as it bought us some time. Six months ago it was thought that the Philippines could not be defended since there were no facilities for defense. But now the battery fortifications are strong, and our airplanes could take control of the air route between the Philippines and south China," and so on. I will report the follow-up to Your Excellency.

T. V.

255. Telegram to Chiang on US plan against Japanese invasion into Yunnan (November 4, 1941)

(1) After my meeting with the President on October 31st, the President discussed with Mr. Cordell Hull. The State Department told the War Department that they should prepare to sideswipe Japan's (imminent) attack of Yunnan. According to the confidential message of someone in the War Department, they plan to adopt two tactics: A. Philippine airplanes bombard the communication route between Japan and Vietnam; B. To dispatch a squad of Air Fortresses stationed in the Philippines to help China to fight. However, none of them is finalized. I will keep finding out and report, and beg Your Excellency to keep it secret.

(2) US Civil Aeronautics Administration (CAA) held a meeting yesterday and decided to alter their previous China policy, which stipulates the supply of military aid to China on the basis of their inventory. They decided to maintain the plan of offering us 500 new aircrafts, and provide us with personnel and aircrafts in a more swift and practical way. As regards to the method of implementation (of the new policy), they are discussing keenly at the moment.

(3) US has promised to allot 66 airplanes (to us). But because the

revolving emplacements and some other weapons on the plane are made in UK, it would take at least several months to assembly them. Therefore, I plan to request some airplanes on the aircraft carrier transfer to us to meet our urgent need. Now I'm doing my best but not sure about the success. I report this in secret and beg Your Excellency's inspection.

Besides, I met Australian Ambassador today, and asked him to telegraph his government to urge Mr. Churchill to offer assistance to our Air Force.

T. V.

256. Telegram to Chiang on US request for Germany-made howitzers and shells(November 4, 1941)

In response to our previous order of artillery gunpowder from the US under Lend-Lease program, the US authorities requested us to send German-made 105 mm howitzer and shells to the US for experiment. I telegraphed chief of Military Lend-Lease Office, Mr. Stettinius, asking him to forward the request personally to Chief of Ordnance Yu Dawei for help. According to his reply, those guns are deployed at various places in the front line, and cannot be withdrawn right away. By my judgment, the experiment is only an excuse, and the US authorities actually intend to study on the gun's performance and structure. They have kept pushing us. For the sake of maintaining good relations with the US and making my office's work easier in the future, I beg Your Excellency to authorize withdrawing these guns and sending them to the US. I look forward to your instruction on whether this is workable.

T. V.

257. Telegram to Chiang on Soong's meeting with Stimson (November 6, 1941)

S445

A friend in War Department just informed me privately of discussion on yesterday's meeting regarding to Your Excellency's request for immediate delivery of airplanes and other weapons to resist Japan's imminent attack on Yunnan. The conclusion was that, since US is actively preparing for war, except those supplies promised to deliver in installment according to list, any (extra) transfer of equipment currently used by US army would disrupt its military plan. I immediately asked for a meeting with Secretary of War Stimson, and was invited for lunch today with him for a long, confidential conversation.

Stimson acknowledged Your Excellency's telegram to President Roosevelt and my talk with President on October 31st. He said, as an US army officer during last world war in Europe, he once believed that it would be more efficient and quicker to win (the war) if American soldiers infiltrated British and French troops to form joint forces. However, much smarter General John Joseph Pershing decided to organize independent American combat unit commanded by American officers. Thus final victory was achieved.

Stimson also said: telling you privately, ninety percent of US military plan in the Philippines is completed. Japanese has not discovered yet. Navy, army and air forces there are exclusively aimed at Japan. Air force alone is strong enough to deter Japanese fleet's ambition to head southward. It would disperse forces and run counter to military principles if transfer airplanes in this area to reinforce China.

I said that if Japanese attack Dutch Indonesia or Singapore, US wouldn't be sitting inactive. But if Japanese attack Yunnan, would US adopt the same attitude? If not, China would need airplanes and other weapons more urgently. Stimson predicted that Japanese invasion into Yunnan is likely difficult due to (negative) topographical conditions. I answered that geographical barrier would do little in face of motorized army with air covering. Stimson asked how long it would take to reach Kunming if they do invade Yunnan. I answered it could happen in a few weeks if we don't have sufficient airplanes and weapons. Stimson said he had told Mr. Hull that US war preparation would be completed within five, or at most six, weeks. If counted by, 10th of next month is key; thereafter US could employ toughest means toward Japan. Should Japanese begin to attack Yunnan from Vietnam, US could deter it before reaching Kunming. I chased down and asked, since it matters much for my country, I want to be sure whether after December 10th US would deter Japan's invasion into Yunnan as she would do when Singapore or Dutch Indonesia was invaded. Stimson answered: "as Secretary of Army, I could not make promises beyond my responsibility since this matter concerns foreign affairs. However, by my observation, Yunnan-Burma Route has immense stake with world situation, even more important than assistance to Russia. Some people say that aiding Russia should take priority over aiding China, and supply bombers and other advanced weapons to Russia immediately. Even some in your country sing the same tone. I am afraid aiding-Russia strategy may not work well due to the length of time. China has been fighting against Japanese invasion for over four years under leadership of Generalissimo Chiang. Yunnan-Burma Route now is lifeline (for China's war), how can we not support? "

I said: "Your determination is highly appreciated. Yet war situation is changing second by second. Please do expedite supply of airplanes and weapons for us, as it is the only and safest solution for China at this critical moment." Stimson replied that it is difficult for airplanes, but he ordered to proceed with other weapons, etc.

Army Secretary Stimson is serious and prudent, with sound moral reputation. What he said is candid. Since it concerned military actions, he asked to keep our conversation off the record and only report to Your Excellency.

T. V.

258. Telegram to Chiang on meeting with US Secretary of Navy (November 7, 1941)

Today President announced the plan to withdraw US Marine Corps from Peking, Tianjin and Shanghai. I attended a lunch meeting with secretary of navy Frank Knox in the company of navy general staff and other officers. I first explained to them the Japanese army's intention of attacking Yunnan Province. The Chinese army now lacks airplanes and other military supplies. Should the Chinese army fail to continue its resistance, the international situation will become more dangerous. Knox said that there were only three and a half Japanese divisions in Vietnam. According to the navy's observations, they can not launch attacks toward Yunnan within two months. I said that the Hainan and Taiwan Islands are so close to Vietnam that the enemy troops could arrive at those places in a single day. The Japanese army can also invade Yunnan from Vietnam via Guangxi by several different routes. Therefore, we are getting extremely anxious to receive aircrafts and other military supplies from US.

We then discussed the planned withdrawal of US Marine Corps. I said Shanghai is China's financial nexus and the withdrawal would have significant effects. Mr. Knox said China should however regard this as a good sign; it shows that US is taking a very active part in realignment (of military forces). In the next two months, the US Far Eastern policy would be clearly demonstrated. He also told me that General McCloy had sent him a telegram, urging US to send some airplanes to assist in China's war.

Because there were too many people at the table, our conversation was not as thorough as that between Secretary Stimson and me yesterday. The above are some important points I chose to report to Your Excellence.

T. V.

259. Telegram to Chiang on meeting with US Secretary of Navy (November 7, 1941)

S446

Today, Secretary of Navy Knox invited me and his chief of staff for lunch. I said that their decision to have the US Marine Corps retreat from Shanghai will leave this economic nexus unprotected. Knox said that previously they had a plan to send the US Marine Corps inland if needed. However, after deliberation they decided that this was impossible to do. The retreat of the Marine Corps is to alert Japan and to let them know our firm determination, and to prevent Japanese troops from taking action in the concessions. In addition, he emphasized that the US Far East policy will take effect in these two months. I told him that I am afraid our country may suffer from a great loss during this period. Then we discussed the Japanese attack on Yunnan. I repeatedly urged the US to provide us with airplanes and munitions at once. Knox said that he received a telegram from General McCloy, in which he insists the US send all the airplanes they can to assist China in military actions. Yet there are many difficulties and so on. Moreover, Generals Knox and Stimson did mention that the US would do her best to help China after December 10th. However, the military and political situation is changing rapidly. We can not sit and wait for the airplanes and other munitions we urgently need. I have entrusted close friends of the President with the task of urging him to allot munitions to us as soon as possible.

T. V.

260. Telegram to Chiang on diplomatic influence of Associated Press news (November 7, 1941)

The telegram from Associated Press in Chongqing briefly stated that according to Chinese source, the Sino-British military cooperation (negotiation) is completed. To prevent Japan from blockading the Yunnan-Burma Road transport and in the event that Japan launches large-scale attack against China, the US will help China with their all strength, and so on. I do not know whether such news will hinder negotiations among Your Excellency, the UK and the US.

T. V.

261. Telegram to Chiang on Hu Shi's press interview in Pittsburg (November 7, 1941)

S447

Ambassador Hu Shi recently addressed journalists in Pittsburgh that supplying armaments and aircrafts to the Soviet Union should be a priority, because China has been fighting against Japanese invasion for more than four years and we can still endure without latest weaponry. Secretary Henry Stimson did hint at this statement in his conversation yesterday. Mr. Currie was surprised by Hu Shi's words. He told me that if China doesn't take concerted actions, it will embarrass those friends who are willing to help China. This is for your information.

T. V.

262. Telegram to Chiang on memorandum for Hu Shi on military affairs (November 10, 1941)

S448

Hu Shi will meet President this noon. I am afraid he is unfamiliar with military and Lend-Lease issues which could be touched on during meeting. I therefore prepared a memo and asked him to submit it to President. The outlines of the memo are as follows:

1. After my last meeting with President, I met Secretaries of Army, Navy and Treasury, Mr. Harry Hopkins, Chief of Military Lend-Lease Office Edward R. Stettinius and other high-ranking officials of the US Army and discussed various topics. All these officials were sincere and cooperative.

2. To date, no response to Generalissimo's request for airplanes and other weapons for defense of Yunnan-Burma Road. We'd ask President to make prompt decision to meet our urgent needs.

3. Japanese could invade Yunnan from Vietnam and northbound toward Kunming. It also could invade from Vietnam via Guangxi province, where

is flatter and broader, accessible to tanks, and indeed a historical marching route (for invaders).

4. US has direct stake in Japanese invasion of Yunnan. Now the only air force that can be relied on to protect Yunnan-Burma route is American Volunteer Group (AVG) commanded by General Clair Chennault. According to telegram from General Magruder, total force of this group are 80 – 90 pilots with a hundred airplanes, a force far from adequate to fight against enemy. In case of defeat, consequence would be grave. If AVG chooses not to engage because of slight chance of winning, what a destructive effect it will have on confidence of Chinese general public and our international reputation, etc. Therefore both Generals Magruder and McCloy dispatched telegrams advocating US reinforcement of airplanes to AVG. Owing urgency, they also suggested using carriers to ship airplanes.

5. During my meeting with President on October 31st, President kindly promised to discuss possibility with UK of transferring British airplanes in Singapore to reinforce China. According to information from sources in both US and China, UK won't dispatch any planes without US participation.

6. Last thing to mention is that after my thorough discussions with US Army and Navy officials, I think the following airplanes and weapons are probably available for immediate delivery to China. Since US Army and Navy currently use them, this is only at President's discretion (to deliver). As regards to airplanes, I'd ask for 80 SBD (A-24 ship-borne dive-bombers) now used by American aircraft carriers, and which can be shipped to the Philippines, or Singapore, Rangoon, then flown directly to China. This model of plane is easy to operate. Earlier maneuvers in Louisiana proved it's perfect for long-range bombing. Each plane can carry 1275 pounds of bombs. Flying range is 1450 miles at the speed of 210 MPH. As to other weapons, please refer to detailed list (i. e., the items listed in my telegram on October 23rd, with minor amendments).

I present above report with honors for Your Excellency's scrutiny.

T. V.

263. Telegram to Chiang on analysis of Japanese invasion into Yunnan (November 12, 1941)

S449

According to various news sources and a recent Associated Press telegram, the Japanese enemy does not seem to have made military preparations for attacking Yunnan. Concentration of troops is likely to aim at area around Thailand. Meanwhile in Liangshan, Tongdeng, and Gaoping of Vietnam, there has been no military deployment. Information from the French embassy is the same. Therefore, our request for airplanes and munitions has not been successful because the President, Secretaries of the Navy, War and State all take this as an excuse. I could only reply that Japan's plan for attacking Yunnan has been secretly completed, and their troops in Hainan and Taiwan could arrive in a day. I beg Your Excellency to inform me by telegram of the latest news, so I have true information and can do my best. Moreover, I believe Your Excellency has received my previous telegrams dated Oct 28th, Oct 31st, Nov 4th, 6th and 7th, and beg Your Excellency to judge whether those measures are appropriate.

T. V.

264. Telegram to Chiang on Kurusu's visit to US (November 14, 1941)

S450

According to an important source, the Japanese envoy Kurusu's visit to the US is to offer fundamental concessions. However, the contents are not directly linked to the Sino-Japanese War. Therefore, he is reluctant to tell me the details. He also said that the prospect of reaching agreement between US and Japan is not hopeless as outsiders conjectured. My guess is that could have something to do with the transport route through Vladivostok or Japan promising not to invade Siberia. However, if the US and Japan do not reach an agreement, Japan will definitely attack the Burma Road. Since the US authorities repeatedly asserted that Japan has not yet prepared to attack Yunnan, I beg Your Excellency telegraph me the information about all the Japanese attack preparations. Then I will be able to explain the situation to the US authorities and persuade them to provide us with aircrafts and other armaments. I feel this is most urgent.

T. V.

265. Telegram to Chiang on Soong's meeting with Hopkins regarding to US-Japan negotiation (November 22, 1941)

1. Harry Hopkins is hospitalized. I went to visit him yesterday and talked about the negotiation between the US and Japan. According to him, the US Navy stands for war against Japan. Yet the Army reckons that the war between the US and Germany is inevitable, and so they hope that there is no war in the Pacific. (This view is different from Stimson's). Some people in the State Department hold similar view. Saburo Kurusu (Japanese envoy to the US) knows very well the differences among Americans.

2. Newly arrived Central News Agency journalist Lu Qixin met with Thomas Connally, chairman of Senate Foreign Relations Committee. According to Lu Qixin, Connally stated that although they want to drive Japanese out of Chinese territory, they cannot ignore realities, such as the Northeastern China issue, and so on.

3. I talked with Henry Luce, leader of the news media, yesterday. He visited Your Excellency with his wife last spring, and had very good impression of China. According to him, Japan hopes to reestablish economic relations with the US. However, without discussing Sino-Japanese problems, there is no way the US government would agree to this, nor would public opinions accept it. Moreover, the US should never supply Japan with oil and iron that help her attack China. Yet, as regards to the Northeastern China issue, it is quite possible that public opinion may support this if Japan promises to return all other occupied areas in exchange for official recognition of the puppet regime in Manchuria (i. e. Northeastern China).

Many Americans think that both China and Japan have their own reasons to persist in claiming their rights in Northeastern China, and so on. By and large, in view of the above arguments, it is imperative for us to disseminate in America our position on Northeastern China, to make clear that the Northeast is an inalienable part of China. Your Excellency has made elaborate and profound point in your manifesto to the Chinese people about the Mukden incident (on September 18, 1931). At this moment, we should not be frugal but broaden our dissemination work here, which would bring great benefit to the final peace treaty. Furthermore, the Japanese representative reportedly only wishes to discuss the recovery of US-Japan economic relations in exchange for the promise of not invading Vladivostok and Siberia. Yet Japan is reluctant to discuss the Sino-Japanese War. Nevertheless, the US thought that unless the Sino-Japanese problem is resolved, Japan has nothing to contribute. Therefore, it is anticipated that Japan will ask the US for conciliation in the end. Hopkins continued to ask, " In your opinion, do you think Japan will bring up the issue of recognizing the puppet regime in Manchuria?" I replied that if the US recognizes the Manchurian puppet regime, then the US violates her fundamental national policy. Moreover, having made enormous sacrifice, China will by no means allow placing 35 million people under Japan's slavery, and so on. Hopkins is the most trusted confidant of the President in the White House. Even though our conversation was casual, we should pay attention to his words. I beg Your Excellency's instructions on whether my above suggestions are feasible.

4. According to the confidential message of Harrison Salisbury, a close friend of the President and editor of *New York Times*, he met the President last Friday and told him, "I always support your tough foreign policy, but in fact it has not been carried out to the full. My newspaper is now in a difficult position. According to our representative in London, Prime Minister Churchill is also anxious about your active standpoint." The President paused for a while and replied to him, "You should have noticed that the US is actually fighting in both Atlantic and Pacific oceans, and so on. "

I hereby recorded what I heard for Your Excellency's reference.

T. V.

266. Telegram to Chiang on expenses of US Air Force Volunteers (November 22, 1941)

S451

I received Your Excellency's telegram dated 21st. It is true that the expenses of the American Volunteer Group (AVG) are huge, and recruitment is also difficult. However, the fact that the UK could allot two squads from Singapore to take part (our war) should be ascribed to the establishment of AVG. Though it is difficult to predict the results of their future military operations, they are of great significance for international public opinion and political effects. James Mchugh and General Magruder have always asserted that AVG won't succeed, and US prestige will be damaged. Their purpose is to elicit attention from the American side. As regards to the newly arrived planes, they first should be handed to the National Aviation Commission's control. Yet for fear the Chinese pilots can be blamed for possible loss of personnel and airplanes, I strongly propose organizing a seperate squad. Moreover, since the US government does not want to command and dispatch the AVG directly to avoid conflict with Japan, we have to bear the expenses of AVG. As soon as the situation changes, then we can formulate different arrangement. I submit my reply here for your inspection.

T. V.

267. Telegram to Chiang to request for intelligence on Japanese activities along the Yunnan border (November 24, 1941)

S450

Concerning the latest intelligence report on the enemy's activities on the Yunnan border, please inform me by telegram as soon as possible. Your telegram dated 20th has been noted. Regarding new order for machinery for the Gansu oil field, I will follow your instructions.

T. V.

268. Telegram to Chiang on Soong's meeting with US Secretary of Navy (November 25, 1941)

S452

I received Your Excellency's telegram on the 25th. Your telegram to Ambassador Hu Shi has not been decoded yet. I just met Secretary of Navy Knox, and conveyed Your Excellency's message to him. Mr. Knox said, "It is very touching. As China's faithful friend, I can assure you absolutely that China needs not worry. Yet from government's position, some words could not be openly stated to ease Generalissimo Chiang's anxiety." I told him, "I do trust your words. However, Generalissimo is the military leader of China, bearing heavy responsibility. At this critical moment, it wouldn't be of any help if you offered cold comfort. According to Ambassador Hu, he learned from Mr. Hull that the US only asked Japan to stop heading southbound and northbound without mentioning China at all. That will make Japan attack China with all their strength. If that happens, Chinese people and soldiers will lose confidence." Mr. Knox said, "I can tell Your Honor that Hull did not tell all the conditions to Ambassador Hu. As far as I know, the US conditions require Japan to fundamentally change its policy. Should the Japanese government accept these conditions, it would fall from power within 24 hours. My assumption is that war between Japan and the US is imminent. Once war breaks out, all problems will be easily solved." I questioned him in every possible ways. Mr. Knox said that one of main conditions is that Japan should resign from the Axis powers. But as Japan has just extended a five-year treaty with the Axis, how can it abrogate the treaty right away? By and large, the time of Japan's collapse is not far away. I said, "According to Mr. Hull's speech forwarded by Ambassador Hu, US has to formulate some interim measures as the general staffs of navy and army need three months at least for war preparations." Mr. Knox said, "There is no deadline for preparations for navy and army. It would be best if we have ample time. But now we have prepared for some time, and it will be easy to deal with the Japanese without making sacrifice (on other issues)." I asked, "According to the message of Ambassador Hu, Hull looked panicked after the negotiations on Monday. I was told the same by the Australian minister to the US." Knox said, "Hull is old and weak. He was nervous but not panicked. Now Japan has come to a dead end, China should be delighted and does not have to worry." I asked, "There is a rumor that Germany seized all French navy. Would that obstruct the American military plan?" Knox said, "Even if this were so, Germany would not be able to make use of the French navy for six months because of some training problems, and so on." Knox is quite active and always a supporter of war, unlike the State Department. Whether his words represent the overall US government's view, and whether the US did not tell Ambassador Hu all the conditions, will need to be proved by facts later. Knox then added that the UK does not have enough military strength to defeat Germany. The US has to immediately take part in the war of the Atlantic and Pacific regions. Mr. Knox also asked that his conversation be off the record. I respectfully submit to Your Excellency the above report.

T. V.

269. Telegram from Chiang on message to US Secretaries of Army and Navy (November 25, 1941)

I hope Ambassador Hu has forwarded to you my telegram to him yesterday. I'd ask you to try to forward the message of that telegram to the Secretaries of Navy and Army, and copy to Mr. Currie. Please also explain to them orally the seriousness of this matter. That is, if the US economic blockade or the freezing of assets toward Japan is relaxed a bit, or such news is leaked from Washington, the morale of our people and military will be deeply affected. For the past two months, Japan has staged propaganda in China that their dialogue with the US will be completed by the end of this month. Therefore, the dissidents in northern and southern China have reached an unspoken understanding. Once the US-Japan agreement is completed, or the American economic blockade is relaxed, then the Chinese and Japanese people will believe the US has reached a compromise with Japan at the expense of China. As a result, the morale of Chinese people would fall apart, and Asian countries would also be disappointed and significantly shift their psychology. One cannot imagine the consequence for the whole world: China's war of resistance against Japan would fail, and Japan's scheme would prevail completely. By then, even if the US would save the situation, there would be nothing she could do. It would be by no means only China who loses the war. For the time being, we can only request the US government immediately state her uncompromising attitude toward Japan, and that it will not relax economic blockade toward Japan unless Japan withdraws its troops from China. Only by doing so, will the Chinese people and military be assured that the overall situation can be reversed. Otherwise, given US ambiguous, hesitant stance and the Japanese incessant propaganda in China, China's four-year war against Japan and unprecedented loss of lives lost in it would become meaningless. There is no end for chaos in the world in this prospect. I don't know how future historians would record this episode.

Kai-shek

270. Telegram from Chiang on coordination with Hu Shi (November 25, 1941)

Please copy my telegram dated 20th to Hu Shi, and discuss with him to find out an effective way to convey a message to United States government that they need to make a quick and clear statement on her uncompromising attitude toward Japan. This is extremely important. Please work with him and try your best.

Kai-shek

271. Telegram to Chiang on Soong's meeting with Roosevelt (November 26, 1941)

My joint telegraph with Ambassador Hu Shi of today is now submitted to Your Excellency. Yesterday I received your telegraph dated 25th. Since it was urgent, I immediately asked Mr. Thomas Cochran[1], the President's trusted aide, to pass on Your Excellency's message to the President. Mr. Hull and I were summoned by the President today. Attention may be paid to the following points of our discussion.

1. The President first said that the Generalissimo might have some misunderstandings because of unreliable information. In fact, the argument of the telegram dated 25th of Your Excellency was based on the two telegrams from Hu Shi dated November 22nd and 24th respectively on Hull's conversation with American, Australian and Dutch ambassadors.

2. Hu Shi's two previous telegrams to a large extent imply that the US has already decided on her principles for US-Japan negotiation and is determined to get things done. Hence, there is no room for further discussions. The President, however, always reiterated that the American proposals should first have the agreement of friendly nations before they are presented to Japan.

3. The major reason held previously by Secretary of State Hull was that the US Army and Navy need three months to make sufficient preparations (for war). The President did not mention a single word about this.

4. The President said that 20,000 to 30,000 Japanese soldiers were reported to have moved southward from Shandong by maritime transportation yesterday. This move shows Japan's insincerity when the US and Japan are holding negotiation. Thus it seems difficult for the negotiation to go on. The President may possibly take this excuse to extricate himself.

5. The President asserted that the US proposal is focused on protecting the Yunnan-Burma Route. But I reiterated that even according to that proposal, the Route will not be free from threat, nor other areas from devastation and oppression. Nevertheless, China would rather make sacrifices to resist the aggression to the end than collapse because of US 's compromising policy with Japan. The President had nothing to reply and appeared embarrassed.

---

[1] Thomas Cochran was then also serving as a legal advisor to China Defense Supplies Inc. in Washington, D. C.

6. Ambassador Hu Shi, putting too much trust in the State Department, thought that Mr. Hull's proposal was in line with the existing US policy and is unchangeable. Therefore, he was reluctant to argue vigorously in terms of the principle, but merely disputed the issue of the number of Japanese troops stationed in northern Vietnam. Such attending to trifles and neglecting essentials won't help. If the misfortune of sacrificing China can be averted this time, this is indeed attributable to Your Excellency's telegraph which speaks out sternly with the force of justice. Hu Shi has rarely interacted with influential US officials. Instead he has only had some brief talks with the British and Australia ambassadors. With no understanding of the actual facts, he would probably hold things up.

7. I invited Mr. Morgenthau, Secretary of Treasury, for dinner last night. According to him, the State Department has always been timid and overcautious. The China's loan two years ago could only be processed and accomplished during Mr. Hull's absense on his trip to South America. It took two years of his painstaking efforts to freeze Japanese assets. The difficulties can be imagined. Moreover, the US-Japan negotiation is very important, but he was not informed and consulted beforehand. This did cause his revulsion. Nevertheless, he firmly believed that it would be rather difficult for the American-Japanese compromise to materialize. The only way of subduing Japan is by force.

8. I am here making strenuous efforts to contact different parties to oppose any compromise (between US and Japan).. The State Department, which inclines toward the Japanese, is naturally reproaching me. But popular opinion tends to be sympathetic towards China. At this critical moment, it is worrisome that Hu Shi is simply incompetent at his job.

T. V.

272. Telegram to Chiang via Guo Taiqi on Soong's meeting with Roosevelt (November 26, 1941)

The President met with Hu Shi and me for about an hour at 2:30 pm today. The President began by saying that because of the critical situation of the

Burma Road, the Generalissimo telegraphed him repeatedly discussing an urgent solution. Then the Japanese envoy Kurusu met with him to express that Japan does not want the US to mediate peace talks between Japan and China. Therefore the whole Sino-Japanese problem could not be touched upon (during negotiation with Japan). One of the interim solutions proposed by Japan includes freezing the number of Japanese troops in Vietnam. The President thought this could help China to ease the immense pressure on the Burma Road. Hence, the Secretary of State discussed an interim solution with Australia, Britain, China, and the Netherlands, focusing on reducing the number of Japanese troops in Indo-China to an unthreatening level. This is meant to help Generalissimo Chiang relieve the critical situation on the Burma Road. The President at first intended to reach a general agreement among China, Britain, the Netherlands, and Australia, and then to begin negotiations with Japan. As of now this proposal has not been raised, but we received a report last night that thirty-odd Japanese warships had headed southward from Shandong and passed Taiwan, carrying roughly thirty to fifty thousand troops. This shows Japan's dishonesty as it increases troops in south even during the negotiation. In such a situation, the negotiation cannot be carried on. A war in the Pacific Ocean is likely to break out in foreseeable future. Therefore this proposal has not been sent out, and the negotiations may well be suspended. The President learned that Generalissimo Chiang has a misunderstanding about this matter. He feels anxious and asked us to explain to you, etc.

Hu Shi explained our government's position which focused on two points: first, the relaxation of (US) trade blockade (towards Japan) would strengthen Japan's endurance ability and diminish the morale of our soldiers and civilians; second, if Japan could advance neither in the south nor in the north, it would attack China with all strength. Then China would be the only victim. The so-called interim solution won't help at all.

The President said: the Secretary of State's proposal could only relieve China's pressure partially and temporarily. It certainly could not solve the whole Sino-Japanese War. The situation is just like this: there are two robbers invading from two sides. If we could pay five dollars to one of them and make him take a detour of ten miles, then we could defend ourselves against the other one with our full strength. Our intention is nothing more than this.

I explained to the President that if the US restored limited economic relations with Japan in exchange for Japan's promise of not invading Siberia, Dutch East India (Indonesia), Thailand and Singapore, our soldiers and civilians would think this an indication to Japan that it could attack China. The three main points of the Japanese military strategy are as follows: first, attacking Siberia, second, advancing to the southward, and third, invading China with full strength. If the first two can not be achieved, China alone will suffer from the calamity. Though protecting the Burma Road is important, restricting Japanese troops only in northern Vietnam only does not help the overall situation. Japan still could use Vietnam as the base for dispatching a large number of troops into Yunnan from Guangxi. This is the route that has been used during wars throughout history. Even if the Burma Road were not attacked for the time being, other areas would inevitably be devastated, and the Burma Road would still be under threat. Therefore Chinese soldiers and civilians cannot understand the (US) restoration of limited economic relations (with Japan). They only know that lifting the economic embargo will enable Japan to obtain fuel quickly to supply airplanes to bomb China. Therefore Generalissimo Chiang is deeply anxious, and thinks that once Japan and the US reach a compromise, China will be sacrificed. Then the morale of Chinese soldiers and civilians for resisting invasion will not be sustained. I dare to say that China would rather defend herself by fighting than to protect Burma Road by lifting the embargo, for the latter would have profound effects on China's morale. Then the future of the war of resistance would be hopeless.

The President did not respond directly to my words. However, he said that at the moment the situation is changing fast and unpredictably. In a week or two there may well be a war in the Pacific Ocean. He hopes that Generalissimo Chiang will not hastily misunderstand him.

After Hu Shi and I left, we recollected and generalized that the President had touched three points. First, the so-called interim solution has not yet been proposed to Japan. The State Department just confirmed this. Second, before the US obtains the agreement from the four countries, negotiations may not start. We will confirm this with the State Department and report to you later. Third, if Japan increases its troops in the south now, the (US-Japan) negotiation will collapse, and war (between them) thus be inevitable.

T. V.

273. Telegram to Chiang on Hull's response to Chiang's messages to Secretaries of Army and Navy (November 27, 1941)

Mr. Currie came to tell me that Secretary of State Mr. Hull was discontented because I passed Your Excellency's telegram on 25th to the Secretaries of Navy and Army and got their responses (without going through the diplomatic protocol). (As remedy,) Currie had to send a telegraph to Lattimore (to explain). Currie added that Your Excellency's telegram on 25th is very effective. Though his telegram (to Lattimore) is out, Your Excellency can simply ignore it.

T. V.   .

274. Telegram to Chiang on Soong's meeting with Morgenthau (November 27, 1941)

Henry Morgenthau arranged a confidential meeting with me today. He said China should take a firm stance (in urging US government). All the cabinet members but (State Secretary) Hull sympathize with China. Morgenthau has drawn up a sincere letter to the President, expressing his view that if the US and Japan reached a compromise, the principles of democracy and world justice would collapse. Even if the President orders him to resign (for this letter), he will have no regrets. I replied that his kindness is highly appreciated, and told him that the current situation is improving, and hope he keeps supporting us.

T. V.

275. Telegram to Chiang on analysis of US-Japan negotiation (November 28, 1941)

Inside information about Japan-US negotiations have been unfolded recently. I hereby present a detailed analysis as follows:

(1) Mr. Hull is an upright gentleman with peaceful personality, but surrounded by the appeasement group in the State Department. This group is eager to compromise with Japan, even at expense of China's interests. Maxwell Hamilton, chief of Far Eastern Bureau, is leader of this group. Political advisor Stanley Hornbeck, though sympathizing with China, was compelled to follow suit. As can be seen from my telegram dated 6th and 12th about talk between Hornbeck and Tamoto, Hull intended to procrastinate. But Kurusu, in excuse of suppressing radical group inside Japan, demanded a solution by 26th, later changed to 29th, which was no less than an ultimatum (to US). Being too anxious, Hull had to defer to the opinions of appeasement group.

(2) Both US Army and Navy are well prepared, as can be seen from my telegrams dated 12th, 24th and 25th regarding my talks with Secretary of Army and Secretary of Navy. State Department skillfully asked navy and army chiefs of staff whether they need more time to get better prepared. Preparation can be indefinite. So those military officers, being straightforward, have no reason to object. Hull then first consulted with ambassadors of UK, Australia and Netherlands regarding interim agreement. UK and Netherlands tended to disagree while Australia agreed. Ambassador Hu Shi was also invited because it matters to China most. Hu Shi, weak in personality, was then reluctant to get fundamental points clarified; only focused himself on modification of interim solution. Hull then reported to President Roosevelt that interim solution was workable.

(3) President knew clearly that US-Japan war inevitable. Nevertheless, politicians are fond of playing games. In addition, believing that interim

solution would not harm China much, President endorsed it. Should Your Excellency's telegram not have been distributed promptly to express our solemn and righteous position, interim solution would have been formally submitted to Kurusu on 25th or 26th.

(4) Mr. Currie told me yesterday that, on 24th, President Roosevelt endorsed interim solution with determined phrases. As subordinate, Currie could not speak out otherwise. I blamed Currie for owing President and China. Currie explained that President had always been strong-minded and he hadn't expected that President would easily change his mind this time. He said he was starting to know more about President and asked our forgiveness, etc.

(5) Learning Your Excellency's determined position, President realized inappropriateness of interim solution. Besides, after learning China's standpoint, some high-ranking government officials realized that this is no more than an "Asian Munich Agreement" and expressed their (opposing) opinions to President. But President still wanted to try, and then summoned Hu Shi and me for a private talk (on 26th). I have submitted my personal judgment in my previous telegram dated 26th. President's statements shown in first two items in my telegram did not conform to facts, which showed President's hesitating mentality. The third point is now proved true since President did want to turn around on that.

(6) After meeting with us, President called for Hull and decided to abandon interim solution and to prepare fundamental principles for break up with Japan. I found that though interim solution had not been proposed formally to Japan, its outlines already appeared in many newspapers. Kurusu must have learned content, as well as news that it was supposed to be proposed to Japan on 25th or 26th. That's why the reporters witnessed Kurusu smiling when he stepped into Department of States and frustrated when he stepped out after receiving a negative answer.

(7) Turnaround of this dangerous situation should be attributed fully to Your Excellency's wisdom, calmness and determination, which saved not only China but also United States. Justice and fairness therefore preserved.

Historical destinies are often defined at moments. Recalling the whole story, I must admire even more Your Exccellency's wisdom.

T. V.

276. Telegram from Chiang on issues regarding to US State Department (November 29, 1941)

Your three telegrams on 26th, 27th are all noted. This time, we are fortunate to have your endeavor and are able to turn defeat into victory. Concerning the complaint of the State Department, there is nothing to care about. I hope that you will continue to keep an eye on the follow-up, thus achieving greater effects.

Kai-shek

277. Telegram draft to Chiang on oil production in Gansu and Xinjiang provinces (December 1, 1941)

As regards to the exploitation of new oil wells in Gansu and Xinjiang provinces, the US authorities concerned introduced a well-known oil well specialist and ecologist Mr. Krappe to China for investigating the oil reserves. The tenure of his service is one year, the salaries, travel expenses of him and other two assistants, and necessary instruments will cost around 60, 000 US dollars. If the drilling facility is concerned, another 90, 000 US dollars will be added. This person is experienced in drilling wells, and is introduced by the US. We can count on him to keep things confidential. If he can come to China, he will bring great benefits to the development of our new oil wells. I beg for your instruction on whether we should hire him.

T. V.

278. Telegram to Chiang to request for intelligence of Japanese activities in Vietnam (December 1, 1941)

The enemy's military situation in Vietnam is crucially important to our negotiation with the United States. I beg Your Excellency to keep me posted.

T. V.

279. Telegram to Chiang on Soong's meeting with Stimson (December 2, 1941)

I just met Secretary of War Stimson. He first stated that he is not State Secretary and therefore, can not talk freely. Yet he could imagine all the difficulties that Generalissimo Chiang confronted. At this moment, he could only request Generalissimo to be patient. The stance and policies of the US are the same as what was said in the telegram of November 6th. Now the army is ready, yet it will be more prepared in a month. He said he spoke the truth out of friendship, and hoped that the secret will be kept strictly. Disclosing the secret would do China no good. I said, "What concerns China most are the improper interim solutions which tear into pieces the morale of Chinese people and the military." Secretary Stimson replied, "China should not ... etc." He halted in the midst of conversation, but his indication is that China does not have to worry about this. In the end, Stimson said, "The enemy would not attack Yunnan and Burma now." When I stepped out of the door, he bade me again to keep the conversation confidential. Moreover, all the newspaper here yesterday softened their tone toward Japan because they sensed that the US-Japan war may be avoided for the time being, and especially because of the propaganda from the Department of State. But today, their tone turned against Japan's insincere gesture of peace.

T. V.

280. Telegram to Chiang on pilot training in India (December 5, 1941)

S454

A friend in the British embassy secretly informed me that if our government intends to send air force pilots to British India for training, the government of India is likely to consent. I hereby report this to Your Excellency.

T. V.

281. Telegram to Chiang on press strategy of Northeastern China issue (December 6, 1941)

Concerning the Northeastern China issue stated in the telegram dated November 22nd. I propose to expand our propagandist work in the United States in a systematic way regardless expenses. As to whether it is feasible, I beg your instructions.

T. V.

282. Telegram to Chiang on US policy towards Japan (December 6, 1941)

The publisher of *New York Times*, after meeting with President Roosevelt, told me secretly that it is impossible for the President to compromise with Japan, and said that there is no hope of peace, and something may happen after Christmas. He also added that the President did not want to see the collapse of the Tojio cabinet.

T. V.

283. Telegram to Chiang on new cross-pacific air routes (December 8, 1941)

S455

The original Pacific Ocean air route has already been obstructed. Henceforth two new routes may be established: one from Honolulu southward via Eastern Dutch Indonesia and Singapore; another from North America via South America, Africa, India and Rangoon. If this is feasible, I propose Your Excellency to officially propose to the US ambassador Mr. Gauss the establishment of the new routes. I beg for Your Excellency's careful consideration.

T. V.

284. Telegram to Chiang on shipment of bank notes (December 12, 1941)

S456

The sea transportation between China and Rangoon may be obstructed. How much is the inventory of bank notes available at home? How many months can the inventory support? And what is the number of bank notes that can be printed domestically? If large denominations of notes are needed, I will endeavor to ask the US government to ship them by air via Africa to the interior to fill the shortfall. Please give me in detail your instructions and also inform me of the amount needed.

T. V.

285. Telegram to Chiang on Lend-Lease affairs after Pearl Harbor Incident (December 12, 1941)

S457

After the sudden change in the Pacific war, the situation of the Lend-Lease program is as follows: (1) President announced clearly that they will not change the Lend-Lease policy. (2) The US military authority has temporarily ceased delivery of many important Lend-Lease military materials. As the war broke out abruptly, the Lend-Lease supplies will not be resumed until the US rearranges the allocation plan. (3) All the shipping lines of the Pacific Ocean are now suspended. However, a plan on convoy is now underway. The air route via South America, Africa to Calcutta in India and Rangoon in Burma is going to be realized. That is the general situation of the Lend-Lease policy, the delivery and transport.

From now on, the Lend-Lease program may depend on the overall war plan and the needs of different war theaters. The Lend-Lease materials will be lend-leased in packages depending on the progress of war, unlike previous method of piecemeal delivery. Take the airplane as example, if a Theatre needs airplanes, all its units such as airplanes, spare parts, pilots and airport technicians will be provided simultaneously. Yet this plan can not be realized until the loss of Pearl Harbor is compensated for. What can be sure now is that this is the trend of future Lend-Lease program implementation. Moreover, the war supplies for China are closely related to the military situation in the Far East. Please inform me of the latest news of Yunnan, Burma and Hong Kong in detail, so that I can deal with it and respond correspondingly.

T. V.

286. Telegram to Chiang on shipment of US military equipment (December 13, 1941)

S458

I hope you received my telegram dated 12th concerning the suspension of (Lend-Lease) supplies by the US War Department. The War Department informed us that the various guns and ammunition supposed to be delivered within this year should be shipped on schedule. Other issues are still under discussion.

T. V.

287. Telegram to Chiang on printing of bank notes (December 13, 1941)

Henceforth the transportation will be difficult. Concerning the issuing of bank notes, we should have a overall plan. I think a large number of bank notes preserved in the office of the Stabilization Board[1] in Shanghai may have been captured by the Japanese enemy. From now on it seems inevitable to use bank notes with large denominations, or immediately put both large and small denomination bank notes in circulation. I beg Your Excellency to make a final decision.

---

[1] The headquarters of the Stabilization Board was then in Hong Kong.

T. V.

288. Telegram to Chiang on military procurement list (December 16, 1941)

S461

Since the US-Japan war broke out, the US will pay more attention to supplying munitions to us. I draft a list according to the needs of our country and the American capability of supply after consulting with Jiang Biao, and will submit it to the US. The items are listed below (according to the first to seventh item in Jiang Biao's draft):

1. 10,000 light machine guns and 100 million bullets
2. 360 75mm mountain artilleries and 600,000 projectiles
3. 360 105mm- or 155mm-howizers and 180,000 shells
4. 360 37 mm Anti-tank guns and 360,000 shells
5. 720 0.5-inch anti-air machine guns and 270,000 shells
6. 180 40mm Bofors Anti-air guns and 270,000 shells
7. 2000 60mm mortars and one million shells

I will request the above guns and bullets be shipped starting in three months. Besides, ammunitions shall be resupplied accordingly. I also hope the supplementary 5 hundred million 7. 9mm bullets and shells be delivered before next March and the shipping will be completed before December. I suggest Your Excellency would bring the plan to the proposed military meeting (in Chongqing) among China, United States, United Kingdom and the Netherlands. I look forward to Your Excellency's decision.

T. V.

289. Telegram to Chiang on training at US pilot school (December 23, 1941)

S462

I received your telegram dated 18th. The training program for the twin-engine planes of the US Air Force is now in preparation, and scheduled to begin next spring or summer. We had previously asked the War Department about training students from our country. They said that the trainer aircrafts were running short, not even adequate for training their own pilots, and so on. It was evident that the US Air Force was not prepared (for the breakout of war). However, now the situation is different, and they will try their best to expand the training programs. I plan to ask them to accommodate more students from our country. Once there is progress, I will report to you via telegram.

T. V.

290. Telegram to Chiang on charge increase of international news telegrams (December 23, 1941)

I have just been informed that the rate for telegram of international news in our country increased by several times. In the midst of war this will become a hindrance to the availability of information (for outside world), and have a bad effect on our international publicity (efforts). It is indeed more of lose than gain. I beg Your Excellency to consider ordering the governmental bodies concerned to call off this measure.

T. V.

291. Telegram to Chiang on destruction of bank notes in the Philippines (December 24, 1941)

S463

Yesterday I instructed the US bank note company to burn the bank notes that the Bank of China was about to ship to China, under the supervision of our consul-general in the Philippines Yang Guangsheng. Previously, I telegraphed Central Bank of China and Bank of Communications to follow suit if the situation required them to do so. Yet so far I have not had any response from them. Now as the situation is greatly dangerous, I have ordered the US bank note company to burn the notes of the three banks in the Philippines simultaneously. Please keep this on record.

T. V.

292. Telegram to Chiang on Chennault's commandership (December 26, 1941)

According to telegram from General Chennault, two divisions will be stationed in Kunming, and one division remains in Rangoon, helping the British fight. As to whether the issue relating to Chennault's commanding power should be discussed with British and American military commanders, I beg Your Excellency to give your instructions.

T. V.

293. Telegram to Chiang on transferring of Xiao Bo to US (December 26, 1941)

S464

Chinese military attaché to the US General Zhu Shiming is rather helpful here in the States. In the future it is expected that the military attaché's office is going to be much busier, and the staff seems insufficient. The third secretary of our embassy, Major Xiao Bo, used to be deputy military attaché, is familiar with the situation here. I wonder whether it is feasible to promote him as deputy military attaché with the rank of lieutenant colonel to assist (General Zhu). Although there is another deputy military attaché, yet by international custom, deputy military attaché is not limited to one. There may be more if needed. I beg Your Excellency to make a final decision.

T. V.

294. Telegram to Chiang on bullet production in India (December 29, 1941)

S465

Director Yu Dawei telegrammed that India is able to produce 7.92 mm-bullets on our behalf. My humble opinion is that if this matter is discussed here, it would need to pass through many hands and places and get delayed. I wonder whether we could approach Sir Archibald P. Wavell[1] directly about the issue, and the US is likely to take care of the expenses. I beg Your Excellency for further instructions.

T. V.

295. Telegram to Chiang on press strategy of Northeastern China issue (January 5, 1942)

The Japanese always made presumptuous propaganda that their country was overpopulated. China, with her vast land and sparse population, should therefore become Japanese colony. People in Europe and US have long been confused by this assertion and ignorant of situation in Northeastern China in particular. For example, when declaring war on Japan, even President Roosevelt in his speech used term *Manchukuo* (Manchuria Nation), let alone other officials. Concerned about this, I gave advice in my earlier telegram. When final peace comes, American moderates may accommodate hard-pressed enemy by sacrificing Northeast China lest Japanese be pressed too much and thus cause feuding. It would be better for us to launch press work as soon as possible to correct the American mindset. I look forward to Your Excellency's further instructions.

T. V.

296. Telegram to Chiang on US confidential memorandum to UK (January 19, 1942)

Today Secretary of War Stimson met with me and stated that in light of the unproductive visit to Chongqing of Sir Archibald Wavell and George H. Brett[2], requisition of our military equipment in Rangoon, and Your

---

[1] British Commander-in-Chief in India.
[2] Senior officer from the US War Department who was invited by Chiang Kai-shek to visit Chongqing in late December 1941.

Excellency's request to President to recommend a candidate for chief of Allied staff in China Theatre, he did his best to draft a confidential memorandum to British authorities, and asked our consent, to promote practical cooperation between Britain, China and US in China Theatre. Translation (of the memorandum) is outlined as follows:

A. Principles

1. Both Britain and US should fully understand that without thorough cooperation with Generalissimo, war situation will not improve.

2. Britain and the US should do their best to strengthen China's military power in both military and political terms.

3. Currently biggest problem is difficulty of transportation between China and Britain and US, together with misunderstanding among these nations.

B. Goals: based on above principles, following tasks should be achieved:

1. To improve measures and means of practical communication with Generalissimo.

2. To protect security of Burma Road and Burma.

3. To improve the administration of the Burma Road transportation.

4. To strengthen army and air force fortress (in China Theatre) and provide sufficient technical supports.

5. To promote China's overall strength of war.

6. To define clearly the measures of smooth communication between China Theatre and Theatre under Sir Wavell's commandership.

C. Plan of Implementation: US Army proposes to implement following plans to achieve above goals:

1. To request Generalissimo accept US senior officer as US representative in China and to authorize him following powers:

    (a) To manage matters relating to US military aid.

    (b) To command all US forces in China and some contingents of Chinese troops handed over to his commandership by Generalissimo. If these Chinese troops have to join war in Burma, their general military plan should be subject to Sir Wavell's instruction, but military operations should be commanded by

American officers.

(c) To represent US in any international military meetings held in China.

(d) To maintain and manage transportation of Burma Road in Chinese territory.

2. Should Generalissimo agree with points listed in Article C1, (US) War Department would:

(a) Strengthen the air forces in southern China and Burma, starting from reinforcing the American Volunteers Group (AVG) with more airplanes and personnel. It is also possible to equip the Chinese troops that Generalissimo may assign (to Wavell's commandership) completely with American weapons and supplies.

(b) Upon British authorities' consent, set up logistical stations (in Burma) to provide supplies to Chinese troops in Burma as well as British and American army and Air Force units in Burma. Moreover, special-purpose facilities and equipment shall be provided to maintain Rangoon port's transport capability and enough troops to secure the Burma Road transport.

(c) It is necessary to obtain British cooperation and commitment in order to implement the above plans. The said cooperation and commitment, preconditioned by Generalissimo's acceptance of article C1, include:

i) To agree that US representative, when executing his duties in Burma and areas north to Burma, should and could cooperate with neighboring theatre commanders to establish and utilize all military fortresses, routes and stations in India and Burma;

ii) To agree that US representative should do his best to increase the transport capacity of the Burma Road from Rangoon to Kunming. To achieve this goal, the US representative shall be entrusted with full authority from Chinese government to administrate the Burma Road within Chinese territory, while the British military and civilian authorities be responsible for the Burma Road in Burma. But the British authorities shall agree to accept all US representative's suggestions, American experts and equipment to improve the transportation in Rangoon Port and the Burma Road;

iii) To consent the US representative, upon communication with British commander in advance, to use all airport facilities and to construct new such facilities in Burma;

iv) To accept US representative as the major contact point between Sir Wavell and Generalissimo Chiang.

Secretary Stimson's memorandum, translated above, is said to be result of careful deliberation on basis of facts. I told him that I will present it to Your Excellency and reverently wait for your instructions. Please consider thoroughly and instruct promptly. Some points should be clarified hereafter:

1. As to senior officer, chief of staff of China Theatre, Lieutenant General Stilwell is recommended. He is generally acknowledged as most talented general in US army, now corps commander and formerly chief of Operations Division under Marshall, Chinese-speaking. Please keep confidential until announced.

2. It is now clear that points stated in my English telegram on Saturday were to avoid any misunderstandings between China and Britain. Therefore I propose to put Chinese troops entering Burma under this gentleman's commandership rather than British authorities'.

3. Your Excellency's dealings with Sir Wavell and the Burmese military and political authorities can be handed over to this person. If Chinese troops enter and are stationed in Vietnam and Thailand, this is different case from Chinese troops in Burma and should be under Your Excellency's direct command.

4. Because of precarious situation in Singapore, General Stimson eagerly wishes to see practical military coordination between China Theatre and Burma. He therefore urged me to beg Your Excellency to send your instructions as soon as possible.

I hereby report the above.

T. V.

297. Telegram to Chiang on proposal of new loans from US and other issues (January 26, 1942)

Situation in Singapore and Burma is critical, and there is danger that our international communication line may be cut off. The effect of this on our troops and people's morale would be by no means insignificant. As remedy, it seems we should immediately negotiate with US about following three issues: (1) expeditious decision on big loans (2) transfer of supplies from Calcutta and Myitkyina to Yunnan using large number of airplanes (3) (establishment of) Sino-American military alliance. First two items are underway. As for third, although US usually would not establish military alliance with other countries, yct (there is precedent that) in summer of 1904[1] when France was under great threat, British used to propose that Britain and France be unified as one nation. In addition, as military alliance itself is not novel, there might be possibility for US to make exception. Should three tasks succeed, it would greatly boost our public morale and fundamentally benefit our military situation. What are Your Excellency's thoughts and what do we need to pay attention to when negotiating with US? Please grant Your Excellency's instructions.

P.S. please be noted that the domestic media's discontent on UK and US's military arrangement is of no good to my assignment here.

T. V.

298. Telegram to Chiang on commander candidate for the Allies air forces (February 5, 1942)

Matters relating to US's promotion of Clair L. Chennault to major general

---

[1] The original script shows "1904", which seems to be error of "1940".

instead of appointing other air force personnel have been detailed in my telegram dated January 30th for your attention. But US chief of staff and General Stilwell originally thought that as soon as counterattack against Japan is launched, air base must be in China. So not only American Volunteer Group (AVG) and Chinese air force need a competent commander, such person is important as well in intensive preparations for sending air force units to China. According to Stilwell, Chennault's qualifications in terms of his skill, experience, prestige and his relations with US Air Force remain questionable. So he would like Major General Clayton Bissell[1] to assume supreme post in Allied air force and supervise everything, while General Chennault continues to command AVG, as well as organize and train China Air Force. My opinion is that the decision (of using Chennault) is just made and should not be changed. Nevertheless, it is also true that General Clayton Bissell has very close relations with high-ranking officers of US Air Force, and his prestige is also well-known. Considering future situation, it would be quite a pity should General Bissell miss opportunity to come to China. I look forward to Your Excellency's instruction on this matter.

T. V.

299. Telegram to Chiang on China's honor awarding to foreigners (March 9, 1942)

Currently we are having more and more interactions with foreign countries. However, honorary medals that our government awards to foreign guests are low in quality and their style is not artistic. Moreover, they are divided into too many ranks. (For the models, some are as low as) seventh or eighth rank. The recipients have often complained that they were awarded with low-ranking medals. Although medals of other countries distinguish with ranks too, but enjoy respective titles instead of specified ranks. Could we consider reforming this system and instructing government organs concerned to work

---

[1] Then serving as commander of the US Tenth Air Force.

out alternative samples or draft new designs in US and then submit for Your Excellency's examination? I beg Your Excellency to make final decision.

T. V.

300. Telegram to Chiang and K'ung on loan negotiation with acting State Secretary (March 21, 1942)

Telegrams from brother Yong (H. H. K'ung) dated March 17th and 18th acknowledged. I have forwarded to the (US) Secretary of Treasury all of Generalissimo's suggestions except the one concerning minimum amount which sounds comparatively weak and was therefore not translated. State Department and Department of Treasury held a meeting to discuss these carefully, and noted that conditions for current loan are far more lenient than for other loans, and do not contain any harsh terms. Aware of this I immediately approached highest authorities and concerned officials for personal explanations and negotiations. This morning Acting Secretary of State Sumner Welles met with me and reiterated US government's stance that Article 2 might be taken out, but asked me to submit letter reaffirming following: (1) Chinese government is willing to exchange views with US Secretary of Treasury at any time on the purposes of loan and to work out effective measures; (2) Chinese government is willing to inform US Department of Treasury at any time of using this loan. I responded that Chinese government by no means keeps secret the uses of loan from US government, and is willing to receive US technical assistance, but there shouldn't be any mention that Chinese Government bears obligation to discuss and negotiate with US government. At my insistence, Acting Secretary of State telephoned and consulted each party concerned, and finally agreed to take out Article 2. After signing of agreement I sent a note to secretary of treasury in which I specified that Chinese government is willing to inform US government of uses of loan in detail from time to time. Full text as follows: With regards to loan agreement entered into between US and Chinese governments today, for the sake of showing our collaborative spirit to work together during wartime, I am instructed to inform Your Excellency that our

Minister of Finance is willing to inform Your Excellency Secretary of Treasury from time to time of detailed usages of the loan, etc. This was US final concession, which did not go against Generalissimo's repeated instructions. Both parties therefore signed loan agreement at noontime today, and agreed to publicize it, whereas my note to Secretary of Treasury is off the record.

T. V.

301. Telegram to Chiang on inviting Cripps to visit Chongqing (April, 1942)

Sir Stafford Cripps[1], unlike other pedantic and stubborn British diplomats, has strategic thinking in mind, and always venerates Your Excellency. He recently returned to UK with high prestige after successfully handling the Indian affairs. It is well possible that he may replace Churchill in near future. Therefore, I advise Your Excellency to invite him to visit you in Chongqing. British politicians do not understand the truth behind the incident of military equipment requisition (in Burma) and the issue of military commandership in Burma (Theatre). Your Excellency could avail this opportunity to tell him the truth explicitly. No matter whether Britain wins or loses the war, the imperial system will collapse anyhow. Yet at this critical moment, it is desirable to keep contact with British lest our enemies would exploit.

T. V.

302. Telegram to Chiang on Pacific War Council meeting (April 1, 1942)

Pacific War Council held meeting today, and President Roosevelt chaired it. Because of meeting's preparatory nature, President only illustrated division of theaters, as reported in my previous telegram dated 12th. Meanwhile it was decided following items should be discussed on next Tuesday:

---

[1] Former British Ambassador to the Soviet Union.

A. Anti-Japanese military plan proposed by Australia and New Zealand;

B. The Korea issue.

President suggested me to propose on the next meeting to discuss how to make use of Korean people to disrupt Japanese enemy, and issue regarding organization of volunteer troops in Northeast China. Concerning above two questions, I beg Your Excellency to give me your instructions as to:

1. Whether Your Excellency agrees that all participating nations of Pacific War Council, or only China and US, should announce they favor independence for Korea, and thereafter decide whether or not the policy of dismembering the Japanese Empire should be publicized before Soviet Union's participation.

2. Whether underground societies in Korea possess real power and have connections with Allied forces; how strong they are. And whether our government intends to supervise them from Chongqing and send personnel to Korea to engage in clandestine activities.

3. US obviously intends to assist in arming Koreans and resistance in northeast with ammunition in order to check Japanese enemy. Please give detailed instructions on how to proceed.

4. What's recent situation and organization of volunteer troops in Northeast? I beg Your Excellency to respond as soon as possible.

I look forward to Your Excellency's earliest reply.

T. V.

303. Telegram to Chiang on explanation of loan purpose to US government (April 12, 1942)

D441

This afternoon I had confidential meeting with Secretary of Treasury Henry Morgenthau. According to him, upon return to US, Mr. Fox told him that Chinese authorities had asked him to proclaim that after signing of loan agreement, China should first consult him (Morgenthau) before withdrawing funds. Morgenthau stressed that he has always trusted

China, therefore he had not insisted on stating this point (of prior consultation) in the (loan) agreement. Yet immediately after signing agreement on March 21st, on 24th our Finance Minister H. H. K'ung, without consulting him in advance, announced a two-hundred-million-dollar budget, then telegraphed him on March 27th about it and asked for disbursement. To comply with agreement, Morgenthau had to allot two hundred million dollars to China's account in Federal Reserve by afternoon of Thursday April 16th. He was disappointed though that China's action did not show spirit of mutual trust. Besides, measures stipulated in agreement contain many loopholes and may not work (as expected). If China fails financially, it is America's failure too, so is his (Morgenthau) personal's. How would we explain to him then, etc.

I replied that negotiation of the loan agreement had lasted long, while China's financial situation was critical and urgent, requiring immediate aids. Minister K'ung was ill and the acting officials at Ministry of Finance are not as experienced or well-thought. But their negligence was not intentional. I will surely report his comments to Generalissimo.

Actually agreement does not stipulate in explicit terms that China should consult US (before any drawdown), but we did imply so beforehand. It seems better to make friendly consultation in advance. Should any disagreement occur, we can still ask for reimbursement of funds according to agreement. They would not refuse (according to the agreement) and we will have shown our good will. Now though Morgenthau has disbursed funds according to agreement, misunderstanding (between us) has been rooted. In a broad and forward-looking view, it may matter in long-run. Thinking broadly, Sino-American relations affect overall situation. And US economic aids to us shall go far beyond this loan.

I have been away from China for two years and am now unfamiliar with China's current financial situation. Its complexity cannot be explained clearly through telegrams. It is impossible for me to make thorough explanation (on this issue to the US side). To make remedy, could Your Excellency please instruct brother Yong (H. H. K'ung) to send someone like Bei Songsun[1] or Gu Jigao[2] who is familiar with China's financial situation to US to explain to Secretary of Treasury? It will not take more than one or two weeks. My thought is that this matter has become question of trust and personal feelings of Morgenthau and American government officials toward China. Sending someone here to exchange views, the misunderstanding would be easily removed, and friendship between brother Yong and Morgenthau would not be harmed.

Please grant me Your Excellency's instructions.

T. V.

304. Telegram to Chiang on dispatch of financial expert to US (April 17, 1942)

Hope my telegram of April 12th has reached your attention. Given intense war situation, I should not have bothered you repeatedly with trivialities. Nonetheless, the recent successful signing of the loan agreement was completely out of the US government's trust in Your Excellency. But Mr. Fox told Secretary Morgenthau upon his return to US, that on January 15th Your Excellency asked to convey message to Morgenthau that, after signing agreement, China would be willing to consult with US about effective execution in advance. However, Morgenthau said that our ministry of finance in practice ignored this point. Therefore he seems to misunderstand us and is critical of measures we have taken. I have been away from China for too long and hence unfamiliar with domestic financial situation. I couldn't make thorough explanation (to Morgenthau). Therefore, I telegraphed brother Yong (H. H. K'ung) requesting him to send someone to US to take charge of this kind of negotiation and communication. I can give assistance as Foreign

---

1 Also known as Bei Zuyi, then serving as managing-director of the Bank of China and one of the Chinese representatives at the Stabilization Board.

2 Then serving as Chinese deputy minister of finance.

Minister. Brother Yong just telegraphed me that he would send Xi Demao[1] here. I again telegraphed him requesting that apart from person who is familiar with financial situation he should send one familiar with general economic issues, such as Gu Jigao, to US to make arrangements. Then Xi Demao could be stationed here and take charge after this mission is accomplished. Please ask brother Yong to do this and I look forward to your reply.

T. V.

305. Telegram to Chiang on Soong's meeting with Hopkins (April 22, 1942)

I just met with Mr. Harry Hopkins. According to him, a large number of British battleships and aircrafts are defending India. Hence it seems that Japanese may not attack India. London's observation is that if Japanese do not attack India and Australia, they will attack China with all their strength through Burma and Vietnam. China should be prepared. I replied that most urgent need is armaments and aircrafts. I'd ask US to expedite shipment. He said many important matters for China, Britain, Soviet Union and US needed to be discussed urgently. He suggested I go to Chongqing with him to request instructions, and then go to Britain and Soviet Union. I think Hopkins is the person President most trusts. This trip is quite important. But things I am managing here would be at standstill because no one could take over. Hence I did not give him a positive answer. But he repeatedly stressed the trip's importance.

Also, about Britain's request of borrowing aircrafts that are supposed to be shipped to China, President has telegraphed Your Excellency directly, which I attach for Your Excellency's information.

T. V.

---

[1] Then serving as direct-general of the Department of Banking, Central Bank of China.

306. Telegram to Chiang on dispatch of Gu Jigao and others to US (April 23, 1942)

I received your earlier telegram and wanted to forward it to Mr. Morgenthau. However, considering that he is one of China's most ardent friends in US government (e. g. he helped to get aircrafts for General Chennault's Volunteers' Group, and made extraordinary contribution to this loan agreement), I weighed repeatedly and believe we had better not to mention it to him. Moreover, in case the two hundred million dollars we have withdrawn would not help to curb inflation, we may still need his support in near future. My request to send people like Gu Jigao to US is entirely for helping reach thorough understanding in complexity between our Ministry of Finance and US Treasury.

T. V.

307. Telegram to Chiang on war situation in Burma (April 28, 1942)

D481

(Recent) setback in Burma battlefield may lower our international standing and affect our Lend-Lease affairs and other work in US. Therefore I need to know urgently the main reasons to cause this setback, such as failure in joint command, (ineffective) air covering, lack of heavy artillery and tanks, difficulty in transportation and logistics, as well as Burmese people's sympathy with Japanese army, etc. Though knowing all these situations in principle, I do not have solid facts to produce a reasonable explanation report for the US authorities. Stilwell was on the field and had a stake in the retreat; he should know the situation more thoroughly and must be willing to cooperate with me and have the facts be known to all allied nations. I look forward to Your Excellency's reply.

T. V.

308. Telegram to Chiang on Lend-Lease Act implementation (April, 1942)

I have been in charge of military Lend-Lease affairs for a year but achieved little, only (obtained) sixty million dollars worth of supplies so far. Reasons might be: first, production is small but demand high. Second, many US generals like Magruder look down on China's fighting ability and send reports here. Third, for many reasons US puts more weight on British and Russian battlefields rather than on that of China. Fourth, before Rangoon's fall, transport capacity of Burma Road was too small; in addition, vicious people spread rumors that Southwest Transport Administration was corrupted by smuggling. There were even rumors that I was in factual charge of this organization and made high profits. I have reported this situation to you many times. Now Rangoon has fallen, transportation is blocked, and construction of new roads lags far behind schedule. US airlift is not efficient enough. Even Burma and India are now in danger of being taken by enemy. Hence (those who advocate against aiding China) would have more excuses. Some even suggested reclaiming the military equipment that already allotted to China but yet to deliver. Fifth, more US vessels have sunk, and maritime transportation is increasingly difficult. Sixth, Chinese complained that US did not render full support, while US said she did, and blamed Chinese for being ungrateful. Being squeezed in between, I have felt mentally and physically exhausted. As to financial affairs, during first four months of my service, Ambassador Hu Shi was not only unhelpful but also failed to behave properly. I was given a cold shoulder (by US authorities) for four or five months and often embarrassed. Now the big loan agreement was finally singed but consultations between Chinese and US finance ministries remains in stalemate. I can hardly sleep because of so many unsolved difficulties. If this situation continues it will damage our national interests. I have been here for two years and feel unable to fulfill a single assignment. Therefore I request you send somebody here as soon as possible to take over various duties. I look forward to your decision.

T. V.

309. Telegram to Chiang on utilization of US governmental loans (May 2, 1942)

It was reported that economic conditions in the enemy-occupied region are improving. (The value of) puppet regime's notes in Northern China is eight times higher than our *Fabi* (the national currency); and that in Central China is two or three times higher than *Fabi*. On our side, the prices keep rising, and situation is getting more and more precarious. Our utilization of US loan is far from perfect, and the effect (of currency stabilization) is almost zero. How would this develop in future? I have asked repeatedly to send officials to US for negotiating with US Department of Treasury and come up with some practical solutions. Gu Jigao is trusted by brother Yong (H. H. K'ung), and is familiar with our domestic economic and financial situation. He must be able to enhance Sino-American financial relations and work out remedies for immediate execution. Although Xi Demao in US is of some help, I am afraid he is not capable enough (to handle this complicated situation). I have been away from home country for too long, and deeply aware that my planning may not be well thought-out. I did not intent to evade my responsibility in the name of not exceeding into other's responsibility. I will still do my best to be helpful. The overall situation is dangerous. Since finance particularly matters to our country's survival, we are not allowed to hesitate and maunder. Nor can hollow words or theory turn the tide in our favor. My blunt words might not be forgiven by others, but hope you will understand my sincerity and painstaking effort.

T. V. by hand

310. Telegram to Chiang on economic situation in China (May 2, 1942)

Our economic conditions are deteriorating and critical; whereas enemy-occupied areas are reportedly better off. If things continue like this, negative effect will be obvious on the morale of our military and civilians. I deeply worry when review the war prospect. Bombardment of Tokyo by US aircraft has produced notable results. As soon as "Air Fortress" bombers are shipped to China, they should be ordered to bomb Shanghai first, with top target being power plants to shock and deactivate enemy's financial center. At the same time cities like Nanjing and Guangzhou also should be bombarded. This tactic of destroying enemy's financial center would bring greater effects for us than that of bombing Tokyo. These suggestions are for your reference.

T. V.

311. Telegram to Chiang on Fox's activities in US (May 2, 1942)

Upon arrival in US, Mr. A. Manuel Fox[1] spared no efforts in offering assistance, and proved himself to be good friend of China. After returning to China, he will make great contributions to many aspects of our economic and financial affairs. Please kindly seek advice from him. I asked him to bring a photograph of signature of loan agreement to you for your reference. Also, Furthermore, twenty-five US B-17 "Flying Fortress" bombers will fly to China in turn from the fifteenth of this month, and may go into service in June. Attaché Mr. Huang Bingheng[2] is traveling with the planes.

T. V.

312. Telegram to Chiang on Pacific War Council meeting (May 5, 1942)

D503

Pacific War Council held a meeting today. President reported following:

1. British occupation of French Madagascar;
2. Outstanding victory of US Navy in southwestern Pacific, details have yet to be reported.

I proposed that one of important points of world war is to supply China with armaments by airlift. This should be achieved at all costs. I also proposed using "Air Fortress" bombers as air-freighters flying directly from Allahabad

---

[1] Then serving as board member of the Sino-American Stabilization Fund.
[2] Then serving as Air Force Attaché in the Chinese Embassy to US.

in northern India to Xufu or Chengdu [in Sichuan Province]. All participants agreed unanimously and advocated this vigorously. According to report from US Air Force, there are some technical problems to be examined. Load capacity may not be much. President ordered Mr. Hopkins, US Aviation Department, and commander of Air Force to speak with me (on details) and report results.

T. V.

313. Telegram to Chiang on issues regarding to airborne transportation (May 6, 1942)

I hope my telegram dated May 5th has reached you. Issue of airlift was discussed at today's Pacific council meeting. It was decided that fifty B-17 "Flying Fortresses" should be immediately assigned solely for transporting military supplies to China. But the Sadiya airport (in India) might soon be raided by enemy air force. Therefore, these planes will have to fly directly from Allahabad to Xufu, 2, 800 miles for round trip. Maximum freight capacity for each journey is three tons, so monthly capacity be 1, 500 tons. The originally planned 100 dual-engine air freighters will still be allocated to us. If so, the maximum capacity may increase to 3, 000 tons per month. The most critical thing is to improve the condition of airfield at Xufu to accommodate new four-engine airplanes. After the cargo arrives at Xufu, they can be shipped to Chongqing along the waterway, more convenient than from Chengdu.

Moreover, according to news from Chen Changtong told (to him) by US military officers having retreated from Burma to Calcutta, an airplane had been dispatched to bring General Stilwell out from Burma but was rejected by him. He is still in the siege accompanied by several staff. His courage in facing desperate situation revealed his quality as a real soldier. Nevertheless, he has many other duties, such as air force aids, Sino-India airlifting and Lend-Lease affairs, that need him to fulfill. Although General Magruder can also help, he would not be as capable as Stilwell. Could Your Excellency (as his supervisor) order Stiwell to return to Chongqing (from India)? Please kindly consider my suggestion. Please also be noted that this (proposal) is not from US authorities.

I am looking forward to Your Excellency's early reply on conditions of the Xufu airport.

T. V.

314. Telegram to Chiang on Stilwell's return to Chongqing (May 6, 1942)

According to news from Chen Changtong told (to him) by US military officers having retreated from Burma to Calcutta, an airplane had been dispatched to bring General Stilwell out from Burma but was rejected by him. He is still in the siege accompanied by several staff. His courage in facing desperate situation revealed his quality as a real soldier. Nevertheless, he has many other duties, such as air force aids, Sino-India airlifting and Lend-Lease affairs, that need him to fulfill. Although General Magruder can also help, he would not be as capable as Stilwell. Could Your Excellency (as his supervisor) order Stiwell to return to Chongqing (from India)? Please kindly consider my suggestion. Please also be noted that this (proposal) is not from US authorities.

I am looking forward to Your Excellency's early reply on conditions of the Xufu airport.

T. V.

315. Telegram to Chiang to request for investigation on Luo Zhuoying's behavior in war (May 9, 1942)

Urgent!

US War Department secretly reported to me that, according to telegraph from General Stilwell, Luo Zhuoying[1] abandoned his army and fled to Baoshan (in

---

[1] Then serving as commander of the 1st Route Army of the Chinese Expeditionary Army in Burma.

Yunnan province). I replied that I thought this was incredible, but it was said to be true. Would Your Excellency please clarify this news and give instructions?

T. V.

316. Telegram to Chiang on confidential report from US ambassador to Secretary of Navy (May 15, 1942)

Upon the arrival of General Xiong Tianyi[1] in US, I especially introduced him to President and important governmental organs, and made great efforts to promote his participation in meeting of Anglo-American joint staff. Up to now there has been no result, and I was wondering on the reason. My close friend just secretly handed to me an abridged telegraph from US ambassador to China Gauss, submitted by navy intelligence to its commander-in-chief. There was some misunderstanding of General Xiong and his entourage, and maybe that is reason why their work could not be carried out smoothly. Attached is copy of the English document with Chinese translation.

[Chinese translation:

Secret Report Submitted to Naval Commander-In-Chief:

Reference: Chinese Army and Navy Delegation (abridged from Ambassador Gauss's correspondence No. 217, dated March 11ᵗʰ, 1942)

Our ambassador to China gave his preliminary judgment on Chinese delegation of army and naval officers to Washington. In relation to negotiation of important matters between that delegation and our navy, this briefing is of great value for reference. Following is abstract.

According to private sources in China, qualifications of the military delegates are not satisfactory.

Lieutenant General Xiong Shihui, head of the delegation, trained in Japan, has little prestige in Chinese army, and did not actually participate in Chinese war

---

[1] Also known as Xiong Shihui, then head of Chinese Military Mission to United States.

of resistance. His identity as administrative officer and politician overshadows that of military man. Before 1937, he allegedly reached a compromise with Japan and was extremely anti-Communist. Major General Xu Peigen, chief of staff of delegation, was suspected of having tendency toward fascism. In addition, he was also suspected of mishandling aircraft purchase deal in 1935. Neither Major General Jin Zhen[1] nor Colonel Cai Wenzhi[2] has seniority or prestige; both are incompetent and unknown.

According to our army attaché in China, purpose of this delegation to US is to take part in discussion of important military plans, as Chongqing announced. Nevertheless, judging from nature and qualification of personnel appointed by Generalissimo, it is clear that the delegation has not been taken serious. Even Chinese themselves share this view.]

317. Telegram to Chiang on Stilwell's return to Chongqing (May 19, 1942)

This afternoon I met with General Arnold, US Air Force Chief of Staff, informed him that since dual-engine air-freighters are sufficient as he asserted, I'd propose a two-week trial period. If results are unsatisfactory, four-engine planes should be dispatched according to original plan.

General Stilwell will soon arrive in India, please order him to Chongqing for detailed discussion on the following:

1. minimum monthly tonnage of airlift from India and types of air-freighters;
2. fighter planes and bombers that we need; and
3. Dispatch of Chinese troops for training in India and detailed plan to equip these troops.

US Army Department often shirks its duties in responding to our claims with the excuse that it didn't receive request from Stilwell, who holds full

---

[1] Member of Chinese Military Mission to the United State.

[2] Member of Chinese Military Mission to the Unite States. He later became acting head of the mission.

authority. So (is its attitude) for airlifting affairs. Since his return, Stilwell shall always be with Your Excellency and available to tackle with problems instantly. He must not be stationed in India. Otherwise, implementation of all plans will be delayed. I beg for Your Excellency's decision.

T. V.

318. Telegram to Chiang on US intelligence personnel's request to enter China's inner land (May 20, 1942)

US Office of Strategic Service (OSS) recently intended to send agents to interior of our country, including Qinghai, Gansu, Xikang, Shaanxi, and Sichuan for inspection tour, under General Stilwell's control and command. I was requested to issue them permits. But I suppose these agents, under guise of investigating countryside, have more to do with political espionage. If they were allowed to penetrate into our hinterland, there would be troubles and disturbances. Their future reports would be inaccurate, incomplete and misleading and might inhibit our work with US. Sino-American interaction has always been frank and open, immune from mutual suspicion. However, it is difficult to ascertain whether it is appropriate to dispatch these agents. Rather than creating unexpected discord in future, it would be better to take precautions. I have indicated that if they are to be under General Stilwell's command, he ought to instruct them directly from Chongqing. If a request is made to Your Excellency, it should be graciously declined. I hereby report the above for Your Excellency's scrutiny. Regards

P. S. attached please find abridged translation of OSS's memorandum.

T. V.

319. Telegram to Chiang on bombing of power plant in Shanghai and on counterfeiting of enemy notes (May 20, 1942)

Japanese troops won momentary gains in South Pacific. Rich resources (in areas) from our four northeastern provinces all the way to the Dutch

Indonesia colonies are in Japanese control, and economic potential of Japanese Empire is ever expanding. If its ferocity unchecked, trouble will be endless, and even more detrimental to us. I met with the President yesterday and discussed solutions. Two things could be done in our country:

1. Since Shanghai serves as financial hub for Japan, no destruction has been brought about there by Japanese. Even British and American technical personnel have not been harassed (by the enemy). The sustenance of industry and commerce in Shanghai largely depends on power companies owned by Americans. If we could destroy them, it would not only shake Japanese morale, but also damage their economic core. President strongly approved this idea and telegraphed General Lewis H. Bereton[1] to dispatch bomber contingent from India to strike at every opportunity. (Perhaps they need refueling in vicinity of Chengdu.)

2. Because of increasing appreciation of Japanese puppet regime's bank notes, we plan to forge them here and ship them back to China, giving them to guerrillas and passing them in enemy-occupied areas to disrupt Japanese finance. President endorsed this as well. I'll proceed right away using samples of puppet regime's bank notes provided by Bei Songsun. I hereby report to Your Excellency the above.

T. V.

320. Telegram draft to Chiang on need list of arsenal materials (May 20, 1942)

Observing developments with Japanese troops, I assume they are likely to take actions all over China in large scale. On one hand, all our ordnance plants should be running at full capacity. On the other hand, please notify me by telegraph the minimum items and quantities of urgently needed materials required from July onward so I can arrange airlifting.

---

[1] Then commander of US Tenth Air Force stationed in India.

T. V.

321. Telegram to Chiang on Japanese army activities and airplane aids to China (May 20, 1942)

Your Excellency must have received my telegram dated 19th. A large amount of aircrafts and weapons were recently shipped from US to India. Upon arrival in India, General Stilwell should discuss with General Wavell on plan to recover Burma in the wake of monsoon. Meanwhile, Your Excellency might dispatch officers to notify him about Japanese attempts in China including gathering vast number of aircrafts in Wuhan. In the meantime, Stilwell could instruct General Bereton to dispatch planes from India to bomb Hankow and other airports, and additional fighters to reinforce China. The number of arrived planes for General Chennault's AVG remains small. (We need to be more resourceful on) how to persuade US War Department to deliver more planes to us, since the Department always takes the excuse that Stilwell is in charge of dispatching freighter and fighter planes in India and China. I look forward to Your Excellency's reply.

T. V.

322. Telegram to Chiang on Pacific War Council meeting (May 27, 1942)

1. At today's Pacific War Council meeting, President read out telegram from sister Mey-ling (Madame Chiang Kai-shek) to Mr. Currie, reporting that three divisions had escaped from the siege in Burma, but large numbers of soldiers starved to death. President asked about the reason (of this tragedy). I explained that Fifth Army broke out along uninhabited route. According to Japanese broadcast, Japan captured only 420 prisoners during Burma battle. This proves our troops would rather die than surrender. President continued that Stilwell had requested last Friday that General Bereton's Tenth Air Force Division be turned over to his command. It shifted too hastily to consult with Britain. However, other air contingents will be dispatched

to India as reinforcements. President telegraphed Generalissimo yesterday about this. No question that future movement of Tenth Air Force directed by Stilwell will be under command of Generalissimo. Furthermore, losses of Tenth Division will soon be filled.

2. (Soviet Foreign Minister Vyacheslav) Molotov is expected to arrive around tomorrow evening.

3. Japanese navy has been built up, and is showing signs of attacking Alentian Island or Soviet Kamchatka.

4. Dutch ambassador said that Japan was reportedly selling rubber gum to Soviet Union.

5. According to report from Department of Navy, some ten Soviet ships transport grain from western US to Siberia every month. Given that they are not carrying weapons, they may have reached agreement with Japan.

T. V.

323. Telegram to Chiang on inviting Hopkins to visit China (May 27, 1942)

Hopkins is willing to visit China, and asked me to request that Your Excellency telegraph invitation to President. Following is draft invitation:

Burma was occupied by Japanese enemy. Enemy troops assaulted Yunnan and Zhejiang provinces, and are preparing to launch all-out land and air offensive in Jiangxi, Hunan and Henan provinces. War of resistance entered its most perilous stage, causing dire straits unprecedented in past five years. I have extremely important matters to discuss with Your Excellency face to face. If you are unable to come, would you please dispatch Mr. Hopkins to China to convey your views and get to know our problems?

If the above draft would work, I can address to President in person. According to previous records, in event of emergencies such as first-time military aid to Britain and American domestic opposition to assisting Russia after outbreak of Soviet-German War, President always dispatched Hopkins on these missions. Given current most critical stage of our resistance war, it is not enough to follow conventional track to achieve all-out US support for China.

This is why we extend this invitation. I beg Your Excellency to give me your instructions.

T. V.

324. Telegram to Chiang on purchase of DC-4 air freighters (May 28, 1942)

Yesterday's telegram must have reached you. When expressing gratitude to President for dispatching Tenth Air Force Division planes to China, could Your Excellency ask President to dispatch dual-engine planes from India to China? The past quantity of these planes was very limited. If he does not agree, Air Fortress planes could be used as air-freighters. US reportedly produced fifteen DC-4 four-engine air-freighters from June to September. We request permission to ship all these planes to meet urgent need in Sino-Indian freight. At same time please notify General Stilwell of this plan and ask him to telegraph his friends in War Department. The British, US Army and Air Force are all competing for these planes. However, because of extraordinary circumstances in China, these planes may be allocated to China.

T. V.

325. Telegram to Chiang on Soong's communication with Stilwell (May, 1942)

General Stilwell informed my representative in India yesterday that:

1. In order to effectively utilize Lend-Lease supplies in China, it is necessary to reorganize the army's logistic organizations and train Chinese troops to use modern weapons first.
2. Because of limitations on airlifting, priority should be given to bomber and fighter contingents.
3. It's a pity that Air Fortresses are used as air-freighters.
4. US bomber and fighter contingents received orders to join Chinese war.
5. Stilwell is opposed to British borrowing of planes supposed to be shipped to China, and also requested Department of War to offer

      fighters superior to P-43.

6. China and Britain should prepare for convergent attack on Burma in order to reopen transportation routes.

7. As to Your Excellency's request for a large air-freighter, he will dispatch one upon his arrival at Chongqing.

I telegraphed Stilwell that the US 3,500-ton monthly military supplies to China were light weapons such as mountain guns, much-needed 79-cartridge and ordnance materials. These are urgently needed, and yearned for by Your Excellency. Concerning airlifting, US is capable of expanding it by using four-engine bombers. It is surely a pity to use them as air-freighters, but track record of carrying capacity of dual-engine freighters was far from desirable. Moreover, with arrival of rain season in India, dual-engine planes would fail to take long-range flights during this period. To maintain morale of soldiers and civilian people, we can't do otherwise than using four-engine planes. As far as I know, this cost is not unaffordable for US.

T. V.

326. Telegram to Chiang on Korea issue discussion on Pacific War Council (May, 1942)

Today President Roosevelt was present at Pacific War Council meeting. The gathering was not precisely in form of a meeting. President explained system of Theatre division, as I reported to Your Excellency earlier. Preparations will be discussed next Tuesday:

A. Military plans of Australia and New Zealand in defending against Japan.

B. Korean issue. President asked me to come up with plans, for instance, for how to mobilize Koreans to disrupt Japanese, as well as organize volunteer army in three Northeastern provinces.

As regards to this matter, I would like to ask Your Excellency for instructions in the following matters:

1. Will Your Excellency endorse Korean independence by issuing declaration either by the Allied nations at the Pacific meeting or by Chinese and US governments respectively? Shall we publicize policy of carving up Japanese Empire before Soviet Union attends meeting and expresses its positions?

2. Do secret working groups in Korea have any practical power? Are they connected with Soviet Union? Your Excellency is willing to offer supervision from Chongqing to control Korea's revolutionary forces and to send agents to operate secretly in Korea.

3. US has agreed to offer weapons and funding to aid Korean revolution. How should we contain Japanese troops?

4. US also want to aid Northeastern Volunteer Army. How to proceed?

I look forward to your quick replies.

T. V.

327. Telegram to Chiang on negotiation with US regarding to airborne transportation (May, 1942)

Situation in Burma has worsened. I will discuss this with US and propose to charter four-engine planes flying directly from Allahabad to Xufu and Likiang (in Yunnan Province). Initial monthly capacity is 5,000 tons, then 7,500 tons since fourth month and 10,000 tons since sixth month. Please advise if you agree. I just spoke with China Defense Supplies Inc. teams. 3,000 tons are for cannons, artillery shells and bullets; 1,200 tons for aviation gasoline and parts; 300 tons for medical supplies; 200 tons for vehicle parts; and 300 tons for radio parts, etc. Materials for military production or gasoline are not included. Few are anyhow better than none.

In case the 100 dual-engine planes can still fly (long range), we will continue to use them. Their capacities are not included in the above forecast. Please manage to upgrade airports in Likiang and Xufu immediately so as to land four-engine planes, i. e. B-17 Flying fortresses. Please inform me of the status quo of the two airports.

Construction of airport for four-engine planes shall has a area size of 25 million square feet, with a runway of 4,000 feet long and 200 feet wide, plus facilities for night landing and taking off, oil depots and all other necessary facilities.

328. Telegram to Chiang on communication with UK and US regarding to war situation in Burma (May, 1942)

The main reason of military setback in Burma is failure of British to thoroughly cooperate with us. However, (1) we still need to use India as our base for air transport in postwar period, (2) British and Americans cannot be divided during wartime. Thus if we flatly blame Britain, we will lose US sympathy. My humble advice is Your Excellency dispatch confidential telegram to President Roosevelt and Prime Minister Churchill, pointing out directly mistakes in Burma campaign. Your wording may be solemn, but without anger. You may also on the ground of China's loss ask US and British governments to send huge number of airplanes to China Theatre, and ask for an immediate planning of Anglo-American-China joint counterattacking Burma after rain season to retake Rangoon and restore China's communications with outside world.

General Stilwell is arriving in India soon. Please ask President and Churchill to instruct him to discuss with General Wavell on the (counter-offensive) plan, then fly back to Chongqing for final decision.

T. V.

329. Telegram to Chiang on Stilwell's trip to Chongqing (May, 1942)

This afternoon I met with Air Force Chief of Staff, who agreed to try two-engine air-freighters for two weeks. If the results were unsatisfactory, four-engine planes should be dispatched.

General Stilwell will soon arrive in India. Your Excellency could invite him to Chongqing for detailed discussion about

1. monthly minimum tonnage of Sino-Indian airlifting and types of air-freighters;
2. fighter planes and bombers that we need; and
3. detailed plans for training Chinese troops in India and equipment of armaments, etc.

US Army Department always evades its responsibility with the excuse that Stilwell holds full authority or he has not made the request. For instance, every time airlifting is mentioned, they respond it is Stilwell's responsibility. Hereafter Stilwell ought to stay permanently by Your Excellency's side, rather than far away in India. Otherwise, it is impossible to carry out any plans.

Look forward to your judgment,

T. V.

330. Telegram to Chiang on Soong's meeting with Roosevelt (June 1, 1942)

I received your telegram dated May 30th. Today I met President with Your Excellency's telegram. He said he is eager to send someone to China. Yet Mr. Hopkins is chronically ill and cannot withstand long flight. Apart from him, anyone who is trusted by Generalissimo could be sent to China. Secretaries of Army and State are both aged. But either Vice President or Navy Secretary can go. I said Hopkins is President's most trusted friend. He is very forward-looking and must be able to carry out President's goodwill to China. Apart from him, it is hard to think of any other proper candidate who could perform such important duty.

Then President said (Soviet Foreign Minister) Molotov has come to US to discuss issues regarding assisting Soviet Union. President took the opportunity to tell him that: (1) China, US, Britain, and Russia should be responsible for world peace and disarming Germany, Japan, and Italy. (2) Small and weak nations should be able to be self-determined and independent. If some nations such as Vietnam and Burma are not ready for independence immediately, there should be collective trusteeship but not colonialism. Molotov agreed with President ardently. Your Excellency can announce this view at Your

Excellency's convenience so as to win Asian people's sympathy, since China is fighting not only for herself. (3) Japan's main fleet is heading north. Military engagement is not far ahead.

I met with Hopkins after meeting President. He said after major surgery he is very weak. However, it is not as bad as President described. Timing is urgent and important, so he cannot use his health as excuse. He would like to appeal to President in person (on his China trip). But he insisted on going with me. Your Excellency instructed me not to leave Washington D. C. and asked Ambassador Shizhi (Hu Shi) to accompany him. He said Shizhi was too idealistic, and he would rather sacrifice his health for resolving several important postwar issues between China and the US with Your Excellency. Moreover, round trip by chartered plane to China only takes three weeks. I told him that I'd love to accompany him but need to ask for instructions from Your Excellency. Hopkins is second most important person in the US. It took me long time to earn his trust after I came here. Over past six months we developed very good relationship. I can assist him if we can come to China together. Since War Department usually misunderstands China's views, and reports of American Military Mission in Chongqing often look down on our fighting ability, this time a politically important person may be able to change their opinions. Otherwise, it will be difficult to solve airlift issue properly.

T. V.

331. Telegram to Chiang on war reports unfavorable for China (June 2, 1942)

Since setback in Burma, US War Department received various reports stating that Chinese troops are incompetent and Chinese commanders are fighting in their own interest. General Magruder always holds an unfriendly attitude towards China. He is reported to have returned to US on sick leave without Stilwell's approval. He will surely give reports unfavorable to us. Belonging to pro-China faction within Department of War, General Stilwell is also reportedly discontent with China recently. Therefore Department is not as friendly to China as it was before. My earlier telegram dated May 19th which requested Your Excellency to discuss with Stilwell to decide some issues upon his return to Chongqing, as well as today's (proposal on) our overall demands for aircrafts and our proposal to US War Department for urgent airlift arrangements in my telegram dated 18th, Your Excellency please reply in details so I can discuss with War Department. Also, today I presented to War Department plan for urgent airlift of military equipments.

T. V.

332. Telegram to Chiang and K'ung on Soong's meeting with Morgenthau (June 2, 1942)

Secretary of Treasury Henry Morgenthau just met with me and said Sir Frederick Phillips[1] stated that Britain's new loans are limited to wartime only due to (limited) affordability, and hoped US would understand. Mr. Morgenthau replied that it is a matter between China and Britain and he has no comment. Sir Philip added that stabilization account entails 5. 5 million pounds sterling. Except for 2. 8 million pounds sterling deposited in (Sino-British) Stabilization Fund, balance is 2. 7 million pounds sterling that is not advised to make up from British new loans. He asked US authorities' opinion. Morgenthau turned to me, saying that given limitation of British loans to only wartime use, Chinese authorities of course would like to use them to make up balance of 2. 8 million pounds sterling. If British authorities do not agree, only alternative would be Sino-American Stabilization Fund. But I know little about this and request Your Excellency's further instructions. I look forward to Your Excellency's reply.

T. V.

---

1 Then serving as British Under Secretary of Finance.

333. Telegram to Chiang on US government's comment on China's war reports (June 3, 1942)

US Army, Navy, and Air Force authorities appeared to criticize Chinese military reports as unreliable. Navy Department ordered its subordinate agencies not to pay much attention to Chongqing's propaganda-style intelligence.

T. V.

334. Telegram to Chiang on press reports of enemy using poisonous gases (June 12, 1942)

D619

On June 9th our government spokesman in Chongqing claimed that Japanese had used poison gas for eight hundred times. People (here) generally believed this sort of information unreasonable. President Roosevelt has already given serious warning against (Japan using) poison gas. If Japanese use it again, we had better present solid evidence or have Allied military surgeons witness miserable victims. That would outrage Allied nations. If we take revenge actions, warning would lose deterrence power. Please instruct spokesmen of government agencies to be careful with any information on Japanese use of poison gas.

T. V.

[On original script, T. V. Soong added a note at the beginning: should we continue to provide reports of Japanese using poison gas and give out no evidence, our allies will not believe. — editor]

335. Telegram to Chiang to propose issues to discuss with Stilwell (June 12, 1942)

According to various sources, India-China airlift was limited to 500 tons a month in June, July, and August. I questioned chief of staff of US Air Force.

He shifted responsibility onto Stilwell. I pleaded to President. He also expressed that Stilwell is Your Excellency's Chief of Allied staff and under Your Excellency's commandership. My earlier telegrams on May 18th, 19th, 30th, June 2nd and 10th suggested Your Excellency discuss following points with Stilwell: first, plan of India-China airlift; second, plan for deploying US air forces in China; third, plan for deploying Chinese army troops in China and Burma and their military equipment. However, I have yet to be informed of result of such discussions between Your Excellency and General Stilwell.

Due to blockade of Burma Road, US authorities took back most of the over 100,000 tons of military equipment that was supposed to be delivered to China. It was agreed that at least 3,500 tons of military equipment should be urgently delivered every month. I gave you details in my earlier telegram on May 18th. However, if the India-China airlift remains as low as 500 tons a month, above-mentioned plan will be cancelled. I followed Your Excellency for two decades, and you must know my upright and frank personality. It is not my habit to shift my responsibilities to others or to be negligent in fulfilling my duties. Yet I could not but offend you once again by asking Your Excellency to let me know clearly your true attitude toward General Stilwell. Have you discussed with him points I raised in my previous telegrams? Are there any difficulties? It is the US government's position that no military aid to China would be possible unless General Stilwell confirmed it after consultation with Your Excellency. Thus I must know your true perceptions toward Stilwell and Stilwell's attitude toward us so I may watch and deal with related matters properly.

T. V.

336. Telegram from Chiang on proposals in next Pacific War Council meeting (June 14, 1942)

Please find below (our) proposal for next Pacific War Council meeting:

Germany is a country with superior land army. Britain and US plan to use their naval and air force advantage to defeat Germany. It may take strenuous effort but gain little. On the contrary, Japan's fighting capacity and country's lifeline lies in navy. With naval and air superiority, Britain and US should first destroy its weakest point while fighting on two fronts. This is unchangeable principle of military strategy. Now in Europe the war between Germany and Soviet Union is at stalemate, they are matched in strength. Since US and Britain's military status in Atlantic Ocean consolidated and it is too early to open second front in Europe, Britain and US, especially US, should take this opportunity to use their superior naval and air forces to defeat Japan and to end its ambition of speedy advancement in northeast Pacific, and consolidate US's west coast defense. Judging from Japan's movement on Midway Island and Aleutian Islands, it is clear that if US does not defeat Japan, Japan can always go on offense against US. Moreover, if Britain and US do not gain initiative, Japan will grow stronger, and US will be in weak position fighting in two oceans during whole war. If Japan advances in northeastern Pacific, US's west coast defense could be threatened. As US now is real pivot of whole anti-invasion camp, security and interests of all Allied nations rest on US security and interests. This is my true observation of overall situation rather than judging merely from China's interests. My opinion is that in overall strategic or political terms, Allies should give Japan's increasing expansion at sea a deadly blow with their full strength, and give up old concept that Japan won't be problem if Germany defeated, or that even if Japan were defeated, Germany could still reverse war situation. Recent military developments proved that such conception should be corrected, and it's necessary first to defeat Achilles' heel of the Axis, Japan, to remove seed of future trouble, and then focus on Germany. Otherwise, if Japan is allowed to grow stronger and abler to use its weaker military power to pin down our Allies' strongest, i. e. the United States, it will not only delay Germany's defeat but also mean that Allies will be trapped in situation of losing control on both sides, indefinitely delaying the war's conclusion. If in the end we have to use strategy of first defeating the weaker one and then dealing with stronger one, why don't we set it correct as early as possible?

Kai-shek

337. Telegram to K'ung and Chiang on termination of Stabilization Fund (June 16, 1942)

I have received your telegram on 12th stating that 1941 agreement of $50 million Stabilization Fund loan is not expected to be renewed. After carefully studying details, I find it still negotiable, and herewith present my views briefly in reply to your inquiry.

A. Stabilization Fund is derived from agreement among four British and Chinese banks[1]. At that time Shanghai's financial market was still important, and stabilizing exchange rate of *fabi* (Nationalist currency) was its goal. Sino-British (Four-Bank) Stabilization Fund was instrumental in sustaining Nationalist currency's credit. However, amount of fund was limited and unable to stabilize exchange rate. Upon my arrival in US, I immediately negotiated with US Treasury for Stabilization Fund loans. Hence in April of 1941, both Sino-British Stabilization Fund Agreement and Sino-American Stabilization Fund Agreement were signed.

B. It took five months for agreement of Sino-American Stabilization Fund loans to be signed since US President approved loans. During that time every detail was carefully discussed, and great pains were taken. In addition, US authorities raised side issues by insisting on disbursement in installments. Fortunately, the Generalissimo telegraphed me some guidelines that enabled me to overcome difficulties. You know all the process. Your earlier telegram states that (a) the US authorities can unilaterally end agreement at any time. This is because funds are part of US Stabilization Fund. When US Congress passed US Stabilization Fund bill with time limit, right of renewal was given to Congress. Therefore, legally US Treasury had to preset term of rescinding when signing agreement with us. (b) Agreement seems not to require that all our earned

---

[1] Refer to the <u>Agreement on Establishment of China National Currency Balance Fund</u> signed in London in March of 1939, which was entered into by Bank of China, Bank of Communications, Hong Kong and Shanghai Banking Corporation, and Standard Chartered Bank.

foreign exchange be submitted to Board of Stabilization for its use. (c) As to the point that decisions made by Stabilization Board should be approved by foreigners, this means that decisions of board need to be approved by more than four board members. Balancing exchange rates entails expertise and experience. We will benefit from technical assistance of US and British specialists.

C. After breakout of Pacific war, Shanghai and Hong Kong fell into Japanese hands and situation suddenly changed. Our external communication was blockaded and foreign trade almost suspended. There is no longer demand for foreign exchange, and value of *fabi* is not linked with foreign exchange. Balancing foreign exchange is no longer a top priority. This is the reason for no full drawdown on both Sino-American fund and Sino-British fund. However, postwar reconstruction will need massive foreign investment hence stable foreign exchanges are prerequisite for foreign government and individual investments in China. Moreover, current domestic prices are rising drastically. We need foreign assistance to stabilize currency after war. The existing Stabilization Board may assume important liaison duties.

D. At the moment I am negotiating with the US authorities about international stabilization fund. In the future, stabilizing foreign exchange among different countries can be assisted by an international organization. Whether Sino-American and Sino-British agreements should exist outside this organization is still uncertain. However, from international point of view, we are only one of many countries that need aid. The only country that really has spare money to help us with reconstruction is US. Our economy has entered into special relations with US through several loans. If we change current status on our own initiative, I am afraid it will be difficult to negotiate with US for continued aid after war.

E. I did my best to deal with US for years. I do not mind any criticism and praise put on me. This matter is related to the future of national economy, so I dare not keep silent. I believe you understand me well.

T. V.

338. Telegram to Chiang on Soong's meeting with Stimson regarding to Stilwell (June 16, 1942)

Your telegram dated June 15th was received. Stimson just dropped by to discuss Stilwell issue. I said it was indeed unprecedented that Generalissimo would allow General Stilwell to command Chinese Expeditionary Army. It was as difficult to conceive of as if US allowing a Russian General to command US Army. I also said as he mentioned to me earlier that, during World War I, someone proposed that American troops be incorporated with British army, a proposal that later almost brewed into huge misapprehension between two countries. Stimson hastily responded that Generalissimo made such resolute decision that US government ought to help China at any cost. He then said both he and US chief of general staff recognized Stilwell as top-ranking general and no one in US Army can match him. This is why he was designated as Generalissimo's chief of staff. Yet their admiration for Generalissimo and enthusiasm for helping China cannot be lumped together with their personal feelings toward Stilwell. If Generalissimo believes that Stilwell is inadequate, please just speak without reservation, and they will consider replacing him with other generals. There shouldn't be any problems. Stimson said when he read dispatches from Your Excellency and Madame Chiang, he felt although both treated Stilwell decently, their wording nevertheless revealed no sign of full trust in him. Stimson therefore asked me to pass on his concerns to Your Excellency and hoped you could respond to him in a straightforward and sincere way.

My thought is Your Excellency's painstaking effort to take overall situation into consideration is well known domestically and overseas. If General Stilwell is indeed not a suitable person to work with, it can be put straightforwardly right now. Given the case of General John Magruder, and other American officers, it could be the same old stuff with a different label. Your Excellency could express trust in Stilwell, and still not have to comply with him on every matter. By doing this, neither party will be hurt, and some leeway may be left in future. After all, Stimson already hinted at recalling

Stilwell, and top US officials from President Roosevelt downward have regarded him as Your Excellency's subordinate. You may command him as your subordinate and need not treat him as honorable guest. Nevertheless, you may try to make good use of Stilwell's standing to promote sufficient US military supply. My humble opinions are for your consideration.

T. V.

339. Telegram to Chiang on five issues including airplane needs (June 16, 1942)

Your telegram dated June 15th received. The followings are my personal opinions for your discussion with General Stilwell:

1. As US decided to maintain air force of 1,000 airplanes in Australia, China Theatre needs 500 airplanes urgently. This is by no means an exaggeration.
2. On Sino-India transportation, according to US capability, there is no question that within three months, monthly transport can reach 5,000 tons. But based on previous experience, if we set this goal for six months, it is highly unlikely to be met. I beg Your Excellency to instruct General Stilwell to telegraph US War Department immediately, urging it to meet first two goals we set within three months. It is also necessary to carefully evaluate monthly loss of fighters, pursuit planes and bombers for replenishment. Besides. The scheduled delivery of air-freighters shall also be reiterated. Please let me know as soon as this plan approved.
3. I just heard that War Department decided to reduce monthly emergent airlift of supplies to 400 tons from 3,500 tons starting in July on the ground that current air transport capability allows 400 tons per month only. I intend to negotiate forcefully and emphasize that it's US responsibility for such low capability. Remedial measure should be enhancing transport capacity instead of reducing minimum amount of ammunition we need. (Current situation is that) the supplies scheduled to be delivered in July will not arrive at Eastern India before September, or even October. Therefore airlift capacity should be increased monthly as

scheduled to meet the original plan. Your Excellency please instruct Stilwell to report this to US War Department too.

4. So far I have not sent telegrams to General Stilwell directly. I plan to contact him directly afterwards at emergencies. It seems that henceforth it would be more efficient and smoother having sister Mey-ling (Madame Chiang) as intermediary. But as to whether this is proper when dealing with Secretary of State, please give your instructions.

5. I had a long talk with Secretary of War, who was rather impressed by idea of sending American troops to India to help us recover Burma. He is aware that reopening of Burma is prerequisite for future counterattack. And it seems worthy in terms of dealing with British and Soviets after war. I beg Your Excellency to consider this and give me your response.

T. V.

340. Telegram to Chiang on Pacific War Council meeting (June 17, 1942)

President of the Philippines joined today's session of Pacific War Council. President Roosevelt said that, first, according to General Stilwell's report twin-engine transport planes started transportation between China and India without hitch. I said unfortunately result is not good up to now because for several months only five hundred tons has been transported. President surprised and ordered investigation and report of actual shipment tonnage immediately. It is clear that US officials' reports to their President are not truthful. I shall inquire again in next session. Second, Japanese increased troops in Northeastern China. President telegraphed Marshal Stalin that according to US intelligence there are signs that Japanese may attack Vladivostok or Kamchatka. Third, Soviet Union has been negotiating transportation route through Siberia. Fourth, Germany and Italy said that Britain and the US 's warning on poison gas means that they themselves are preparing to use it. Therefore we Allies should be careful about making announcements on enemy's using poison gas. I continued to say that Japanese did use poison gas in China. For example, in Burma when Chinese army division launched offensive, Japanese pretended to withdraw but applied arsenic gas and incurred Chinese troop losses. Fifth, US general staff said that, according to their evaluation, my proposal for bombing power plants in Shanghai is not as important as attacking arsenals in Japan. I replied that bombing Shanghai has two significances: (1) airplanes could use Chengdu airport as their base for Shanghai target, while Japanese target is difficult to reach because Quzhou airport (in Zhejiang province) has fallen into Japanese hands; (2) Shanghai is economic center and logistic headquarters of Japanese invasion. Shaking Shanghai would be enough to influence Japan's finance situation. In conclusion, this matter is supposed to be referred to Your Excellency for evaluation and for instruction to Stilwell to execute it.

T. V.

341. Telegram to Chiang on UK dispatching Air Forces troops to China (June 18, 1942)

Head of Asian Affairs Department of British Foreign Ministry told me that misunderstanding between Britain and China is warrisome. I told him that this issue cannot be solved by empty words and British authorities had better dispatch bombers to China to join war. I also telegraphed Ambassador Shaochuan[1] asking him to indicate this to British Foreign Secretary Anthony Eden. Soon after that, Shaochuan telegraphed me that British government decided to dispatch a group of bombers to join war. Though number of bombers is small, this is first time British government has dispatched air force to China. I hope Your Excellency may express welcome.

T. V.

342. Telegram to Chiang to request for intelligence regarding to Japanese invasion into Siberia (June 19, 1942)

US War Department inquired whether we have reliable information on

---

[1] Shaochuan, i. e., Wellington V. K. Koo, then Chinese Ambassador to UK.

Japan's intention to attack Siberia.

T. V.

343. Telegram to Chiang on China's request to up-scale airborne transportation (June 20, 1942)

1. I just received information from US War Department. When department was considering dispatching aircrafts Your Excellency requested, i. e. fifteen four-engine transport planes plus another ten converted from Air Fortresses, they received reports from their officers stationed in Chongqing that only seventeen twin-engine transports can be effectively used. Therefore they decided to dispatch seventeen twin-engine transporters to China on July 1st. I think this decision does not conform to your instructions. This may result from lack of communication and coordination. Your Excellency confirmed with Stilwell that monthly tonnage of airlift is raised to five thousand tons. Why US side received above-mentioned report? Please ask Stilwell directly for the truth.

2. Your Excellency agreed with General Stilwell that monthly tonnage of airlift should be maintained at five thousand tons, and that five hundred fighters should be sent to front line. However, War Department said such report from Stilwell has yet to be received.

3. Upon receipt of your telegram I learned that only five bombers of General Lewis Brereton's US Tenth Air Force Division arrived in China, but President ordered all of them dispatched to China a month ago.

Above three issues show a lack of communication between US Military Mission in China and our side. I'm anxious about how to improve this situation. Please give orders to handle this as soon as possible. I look forward to your further instructions.

T. V.

344. Telegram to Chiang and Mme. Chiang on Soong's meeting with Currie regarding to US air force aids to China (June 22, 1942)

After yesterday's Pacific War Council, newspaper reporters asked for results. Many participants gave optimistic responses. I provided a different view, and explicitly told them that I requested aid of British and US air forces. Asked whether we were satisfied, I replied this was military secret and therefore I had no comment. Since my words carried an implication, President summoned Mr. Currie last evening and ordered him to go to China to explain. Currie visited me and I told him that his trip was unnecessary, because what China urgently needs is real assistance. As to explaining US 's difficult situation, he and I have worked hard for more than a year. Words alone are useless, and traveling would prove futile. As to issue of air force, first, twenty-four air fortresses supposed to fly to China with Huang Bingheng were diverted to Mediterranean at Britain's request. Second, sixty-two light bombers agreed to be dispatched to China eight months ago were reduced to thirty-two because of Pearl Harbor (Incident). Now they were dispatched to Mediterranean instead. Third, seventeen twin-engine transport planes designated for air transport over Hump were also sent to Mediterranean. Fourth, Generalissimo summoned General Brereton upon his arrival in Chongqing but he refused to meet on ground of not having Stilwell's order. It seemed an excuse for evading. There are signs that US authorities intend to divert US Tenth Air Force Division to Mediterranean. As fact is any explanation will be useless. Fifth, for the good of Sino-American relations, President should give me certain plan for assisting China with air force. Then we can discuss Currie's visit to China. I asked him to relay my opinions to President.

I also asked sister May-ling in my English telegram to her today to request Your Excellency discuss with Stilwell and confirm plan for air force support and India-China air transportation over Hump, and approve it for immediate implementation. Then I can push here for putting it into execution. President treats me like family member, keeps no secrets in conversation, and addresses me by my first name. This shows his intimate relations with me. However, as our country is in critical situation, there should be no room for inaction caused by private feelings. Also, please ask sister May-ling not to communicate with Currie by telegraph to avoid being taken advantage of by the other side and hinder my urgent work here. For our country's interest, I must be authorized to be in charge of negotiating everything. If our side can act coordinately and make right judgment according to priority, we might get real results. I look forward to your instructions on how to deal with this matter.

T. V.

P. S. If the US government telegraphs you inquiring on Mr. Currie visit, please ask them to discuss it with me here in Washington D. C.

345. Telegram to Chiang on Pacific War Council meeting (June 25, 1942)

President said at today's session of Pacific War Council that Japan lost five of its twelve aircraft carriers. This shows that strength of its air force is gradually diminishing. The battle in Aleutian Islands has had no significant effect. Then he asked British Prime Minister Churchill to express his view. Mr. Churchill said that war situation in Pacific has improved since his last visit to Washington. After Singapore fell into Japanese hands, Japanese naval forces and five aircraft carriers attacked Ceylon but were repelled. US naval forces won battles in Coral Island and Midway Island and greatly frustrated Japanese momentum. Britain increased troops in India by several divisions. Major British naval forces were supposed to gather in Ceylon in July but were delayed for two months because of other deployment, and to be completed by September. This won't affect retaking Burma and assisting China because monsoon prevents fighting in India. Sir Wavell was appointed as British commander-in-chief in retaking Burma and Sir Harold Alexander[1] as commanding general. Churchill said he and President will never forget to help China. Jan Christiaan Smuts of South Africa also expressed concerns over China. Churchill read out Mr. Smuts's telegram, which pays attention to China's war and her important postwar role.

1 Then serving as British commander-in-chief in Burma.

Churchill continued that Japan moved four more divisions of troops from Japan to Northeastern China, totaling twenty-five divisions there. Indications show that Japan is going to attack Russia. Russia does not want to see this happen. But if it does, Japan will have one more rival in the Pacific. President inquired about war situation in China. I gave a briefing and expressed our wish to have more US and British air force support and air transportation. President said aircraft production in US and Britain has increased thus something can be done. After conference I stayed at White House for dinner. According to various sources, (1) Britain and US concluded that at the moment they are unable to open second front; (2) after dinner Soviet Ambassador was summoned to discuss maintaining military strength in Near East; (3) Churchill is leaving Washington D. C. very soon.

T. V.

346. Telegram to Chiang on purchase of air freighters (June, 1942)

Under the Lend-Lease framework, (we have) 260 pursuit planes shipped or to be shipped, 33 light bombers to be shipped to India and 150 pursuit planes that General Stilwell demanded (resupplied with 50 every month). If all above are shipped to China, we would need roughly 3,500 tons of fuel, ammunition, and other equipment every month, or 21,000 tons from May to October of this year. I am negotiating with the War Department to lease fifty B-24D bombers, and convert them into transport planes to ship above supplies to China via India to meet urgent needs. Details will follow. The above is just for Your Excellency's information.

T. V.

347. Telegram to Chiang on Stilwell issue (June, 1942)

Your Excellency's earlier telegrams dated 12th and 13th represent our consistent position. I have explained it to President Roosevelt orally. His view is that US and Britain's opening of second front in Europe is not only to defeat Germany. Last winter Germany lost more than three million soldiers in its war against Russia. This summer Germany will attack southern Russia with its full strength. Situation in Russia is critical. If Russian army defeated, then overall situation would be shaken. This is why Britain and US have agreed to open second front to save Soviet Union. This plan is already set and hasn't changed. My humble judgment is that, apart from fighting Japanese around Aleutian Islands and weakening Japanese naval forces, US does not intend to launch large-scale offensive. In September this year, number of US carriers could increase, and take dominant position by next spring. Japanese naval forces tend to fight a quick battle to force quick decision, whereas US goes the contrary. Yesterday I met Soviet ambassador (to the US) and asked him about situation in Turkey. He said if Sevastopol[1] falls, Turkey would turn to Germany. This shows his pessimistic view about war. My humble opinion is that we cannot expect US and Britain would launch offensive against Japan within this year. If we try to persuade them to do so, such attempts would be difficult and yield nothing. We should do our best in following work: (1) Conducting air transportation over Hump; (2) urging US air forces to send more divisions to China to join war; (3) according to General Stilwell's request, urging US to send two or three divisions of army troops to India to help us to retake Burma in order to make ground transportation easier. For achieving these goals please be patient with General Stilwell to avoid any delay.

T. V.

348. Telegram to Chiang on Soong's meetings with Stimson and with British ambassador (July 1, 1942)

1. I met Stimson today. He informed me that because of precarious situation in Egypt, warplanes originally supposed to be allotted to China have been transferred to Egypt as reinforcement. For fear of causing

---

[1] Sevastopol is a Russian port and naval base.

misunderstandings, he specifically tried to comfort me, and said that Generalissimo may have already made comments to General Stilwell. I replied that this must be temporary measure. Generalissimo just asked Stilwell to convey immediately China's three urgently needed requests which we hope be satisfied. Stimson said he has received Stilwell's telegram, and will discuss it in detail with Crabbe upon his arrival in US He implied that Britain and US will soon take big steps against Japanese that might relieve Japan pressure on China. He also said that Marshal Erwin Rommel's attack on Egypt led to concentration of British navy in Ceylon. Yet he didn't go into detail.

2. I met British ambassador who will return to Britain within days. I showed him Mr. Gandhi's letter and words from British ambassador in Chongqing to Your Excellency. I stressed this matter is Britain's internal affair and Your Excellency does not want to interfere. Yet arrest of Gandhi not only cause internal dispute in India, but will definitely influence American public opinion on Britain. It should be cautiously dealt with. While I repeatedly stated what's at stake in this issue, ambassador said that it might be fruitless at this moment to hold any negotiations between British and Gandhi. He asked whether Generalissimo could give advice so he might suggest some solutions to Churchill after his returning to Britain. He will keep me posted about the possible solutions. I think it might be best chance for offering our mediation. I beg Your Excellency to consider this.

3. Sources from State Department said that Japanese would attack Siberia within hours. My opinion is that British defeat in Mediterranean and Japanese attack on Soviet Russia would prompt the British and US to take drastic actions against Japanese and would benefit us.

T. V.

349. Telegram to Chiang on management of military procurement affairs in US (July 1, 1942)

US War Department telegraphed its military attaché in Chongqing to inquire General Yu Dawei what sort of munitions we need most urgently. General Yu replied that rifles are most urgent item, with machine guns the next, followed by mortars. War Department thought this statement is different from that of General Jiang Biao, our military commissioner stationed in Washington. General Yu might have made random statement without deliberation. Yet his words were taken seriously and briefed. Concerning such specific issues as ammunition, our government organs have commissioners stationed in the US. I beg Your Excellency to instruct all bodies concerned that in case of foreign inquiries they should let their commissioners answer to avoid any unnecessary discrepancies.

T. V.

350. Telegram to Chiang on Roosevelt's stance on India issue (July 5, 1942)

White House chief of staff just dropped by and passed on President's message about Mr. Gandhi's statement that not only would India expel British imperialists but also would not want to let American imperialists invade India. President is not clear what this means, and said this gentleman is not pragmatic although we are collaborating with him. He hopes Your Excellency will take every opportunity to advise Gandhi on behalf of President not to go to extremes in order to avoid being exploited by Japanese and harming hundreds of millions of Chinese and Indian people. I presume that President's intentions are:

1. He does not want to push British Prime Minister Churchill when situation in Near East is critical. However President still asked Mr. Frankfurter to meet British ambassador to grasp British authorities' intent.

2. In short term, India truly has too many things to take care of at the same time. If Gandhi's wish is fulfilled, those Muslims who serve in Indian army will be disappointed. It is also possible that most influential Islamic powers in Near East would become involved. Therefore President has to find pretext to procrastinate.

T. V.

351. Telegram to Chiang for Chiang's decision on Stilwell (July 6, 1942)

I received your telegram dated July 5th. General Stilwell's attitude is bizarre. His letter resorted to sophistry, and misinterpreted his authority. If not insane, he would not be so arrogant. I will soon call on US authorities in hope that they will correct him. But I am eager to know whether Your Excellency still wants to keep Stilwell's post in China after redefining authority of chief of staff or will take this opportunity to replace him. Please give clear instructions then I can act accordingly. Stilwell's attitude toward us has long been my concern. If we had found out earlier, perhaps US would not have procrastinated about aid for us. When guests are treated too well, they lose loyalty to us. It is clear that people like Stilwell are not grateful. This incident also revealed that the Foreign Affairs Department did not perform its (of the Military Committee) duty well, being unable to help Your Excellency. Reorganization seems necessary. This is my humble opinion for your consideration. Look forward to your reply.

T. V.

352. Telegram to Chiang on US government sending investigation personnel to India (July 16, 1942)

Dear brother Kai-shek,

Regarding transportation of Lend-Lease supplies from India to China, several months ago an American Shaugnessy was sent to India to investigate. Extremely unsatisfied with careless and perfunctory attitude of War Department, this American repeatedly telegraphed me providing true information for negotiations with the Department. I urged him to go to Chongqing to report everything. This gentleman is loyal to us and is familiar with situation and relations among General Stilwell, George H. Brett[1], and other British and US officials in India. I have asked him to report Your

---

[1] Then serving as a US senior military representative to China.

Excellency all the truth if he could be summoned for an interview... (the original script does not end here)

T. V.

353. Telegram to Chiang on US sending sanitary experts to the Burma Road (July 17, 1942)

During construction of Vietnam-Yunnan Railway, more than 50,000 workers died of malaria. Now malaria is more serious in area along Burma Road. An estimated 250,000 workers could catch it. Thus I requested US Public Health Service (PHS) to take responsibility for controlling malaria and preventing epidemics. PHS planned to send 15 specialists to control the epidemic for two years. Their salary, roughly $100,000, medications and supplies are advised to be paid by Lend-Lease aid. But large numbers of Chinese doctors, nurses, and other personncl are needed as well, and this entails Chinese currency equivalent to 150,000 US dollars on our side for their discretion. In my humble opinion, PHS agrees to take responsibility with foreseeable results and preferable terms, it might work out. I look forward to Your Excellency's decision on this matter.

T. V.

354. Telegram to Chiang on plan to recover Zhejiang and Jiangxi provinces (July 19, 1942)

President received frequently British and American reports that Japanese enemy has not yet employed large number of troops to attack China and all battles happening are no more than large-scale guerrilla warfare. Therefore China is not in danger and does not need too much attention. Moreover, already having fought for five years, China could still stand for another one or two years (under existing conditions). To correct this view, I repeatedly explained that after the Pearl Harbor incident, Shanghai, Hong Kong and Burma fell into Japanese hands one after another. China's international communications have been cut off and armaments are exhausting. Puppet government prohibited use of our *fabi* (Nationalist currency) in occupied area and economically blocked our administrated zones, which has caused rising prices and inflation. After seizing Zhejiang-Jiangxi Railway recently, Japanese occupied the important rice production area around the Buoyang Lake. Supplies from coastal areas, especially salt, were cut off. In the past, Changsha was only threatened by enemy from Yuezhou, but now is under attack from east that threatens food production area of Dongting Lake. Japanese also increased troops in Guangzhou and Vietnam so as to attack Yunnan from three directions. I have also asked Crabbe to help explain. I'm afraid US authorities always believed that China could endure warfare. Therefore, we need to explain with facts. Since this passive persuasion may not convince US authorities to support China, we must actively indicate the immensity of the stake. Now it seems that Soviet troops may collapse. Then American public would be discontented with their government, and congressional election is in sight. For the sake of US government, the only choice is frequent large-scale bombing of Japan that would earn American people's trust. Although our air bases in Zhejiang and Jiangxi provinces are now occupied by Japanese, it would not be difficult for our troops to retake them if US authorities meet Your Excellency's three demands. We should also show plan for retaking Zhejiang-Jiangxi Railway and air bases to reinforce US determination to assist us. If Your Excellency agrees, please tell Currie the plan for retaking military positions in Zhejiang and Jiangxi. I look forward to your further instructions on how to deal with this matter.

T. V.

355. Telegram to Chiang on Pacific War Council meeting (July 22, 1942)

At yesterday's session of Pacific War Council,

1) I stated China's military and economic difficulties according to Your Excellency's earlier telegram dated July 19th. I also produced a map to show how Japanese blockaded our external communications, emphasized that

munitions will soon be exhausted unless supplies arrive from India. How could China fight against aggression in these circumstances? Many conference participants were moved.

2) President said last month thirty of thirty-five transport vessels sailing to Murmansk were sunk. However, Soviet ambassador to the US, with Stalin's instruction, still asked US to ship armaments there. President had no alternative but to reply that, if without using Murmansk Soviet Union would not be able to sustain war, President would have to take this great risk, but Stalin should bear responsibility (of making that judgement). President also said that Soviet ambassador is very pessimistic about war and he does not know ambassador's intention. After Conference session I visited Soviet ambassador. According to him, as north-south railway line severed, Soviet Russia's battle line has in fact been cut in two. Although Russia will still fight to death but she already has lost strength. Opening of second front may become an illusion. There is no need for Japanese to attack India. They will soon attack Siberia.

3) A friend in War Department secretly told me that Russian army would collapse. Then US will make most important decision soon. Future strategy may be one of the following three options: (a) attacking Germany through France with full strength; (b) attacking Japan with full strength; (c) employing part of forces to support India and China; and another part, an estimated ten divisions, to retake French North Africa and attack Rommel's troops, capturing whole Mediterranean coast and restoring sea lanes in Mediterranean. I told him that it's too late to land on French coast to reinforce Soviet Russia, and it's extremely dangerous fighting on the edge of coastline against powerful enemy troops. If operation fails then we will lose the war. Plan (c) will dissipate military strength and may fail on both sides. Under such circumstances, only plan (b) is workable. If we follow Generalissimo's plan to consolidate Chinese, British, US and Russian forces to attack Japan, we will win within a year. Then we can rally all powers outside European continent to attack Germany. Although Germany is powerful now, it is only a question of time before it collapses. For Allies, this is a completely safe plan.

I look forward to Your Excellency's comments on above idea.

T. V.

356. Telegram to Chiang on US clarification on Stilwell's responsibilities (July 23, 1942)

With regards to Stilwell issue, US War Department conveyed President's remarks that, as chief of staff of the China Theatre, General Stilwell should defer to Your Excellency. Yet as US representative of Lend-Lease Act in Chongqing and at international military conferences, he also should defer to the US government. If Your Excellency feels this inconvenient, General Stilwell's functions could be split and given to two persons: first, chief of staff, second, US representative in China. However, since President Roosevelt believes Stilwell friendly toward Your Excellency and China, and familiar with Chinese affairs, he very much hopes that Your Excellency will continue to allow General Stilwell to work in China.

Feeling that the tone of above explanation obviously favored General Stilwell, I later went to visit him and explained in detail the inappropriate wording in Stilwell's letter. President said that Stilwell's position as US representative in international military conferences is nominal, since there are actually no such conferences. Regarding Lend-Lease affairs, President said I (T. V.), representing Your Excellency and Hopkins, representing President could henceforth resolve all problems in Washington D. C. As these two functions are clear-cut, Stilwell could actually act only as chief of staff. If Generalissimo still thinks Stilwell inadequate, he will replace him. Yet because of scarcity of qualified and capable officers like Stilwell in US, it's difficult to find appropriate replacement. I promised to convey his remarks to Your Excellency, and asked President to instruct his chief of general staff and Hopkins to discuss with me upon their return to US the three proposals made by Your Excellency, and reply to Your Excellency. I also said since Vice-Admiral Crabbe is here, he could offer some advices for consideration. President agreed.

I hereby report the above and look forward to Your Excellency's instructions.

T. V.

357. Telegram to Chiang on Burma Road transportation (July 29, 1942)

I found out that our Directorate of Military Ordnance stockpiled many materials in Rangoon. Average monthly tonnage of transportation from Lashio to Kunming is between four to five hundred tons. Materials in Rangoon are for making ammunition, which are urgently needed at front. After seizure of Vietnam by Japanese, Burma Road is under threat. I earnestly request Your Excellency to order the Administration Bureau to ship inland as soon as possible. They should use at least 50 percent of total tonnage to deliver military materials.

I look forward to Your Excellency's decision.

T. V.

358. Telegram to Chiang to propose communication with Currie regarding to Stilwell issue (July 30, 1942)

Assistant Secretary of War John J. McCloy secretly told me that US general staff is discussing whether to agree to Your Excellency's demand for 500 fighter planes. He is surprised that they are inclined to agree and asks us not to disclose any information about it. Moreover, friend in Department of War also secretly told me that since Your Excellency expressed your discontent with Stilwell to President, general staff has no choice but to pay more attention to meet China's demand for aid. Your Excellency may want to take the opportunity of Currie's stay in Chongqing, to tell him honestly the facts about our discontent with Stilwell, because Stilwell is going to India with Currie, and may tell Currie his one-sided story.

T. V.

359. Telegram to Chiang on British proposal on India issue (July, 1942)

Your Excellency must have received my earlier telegram. British ambassador (to the US) left for London. His proposal on India is based on memorandum of Justice Frankfurter, Supreme Court judge. Mr. Frankfurter is a close friend of President. Content of proposal is what President has told me about many times. President read Gandhi's letter to Your Excellency and British ambassador to Chongqing told Your Excellency that it is better the proposal is not presented directly by President to Churchill. This is why he asked Mr. Frankfurter to address the issue. Summary of memorandum is as follows:

1. If Mr. Gandhi recklessly takes any action and Britain is forced to detain him, US authorities will resume their previous unsympathetic attitude toward Britain's Indian policy, even though Sir Stafford Cripps made successful negotiation in India and US public opinion on Britain improved.

2. For sake of British interest, it is better to involve US in Indian issue. If India's attitude becomes unreasonable, it is expected that US will understand difficulty of dealing with this problem.

3. Leaders of Allies, led by the US and Britain, maybe with China, should adopt following principles:

   a. Indian issue is an Allies' issue.

   b. India should be independent.

   c. World peace entails unified, integrated India.

4. Thus Britain could state that it is Indian policy just like US 's Philippines policy. This is to show world that British imperial system is good at adapting to changes, not like decayed Austro-Hungarian Empire during World War I which went against global trend.

5. Therefore, we suggest British Prime Minister Churchill announce following points on behalf of the Allies, especially Britain, US and China:

   a. The goal is to seek India's independence and territorial integrity.

   b. The date for India's autonomy should be decided. This date should be in near future and must not be changed.

   c. Allies will guarantee plan and date of autonomy. With this responsibility the Allies will have right to be consulted and making comments.

   d. Before autonomy, India should draw up its constitution defining limits of authority of central, provincial, and regional governments. Constitution should suit India's conditions and does not have to follow model of US 's or other countries' constitutions. But national defense and foreign affairs should be at discretion of central government.

e. If Indian political parties cannot complete a constitution by designated date of autonomy, every province or region is entitled to proclaim autonomy unconditionally.

f. If India cannot conduct its foreign relations independently, Allied countries, especially Britain and US, will assume this responsibility.

Should above terms be accepted, British-US relationship would be much closer.

British ambassador to the US and Mr. Frankfurter showed me above memorandum as courtesy, and requested me to forward to Your Excellency and keep off record. Please don't mention it to Indians either.

T. V.

360. Telegram to Chiang and Zhou Zhirou on delivery of US airplane to China (August 10, 1942)

1. A friend in US War Department privately informed me that as US Air Force gained excellent results in China Theatre, Department is considering sending more air troops to China. We Chinese Air Force using P-43 airplanes should achieve comparable results in military operations so as to make it possible for us to make more requests to US. According to War Department, currently 82 P-43 airplanes have already been assembled. Among them, 67 planes were taken over by us.

2. Yet according to our own report, only 29 P-43 airplanes arrived in China, among them 12 already damaged. Those P-43 airplanes deployed in India were returned to US because they are not suitable for our pilots. Moreover, their engines were disassembled for C-53 airplanes' use.

3. War Department will report that 65 P-66 airplanes have reached India. But our report indicates that we only received 9 P-66 and all deployed in

Karachi. Please pay attention to such huge discrepancies between two reports.

4. Original confidential plan for US air force in China and supplies for Chinese Air Force is as follows:

a. 150 P-40 airplanes, with additional 32 planes every month.

b. 32 light bombers.

c. 48 heavy bombers to be divided into four units, 12 bombers for each unit, 9 of them in operation in frontline and 3 as backup.

d. To supply Chinese Air Force with 100 pursuit planes in forefront, 50 back-up planes including P-43 and P-66 models, and 33 A-29 light bombers.

5. My friend privately informed me as expression of goodwill that A-29 bomber is more difficult to operate than P-43. It is an old model, and less effective compared with newly arrived B-25 bomber. So far 4 A-29 bombers already crashed on their way to China, causing 12 casualties. He advised that upon arrival in China A-29 bombers are better be allotted to General Chennault's unit for American pilots to operate. They have already flown these bombers to China and thus are familiar with them. If Chinese pilots make any mistake in operation, US may use this as excuse to reject further requests for more planes. Whether such advice is feasible, I beg Your Excellency to make final decision. But please don't let American Military Mission in China know about this. Moreover, if we can come up with an excuse to give up A-29 and request B-25 instead, there might be more effective results.

T. V.

361. Telegram to Chiang and Zhou Zhirou on A-29 bombers (August 11, 1942)

1. Please inform Director Zhou Zhirou of this message conveyed secretly by friend of War Department, that A-29 light bomber is quite old and more difficult to operate than P-43. Moreover, 4 A-29 bombers crashed on their way to China, and 12 pilots killed. He secretly advised that upon arrival in China, it is better to use excuse to transfer these planes to General Chennault's unit and let American pilots who had operated these planes on

way to China fly them. Also we should request B-25 as substitute. Once our pilots make mistakes, US may have excuse to decline our request for more planes. A-29 is first bomber ever to be allotted to us, and we waited for two years. It's unclear if we can wait any longer. Yet friend's advice is sincere. Please take it into consideration.

2. Most P-66 and P-43 allotted to us are reportedly unworkable. Please inform me of the detailed reasons, then I can negotiate with US.

T. V.

362. Telegram to Chiang on Roosevelt's talk regarding to India issue (August 13, 1942)

I believe President's reply in English must have reached Your Excellency. In yesterday's Pacific War Council session, President said, "I communicated with Generalissimo frequently over India issue, and learned our ultimate goal is the same, that is, India should become autonomous. I always pay attention to timing. Gradual unification of federal states of America, and 40 years' preparation in the Philippines autonomy are precedents. British are our ally, and if US and China are invited to offer mediation, we should fulfill our responsibility (as Britain's allies). Otherwise, it would be inappropriate for us to do so. Therefore, my suggestion is to keep quiet for the time being." His wording implied that it is better for US and China not to openly express their viewpoints to British. President is taking wait-and-see attitude because he was informed by British that India issue will be settled soon. My opinion is that, if British cannot effectively check Gandhi's movement within two or three weeks, American public opinion will change. By that time, I will choose opportune timing to sincerely express to President our viewpoint based on Your Excellency's instructions. Then it will be more effective. I beg for Your Excellency's final decision.

T. V.

363. Telegram to Chiang to request for intelligence of enemy activities (August 18, 1942)

1. British shipment of large quantities of ammunition and warplanes to Malta, escorted by their main fleets, has been bombarded incessantly by German air force, causing heavy losses to British navy and was forced back. As a result, eastern Mediterranean is controlled by Germans.

2. Meanwhile, two German divisions reached Egypt as reinforcement. Marshal Erwin Rommel will keep on offensive, and general opinion here is rather pessimistic, believing that Suez Canal will be captured soon.

3. Japanese enemy seems to have suspended their plan of attacking Siberia. Yet there is no sign they will attack India. Recently, US Air Force has been quite active in China. Seeing that China might be final base for counterattacking them, Japanese enemy might concentrate their forces to press us (in near future). Your Excellency may not have such information. Please give your instructions as soon as possible so that I can prompt US to reinforce our air force.

T. V.

364. Telegram to Chiang on memorandum draft to Currie (August 20, 1942)

Your Excellency's telegrams dated August 12th and 14th acknowledged. Since fall of Burma in May, given difficulties in air transport, I persistently requested air transport of 5,000 tons per month, 500 fighter planes and 3,500 tons of urgently needed ammunition per month. Apart from this we don't have any extravagant claims. Nor is there any estrangement between US War Department and us. It seems we might disregard Lauchlin Currie's claim that there might be misunderstanding. US Chief of General Staff complained to me that everyday there are quarrels between War Department and authorities of British, Soviets, Australia, Netherlands, and South American nations. It is a commonplace that each country acts in its own interests, and all those quarrels are forgiven afterwards. Now since US hoped that henceforth requests for supplies should first be negotiated between our Ministry of Military Affairs and American Military Mission to China, and then War Department and I should be informed for further execution, we might follow suit in order to reach the goal. Your Excellency has negotiated with Currie for some days, and there must be lot of details. For reaching consensus, I drafted memorandum for Your Excellency based on your telegrams dated 12th and 14th. Please let me know as soon as possible Your Excellency's opinion. The memorandum reads:

To notify Chinese Military Ministry and China Defense Supplies Inc. of our conversations in Chongqing during these days, I have prepared following memorandum for your reference:

1. *Given difficult circumstance of current air transport between China and India, it has been decided that the most urgent task is to transport 5,000 tons of ammunition per month and 500 planes for air force frontline.*
2. *3,500 tons of urgent ammunition per month should be transported as usual without suspension.*
3. *After Lend-Lease goods reach India, US should take charge of stockpile and copy stock records to us. These goods should not be appropriated by other organizations without consent of Generalissimo. These goods can be employed for needs of Chinese troops in India only on notification by Generalissimo or his representative in India.*
4. *Americans should take charge of these Lend-Lease goods on China's behalf. Yet air transport between China and India should be managed according to priority and ratio given by Chinese Transportation Administration Bureau.*
5. *Above points are interim plan during period of difficult transportation, and should be amended once transportation improved.*

If Your Excellency regards above memorandum appropriate, please modify as needed and let me send it to Mr. Currie on Your Excellency's behalf.

Please inspect it and give me your instructions.

T. V.

365. Telegram to Chiang on issues regarding to Thailand (August 29, 1942)

Your Excellency's previous telegram acknowledged. I talked with Thai minister to the US. According to him, currently funds Thai government deposited in the US amount to about 10 million dollars, and 3 million dollars cash. US government tenders special permission to draw the money to support Free Thailand movement. Young Thai emperor and his mother are still in Switzerland, where they are besieged by Axis powers, and there is no way for them to escape even if they wish to. The abdicated empress is now in Britain. Since Thai people do not support her, it is not easy to establish her as legitimate government émigré to appeal to people. For the time being, center of Free Thailand movement is in Thai embassy in US. Now there are 40 Thai students receiving military training in US. Among them, 5 will be sent to China, Burma and other places for clandestine operations. It is said that this mission is conducted by US military intelligence in connection with General Stilwell. Thai Minister also said that its funds now deposited in Britain roughly amount to 50 million pounds, but are still frozen by British authorities. Thais in England used to be regarded as Japanese enemy's puppet, but now Thai people in Britain are allowed to be enrolled in British army. About a month ago, Thai minister managed to send an envoy to visit Britain with British support. Currently Minister is planning to appoint a Free Thai representative to be stationed in China to cooperate with us and to promote anti-Japanese movement launched by Thai refugees on Yunnan-Assam border. This requires permission from our government, I beg Your Excellency to give me your instructions.

T. V.

366. Telegram to Chiang on India-China airborne transportation (August, 1942)

Following are messages from US War Department regarding to the air transport between China and India:

1. US War Department proposes to complete plan of having 100 freighters for Sino-Indian air transport within shortest period of time. Among them 75 freighters belong to Transport Unit of War Department, and 25 are

under China National Aviation Corporation.

2. General Stilwell intended to sign contract with China National Aviation Corporation, according to which transport fee will be based on costs. But this contract should be approved by Your Excellency, and priority of China National Aviation Corporation's transportation will be decided by Your Excellency as well. General Stilwell also said Your Excellency has approved in principle.

3. According to reports of pilots of US Transport Unit, in China-India air route, it's difficult to operate whenever load of each flight exceeds one ton, and two tons at most. I told them that recently, when testing the line between Sookerating and Kunming, our pilot Xin Keye used to load 3. 5 tons of goods, excluding petroleum used for round trip.

T. V.

367. Telegram to Chiang on reply letter from Currie (September 7, 1942)

In my telegram dated August 20th I drafted a memo for Lauchlin Currie. Now memo has been revised according to your telegram dated August 23rd, translated and forwarded to Mr. Currie. He replied on September 4th as follows:

" Points made in memorandum generally concur with opinions Generalissimo expressed to me in Chongqing. Yet there are still some points to be clarified in advance as they might cause misunderstanding:

1. I was not authorized by my government to make a decision during my trip to Chongqing. Generalissimo should have been aware of this.

2. With reference to first point of third section, I explained to Generalissimo a new way, that is, those Lend-Lease supplies transported out after May 1st of this year should be controlled by Munitions Control Board before its ownership be transferred to Chinese government. "

The last paragraph means that, although the supplies shipped out after May 1st arrived in India, they still belong to US government. US has right to allocate them to other parties without getting permission from our government. Supplies that arrive in China are instantly owned by Chinese government. Supplies already shipped out before May 1st also belong to China. Without permission of Chinese government these goods should not be allotted to other parties.

I beg for Your Excellency's further instructions.

T. V.

368. Telegram to Chiang on US media reports on India issue (September 16, 1942)

With reference to India issue, shift of American public opinion is exactly what I expected in my previous telegram dated August 13th. At beginning, Americans were fooled by Sir Cripps. After arrest of Gandhi as well as other oppressions, it is generally believed that although Gandhi is indeed difficult to deal with, it is British who are to blame as they repeat in India their unsuccessful policies in Hong Kong, Malaya, and Burma. Speeches made by Prime Minister Churchill and Secretary of India Affairs Sir Amery the other day generated bad impression among Americans, who believe Mr. Churchill and his fellows prefer merely repressive means. British especially made clear in their speeches that their government already sent huge number of troops to India. This revealed British intention to control India permanently. Those who originally sympathized with British, such as *New York Times* in their editorials, have changed their tone. I advised Central News Agency to submit related information for your reference.

T. V.

369. Telegram to Chiang on Soong's trip to China (September 18, 1942)

After Mr. Currie returned to US, I discussed frankly many times with him three demands proposed by Your Excellency. He frankly told others and me that in Chongqing he was unable to solve misunderstanding between Your Excellency and General Stilwell. After his return to US, apart from some progress War Department made in air transport, they nevertheless could not accept plan of retaking Burma and delivering 500 warplanes. Even President could not urge them to do so, because their focus is still on Germany. Before such deep-rooted notion is altered, it is difficult to make significant progress. I deeply felt that, since fall of Burma, issue of assistance and supply here is getting more and more difficult. To overcome this difficulty and to understand real situation, I feel necessary to come back and ask for Your Excellency's instructions in person.

Please inform me of Your Excellency's decision on whether approve my request.

T. V.

370. Telegram to Chiang on transportation of Russian goods via China (September 24, 1942)

Your telegram dated September 22nd acknowledged.

1. I received telegram dated September 19th from our ambassador to the Soviet Union Shao Lizi, who said he submitted to Soviet new proposal on transit cargo. According to existing agreement, we are required to deliver 24,000 tons of agricultural and mineral goods to Soviet Union every year. If 5,000 tons of fuel we buy from Russian merchants is deducted (from the transport capacity), the remaining 19,000 tons capacity are defined as transit cargo. Soviet government deems this proposal surely practicable. According to my observation, limitation of tonnage may be calculated according to loading capacity of their empty vehicles coming to China to ship agricultural and mineral products. If we can use our own vehicles carrying goods from Russian border to China proper, we may go beyond this limitation.

2. British embassy in US and UK Commercial Commission (UKCC) contacted me on preparation of first section of transport via Iran, outlined as follows:

   A. They will telegraph London to instruct UKCC representative in India to contact Shen Shihua, our commissioner in India. Please instruct Mr. Shen and ask him to find out cargo capacity of railway and road transportation from Karachi to Meshed, as well as whether UKCC has enough vehicles and facilities.

B. The transport for 80 miles between Meshed and Ashkhabad be charged by Russia or Britain, which should be negotiated between British ambassador to Soviet and Soviet authorities.

C. We provide vehicles for transportation in our territory. As to the transportation between Sargiopol and Sino-Russian border, please instruct Ambassador Shao to negotiate with Soviet authorities.

3. Since transport issue between China and Russia is complicated, please give your instructions on whether it should be delegated to Ministry of Transportation.

T. V.

371. Telegram to Chiang on gifts to Currie and others (October 23, 1942)

Christmas is approaching. Some of our close American friends, including Mr. Currie, one general, 23 colonels and lieutenant colonels, 10 majors, and 7 captains, have always warmheartedly helped us very diligently. I propose to present gifts to them on behalf of Your Excellency as a sign of comfort and encouragement. I beg Your Excellency to instruct Jiang Biao to buy and bring gifts to America. I look forward to Your Excellency's decision.

T. V.

372. Telegram to Chiang on trip to Canada and on meeting with Stilwell (February, 1943)

Upon arrival at Calcutta, I passed on your message to General Stilwell. He was very depressed and regretted his manner and attitude during conversation. Yet he believed that Your Excellency would forgive him considering his honesty and devotion. He also said if Your Excellency did not make serious statement,

Britain would take it as excuse to procrastinate. As to your instructions of obtaining ten thousand tons of supplies, Stilwell brought up this issue at conference in Calcutta and said that it's indispensable for China to receive ten thousand tons of aid every month. General Wevall mentioned many difficulties, and his Chief of Staff General Morris said how railroads and waterway would catch up with air transport. Hence I seriously stated to General Arnold that since British authorities expressed their responsibility for this, subsequent transportation of ten thousand tons of aid would depend on your effort. Arnold said Britain needs to add three air bases and China also needs to add more air bases. I replied that as Generalissimo already showed willingness to take this responsibility, will Britain make their effort? Wavell said he will do his best. Later Stilwell told me that British and US high-ranking officers held meeting in afternoon of 9th and British authorities agreed to open another three air bases and that US also decided to increase number of aircrafts. Thus Your Excellency's conversation with Arnold in morning of 7th achieved full results. Military meeting in morning of 9th went very well. General He (Yingqin) will submit translation of meeting's minutes to you. After arrival in Ramgarh I was ill with high fever that nearly turned into pneumonia. Fortunately I took a new medicine Sulpha and recovered.

T. V.

373. Telegram from Chiang on Chiang's interview with Stilwell (April 20, 1943)

I add hereto a copy of transcript of my conversation with General Stilwell. Since enemy occupied Huarong [in Hunan Province] and Shishou [in Hubei Province] on south side of Yangzi River last month, its naval vessels could reach Yichang [in Hubei] through Yuezhou [in Hunan]. The most dangerous time would be summer when river water rises. We now urgently need three divisions of pursuit planes as contingency air forces, to cover army troop sweeping away enemy troops around Huarong and Shishou, and dispatched there by June. The rest of conversation recorded in transcription here hence I will not repeat again.

Kai-shek

[The transcript of the conversation between Generalissimo and Chief-of-Staff Stilwell

Time: *5. 00 pm, April 19*[th]
Venue: *residence of* the *Generalissimo, Zengjiayan (Chongqing)*

Stilwell: *Does Your Excellency have any opinion on candidate for commander-in-chief (of the allied troops) to retake Burma? If Britain appoints Auchinleck (former commander-in-chief of British forces in Northern Africa) to this position, will Your Excellency agree? In the future when China's expedition army enters Burma from India, whose commandership shall these troops be subject to?*

Generalissimo: *I have no opinion about candidates for commander-in-chief for retaking Burma. This can be discussed and decided between Britain and US. Chinese Expedition Army in India is still under your command as Chief of Staff. As to overall military operation of Chinese troops during counterattack, I will command in person. I hope you convey my wish to President Roosevelt and General Marshall that when attacking Burma, apart from US Navy and Air Force, as US chief of staff of air force General Henry H. Arnold reported in his plan in Chongqing, US can dispatch three army divisions to India to reinforce British troops in retaking Rangoon.*

Stilwell: *There is difficulty in dispatching army troops because of lack of vessels. Of course I will follow your instruction to report to President Roosevelt and General Marshall.*

Generalissimo: *Please tell President Roosevelt and General Marshall that current situation in China is critical. Morale of both Chinese military and civilians is extremely low, a state never seen in past six years. Since Japanese crossed Yangzi River around Huarong and Shishou, water way from Wuhan to Yichang has been opened (to them) . In summer, when water rises, Japanese gunboats and vessels could cruise upstream and threaten outer defense line of Chongqing. This is indeed worrying. Now we request US must dispatch by this*

June three divisions of pursuit aircraft to China to assist our troops. Then our troops can drive Japanese troops around Huarong on south side of Yangzi River to north side and thus remove this serious threat and boost our morale. Otherwise Japanese would use Wang (Jingwei) puppet regime and strengthen its puppet troops to sway our people and troops' will to resist Japanese invasion. If Japanese launch offensive along Yangzi River in summer, China may not stand. Now both Chinese government and Chinese people hope US will provide more aid. Even with so high an output of aircraft, US has remained reluctant to meet our appeal for only three divisions. I am unable to explain this reluctance to Chinese soldiers and people. I hope you will earnestly express this point to President Roosevelt and General Marshall.

As to proposal for military operations in retaking Burma, Arnold discussed this with me in Chongqing, I hope we can formulate more detailed plan with your country's military authorities, and complete all preparation work before rain season.

Stilwell: Yes, sir.

Generalissimo: When you see Madame Chiang and Minister Soong in US, please notify them of our conversation today. And it's preferable if Madame Chiang can come back to China with you. Please convey my regards to President Roosevelt and General Marshall.]

374. Telegram to Chiang on availability of military aids from Canada (April 24, 1943)

D1127

Canada is a rising nation in terms of armament industry after WWI. I have good relationships with Canadian Prime Minister, Minister of Defense Industry and others, and have often told them that defense industry will come to a halt after war and turn into ordinary industry. Then Canada can cooperate with us, helping us build a new China and so benefiting us mutually. Canadian people also admire Your Excellency and our fight against aggression. Given supremacy of US and Britain, they have quite a lot of grievances. Canadian Prime Minister and senior officials invited me to visit Canada. After discussion Canada agreed to provide us with large amount of military equipment. Equipment listed below will be delivered during next twelve months. This proposal is to be approved by parliament next month, though it is only a formality. Please keep it secret before that.

1. 30,000 79mm light machine guns.
2. 180,000 hand guns with 54,000,000 bullets.
3. 240 3.7-inch anti-aircraft guns with 480,000 shells.
4. 2,000 one meter rangefinders.
5. 50,000 6X-magnification telescopes.
6. 360 anti-tank guns with 240,000 penetrator shells.
7. 60,000 9mm hand-held machine guns with 50,000,000 bullets.
8. 720 25 pound grenade-launchers with 1,152,000 grenades and 144,000 smoke grenades.
9. 1,200 machine gun caterpillars.
10. 600 40mm antiaircraft guns with 1,620,000 shells and 180,000 penetrator shells.

Above guns and ammunition will be equipped with auxiliary accessories, vehicles, and communication appliances in accord with the British standard.

I also asked Canadians to provide us with three ten-thousand-ton cargoes on the grounds that maritime transportation carried out by US is having difficulties. They agreed. I will telegraph again about issues of staffing for three cargoes. Canada, a country of only ten million populations, so devoted to supporting us and advocating justice, is truly admirable. I suggest Your Excellency express gratefulness to prime minister as soon as this proposal is formally approved. I look forward to your further instructions.

T. V.

375. Telegram to Chiang on meeting between Chennault and Arnold (April 30, 1943)

Results of meeting between General Chennault and General Arnold and other senior officials were satisfactory. Arnold agrees to all Chennault's demands. He also said that President is willing to use air forces attacking enemy in China Theatre. Although US Air Forces endorse this plan, Marshal has not agreed. Whether this plan is workable depends on air transportation over Hump. Herewith I attach my memorandum (abridged translation) to President:

After careful consideration, Generalissimo Chiang thinks that all military resources should be focused on preparation of air strikes. Therefore air cargo capacity in May, June and July should be used to deliver gasoline and aircraft parts in order to launch effective air strikes as early as possible. After July air transportation could deliver army equipment, apart from small amount of air force supplemental materials. Judging by US industrial capacity, amount of aircraft and materials required to launch air strikes is not large. Therefore we earnestly hope expediting delivery in order to complete all preparations. Generalissimo Chiang also asks me to stress that if Japanese troops launch land attack on our air bases and hamper our plan for air strikes, Chinese army is capable of handling the situation.

Generalissimo Chiang previously requested that President order General Chennault to return to US to report plans for air strikes. Now General Chennalut has arrived and would report in detail.

When this memo submitted, Stilwell has not shown Your Excellency's instruction and records of conversation. Thus I would report to President in person soon about grave situation after Japanese crossed Yangzi River.

T. V.

376. Telegram to Chiang on Soong's meeting with American generals (May 1, 1943)

D1140

(1) Stilwell, Chennault expressed their views at general staff's conference, which lasted for three hours yesterday. Chennault proposed that China-US air forces use 500 airplanes for massive air attack in China

Theatre. It should destroy most of Japanese air force in China and deal heavy co-blow to enemy's marine transportation. If enemy's communication lines destroyed, ground movement will be easier in Burma and China.

(2) Stilwell asserted that it would be impracticable to launch massive air attack before ground force is reinforced. He thought that currently training and logistics of Chinese troops will not support sustained defense and protection of air bases in forefront. Stilwell highly praised Chinese troops now being trained at Ramgarh, and believed that when they return to China after fighting in Burma they will be able to protect air bases in forefront. At that time massive air attack would be practicable. If such attack launched too early, Japanese might be shamed into anger and capture our airfields. Then it's not easy to retake them, and chances to launch massive air attack on Japan proper from China will be lost.

(3) General George Marshall had previously told Chennault that he agreed with Stilwell. He left the meeting even before Chennault spoke.

(4) I insisted before President Roosevelt and Harry Hopkins on immediate preparation for air attack before too late. Hopkins told Chennault that my memorandum submitted to President Roosevelt earlier embarrassed President, because he has to refute his top military advisors' ideas.

(5) Sister (i. e. Madame Chiang) is arriving in Washington D. C. on Monday, to join me in persuading President that if we fail to start air attack sooner, then Japanese may attack Chongqing at time of water rising in Yangtze River in summer. No situation is more precarious than this. Maintenance of China Theatre will entirely depend on whether or not US government accepts our proposal.

T. V.

377. Telegram to Chiang on UK-US Joint Staff meeting (May 17, 1943)

D1185

All high-ranking officers, except President and Prime Minister Churchill, joined today's British and American Joint Chiefs of Staff Conference.

Chairman Leahy, Chief of Staff to President, asked me to report on Your Excellency's opinions.

I stated that "since enemy occupied Burma, China has been blockaded completely. As a result, China could not obtain supply of ammunition and goods. Moreover, our domestic economy is declining and inflation surging. The enemy again altered its strategy of invasion by using puppet regime to agitate public feelings. They concentrated troops to launch incessant attacks on Shanxi, Henan, Hebei and Hunan provinces in order to threaten Chongqing. These facts have been generally acknowledged. China is in such great danger, yet we do not make any unreasonable requests but ask Allied nations to live up to promises made by US president and Prime Minister Churchill in North Africa. Here are all I can address all of you on behalf of Generalissimo. Now permit me to make some comments on two resolutions concerning China decided in North Africa:

1. The decision to reinforce air force in order to attack enemies in China and in Japan proper has not been carried out yet because of insufficient air transport. For the time being, US air force in China can only protect air transport route between China and India. Chinese Army has never been protected by US air force. Yet while enemy intends to launch assaults on many important cities and provisional capitols, what is needed most is that US air force should assist Chinese army in military operations and in destroying enemy's communications. However, this is very unlikely to be carried out at the moment. Moreover, at this time, within months the only support that Allied nations could provide is air force. For this reason, Generalissimo Chiang requested to US president that air transport in next three months should be used entirely to support air force, so that General Chennault's air force can be strengthened. As regards to air force operational plan, General Chennault has elaborated on that point in details.

2. The decision to recover Burma:

   President Roosevelt and Prime Minister Churchill telegraphed Generalissimo Chiang from North Africa that they decided to recover Burma by sending the land, naval and air forces and to connect Yunnan-Burma Road. Moreover, they sent Field Marshall John Dill and Commanding General of air force Henry H. Arnold to Chongqing personally to state the details. Furthermore, they held a conference in Calcutta. Its participants included many high-ranking officers of US and Britain, Minister He Yingqin and me, where we decided on responsibilities of each nation. I thus read out records of Calcutta Conference noted down by British military attaché on February 9th. I pointed out:

a. The opening speech by Wavell mentioned the decisions made in north Africa and Chongqing.
b. Minister He reported on military strength of Chinese forces.
c. Wavell decided to send 10 divisions from India.
d. Minister He proposed that participation of strong navy force is necessary. The suggestion was promised by an Admiral of British Royal Navy.
e. Minister He said that air supremacy is indispensable. Arnold has promised to achieve the goal. "

Also, I pointed out that since Wavell's conclusion was agreed on by all parties, we need to make the most efforts to prepare for the counterattack.

I continued by saying, "Please pay attention. The counterattack against Burma is not an ordinary plan. Instead, it is resolution reached by three countries. Chinese forces have been concentrated for the military action. Also, airports have been consolidated and expanded. I stated again that Generalissimo does not have new demands now except requesting British and American Allied nations to carry out their concurrent resolutions and to provide information about deployment of the navy and air force for Burma counterattack. Those high-ranking officials in US and British governments repeatedly announced to world that counterattack against Burma would take place this year. Therefore, please forgive my blunt statement that once counterattack against Burma is retracted, Chinese people and soldiers will view the UK and US as unfaithful and breaking promise. UK and US both expressed that if they are not determined to force Japanese enemy to surrender, not only Chinese forces will become hopeless and begin to disintegrate, but Allied nations will also be unable to eliminate the Japanese enemy if they lose Chinese as military base. "

"In addition, before North Africa conference, General Stilwell proposed attacking north Burma. Yet Generalissimo did not grant his permission. That was because enemy controlled communications routes of railway, roads and Irrawaddy River. If we do not capture south Burma to intercept their retreat route, the plan is destined to fail and our efforts will turn out to be in vain. Generalissimo Chiang was determined to believe so, and now is even firmer. "

It is on record that in British and American military council held last Friday, General Stilwell criticized Generalissimo Chiang openly for being hesitant in making decisions, and having no definite views on military strategy. I took advantage of this conference to supplement our assertion that it is not the first time Generalissimo Chiang has cooperated with foreign military experts. General Vassili Galen (aka Bluecher), who defeated Japanese enemy in Nomonhan near Zhanggufeng in Northeastern China, had followed Generalissimo Chiang for several years. In addition, General Hans von Seeckt, who founded the modern German army; Wetzel, who had been appointed as operation officer under German Chief of General Staff E. Ludendorff; and Vasily Ivanovich Chuikov, who defeated Germany at Battle of Stalingrad, have all served as our advisors. They have all been following Generalissimo Chiang's instructions. If you consider that we are wrong to obey Generalissimo Chiang's instructions, then we are not the only ones to have made mistakes. Those aforementioned famous generals of world have made such mistakes as well. Moreover, Generalissimo Chiang is responsible for safety of China Theatre. All his preparation has taken overall situation into account. If people like us are suspicious of his ability or object to his claims, then we should have corresponding ability in protecting China Theatre. My speech not only is against Stilwell, but also warns US Army and Air Force authorities that they should not look down on China because of their own limited views.

T. V.

378. Telegram to Chiang on debate with Churchill on Tibet issue (May 21, 1943)

D1195

Pacific War Council session took place today. President Roosevelt reported general situation in Pacific and warfare in Attu is rather good. Concerning China Theatre, now measures are being taken to enhance air force and transport capability. Air transport will be greatly increased, and General Chennault's air force will be three times stronger than before. Prime Minister Churchill also showed his willingness to send three units of pursuit planes to China.

I warmly welcomed the above decisions and recalled that Prime Minister Churchill intended to send Royal Air Forces to China even before the Pearl Harbor incident.

Mr. Churchill said that recently it has been alleged that Chinese have concentrated troops to attack Tibet, causing this independent nation to panic. He hoped that China could guarantee there would not be any misfortune happening. I replied that I have never heard of such a message. And meanwhile I said that Tibet is not an independent nation as Churchill had claimed. All previous agreements between China and Britain have all recognized that China possesses sovereign rights in Tibet, and I believe this fact has already been under his careful examination.

Mr. Churchill said that Tibet is a barren land and British have no ambitions there. I just hope that at this moment we should concentrate our strength to deal with our common enemy. I am now trying to increase air transport to China, the result of which would exceed any previous loading capacity through Burma Road. We should know that Burma is a place with malaria and disease. For launching warfare in such bad circumstances, our troops are not comparable with those of Japanese. Currently there are quite a lot of British troops on British Indian border, yet because of difficult transportation it is not an easy job to mobilize these forces. Our failure in Arakan battle was a hard lesson.

I said that although recovery of Burma is difficult and will take great efforts, it is most imperative task and worth striving for in order to accomplish something once and for all. It is certainly important to increase current air transport to China, yet once Burma Road has been restored, ground transport will be elevated to 100,000 tons per month. Now what Chinese have expected from Britain and US is a counterattack on Burma. Ordinary Chinese and people in the world have roughly been aware of this, and if we fail to carry on, Chinese morale will be shaken, and the future of our warfare will be in great danger.

Churchill said that this (recover Burma) plan is not an official commitment (for British government), and is adjustable according to development of situation.

I said President Roosevelt and you once telegraphed Generalissimo Chiang of your decision in North Africa (on Burma recovery). After that, British and American senior officers flew to Chongqing and consult (with Generalissimo) personally. In addition, Chinese Minister of Military Affairs He (Yingqin) and I attended the military conference hosted by General Wavell in Calcutta to detail this (Burma) plan. (Based on all those facts), Chinese government naturally regarded this as an officially endorsed resolution.

Churchill insisted that there was only a plan but not an (official) resolution. He added that if the British and American military authorities had made some commitments, (it was unlawful because) they exceeded their responsibilities. I said that on the Calcutta meeting it has been decided each participant should start actions immediately. Therefore, in the past a few months, China has been making preparations with our full strength.

Churchill said he had not read the Calcutta meeting minute until several days before. I replied it was difficult to believe that such an important document, which was composed on February 9th, had been delayed for so long for (British Prime Minister) to read. Churchill could not make any response on that.

I continued that all difficulties in combating in Burma would be the same even we postpone the offensive to next year. Winning the war is really depends on the resolution and techniques of the soldiers, so as to overcome all sorts of difficulties. Malaria and disease applies to the Japanese troops too. The difference of impact is not on human races, but on amount of human will. The Allies' victory in North Africa was mainly because of sound commandership. Besides, according to prior experiences, army troops from America and Australia are equally able to combat as the enemy soldiers. China regards recovery of Burma as the only solution for current crisis, and thus yearns to witness Britain and US to execute what they have promised. The consequence otherwise would be unimaginable.

Churchill said what he considered is not only (strengthening of) air force and airlift capacity. He also thought of linking up Chinese troops and Indian troops, or (making join efforts) through Northern Burma. President also told me not to worry (about the Burma plan). The military strategy of recovering Burma is already set, but the exact tactic might adjust. It was still uncertain whether the offensive be via Rangoon or elsewhere.

I responded that China's largest hope is to recover Burma and that our allies to implement immediately the decided plan of assisting China. I might have been emotional in my words, but this relates to the fate of my country and I was obliged to argue for her. President and Prime Minister, being top leaders of our Allied nations, must know well the importance of this issue.

Churchill said that, though without definite information, he was confident that if Soviet Union could pull through this summer, she would surely attend the war against Japan (in the future). He would of course do his best to assist China when applicable. But even Burma is recovered, the transportation on the Burma road could not be fully revived before 1945, allegedly at the level of 20,000 tons a month. President then asked me whether Chinese army had destroyed the Burma Road when they retreated (in 1942). I said only a part was destroyed, but has been repaired by the Japanese enemy. According to source from US, after improvement, the monthly transport could reach 100,000 tons, which is by no means replaceable by air transport.

After the meeting, Churchill asked me not to report today's discussion to our authorities, and wished to talk with me some other time.

For Your Excellency's reference.

T. V.

379. Telegram to Chiang on Soong's meeting with Roosevelt regarding to Churchill (May 21, 1943)

Your Excellency must have received my previous telegram dated 21st. I met with President at noontime today. He said, though Prime Minister Mr. Winston Churchill spoke inappropriately yesterday, his objectives were more or less in line with what I (T. V.) was advocating. Henceforth, President made efforts to mediate. I indicated Churchill's statement can be summarized into three points:

1. No promise has been made.
2. Even if there were any promises at the Calcutta Meeting, he has not approved them.
3. Report of Calcutta Meeting held on February 9th had not reached him until late May.

After yesterday's meeting, Churchill asked me not to report this to Your Excellency for the time being. (I told President that) I had to report immediately because just two days ago I telegraphed President's plan of retaking Burma to Generalissimo. Only one day after, there came Churchill's (reversed) statement. One can easily imagine how Generalissimo would feel and think. To implement this (attack) plan decided at Calcutta Meeting, Generalissimo has already dispatched troops to Yunnan, even at the cost of weakening forces on other battlefields. (This maneuver) was completely based on his trust on Britain's loyalty (to her promises). If Britain breaks her words this time, it would undermine not only the military plan of retaking Burma, but also the mutual trust among the Allies. This is by no means a minor issue. Should Britain turns around this time, how could we be sure of the sustainability of her next promise, maybe just in next week? And if the

Chinese people learn the truth, there will be tremendous negative influence (on their morale). The President said I could report to Generalissimo Chiang (with confidence) that the retaking Burma plan would surely be implemented. The US Army staff are now working vigorously on composing of detailed operation plans, which would finish by next Monday. What can be revealed to me now in private is that though General Wavell would return to commanding position in name, the actual commandership of operations would be entrusted to a young and able division commander aged 42, who would be soon promoted.

He asked whether it is true that Japanese troops are only 127 miles away Chongqin as newspaper reported. I answered that situation in area south of Yangtze River is indeed critical as reported earlier. Churchill abandoned plan of attacking Burma yesterday, and laid hope on Soviet participation in war as alternative. It's nearly wishful thinking. We are quite familiar with situation in Soviet Union. Prior to war with Germany, Soviet Union did assist us with large amount of weapons. Nonetheless, Soviet Union will not join war against Japan until it defeated Germany. President said Soviet Union would be willing to take part after defeating Germany. By then, however, what we need are air bases instead of Soviet troops.

I said I like to add something. While General Stilwell was in China, he drafted limited offensive plan against northern Burma. Generalissimo already informed him of his disapproval, and asked him pass on reasons for objection to President upon return to US. The reasons lie in importance of terrain of Burma as well as logistics and supply in the rear. Secret of success over past six years of our battle against Japan is to press technologically advanced enemy to operate in poor communication conditions which virtually broke down their machinery and equipment. If we look at map of Burma, terrain of northern Burma is just opposite of the case. Japanese may use Irrawaddy River and the Rangoon Railway; whereas only two roads, Ledo and Imphal Roads now under construction are available to us. Even if we could win bliz attack in north Burma, Japanese would still be able to deploy reinforcements through transport facilities in Malaya and Thailand. Thus Generalissimo repeatedly reminded Stilwell not to take the same disastrous road. President inquired whether it is impossible to win in northern Burma. I replied that unless we fight in southern Burma simultaneously and cut off enemy's route of retreat. President emphasized necessity of mobilizing navy in this connection, and it has to rely on US navy because he British have only some old naval vessels and no aircraft carriers in Indian Ocean. Besides, since there are reportedly twenty-three airports in proximity of Rangoon, navy would suffer severe blow. I answered all airports near Rangoon could be bombed from China or Calcutta, and currently our air forces have gained upper hand. One evidence is that Japanese planes failed to intercept our airlifting.

President said he told staff officers that, "Why don't we construct a huge air base in Calcutta so as to bomb and smash Rangoon into pieces?" I said at the same time General Chennault's contingent should bombard communication lines of Japanese troops. President said there should be no problem in supplying fighters and air-freighters Chennault needed. He will do his best. I reported that Mr. Churchill proposed to dispatch three British air force contingents to China. For that we are definitely grateful. However, it would inevitably hinder unified command of air forces. Would it be better to assign British air force to protect airports in Assam Province to replace US air force currently stationed there? In so doing, US air force could be transferred to China. President said that's the point, and would offer us 1,500 trucks for transportation in Iran. As result, monthly carrying capacity could reach 4,000 tons. In case of gasoline shortages, US could provide charcoal engines. I reiterated that Stilwell's plan of attacking northern Burma would simply exhaust our military strength, and Generalissimo would never accept. President said it's indeed difficult to recover Rangoon, but offensive could first be launched in southwestern coast and then Rangoon be attacked from rear. He added that Britain proposed to transfer New Zealand troops to take part in battle in North Africa. But he told British that those soldiers fought for long time and need to take a rest, thus he dissuaded them to do so. He also would order American troops currently in North Africa to take rest and recuperate. If he were to dispatch contingents to Burma in future, it would be fresh and crack troops. He asked me to inform Generalissimo of plan to attack Burma and his resolution to carry it out. The Anglo-American staff officers will table a proposal next Monday.

T. V.

380. Telegram from Chiang on stance against Churchill's Tibet Policy (May 22, 1943)

By treating Tibet as an independent country, Churchill has denied territorial integrity and sovereignty of our country. It's a great insult. I did not expect Britain would make such statement. It is indeed a humiliation placed on all Allied nations. We should ask President Roosevelt about his views on Churchill's statement and how to deal with it. Tibet is part of China's territory, and Tibetan affairs are China's domestic affairs. Now, Churchill's statement is interfering with China's domestic affairs. That is also breaking the principle of Atlantic Charter in the first place. China cannot regard it as an ordinary matter and must oppose it. We can not ignore this event. Moreover, when at beginning of this month British ambassador met with Vice Foreign Minister Wu Guozhen, he claimed that Tibetans had heard about arrival of Chinese troops at surroundings of Chamdo and were extremely panicked. At the moment that US is reinforcing China's air transport, it is indeed inappropriate for China to dispatch troops to fight with Tibet. His way of speaking was just like Prime Minister Churchill's. Vice Minister Wu rejected his request right away and claimed that this was our domestic affair. Thus, we could not accept such advice. After that, Wang Xueting[1] sent Hang Liwu to warn British ambassador in personal name not to raise this matter again. That is why he has not dared to refer to it since then. Please forward this telegram to sister Mey-ling.

Kai-shek

---

[1] Wang Xueting, aka Wang Shijie.

381. Telegram to Chiang on Soong's meeting with Assistant Secretary of Army (May 23, 1943)

D1202

1. I just met Deputy Secretary of War and General Stilwell, to whom I reported instructions given by Your Excellency. They have agreed to transfer two units of pursuit planes and one unit of light bombers from Kunming to Chongqing to assist in warfare. Meanwhile, additional air forces will be transferred from India to China. Their opinion is that air force will be used as cover, and 9th and 5th war zones used to launch a converging attack so that Japanese enemy will not be able to reach its purpose.

2. Concerning Tibetan issue, I sincerely beg Your Excellency to avoid any clash in Tibet at this critical moment. I observe that, when negotiating Tibetan issue in the future, British would surely make concessions. In addition, it will be pointless to construct Sino-Indian roadway without full cooperation of British. President Roosevelt also admonished that accident must not happen. After matters have been settled here, I propose to visit Britain and negotiate with British authorities. With Your Excellency's instructions I will endeavor to complete my job. And I am confident to do my duty well. Please let me know your decisions.

3. Deputy Secretary of War just informed me that attitude of Anglo-American Joint Chiefs of Staff toward counterattacking Burma has been much more positive than before.

T. V.

382. Telegram from Chiang on communication with Roosevelt (May 23, 1943)

R1182

I am aware of the situation from your telegram dated May 22nd. Our government only paved roads in Tibet for transport, and we have never concentrated 11 divisions of troops to attack Tibet. Such rumor was made up entirely by British. They intend to force us to announce that we do not have intention to attack Tibet. We must not make any such announcement or assurance to UK. Please follow my previous telegraph and make serious statement to President Roosevelt that British have *de facto* broken Atlantic Charter in the first place. The wording of "in the first place" should be particularly emphasized.

Kai-shek by hand

383. Telegram to Chiang on analysis of UK governmental policy (May 24, 1943)

Yesterday I had a meeting with President Roosevelt and Prime Minister Churchill. Today I had another discussion with British and American chiefs of staff. This time British seemed more sincere than before. British and Americans have a thorough plan for fighting Japanese, and not limited to Burma only. For fear of leaking this information, I will not say anything about it via telegram. I propose to have our military attaché, General Zhu Shimin, fly back to Chongqing next week to report details in person. Please instruct if this is appropriate. I did not express my own opinions on the plan, and simply said I should report to Your Excellency before making any response.

T. V.

384. Telegram from Chiang to reiterate importance of Tibet issue (May 25, 1943)

R1190

I am aware of situation from your telegram dated May 23rd. We cannot overlook Tibetan issue, and should follow my previous telegraph to make serious statement to President Roosevelt and asking him to pay attention to this issue. Since President Roosevelt said "accident must not happen", it is most necessary for us to assert our stance and sovereignty. Otherwise, our other military demands and assertions would be looked down on, and all negotiations from now on would fail. Please follow and execute my orders. Do not make mistakes and do reply to me.

Kai-shek by hand

385. Telegram to Chiang on reiteration of China's stance on sovereignty (May 25, 1943)

D1280

I received your telegram dated May 25th. As regards to Churchill's reference to Tibet on that day, I made a serious proclamation immediately that Tibet is under China's sovereignty. Lord Halifax also recognized this. On next day, President Roosevelt said that Churchill's speech was inappropriate as well. I plan to reassert the stance and sovereignty of our country according to your instructions when I meet President next time. I would not make any statement to any one that we do not intend to attack Tibet. Yet please do instruct our troops not to cause any conflict under any circumstances. Those British and Americans who opposed us said that once becomes a powerful country, China will become aggressor. Tibet is part of our territory, and even if we resort to force, it would not be aggression. Yet those who do not know the truth will surely misunderstand us. Moreover, they will say that in this critical moment for survival, China does not act concertedly against the enemy, but instead dispatch military forces to a peaceful border. In legal term, Britain has no right to interfere with our domestic affairs. Yet if there is any conflict between China and Tibet, it will become an excuse that British can make use of, and at least obstruct China-India international communications and sabotage plan of attacking Burma. It is unnecessary to belabor the obvious to Your Excellency. I beg for your inspection.

T. V.

386. Telegram to Chiang on US government decision on invading Burma (May 25, 1943)

Today President Roosevelt told me in person that plan of attacking Burma has been decided. He gave me notice of plan; yet, original notice will be delivered separately. I heard that US Military Mission to China would submit the notice to you. I said that Generalissimo Chiang is eager to know detailed plan of action. First, we need to know whether US army will send three divisions to join Burma attack. President said that he has decided to send only engineering corps for now, and has not decided on the rest yet. I asked whether he would send combat troops. President said that even if Americans are willing to do so, British claimed that they have 600,000 fine soldiers in India, and there is no need to send troops all the way across the ocean. In his personal view, one division of American troops is equal to three divisions of British Indian troops. I said that they are equivalent to five divisions. President said that he can send more troops, but it depends on how situation develops. There are five to six locations close to Rangoon where US Marine Corps can execute landing actions. The British-US Joint Staff are doing research and will finish the work in four to five days. (President recalled that) he once promised US Navy would help British troops to fight.

I expressed my interest in knowing details of the plan, so that I could report to Generalissimo. President replied that he could not tell me in advance. Military information is usually restricted to those are directly involved. Generalissimo must understand and forgive me. For example, as regards to landing location, since it is yet to decide, thus no information to tell. (Even having been decided,) it will not be informed (to China) until twenty to thirty days before the action day, so as (for Chinese army) to launch attacks behind the enemy's line. Nevertheless, the specific location of first landing will still be confidential. As a military principle, the fewer know, the better.

Prime Minister Churchill has decided to appoint Wavell to command all the Indian troops inside India, whose position is like a supervisor. Meanwhile, Churchill has sent an urgent telegram to Harold Alexander and Bernard Montgomery, asking them to recommend a most established division leader in the Northern African campaign and an able logistics organizer to take the position of field commanders for Burma operation. Therefore, the dispatch of American troops also depends on the choice of these two commanders.

As regards to Stilwell issue, General Marshall stated to President that if US could transport large quantity of air force supplies to China through India-China air route, he is not certain on recalling Stilwell. President replied that he had no preference on this issue. I said this is good, but General Chennault better go back to China as early as possible. President said he would dispatch Chennault and Stilwell to UK first to discuss with the British side on transportation on Brahmakulia River and in Assam region.

President at last said that in past two days he had been discussing with Churchill on Burma attack plan. Not until 3:00 am on last day's morning did Churchill give in and promise to cooperate.

President asked about Japanese enemy's threat to Chongqing. I replied that the situation is still critical. In past months, we have appealed repeatedly to US on checking enemy troops to attack Chongqing. But some senior American officers are not far-sighted (to take actual actions), which resulted in our awkward situation now, etc. President said he sincerely hoped China could understand US is now trying best to aid China.

T. V.

387. Telegram to Chiang on Soong's meeting with Roosevelt regarding to Tibet issue and other topics (May, 1943)

I called on President this morning and handed Your Excellency's telegram on the 29th to him first, then conveyed several points according to your second telegram on the same day. His replies to those points are as following:

1. UK has decided to send strong navy fleet to control the Burma Sea. "As for occupation of Rangoon, they have decided to intercept enemy's route of communication. About whether to occupy Rangoon, or surrounding cities around Rangoon, this is a military tactic issue. The most important thing is to occupy Southern Burma." Now Churchill is in North Africa, and he should have told me the new commander of British troops for attacking Burma. But he might be busy these days in mediating arguments between two factions of French and North Africans, and that is why he has not sent

telegraphs yet. But we will hear from him within days. As soon as British decide on candidate for commander, he (the commander) and Stilwell will formulate a perfect plan.

2. The navy force for attacking Burma this time is mainly composed by British fleets, and then Americans. Now British and Americans have done their best to damage Italian main fleet. They feel quite confident. If they would succeed, there will be a larger fleet than originally planned to control Burma Sea.

3. It is important to push British to keep their promise at every opportunity.

4. Though "simultaneous military actions" means launching attacks at the same time, it is difficult to be precisely at the same time, but the interval may not be more than two to three weeks. President said though he is not a military man, by his judgment, when British India and China launch attacks in Burmese territory first, enemy's redeployment of troops would be impeded. Then in two or three weeks, landing forces will carry out military actions backing the sea.

Finally, as regards to participation of American troops, President said that now he has only sent engineering corps. However, he will also consider sending one or two divisions of Marine Corps.

President continued to ask about progress of battle around Yichang. I replied that this battle proved that War Department had been wrong when they judged that enemy had no intention of attacking Chongqing. It also proved President right to send US air force to assist. However, it is necessary to keep reinforcing air force in China, (for instance), to transfer all planes of 10th Division to China. President endorsed that suggestion and ordered Deputy Chief of Staff to execute.

Finally, I described Your Excellency's views of those telegraphs concerning Tibet, asking him to pay attention to this issue, and informed him that China would not accept any proposals brought up by British regarding Tibet. President said, "I asked Churchill before he departed why he brought out Tibet issue". Churchill answered that Britain has no intention of occupying Tibet. President continued to say that Tibet was part of imperial China and now is part of Republican China, which has nothing to do with Great Britain. Churchill replied that Chinese government has no *de facto* administrative power in Tibet. Presidnet said, "Whether Chinese government has actual power or not has nothing to do with Britain". Churchill could give no reply.

I said Churchill's assertion that China has concentrated 11 divisions to attack Tibet is indeed ridiculous. China is merely building roads in Tibet, because President has suggested China repeatedly to build roads between China and India to make transport easier. President said he looks forward to meeting Generalissimo Chiang, Stalin, and Prime Minister Churchill to discuss this sort of matters as early as possible. However, Churchill constantly bears in mind the traditional idea that Great Britain should dominate the world. President said it would be better if he could talk with Your Excellency two or three days before the summit of four.

T. V.

388. Telegram to Chiang on Soong's meeting with Eden and others (May, 1943)

1. British Foreign Secretary Anthony Eden went to Canada and proceeded to England. I have talked with him four times.
2.
   a. Eden said plan of attacking Burma will surely be carried out within this year, with participation of massive navy and air forces. The goal of this attack is only to retake Burma and to revive China's land transport. As to recovery of Thailand, Vietnam and Malaya, this has to wait until the first goal is achieved.
   b. Britain has no intention of appeasing Japan, and would like to exert the same means against Japanese as they have against Germans. After the war, the ways of dealing with Japan will surely follow China's will.
   c. According to USSR's proposal, British-Soviet alliance covers Europe. They did not mention Far East issue.

    d. The four great powers should become mainstay of postwar international organizations, and play leading role. Previous experience of many small nations dominating the League of Nations should not be repeated again. For this reason, the four great powers should formulate coherent policies as early as possible.

    e. War developments are going well. However, it will be a painstaking task to solve postwar problems. As regards to US and Soviet Union, US is too idealistic, USSR too practical.

    f. I mentioned Tibet issue and asked him why India challenged China's sovereignty. China has no territorial ambitions outside China, but will never give up her own territorial sovereignty. He said he is not aware of this question and will discuss it with me when I go to England. Later he told Under Secretary of State Welles that I had mentioned this question, and he has telegraphed London for further inquiry. In his view, if there is any interference with China's sovereignty, that must be action of some subordinates.

3. After Eden came to US, I met with President Roosevelt, Secretary of State Hull, Mr. Wells and Mr. Harry Hopkins several times inquiring about contents of discussions between US and Britain.

4. Eden focused on Europe and Asia issues during discussions. Hull said that UK and US should respect China's rights. Taiwan, Ryukyu, three Northeast provinces, and Dalian shall be returned to China. As regards to three Northeastern provinces, President and Welles mentioned that China and Russia should negotiate Russia's previous railway privileges directly. I said that Russia has sold Chinese Eastern Railway to Japan, and therefore it's no longer a question. With reference to Outer Mongolia, President also said that this has to be negotiated by China and USSR directly. I pointed out that there should be a solution that anticipates postwar problems. The boundary problem between two countries is therefore an issue of concern to every country. Hopkins could not agree more with that proposal. UK and US believe that Korea should be independent, but for the moment, the Allied nations' collective trusteeship is necessary. As to Hong Kong, President said this would be decided by British, yet date of

announcement is absolutely secret. China may take initiative in announcing Hong Kong as a free port. The date could be one or two weeks after UK's announcement, and should not be leaked out beforehand to keep to the original idea of "initiative".

5. As regards to India problem, President told us that before Gripps left for India, he had sent a letter to Churchill. He advised UK to announce India's autonomy without mentioning India's departure from British Empire in order to avoid religious arguments in India. Eden said that Churchill did not tell him about President's letter.

6. President and Mr. Eden talked about problem of dependencies. Eden seemed to be able to accept establishment of trusteeship under Allied nations. British believed that Malaya and Singapore could be put under Allied nations' trusteeship. However, according to what Hull told me, as long as Churchill clearly shows his unwillingness to give up dependencies, this idea won't work out for the British. Yet it can be implemented in French dependencies, as well as former German dependencies, which were under trusteeship of League of Nations.

7. Americans are strongly opposed to looking down on China as revealed in Churchill's speech. I told President that Churchill's insistence on establishing one European international bloc and one Asian international bloc is equal to policy of restoring super power politics. China could not agree with that idea. President said he told Eden that US would never join European bloc.

8. President told Mr. Eden that US can join only world bloc, not European bloc. Even if the President agreed, US Senate would never approve. Eden was very surprised by his determined attitude and so on. British intend originally that US and UK dominate the world, and later on, they want UK, US and Russia to dominate the world. However, US believes if white people try to control the world, it will inevitably lead to a racial war.

9. Welles said that UK and Russia in their attitudes toward all kinds of postwar problems cannot be oblivious of what has taken place before. It was the policy after World War I that US return to isolation. American politicians and public should demonstrate their responsibility in joining

world bloc after the war.

10. Eden wants Britain to mediate discussions between US and USSR. Yet Americans would prefer direct negotiations. Hopkins may go to Moscow soon to negotiate with Stalin directly.

11. Eden came to America. Everything goes quite well. Progress could be made toward partial understanding between British and US. As regards to questions of world bloc and bloc security and so on, there are no concrete conclusions yet.

12. Hopkins told me in secret that he and President thought that US and China did not have to exchange ideas in an unofficial way any more. China can discuss the practical problems of Far East with the US and express China's views on world bloc. Once China and US reach certain understanding, I should go to England for official negotiations. Though such negotiations will be formal, we should still keep them secret. Meanwhile, it is hoped that China could begin to exchange ideas with USSR.

T. V.

389. Telegram to Chiang on Soong's speech on UK-US Joint Staff meeting (May, 1943)

1. Except Roosevelt and Churchill, all important figures participated in UK and US Joint Chiefs of Staff Conference. Chairman Leahy invited me to report on Your Excellency's opinions. I said that China has been besieged partially for five years, and enemy's occupation of Burma blockaded China completely. Therefore, supply of ammunition is interrupted, China's economy is declining, with inflation surging. Enemy altered their policy by making use of puppet regime to agitate public feelings, also oppressed governmental regions by military force, such as their attacks on Shanxi, Henan, Hubei and Hunan provinces. The crisis is obvious. Yet, China does not have new demands now, but only hopes Allied Nations to carry out resolution made by President and Prime Minister in Casablanca.

2. The decisions made in Casablanca are:

a. To reinforce air force and attack enemy in China and in Japan proper;
b. To recover Burma. Owing to insufficient air transport, the reinforcement of air force is not carried out by now. Therefore, US Air Force in China could only protect air transport route between China and India. Chinese Army has never been protected by US Air Force. As regards plan of air military operation, Chennault has elaborated in details. While enemy is launching attacks on provisional capital, Changsha, and other important cities, what is needed most and most important is assistance from US Air force. It is known that within these months land transport is interrupted, and sea transport stopped. Allied Nations could only use air force to assist. As China is in such great danger and isolation, what is most needed is only the air force. For this reason, Generalissimo Chiang requested US President that air transport within these three months should be allotted entirely to support air force in order to consolidate General Chennault's Air Force.

3. I heard that General Stilwell opposed Generalissimo Chiang's plan openly in last Friday's US Joint Chiefs of Staff Conference. He asserted that Generalissimo is hesitant in making decisions and has no definite views on military strategy. I thus supplemented by saying, "Please pay attention! It is not Generalissimo Chiang's first time to cooperate with foreign military experts. General Vassili Galen (aka Bluecher), who defeated Japanese enemy in Nomonhan near Zhanggu peak, had followed Generalissimo Chiang for several years. In addition, General Hans von Seeckt, who founded modern German army, Wetzel, who had been appointed as Operation Officer under German Chief of the General Staff E. Ludendorff, as well as Vasily Ivanovich Chuikov, who defeated German at Battle of Stalingrad, have all served as our advisors. They all followed Generalissimo Chiang's instructions. Thus, if you consider us wrong to obey Generalissimo Chiang's instruction, then those who made mistakes are not only us. Those aforementioned famous generals of world have made such mistakes as well. Moreover, His Excellency is responsible for safety of China Theatre. If we do not follow His Excellency's instruction, then we should have corresponding ability in protecting China Theatre."

4. The decision to counterattack Burma:

US President and Prime Minister Churchill telegraphed Generalissimo Chiang from North Africa about decision of recovering Burma by sending Armed Force and breaking through Yunnan-Burma road. In addition, they sent Field Marshall, John Dill, and Commanding General of Air Force, Henry H. Arnold to, go to Chongqing personally to make briefing. Furthermore, they held conference in Calcutta. Its participants included high-ranking officers of US and Great Britain, Minister Ho and me. The conference decided responsibilities of each nation. I thus read record of Calcutta conference noted by British military attaché on February 9th and pointed out:

    a. Opening speech by Wavell mentioned decisions made in north Africa and Chongqing.

    b. Minister He reported on military strength of Chinese forces.

    c. Wavell decided to send 10 divisions of troops from India.

    d. Minister He proposed that participation of strong navy force is necessary. The suggestion was promised by Admiral of British Navy.

    e. Minister He addressed that air supremacy is indispensable. Arnold has promised to achieve the goal.

Also, I pointed out that since Wavell's conclusion was agreed by all parties concerned, we need to do our best to prepare for counterattack.

I continued to say to all participants, "Please pay attention! Counterattack against Burma is not an ordinary plan. It is joint resolution reached by the three countries. Chinese forces have been concentrated for military action. Also, airports have been consolidated and expanded." I stated again, "Generalissimo does not have new demands. He only requests British and American Allied Nations to carry out their concurrent resolutions in order to save China from crisis. Moreover, those high-ranking officials in US and British governments have repeatedly announced to world that counterattack against Burma will be taken place this year. Therefore, Chinese people look forward to seeing deployment of navy and air forces. Please consider that once counterattack against Burma is retracted, Chinese people and soldiers would reckon U. K. and US as unfaithful and breaking the promise. US expressed that if they are not determined to force Japanese enemy to surrender, not only Chinese would become hopeless and disintegrated, but Allied Nations would lost Chinese military base and unable to eliminate Japanese enemy. "

"In addition, prior to North Africa conference, General Stilwell had proposed to attack north Burma. Yet, Generalissimo Chiang did not approve at that time. That was because enemy controlled communication route of railway and Irrawaddy road. If we do capture south Burma to intercept their retreat route, the enemy would be defeated. Generalissimo Chiang was determined to do so, and now is even more so. "

T. V.

390. Telegram to Chiang to propose recovery of Yichang (May, 1943)

There are still several months before planned attack on Burma. During this period, US air force will be either attacking surrounding area of Guangzhou and enemy's ships near coast, or moving around Yangtze River. In light of all domestic economic and political difficulties, if we can recover Yichang, it will have significant effects. General Chennault deeply believes that he should order air force to obstruct enemy's transport in Yangtze River while using bombers to help army to recover Yichang. If Your Excellency regards this proposal as appropriate, please summon Chennault and Chen Cixiu (Chen Cheng) to hold a meeting in Chongqing. I beg for your decision.

T. V.

391. Telegram to Chiang on Stilwell issue (May, 1943)

I received your telegram dated May 18th.

1. General Crabbe arrived yesterday, and we had a pleasant talk this morning. His opinion is quite similar to ours and we agreed to act

concertedly. Stilwell's letter can only be replied in next week because Chief of Staff would return from London next week, and because this matter related to Crabbe's report to War Department.

2. Prime Minister Churchill's trip to US was originally to negotiate opening of second front. However, upon his arrival, Tobruk was captured, thus his discussion shifted onto how to reinforce Near East. As regards to British and Soviet alliance, American's policy is not to develop solitary allied relation with any single country, the USSR in particular. US made this clear when British and Russians discussed on alliance. Therefore, Prime Minister Churchill this time intended to explain the necessities for UK to form alliance with USSR. As regards to China-US alliance, US would not make such decision unless the world war situation has come to desperate stage, same as Anglo-French alliance, which was (not until most critical time, did) Britain proposed to form and even propose unification of two countries.

I hereby present to Your Excellency my observation.

T. V.

392. Telegram to Chiang on communication with US military personnel (May, 1943)

In today's Pacific Council meeting, President informed us of developments in Egypt and said that because of need for haste, a part of 10th Air Force Division had been dispatched to reinforce Egypt without notice. Therefore, Generalissimo Chiang was quite worried. But Egypt does matter to China because if Near East were lost, transport routes to China would be cut off. Furthermore, President said he telegraphed Stalin to request the returning of 45 pursuit planes that have arrived in Persia, and Stalin agreed. It is therefore clear that (1) USSR is more concerned about the total war than before; (2) warfare between USSR and Germany is not as tense as we had heard. I was not willing to show my disagreement, and said I would brief him after the conference since I just received Generalissimo's telegram.

Moreover, President said that China's war against Japan has been going on for five years, and though there are still difficulties, overall situation is quite optimistic. China could win final victory as long as she receives assistance. I said that undoubtedly Chinese leaders and people all have firm determination, but there are also many difficulties after five years' long war. Since fall of Burma, supply of ammunition for China has been cut off. After Shanghai, Hong Kong, Singapore, the Philippines, and Dutch Indonesia fell in succession, our finance has suffered from great blow. The currency war in enemy-occupied areas has failed. Inflation is surging. Also, since enemy captured railway between Zhejiang and Jiangxi provinces, salt and food supply are in great scarcity. In such difficult circumstances, though enemy has not increased its forces around provisional capital (Chongqing), the capital is under tremendous pressure.

President continued to say that judging from various sources, Japan is likely to attack Siberia in August. Should this happen, pressure on China may be greatly released, and so on.

Though Americans are deeply sympathetic with China, most of those Americans recently returned from China, particularly military, have negative thoughts about China. This is a fact and needs to be remedied. Their ideas include the following: (a) Recently, Japan's attacks have mostly been small-scale, such as sending small troops to attack Zhejiang and Jiangxi. Yet China could not resist effectively. (b) Since December 8, 1941, China has heavily relied on US for counterattack against Japan. China did not want to sacrifice. (c) Chinese army could not be organized for war, and therefore, their power is fairly weak, even though supply of massive ammunition would be of no great use. (d) Chinese military and political circle is undergoing a split.

When Huang Bingheng returned, I asked him to deliver a letter advising that when US governmental bodies send officials to inland China for investigation, we should not be completely open to them. Experience of the USSR, who did not allow foreigners, i. e., US military mission, go either inland or to their frontline, could be our reference.

T. V.

393. Telegram to Chiang on American aids on China's army pay (May, 1943)

I have been negotiating with all parties involved in these days and concluded the following:

1. Judging by their mentality, Roosevelt, Churchill and Treasury Secretary would enthusiastically agree that Allied nations should take care of Chinese soldiers' pay and provisions. This will not be a loan. This attitude is assumed to show their warm-heartedness toward allied countries. We can make use of that point and expand the scope by asking them to take care of all Chinese military salary expenses and to prorate monthly, without mentioning calculation based on number of troops.
2. To rectify already issued fiat banknotes, we plan to ask US and UK for a loan of so-and-so millions of dollars.
3. We should not neglect the zealous attitude revealed in above first item. To stabilize mindset of Chinese soldiers and civilians, getting funds for military expenses from allied countries is more practical than borrowing loans casually. We can gain credibility from them. The total of monthly military expense assistance plus requested one-time loan could reach Your Excellency's expectations.

T. V.

394. Telegram to Chiang on Soong's meeting with Mme. Chiang in New York (May, 1943)

I have received your telegrams dated 7th and 9th. I met sister Mey-ling in New York yesterday. I handed her all telegrams regarding the Four-Leader Summit as well as our request to US for strong naval support. I also proposed to prompt President Roosevelt to send land force to join the war (in Burma). Both Mey-ling and I agreed that we don't have to be too polite when touching the Four-Leader Summit topic. With regard to land force's participation in Burma campaign, Mey-ling said in her previous discussions with President she had already requested sending US forces to Northern Burma. Thus this time we'd better request sending army to Northern Burma too. However, my opinion is that since Allied forces will launch counterattacks both in Northern and Southern Burma simultaneously and their interval must be only two or three weeks, we should not specify that US troops will solely undertake Northern Burma campaign. If we insist only on (action in) Northern Burma, US general staff may argue that transportation conditions there are poor, and that Chinese and British forces have already been there so it is pointless and difficult to send US army to this region. I beg Your Excellency for instructions.

T. V.

395. Telegram to Chiang on discussion among American generals over Chiang's proposals (May, 1943)

Yesterday afternoon general staff conference invited Stilwell, Chennault and me to discuss Your Excellency's two requests on army and air force. I made a detailed explanation (on these two issues) in accordance with Your Excellency's instructions in all related telegrams and the transcript of meeting with Stilwell on April 19:

1. The India-China airlift in June, July and August shall be exclusively for air force supplies. Since September, the airlift capacity be raised to 4,800 tons monthly. (Only by doing so), the target of increase 3 pursuit plane divisions in June, and maintaining the air forces in China at 500-plane level can be achieved.

2. The Allied forces in India are not adequate to execute the Burma plan. The latest illustration is British India's defeat in Arakan of Southern Burma by a small amount of enemy troops. Therefore, according to resolution passed on Casablanca Summit, I propose to send British and American army and navy to occupy Rangoon, cutting enemy's retreat route. I asked specifically for three American divisions to India to fulfill this task.

(I also said) China has been exhausted during the six years of war against Japanese aggression. Now the enemy is controlling the route from Yuezhou to

Yichang and threatening Chongqing. Chinese army is lack of air force cover, thus being unable to attack. If the international communication on land can not be reopened by year-end, the situation in China would be extremely dangerous.

Stilwell kept silent on sending three American divisions, but said Chinese army has not received (large scale of) military supplies for six years. If our air forces increase activities, the enemy would surely launch offensive to us with full strength. At that time all airports in Yunnan, Guangxi and Hunan may likely be lost.

I said that Japanese were deeply aware of strategic importance of China Theatre. If they are capable of occupying our airports, they will attack with full strength, no matter whether air force has activities or not. Generalissimo explained seriously to President that Chinese troops would be able to protect airports if covered by air forces. Stilwell then said, if Chinese troops have such capability, why was Generalissimo so anxious when Huarong and Shishou (in Henan Province) fell to enemy's hands? I replied that, first, it entails cover of air force in order to defend airports in Yunnan, Guanxi, Hunan and recapture Huarong and Shishou. Second, unlike in Yunnan, Guanxi and Hunan, with their transportation and difficult terrain, Japanese were able to use Yangtze River as their line of transportation in Huarong and Shishou.

Stilwell continued by saying that, brave as Chinese soldiers were, they had suffered a great deal of losses. The 32nd Division's artillery now concentrated in Yunnan and Guanxi is in serious need of light weapons and soldiers. At present it cannot withstand a single blow. But the division can become a strong and capable force by September or October of this year, he believes, if it is supplied with war materials from India month by month. Otherwise, if in June, July and August we are engaged only in air force transport and supply, there is no guarantee that counterattack on Burma will succeed.

I said that Chennault's air force is for helping China, and Stilwell's effort is also for helping China. Generalissimo appreciates equally both of their endeavors. But as supreme commander of Allied forces in China Theatre, Generalissimo has to weigh the whole matter carefully. For the sake of safeguarding Chongqing, supporting each Theatre in China, as well as boosting Chinese morale, what's·most imperative at present is to strengthen our air force for three months. After that supplies for army and air force could still be delivered. Thus this would not inhibit Stilwell's plan. Besides, I think General Stilwell is too pessimistic on China's army troops. The so-called "troops that can not withstand a single blow" is the very troops that Stilwell pushed hard in Chongqing for the Burma attack plan. At the moment, the Chief of Staff expressed gratitude to my presence and I thus exited the meeting.

Sister Mey-ling just told me her conversation with President last night. After long time of advocating, President finally agreed:

a. 50% of the India-China airlift cargo be air force supplies, while the other 50% for army;

b. The plan for full recovery of Burma is adjusted to recover only Northern Burma, of which the border is set at Mandalay. The dispatching of American ground troops would be discussed with Wavell when he visits Washington;

c. The Chinese pilot trainees now in US will be organized into two division by using the planes now in Karachi.

It is reported that current monthly air transportation is between 4,000 and 5,000 tons. If half is used on Chennault's AVG, it can barely maintain its current level, but no chance to achieve Your Excellency's wish of increasing three more pursuit plane divisions in June and marinating 500-strong fleet by September. As to the third item, there are only a few and out-of-date airplanes in Karachi now; thus organizing two new divisions are illusionary too. Regarding to the scaling down of Burma plan set in Chongqing and Calcutta into "Northern Burma plan", Your Excellency has repeatedly stated to oppose, for without naval and air covering to occupy Rangoon and cut off enemy's enforcing line, the offensive in Northern Burma would doom to fail.

Prime Minister Churchill is visiting Washington next week. Please instruct me urgently before his arrival whether we should accept President's proposal or insist on Your Excellency's prior proposal.

T. V.

396. Telegram to Chiang on Soong's meeting with John Davies (June 8, 1943)

John Davies, political consultant for General Stilwell appointed by State Department, talked with his friend about China's recent situation. According to him:

1. Communist troops made great efforts to fight against enemy. Yet central government monitored Communist Party with 400,000 troops. According to *Doūmei sha* (aka the Allied News Agent) of Japan, Japanese army has had more than twice the number of engagements with Communist troops as with central government's army troops in recent months. City Bank employee Hall and son of Lindsey, master of Balliol College of Oxford University, both toured communist-controlled area, admired result of Communist army in fighting against Japan.

2. Communist Party believes that Generalissimo Chiang is the only leader who can unite China. However, Generalissimo Chiang is still anti-Communist. Communist Party has urged central authority to enforce democracy strictly.

3. Generalissimo Chiang's position is quite difficult. He is practical in political terms, and likes neither Communist Party nor Nationalist Party. However, his political power is still based on Nationalist Party and he tries to maintain balance among all factions within party.

4. Generalissimo Chiang's demand of strong air forces is to maintain his own power in future domestic arena. US War Department decided supply of army ammunition to China is top priority. General Stilwell's position is in accord with War Department's decision. General Chennault is quite active in Chinese political arena, and obstructed plan of War Department. While in China, Minister (T. V.) Soong supported Stilwell, but now disagrees with him. Chinese army is quite weak. Once air attack launched, it's not difficult for Japanese to capture airports in Yunnan and Guangxi

provinces.

5. US War Department ordered Stilwell to make every effort to take charge of Chinese troops.

6. Stilwell had talked with President Roosevelt and was quite disappointed. He reckoned that President Roosevelt had hollow views on Far East problems, yet appeared to be indifferent to solutions Stilwell brought up on major issues.

7. Stilwell criticized President Roosevelt strongly, and said President should make choice between him and Chennault. Yet at same time he felt President is fairly lenient to all parties, and therefore he would not insist that President should take drastic measures.

8. Stilwell's relation with China is not as friendly as Chennault's, because Stilwell always wants Chinese to assume tasks that Chinese are unwilling to undertake. Yet Chennault always makes compromises.

9. Inflation in China is getting worse. US Department of State discussed whether such situation would cause revolution or civil war, and concluded that inflation would surely lead to people's suffering, though it is unlikely to reverse overall situation.

10. Japan dispatched three divisions of troops, and is ready to attack Yunnan at any time. Yunnan governor may switch side once attacked. The Chinese 60th Army has no combat strength, and now they collude with Japan to undertake smuggling, trafficking in bootleg from Annan and selling it to US air force in China.

11. US officers residing in China mostly have ill feelings toward Chinese. That is because Luce family periodicals such as "Life," "Time" and "Fortune" have made excessive propaganda about China. As soon as they arrive in China, what they have seen disappoints them.

12. Generalissimo Chiang's intention to develop air force is for no other reason than to maintain his regime after war and to eliminate Communist Party and local anti-government personnel. The person whom US supports by that time would be China's "Francisco Franco." That would cause Russians' resentment and lead to chaos.

Above points are worth paying attention to because Stilwell and Davis's formal report to the US government may be quite similar. I state matters in this correspondence and beg for your inspection. I pray for your health.

T. V.

397. Telegram to Chiang on Soong's meeting with Roosevelt regarding Sino-UK negotiation over Hong Kong issue (June, 1943)

I met President Roosevelt yesterday. According to him, Mr. Anthony Eden is coming to US and plans to discuss postwar settlement in Europe. Though Prime Minister Churchill cannot get rid of nineteenth century mode of thinking, President can exchange views frankly with Eden about reconstructing a new world. As regards to Sino-British relations, President plans to bring up issue of hand-over of Hong Kong. British may not agree at beginning. He told Madame Chiang his opinions that on one hand, British hand over Hong Kong to China of their own accord, and on other hand, China delimits part or the whole of Kowloon and Hong Kong as free port where no duties are levied. After one-hundred-year rule of Hong Kong by British, free port status of Hong Kong announced by China could ensure part of privileges of British nationals. That is contribution of China for constructing a new world. He inquired about my opinions on that. I answered: (1) British ambassador to China Sir Clark-Kerr expressed in Chongqing that British are willing to give up Hong Kong. Ambassador Koo got the same impression in England. (2) During negotiation of abolishment of unequal treaties, Britain expressed that hand-over of Kowloon would be negotiated after war. (3) Hong Kong does not have military importance any more. As to its economic position, if China regards Hong Kong as a foreign territory, Hong Kong will inevitably go bankrupt. I do not want to make any comment on Hong Kong's status as free zone before I receive instructions. On this point, I beg for reply on Your Excellency's decision.

President added that as regards to requests of Your Excellency passed on by General Arnold, he decided to fully comply with them. Capacity of transport planes increased to 10,000 tons per month, and War Department promised to increase number of warplanes in China to five hundred before December. President earnestly wants to bombard Japan and their sailing ships. I said it is best to make use of Kunming Lake, and dispatch navy force, torpedoes and warplanes to sink enemy's ships. He could not agree with me more and said that he will discuss with Navy Department.

I continued to say that China is very serious about plan of attacking Burma. However, British combat troops are mainly composed of Indian forces. Since there is estrangement between British and Indians, it is feared that troops used for fighting against Japan cannot be efficient. To occupy Burma and ensure America's voice in Asia and Pacific regions hereafter, it is necessary to dispatch a US corps to India to join Burma battle. President said that is also what he intends, and it would not be a problem to dispatch one or two divisions. I'll discuss it with War Department.

Finally, President said that Madame Chiang's visit to US this time impressed Americans. Yet her goal of this trip already achieved. It is better for her not to make any public speeches, as it may hinder recovery of her health. Both President and his wife would advise Madame Chiang not to go to other Western countries, and even trip to Canada is not of great importance. I said my third younger sister's trip this time was only to cure her illness. She is fortunate to receive special reception from President, the first lady and all American officials and ordinary people. We owe them a lot of gratitude.

T. V.

398. Telegram to Chiang on Soong's meeting with Roosevelt on June 18, 1943 (June, 1943)

1. I called on President on 18th. President told me that he fully understood difficult situation Your Excellency faced militarily and economically. Therefore, he is eager to reinforce air forces in China and decided that:
   a. From July 1st on, capacity of air transport between China and India fixed at 7,000 tons per month. First, 4,700 tons for General Chennault's air force, then 2,000 tons for army and 300 tons for (Chinese) air force.

    b. From September 1st onward, capacity of air transport set at 10,000 tons per month and to be increasing incrementally.

2. I asked President whether air transport in May and June could be entirely devoted to air force. President said that he has to consult with deputy chief of staff, and certain amount still has to be allotted to army.

3. I negotiated with deputy chief of staff immediately. We both agreed that if in May and June they supply 500 tons to army, the rest should be subsumed under air force. Starting from July 1st, air force should have priority of 4,700 tons per month, and rest for army. By the end of October, army can get total of 10,000 tons.

4. President ordered General Raymond A. Wheeler to repair several airports in India. As for other airports, Prime Minister Churchill will order them repaired promptly.

T. V.

399. Telegram to Chiang on delay of Canadian weapon delivery (July 1, 1943)

I reported to you about allotment of all kinds of ammunition by Canada in my telegrams of April 24th and May 28th. Soon afterward, I received formal notice from Canadian minister of National Defense Industry explaining reason for delay. It said US War Department asserted that some components and materials of ammunition manufactured by Canada always rely on US supply. Moreover, as US is responsible for transport between China and India, it should be involved in this matter. In fact, some military officers who do not understand overall situation intend that all ammunition supplied to China be inspected by Stilwell. Purpose of this is to enhance Stilwell's power and position, so he can hold sway in China. As soon as I received this confidential information, I disclosed the inside story to Canadian Prime Minister and Hopkins, and said such manipulation runs counter to US principle of cherishing allied countries. War Department was aware that they were in indefensible position, thus no further twists and turns occurred, and now the matter has come to an end. Yet this shows how difficult it is to cope with all such things here. I previously asked Your Excellency to thank Canadian Prime Minister and minister of National Defense Industry via telegram, and will attach English draft by another telegram for your inspection and decision. Upon arrival of ammunition in India, I plan to negotiate with concerned authorities when I go to England. Ammunition will be taken over and stored by personnel from our Arsenal Division, and shipped, distributed upon Your Excellency's instructions to avoid Stilwell's manipulation. Please instruct if this is appropriate.

T. V.

400. Telegram to Chiang on possibility of Roosevelt-Stalin summit (July 26, 1943)

D03

I received your telegram dated June 24th. My confidential correspondence of June 21st mentioned that President has intention to meet Stalin. Recent development of war as well as Soviet's promotion of organizing a free German government in Moscow, which contradicts British and American ideas, make Roosevelt's meeting with Stalin even more necessary. Location for meeting will be in Siberia. It seems that Roosevelt may want to meet Your Excellency in Alaska on his way back to America. Before I left US, Mr. Hopkins enquired Your Excellency's opinion. I replied to him according to your telegram dated June 21st.

T. V.

401. Telegram to Chiang on Churchill's political attitude towards Russia (July 27, 1943)

At banquet in honor of Polish Foreign Minister yesterday, Churchill expressed his misgivings about Russians' attitude. Moreover, he said that USSR lacks diplomatic ethics and never fulfilled any agreement signed by Stalin. He also implied that it would be extremely horrible if the Russians enter Berlin first, and so on.

T. V.

402. Telegram to Chiang on letter from Qian Duansheng to Churchill and his cabinet (July 29, 1943)

D07C

Shaochuan (V. K. Wellington Koo) said that Sir Stafford Cripps told him about correspondence sent by Qian Duansheng[1] to Prime Minister Churchill, other important cabinet members and himself, briefing about China's political situation as follows: 1. Nationalist Party is autocratic; 2. nonparty elites cannot take part in government; 3. economic situation is critical, with abuses ubiquitous. Moreover, senior government officials are involved in embezzlement. Sir Cripps said that naturally such matters damage British perceptions of China. He had done his best to argue but cannot offset effects of such correspondence by Chinese and so on. I beg for your attention.

T. V.

403. Telegram to Chiang on Churchill's speech on war against Japanese (July 29, 1943)

D08C

Today Prime Minister Churchill told me about developments in the Italian warfare recently, and said that British have firm determination to attack Japanese enemy. Except for navy and air force, they are planning to dispatch massive army to take part in war pending next meeting with President Roosevelt to make final decision. I asked about preparation for Burma attack. Churchill replied that it would proceed after rain season. Considering his wording ambiguous, I told him that Your Excellency would like to know detailed plan of British attack against Burma. Churchill said, "I would like to defeat Japan completely. However, we should make surprise attacks when enemy is unprepared, and not limited to the expected targets. Recent victory in North Africa was based on this strategy. I will summon important generals

---

[1] Qian Duansheng, a professor at Southwest United University and member of National Consultation Congress.

for Pacific Conference on next Tuesday and invite you to join, and then you will know details. " I said, in my experience, important policymaking is usually made outside formal meetings, which are only supposed to communicate the outlines of those matters already decided. Churchill said, "Your comment is true. You may consult with highest navy and air force authorities first next Monday, and join Pacific conference on next day. " Moreover, Field Marshall John Dill, was in London and came to meet me. I asked him about plan of Burma attack. According to him, there is no problem about attacking Burma after rain season. Yet goal and forces to be used depend on idea of incoming commander in chief who should be appointed in one or two weeks, as well as on developments in Italy. Situation in Italy should become clear within two weeks. If it can be solved soon, then strong navy and air force and landing fleet there could be deployed to India, and so on. I elaborate these points for your inspection.

T. V.

404. Telegram to Chiang on intelligence of Chinese Expeditionary Forces (July 30, 1943)

I made appointment with chiefs of general staff of army, navy and air forces for next Wednesday to examine both sides' preparation for Burma attack. I request Your Excellency inform me of our troops' war preparedness, including index number of military forces, their present positions, level of training, amount of establishment, and future supplies, as soon as possible, as well as detailed figures for food, ammunition, communications, sanitary and equipment reserves. Also, we should know British situation. Look forward to your prompt reply by telegram.

T. V.

405. Telegram to Chiang on improvement of press reports of military activities (July, 1943)

I am aware of your previous telegram. According to United Press news on July

2nd in Chongqing, US War Department spokesman mentioned that the battles between May 4th and June 30th in west Hubei province were fierce. Japanese army suffered casualty of 55, 870. Among them, 48 were captured and we acquired large amount of war trophy, including 646 rifles, 30 machine guns, 10 mortars, and over 300 warhorses. In addition, three enemy's aircrafts shot down, and ten river ships sunk. My opinion is that those who have common sense would feel odd that with such few war trophies, it was impossible that enemy could suffer more than 50,000 casualties. Judging from war experiences of other countries, enemy's casualties would not exceed five thousand. No wonder that US War Department and Stilwell do not believe in fierceness of west Hubei battles, let alone enemy's intention to threaten provisional capital. Again, when I described military situation of west Hubei to War Department and those who concerned, I was regarded unfaithful or incomplete. I feel our military propaganda has long been naive, and always treated as child's play. Moreover, its reports damaged credibility of our government more than enemy's propaganda did. Its effect is equal to Fifth Column's job. I resided overseas for three years representing Your Excellency. During the period, my activities were overshadowed by our naive military propaganda. For this reason, I sincerely requested Your Excellency to make serious rectification, appoint able and efficient personnel to take charge of military propaganda. For those who lack common sense, we can not rectify their mistakes by instructing them with several guidelines. I beg for your special attention to this matter.

T. V.

406. Telegram to Chiang on Soong's meeting with senior British military officers (August 3, 1943)

This afternoon, accompanied by our Ambassador Wellington Koo and General Cai Wenzhi[1], I attended meeting with British army, navy and air force chiefs

---

[1] Wenzhi, then acting director of Chinese Military Mission to the US.

of staff. British army chief of staff chaired meeting.

1. I first reported that Chinese side had prepared intensively according to accord reached in Calcutta on counterattack against Burma, and that our troops and provisions are in good shape. In return, Generalissimo wishes to know preparedness of British side. I also stated that some British officers thought Burma Road completely damaged, and even if restored, total capacity of military transport would remain only about 10,000 tons per month. I said this is not the case. We should be aware that Burma Road is actually not that easily damaged. To improve military transport for forefront, we have already increased our workload on China-controlled section, and so has Japanese enemy on their section. Although Salween Bridge is damaged, it is not difficult to build a temporary military bridge. Currently Chinese Second Preparatory Division is stationed on west bank of Salween River.

In past, owing to shortage of vehicles and gasoline, capacity of transport on Burma Road was not large. Yet now US Logistics Department made thorough plan to transport up to 100,000 tons per month. Methods are: (A) to improve quality of construction of Burma Road; (B) to use Burma railway's roadbed to build second Burma Road; (C) to use pipeline along Burma Road to fuel trucks; and (D) to organize a huge transport convoy.

I said although it might take a few months to reach 100,000 tons per month, yet even 50,000 tons per month would produce great effect for counterattacking Japanese enemy in China, bombarding Japan proper, cutting off Japan's communications with Southeast Asia, and covering Allied naval movement along South Chinese coast. In addition, once Burma is restored, air transport to China would be able avoid high mountains and risks. British chief of army said that the British source on capacity of transport and general situation of Burma Road tells rather different story, and asked me to make detailed report. He then added that, on July 31st, railway west of Calcutta was destroyed by river flood, but railway between Calcutta and Assam was not affected. Currently group of British and American engineers organized a committee to investigate and solve problem. One possibility is to use maritime transport to Calcutta as remedy. Yet there is no doubt that this incident seriously affected preparations for counterattacking Burma. In some places, airports destroyed by floods too. As to what extent our military project has been affected, a report will be given in a few days.

2. I then asked about preparations of British Navy. British navy chief of staff replied that because of new developments in Italy, British navy won't use too much naval force in Mediterranean and could allocate them to Indian Ocean, although redeployment and repairing work entail some time. But if army and air force completed preparations, navy would not lag behind. I further asked if there is any possibility that Italian navy could be captured by Germans. He said no such concern, although he cannot predict when Italians will surrender.

3. I went on to ask about preparedness of air force. Chief of staff of air force said that though some airplanes damaged by flood, total number of airplanes increased. However, increases in heavy bombers are necessary. This also relates to current situation in Italy. If war in Italy could finish sooner, we may transfer a part of our air force from there. Allied air power in Burma has gradually been enhanced. Reportedly in January there were in total 270 Japanese warplanes in Burma, but now reduced to 140 or so. Between February and April, Allied air strikes were 6 times more than those of Japanese, and between May and July 25 times more than those of Japanese.

4. According to Churchill, British and American Governments are discussing using other strategies to attack Japan. I would like to know details. Chief of army replied that there are several options for Far East Theatre now under consideration: (A) attacking Burma; (B) cutting off Kra Peninsula in south Thailand; (C) restoring Sumatra; (D) attacking Southeast Asian islands and capturing their raw materials, such as oil and rubber. So far two governments are still negotiating, and decision has yet to be made. Churchill preferred surprise tactic used in North Africa battles to force enemy to respond and then destroy them at one stroke. I asked if we choose B, C and D options, does A option proceed simultaneously. He answered that Allies will not alter original plan before any new strategy

finalized. I continued to ask will British dispatch large number of ground troops to Far East to attack Japan. He replied that if we decide to take A option, troops could be dispatched from India. For B, C and D options, troops have to be transferred and provisioned from England. As to how many troops could be transferred to Far East, this depends on tonnage of ships. Currently our maritime transportation has greatly improved.

5. I asked whether British troops dispatched from India reached their due positions ready for offensive as agreed at Calcutta meeting. Chief of army replied that not yet because that area plagued with malaria, and troops moved back to rear for training and keeping fit.

6. I said that since Allied air forces are supposed to do their best to bomb Japanese positions and supply line, I'd like to know how it's going. Chief of army replied that it's going smoothly, focusing on enemy's docks and ships, and from February to July, 773 enemy's ships destroyed. He then added that at recent meeting in Washington there was discussion for candidate of commander-in-chief for attack on Burma. Because of participation of US troops, Allied forces will not be led by commander-in-chief in India. New commander in chief is to be appointed. British government is now negotiating with US government and wants a decision as soon as possible.

7. Chief of army asked me current situation of Japanese-built railway between southern Thailand and Burma. I replied that according to Chinese sources railway has begun to function, although related facilities are yet to be completed.

8. I asked whether barges used in landing in North Africa and Sicily, given their high efficiency and low rate of loss, could be used in future attack on Burma. Chief of army replied that it's indeed a surprise that battle in Sicily incurred few losses, but expended lots of barges. It is uncertain how many barges could be transferred.

9. Chief of army asked me about Japanese activities in China, and transport lines in Tibet and Central Asia. I responded accordingly.

10. Summing up results of today's meeting, although according to British they are preparing Burma attack, the flood did affect transportation. Also,

reinforcement of naval and air force is connected with warfare in Italy and depends on when battles in Mediterranean finish. I am afraid that it may not launch counterattack on Burma after monsoon season ends. Other options for defeating Japan discussed with US have yet to be finalized. On surface, chief of army pointed out purpose of counterattack against Burma is to restore communication with China so there is no intention to change existing plan

T. V.

407. Telegram to Chiang on transferring of troops in Kunming to India (August 10, 1943)

D22C

I just received urgent telegraph from General Marshall, stating that some regiments of 38th and 22nd Divisions of Chinese Expeditionary Army in India are still short 5,000 infantries, and that only 900 soldiers of 30th Division arrived in India. As war is approaching, General Marshall asked me to report this problem to Your Excellency and dispatch troops to fill vacant positions immediately. We repeatedly assured Britain and US that China is rich in human resources and we would make up vacant positions in each division by spring. This might become cause for gossip. In addition, Roosevelt, Churchill and other top officers from both US and Britain are going to meet in Canada, and the meeting is in no way to procrastinate about this matter. I beg Your Excellency to direct that our troops stationed in Kunming be transferred to India and make up deficiency immediately. This will take more time if dispatch is from interior.

My job here more or less completed, and I'm leaving London on 11th and leaving for Washington via Scotland on next day.

T. V.

408. Telegram to Chiang on Soong's meetings with British politicians in London (August 17, 1943)

During my three weeks' stay in London, I met and talked with many British government and opposition politicians, foreign ambassadors, and leaders of some governments in exile. What I have seen and heard may be of some value for Your Excellency's reference. And hereby I selected some items as follows:

1. Main purpose of my trip was to probe true attitude of British government toward warfare in Far East. I have reported my conversation with Mr. Churchill in my previous telegrams to you, and from our conversation you may have a general idea about British government's true intention. Ostensibly, from King down to Mr. Churchill, Mr. Eden, army, navy and air force ministers, and leaders of various parties, they have unanimously reiterated their determination to continue fight with Japanese until last minute. Nevertheless, the proposed new option for counterattack on Burma, even if implemented right now, would have long way to go. The general viewpoint is that current warfare in Europe is a matter of life and death. If Germans are defeated, Axis powers will soon collapse. War in Far East is not most critical matter. Even British Empire's interests in Asia could temporarily be disregarded. Perception of this kind is totally different from that of US, whose people insist on fighting with Japanese, and regard this as national policy. American society has greatly sympathized with assisting China, and public opinion played influential role. Meanwhile, British war cabinet possesses huge power, and although common people sympathize with our war effort, political parties' advice and people's opinion have little influence. As a result, final decision on Pacific war hinges on US. If Americans will reinforce army, navy and air force strength, Britain will cooperate in fighting. Therefore, only person who can influence British government is President Roosevelt.

2. The unexpected failure of Mussolini no doubt is a sign of final collapse of Italy. Recent massive bombing of Germany, staunch resistance of Soviet troops, recent failure of Axis's submarine tactic, and rapid increase of Allied war necessities production, have all convinced British that Germany

will not be able to sustain further attack. British chief of air force once asserted that if Germans cannot improve their air defense, then with successful Allied land and naval joint attack, it will not be impossible that Germans will surrender by end of this year. His words may be over-optimistic, yet most of the British truly believe that war with Germany will come to an end no later than next spring or so.

3. The war has entirely changed British society as well as people's daily life. British people who aged under 55 are obliged to undertake public service. This policy is strictly carried out by Ministry of Labor, regardless of social status and all are treated on an equal footing. Daily necessities, enterprises, finance and transportation are under government's strict and effective control. Whole society is well ordered and managed, better than in US. It is indeed good example for us to follow suit. Political leaders, businessmen, bankers and church authorities generally believe that advanced social security policy is a requisition for postwar period. But during wartime, they are convinced that it is appropriate for government to plan and manage everything, unlike Americans, who generally tend to favor private entrepreneurship.

4. One main British foreign policy during wartime is to check rise of Germany. British originally regarded signing of Anglo-Soviet treaty as only remedy against such a tendency, yet now they are gradually convinced that Soviets are merely pursuing material assistance. When Allied force failed to open second front, Soviets were greatly disappointed. Now Soviets are growing stronger, and are much more likely to be in position to take unilateral action. Mr. Eden therefore wishes to see a restored France to counterbalance Soviet Union, then demarcate rest of European continent as two spheres of interest controlled by Britain and Soviet Union, with world security guaranteed by international powers.

5. British have got into debt in India and many other colonies for over 4 billion US dollars, plus wartime annual debt of 1. 02 billion US dollars. Their debts to US are becoming even more amazingly huge. Currently British authorities are seeking ways to write off these debts. Postwar restoration will certainly depend on foreign markets, including market in

Japan. President Roosevelt once told Mr. Eden that he wishes China, under American assistance, to become a strong power within 50 years. His words may cause some misunderstanding among British high officials. Yet Churchill is also fully aware that any final decision regarding China will be made in Washington. British would only try their best to maneuver it.

6. On several occasions I met and talked with some European and former Spanish Republican Party leaders who were exiled in London. They were extremely fearful of rise of Germany, and of growing Soviet influence in Europe, although they understood that without Soviet participation in the war, Allies might have already been defeated at very early stage.

7. The most difficult issue is dispute between Soviet Union and Poland. Soviets either wish to establish an independent Polish nation with which they could develop a military alliance and concerted foreign policy, or intend to divide Poland into small and weak nations that will not be able to threaten Soviet. At beginning, British government, influenced by US, was against any proposal relating to boundary demarcation in wartime Europe. Yet recently British seem to have gradually changed such policy.

8. German military force is now divided into three groups. Officers of the traditional school have gradually lost their influence. Regarding the other two factions, one proposes that Germany should come to terms with Western European countries and collaborate with them in fighting against the Soviets. Another group suggests that Germany should ally with Soviet Union as the only way for Germany to dominate the world. Now Moscow intends to establish a "Free Germany Committee" to manipulate this issue, and this plan has caused much uneasiness among British and American officials. And because Stalin has repeatedly rejected idea of having a meeting with President Roosevelt, Eden would have to go to Moscow after Quebec meeting.

Based on above analysis, my feeling is that warfare in Europe has made some progress, yet political sequence of events is getting more and more complicated. Regarding fighting against Japanese, Britain and US have not yet reached consensus, and final decision has yet to be made by President

Roosevelt.

T. V.

409. Telegram to Chiang on arrival in Quebec (August 22, 1943)

I arrived in Quebec at 4 o'clock this afternoon. Canadian Prime Minister Mr. King personally came to pick me up at airport. So far I have not met other important figures. The general atmosphere at meeting here is extremely unfriendly toward Soviet Union. Soviet Union has just recalled its ambassador to US, M. Litvinov, and now it also recalls its TASS correspondents in Quebec as an expression of cool-shoulder toward US and Britain.

An important American general just secretly told me that British and US are determined to launch counterattack on Burma. Today US telegraphed US Commander-in-Chief in India to actively prepare for military supply lines and to install a new pipeline between Calcutta and Yunnan, via Fort Herz. With new pipeline, 18,000 tons of aviation gasoline can be supplied every month. If via line between Kunming and Burma Road 36,000 tons of gasoline can be shipped per month. For troops at forefront, 9000 tons can be transported per month.

T. V.

410. Telegram to Chiang on Soong's meetings with Roosevelt and Churchill (August 23, 1943)

Today President Roosevelt and Mr. Churchill invited me to have lunch with them, and the only other company was Mr. Harry Hopkins. Before lunch President Roosevelt met me and told me in a confidential manner that war plan is going smoothly, but concerning postwar political framework Mr. Churchill's attitude remains stubborn. When we were all seated, Churchill first stated that they have spared no efforts to prepare war against Japan and then left President Roosevelt to further the conclusion. President Roosevelt said:

1. US will transport pipeline starting from today for installing lines between Calcutta and Kunming, via Assam and Fort Herz. Shipment will take about three months to reach Calcutta, and then installation will take another five months. By summer of next year 15, 000 tons of aerial gasoline could be transported per month to meet war needs.
2. It is decided that Ledo motorway (in north India) be broadened to connect kunming and Upper Burma.
3. A certain number of US troops trained for forest operation will be sent to Upper Burma to join British army there for the purpose of opening up road to China. Mr. T. V. Soong should contact the British and American chief of staffs as soon as possible for details.
4. The current tonnage of Sino-Indian air transport is 7, 000 tons per month, and it will be increased to 10, 000 tons by next month. By next spring tonnage will be up to 20, 000 tons per month. Increase of air force stationed in China will depend on capacity of airlift in China.
5. After Chinese Expeditionary Army is sent to fight in Burma, Chinese government may continue to send troops to Ramgarh for training.

Mr. Churchill then told me that British government has appointed a member of royal family as new commander in chief of expedition army (in Burma). While I was in London Churchill had introduced him to me, and we had a conversation then. This man is young and energetic, and has considerable prestige. Churchill told me that time has not yet ripened for this announcement, and hoped that I will not mention new commande's name in my dispatches so that his name will not be leaked. I asked President Roosevelt and Mr. Churchill when counterattack on Lower Burma could be launched. Both replied that it depends on when Allied fleet in Mediterranean Sea can be transferred. I told them that I would request Your Excellency's instructions after I met Joint Chiefs of Staff tomorrow.

T. V.

411. Telegram to Chiang on Mountbatten's trip to Chongqing (August 25, 1943)

This morning I arrived in United States. During Quebec meeting, Mr. Churchill informed me confidentially that Lord Louis Mountbatten has been appointed as British new commander-in-chief in Far Eastern Theatre. Lord Mountbatten was former captain of famous aircraft carrier *Illustrious*, now chief of staff of British Joint Landing Force, vice admiral, and soon will be promoted as admiral. He is fully trusted by Mr. Churchill. While I was in London Churchill introduced him to me. He was present at this (Quebec) conference, and through several conversations I believe he is indeed an able man, young and energetic, and always admired Your Excellency. US also regards his reputation qualified. He will soon go to India, and then arrange a trip to Chongqing to meet Your Excellency. Please keep this confidential. My opinion is that he will be of crucial importance to war in Far East. I suggest that we should now select some capable and well-trained officials to be ready to deal with him.

T. V.

412. Telegram to Chiang on discussions with US and UK on postwar ship routes arrangement (August, 1943)

When I was in London representatives from Swire Group and Jardine Matheson Ltd dropped by, asking final plans of Chinese inland and coastal navigation, as well as projects in cooperation with these two companies. I believed this issue closely related to China's postwar construction and economic restoration, and therefore I put off their requests for further discussion. Now people at US Wartime Navigation Bureau also expressed their willingness to offer their assistance in training navigation and management staff, and to provide ships we may need in postwar time in form of lease or manufacture. Their main purpose is to connect their Pacific shipping lines with our domestic lines. I gather that after war Britain and US will be competing for shipping lines in Far East. So at this moment we don't have to express our clear position. Yet for sake of taking advantage of the opportunity, I beg Your Excellency to dispatch Mr. Zeng Yangfu to US immediately to assist me with planning. Please also do not reveal this issue to any other officials in Chongqing.

T. V.

413. Telegram to Chiang on US proposal of postwar international organization (September 3, 1943)

Secretary of State Cordell Hull informed me that, within days, President Roosevelt would hand over to me a written document about establishing an international organization. President wishes this organization be set up in near future, according to *modus vivendi* signed by Great Four. The general principles are:

1. Supreme Committee will consist of Great Four, who have responsibility to use military force to maintain world peace.
2. Eleven nations are Council members.
3. All of Allied nations are Assembly members.
4. All nations are members of the assembly, which is provisional. And the permanent entity will be established after war.

T. V.

414. Telegram to Chiang on Soong's discussions with Wei Daoming, Liu Kai and others (September 9, 1943)

Today I summoned Ambassador Wei Daoming[1], Minister Liu Kai[2], Xia Jinlin[3] and Lu Qixin[4] to hospital for a meeting. I have conveyed your instructions to them, urging them to get prepared to keep in touch with all media contacts.

---

[1] Chinese ambassador to the United States.
[2] Chinese Ministe-Counselor of Embassy in the United States.
[3] Head of the branch office of KMT Central Propaganda Department in New York.
[4] Director of China Central News Agency in the United States.

They mentioned that recently local mass media reported news of armed conflict in Shandong between Communist troops and local security forces. Since Americans paid attention to this incident, I was worried about possible impact of this conflict.

After meeting, I was thinking about most practicable way to respond. The KMT Plenum issued a declaration emphasizing constitutionalism and guidelines for postwar political and economic restorations. If we make full propaganda of these points here, we might be able to obtain greatest international sympathy. Yet on other hand, if we hastily involve in Communist Party issue, those leftists who do not know the truth would misunderstand general policy of our party as a means to settle Communist party. I suggest that declaration ignore issue on disposition of Communist Party. After one or two months, following our general policy, on one wand, we can push Communists to give in, but the other, we may also propagandize our efforts. I am sure by then we will be able to achieve good effects.

T. V.

415. Telegram to Chiang on military relationship with US and UK (September, 1943)

As Allied offensive against Japan has been intensifying, our military relations with US and Britain are in need of readjustment. I planned to visit President Roosevelt next Monday and broach this subject to him. Your Excellency may further discuss this matter in detail with US Deputy War Secretary, when he visits Chongqing next month. My proposal is that adjustment could be divided into two main categories:

(A) With regard to supreme organs, such as Joint Chiefs of Staff and Munitions Control Board, China should send representatives to participate. Chinese government should directly apply for ammunition needed without intervention from General Stilwell or other US officers stationed in China.

(B) General Stilwell should be replaced immediately. Yet replacement of

Stilwell himself will not fundamentally improve Sino-American military relations in China Theatre. In near future China will become biggest Theatre of Allied forces in fighting with Japan. By then, large number of American and British troops will join war. If foreign troops in China continue to be commanded by British or American generals, as has been the case with air forces in China, Burma and India commanded by General Stilwell, then Your Excellency's position as supreme commander of China Theatre will exist in name only. It's dangerous. To improve such a situation, my opinion is that we should emulate how General MacArthur, Eisenhower and Mountbatten command their Theatres, and reorganize China Theatre. Your Excellency will remain supreme commander, with an American general as your deputy. A Chinese general should serve as chief of staff, with another American general as his deputy. In each department or organ, Chinese and American officers should serve as chiefs and deputy chiefs.

T. V.

416. Telegram to Chiang on Soong's meeting with Roosevelt regarding to China Theatre affairs (September, 1943)

I just discussed various important matters with President Roosevelt. Please allow me to report details in person later. The following are some brief conclusions.

1. There is no change in China Theatre, which still encompasses Vietnam and Thailand. Although Mr. Churchill intends to transfer above two nations to Lord Mountbatten's direct command, US government will not agree.

2. Entry of Chinese troops into Burma is in no way unwelcome. I agree to this point.

3. General Stilwell will be recalled.

4. Washington is considering setting up Pacific Joint Chiefs of Staff with China's participation. With regard to this, please let me discuss it with you after I return to China.

5. China Theatre would be reorganized according to my proposed ideas.

Concerning my trip back to Chongqing, as Lord Mountbatten is going to visit Chongqing and because his visit to China is extremely important, I will not change my schedule. In addition, I wish to fly back to report international situation to you, and discuss with you future meetings with President Roosevelt and Churchill. I decided to set out for New Delhi on Friday, and then accompany Lord Mountbatten to fly to Chongqing.

T. V.

417. Telegram to Chiang on Mediterranean Council meeting (September, 1943)

TASS report concerning the establishment of a Military and Political Council is generally correct, and US government also confirmed it. The so-called Military and Political Council is actually the Mediterranean Council. When Prime Minister Churchill addressed House of Commons on 21st of this month, he stated that this body was proposed to be set up by Soviet Union. Mr. Hull in press conference on 22nd further explained that this new council is only a coordinating organization to gather important and valuable information without any policy-making power for making reports and recommendations to governments concerned. It is believed this new organ would be of great benefit to Russia, Britain, America, and China. When asked whether China would join this council, Mr. Hull replied that he had not discussed this with President yet. As to development in Mediterranean, whether related to China's vital interest or not, it will do its best to keep China informed. US State Department informed me that the new council would focus on political developments in Italy resulting from military situation, and US representative has not yet been appointed. Soviet Union is especially concerned with this new council, as developments in Mediterranean will have important effects on future military movements of Balkan region. I said that Chinese government highly stresses the global nature of this war, and is very concerned about situation in Mediterranean. So China should have her representative in the council to show solidarity of the Great Four. US State Department agreed to take my opinions into consideration.

With regards to conditions on Italian request for armistice, according to State Department, secret agreement already signed on September 3rd, earlier than scheduled, between General Eisenhower and Italian representative, which is confined to military affairs only. Contents have been telegraphed to US Ambassor to submit (to Y. E.). Matters relating to political and economic issues are supposed to be negotiated. Yet current Italian government is virtually no longer able to rule the country, and both king and prime minister have fled to the south. In such conditions, it is presently unnecessary for signing of formal documents except the military one. In future it is proposed that an administrative committee be established under command of Allied commander-in-chief to handle civil affairs. Then other countries concerned could send officials to contact the council about protecting interests of these countries.

T. V.

418. Telegram to Chiang on US media reports on KMT Plenary Session (September, 1943)

The declaration and resolutions approved by the KMT Plenary Session concerning Communist issue have not yet been reported in newspapers here. Yet instructions given by Your Excellency regarding carrying out Constitution as well as settlement of Communist Party issue in postwar period are widely reported and have generated favorable comment and hope in all circles here in US. Resolutions concerning postwar economic reconstruction and no limitation on ratio of foreign capital investment in China have also earned credit from US side. The following are some of my observations.

1. It is well known all around the world that Your Excellency has long been mainstay of Chinese government. Now you are elected chairman of Nationalist government, taking full charge of both political and military affairs. It is indeed a perfect choice and no one else could serve except

Your Excellency. Nobody would exceed your supreme authority before execution of constitution.

2. Much American public opinion has shown suspicion of China's one-party rule. They thought it would lead China to autocracy, run counter to democracy and delay materialization of constitutional system. This KMT Plenary Session worked out concrete timetable for convention of National Assembly and promulgation of constitution, with specific date of its execution. This development will surely relieve such a suspicion, and generate hope that Americans will be able to cooperate with democratic China in postwar period.

3. Americans have long been paying attention to how Chinese government would dispose of Communist Party issue. This plenary session decided to take tolerant stance, using political means to solve the issue. This is greatly applauded by US mass media. New York Tribune reported that the "tolerance stance" better be applied to the battlefield, so as to have the Communists be blamed for destruction of peace.

T. V.

中文索引①

---

① 本索引索引词后所标的号码为本书所收电报的序号

七 画

九　画

Index[1]

---

[1] The figures in the index are the telegram number.

图书在版编目（CIP）数据

宋子文驻美时期电报选(1940～1943)/吴景平,郭岱君编.—上海：复旦大学出版社,2008.3
（复旦—胡佛近代中国人物与档案文献研究系列）
ISBN 978-7-309-05956-4

Ⅰ.宋… Ⅱ.①吴…②郭… Ⅲ.①蒋介石(1887～1975)-电报-汇编-1940～1943②宋子文(1894～1971)-电报-汇编-1940～1943③抗日战争-史料-中国-1940～1943 Ⅳ.K827＝7 K265.06

中国版本图书馆 CIP 数据核字(2008)第 029232 号

宋子文驻美时期电报选(1940～1943)
吴景平 郭岱君 编

出版发行	**復旦大學**出版社　上海市国权路 579 号　邮编 200433
	86-21-65642857（门市零售）
	86-21-65100562（团体订购）　86-21-65109143（外埠邮购）
	fupnet@fudanpress.com　http://www.fudanpress.com

责任编辑	史立丽
出 品 人	贺圣遂

印　　刷	上海浦东北联印刷厂
开　　本	787×960　1/16
印　　张	36.25
字　　数	650 千
版　　次	2008 年 5 月第一版第二次印刷
书　　号	ISBN 978-7-309-05956-4/K·224
定　　价	55.00 元